Be
N
E
Te

BBC

DOCTOR WHO

THE DOCTOR

HIS LIVES AND TIMES

BBC

DOCTOR WHO

THE DOCTOR

HIS LIVES AND TIMES

JAMES GOSS AND **STEVE TRIBE**

ORIGINAL DESIGN BY
PAUL LANG

ORIGINAL ILLUSTRATIONS BY
MATTHEW SAVAGE

BBC
BOOKS

10 9 8 7 6 5 4 3 2 1

Published in 2013 by BBC Books, an imprint of Ebury Publishing
A Random House Group Company

Doctor Who is a BBC Wales production for BBC One.
Executive producers: **Steven Moffat** and **Brian Minchin**

The Random House Group Limited Reg. No. 954009

Addresses for companies within the Random House Group can be
found at www.randomhouse.co.uk

A CIP catalogue record for this book is available from the British
Library.

ISBN 978 1 849 90636 4

The Random House Group Limited supports The Forest Stewardship
Council® (FSC®), the leading international forest-certification
organisation. Our books carrying the FSC label are printed on FSC®-
certified paper. FSC is the only forest-certification scheme supported
by the leading environmental organisations, including Greenpeace.
Our paper procurement policy can be found at
www.randomhouse.co.uk/environment

Commissioning editor: **Albert DePetrillo**
Designed by **Paul Lang** and **Richard Atkinson**, with **Lee Binding**,
Michael Dinsdale, **Stuart Manning** and **Dave Turbitt**
Original illustrations by **Matthew Savage** © Woodlands Books Ltd, 2013
Additional interviews by **Darren Scott** and **Tom Wicker**
Additional research by **Andrew Pixley** and **Tim Leng**
Jacket design by **Lee Binding** © Woodlands Books Ltd, 2013
Production: **Phil Spencer**

Printed and bound in the UK by **Butler Tanner and Dennis Ltd**

To buy books by your favourite authors and register for offers,
visit **www.randomhouse.co.uk**

With thanks to our contributors:
Colin Baker: 'The Empty Child and The Doctor Dances' (p.184)
John and Carole E. Barrowman: 'The Time Warrior' (p.78)
Sir Tim Berners-Lee: 'The War Machines' (p.30)
Nicholas Briggs: 'Inferno' (p.74)
Nicola Bryant: 'Full Circle' (p.110)
Paul Cornell: 'Horror of Fang Rock' (p.107) and entries from 'A Journal
of Impossible Things' (pp.196–198)
Bernard Cribbins: 'Daleks: Invasion Earth 2150 A.D.' (p.28)
Russell T Davies: 'Fake ending' to *The Parting of the Ways* (p.185)
and 'Sycorax-English Vocab' (p.189)
Terrance Dicks: 'The Eleventh Hour' (p.248)
Neil Gaiman: 'The Tomb of the Cybermen' (p.51) and prelude to
Nightmare in Silver (pp.242–243)
Mark Gatiss: 'An Unearthly Child' (p.26)
A.L. Kennedy: 'The Christmas Invasion' (p.214) and 'David Tennant'
(p.220)
Tom MacRae: 'The Happiness Patrol' (p.161)
Katy Manning: 'The Crimson Horror' (p.253)
Paul McGann: 'Paul McGann was the Eighth Doctor' (p.164)
Harry Melling: 'The War Games' (p.54)
Steven Moffat: 'Fake ending' to *A Good Man Goes to War* (p.251)
Georgia Moffett: 'Georgia Moffett on Doctor Who' (p.131)
Anjli Mohindra: 'School Reunion' (p.216)
Marc Platt: 'Kinda' (p.130), 'Snakedance' (p.132) and
'London's Greatest Ghosts: Gabriel Chase' (p.152)
David Roden: 'Dimensions in Time' (p.163)
Gary Russell: 'Ghost Light' (p.162)
Robert Shearman: 'Carnival of Monsters' (p.76)
Andrew Smith: 'Starliner System Files' (pp.100–101) and
'The Ribos Operation' (p.108)
Dan Starkey: 'The Two Doctors' (p.146)
Donald Tosh: 'The End of the World' (p.180)

BBC Books would like to thank the following for providing photographs
and for permission to reproduce copyright material. While every effort
has been made to trace and acknowledge all copyright holders, we would
like to apologise should there have been any errors or omissions.

All images © BBC, except:
Original illustrations by Matthew Savage on pages 12, 20, 21, 43, 69, 97,
102, 114, 120, 149, 152, 166–7, 196, 203, 228, 239, 241, 242–3, and 245
Map of 'The Travels of Marco Polo' (page 13) by Dean Rose

CONTENTS

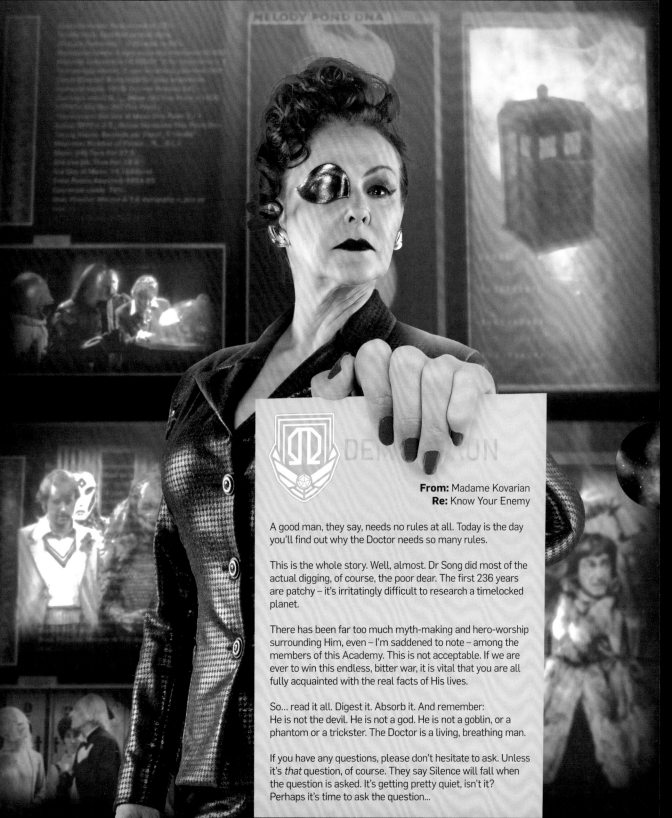

From: Madame Kovarian
Re: Know Your Enemy

A good man, they say, needs no rules at all. Today is the day you'll find out why the Doctor needs so many rules.

This is the whole story. Well, almost. Dr Song did most of the actual digging, of course, the poor dear. The first 236 years are patchy – it's irritatingly difficult to research a timelocked planet.

There has been far too much myth-making and hero-worship surrounding Him, even – I'm saddened to note – among the members of this Academy. This is not acceptable. If we are ever to win this endless, bitter war, it is vital that you are all fully acquainted with the real facts of His lives.

So... read it all. Digest it. Absorb it. And remember: He is not the devil. He is not a god. He is not a goblin, or a phantom or a trickster. The Doctor is a living, breathing man.

If you have any questions, please don't hesitate to ask. Unless it's *that* question, of course. They say Silence will fall when the question is asked. It's getting pretty quiet, isn't it? Perhaps it's time to ask the question...

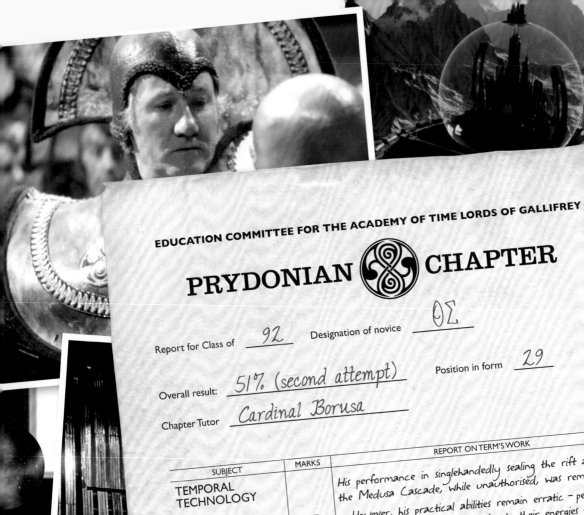
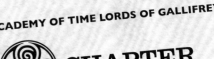
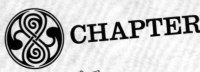

EDUCATION COMMITTEE FOR THE ACADEMY OF TIME LORDS OF GALLIFREY

PRYDONIAN ⊗ CHAPTER

Report for Class of ___92___   Designation of novice ___ΘΣ___

Overall result: ___51% (second attempt)___   Position in form ___29___

Chapter Tutor ___Cardinal Borusa___

REPORT ON TERM'S WORK

SUBJECT	MARKS	
TEMPORAL TECHNOLOGY		His performance in singlehandedly sealing the rift at the Medusa Cascade, while unauthorised, was remarkable.
Practical	43	However, his practical abilities remain erratic – perhaps because he and his associates devote their energies to creating time-flow analogues to spoil one other's time experiments.
Theory	39	He dismisses Artron energy as 'silly', and seems content to allow his tutors to understand such concepts on his behalf.
Quasitronics	2	'I don't know much about Quasitronics' in no way constitutes an adequate examination response under test conditions.
MATHEMATICS	84	Only in mathematics will we find truth. Is he at last learning this simple actuality?
LAW	66	While he has the constitution at his fingertips, he has a fanciful and dangerous notion that vital texts such as "The Worshipful and Ancient Law of Gallifrey" are fit merely for Time Tots.
PHYSICAL INACTIVITY	7	Seems to believe he is some sort of mountain goat – see General Remarks below.
CONDUCT	7	Responsibility, duty, detachment – all subsumed in his absurd faith in 'instinct'.

DRIVING	Fail	It will be a sorry day for the universe if he ever gets his hands on a dematerialisation circuit.
THERMODYNAMICS	97	Perhaps the only subject in which he truly shines. All his tutors agree that this should become his specialist focus.
CYBERNETICS	17	It is almost a century since he was first instructed that, when replacing a robot brain, always make sure the arrow 'A' is pointing to the front. A simple concept he still has yet to grasp.
TELEPATHY	42	Shows some promise in partial mental shielding, although compulsive lack of discipline and compulsive inattention will probably always leave him weak and vulnerable.
HISTORY	49	Highly enthusiastic and often motivated, but his results suffer on two counts: 1. A wilful (or feigned?) ignorance of Rassilon, Omega and the Dark Times 2. Disturbing signs that he is beginning to formulate an argument in favour of adjusting the truth to suit his own philosophies. He will learn, in time, that he cannot rewrite history — not one line.
LANGUAGES	89	Displays a remarkable linguistic aptitude, which is sadly pointless, given that each Time Travel Capsule is now equipped with translation circuits. His (admittedly sound) grasp of Old High Gallifreyan seems especially futile — unless, of course, he intends to unearth the Black Scrolls of Rassilon one day!
ART AND ARCHITECTURE	11	Undoubtedly keen and well read, but exhibits a perverse preference for primitive creative methods. He must remember that computers <u>can</u> draw.

General Remarks   I have had cause, in all too many circumstances, to remind him that he will never amount to anything in the Galaxy while he retains his propensity for vulgar facetiousness. We all, regrettably, recall the events attached to his Initiation into the Academy at the age of 8 — he ran away from the Untempered Schism on that occasion, and the intervening decades have done little to improve his unfortunate and reckless disposition.

I strongly recommend that he be discouraged from his continuing association with his several close associates — his hopes for his Doctorate can only be compromised by those rivals already taking Rani- and Master-ships. Yet he revels in his membership of this unusually disruptive clique, whose least destructive preoccupation is, we are told, running across the fields of Mount Perdition, bellowing vulgarities at the sky. He has also been improperly influenced by an Outsider, a renegade from proper society, a self-styled 'hermit', who perches halfway up a mountain, dispensing platitudes about the nearby flora and fauna. I fear for the future of Gallifrey should ever it fall into the hands of a young man who now claims to perceive the meaning of life in a daisy.

Could do better. Three out of ten.

— Borusa

THE FIRST DOCTOR

So many worlds to see! And all SO NOISY! Grandfather and I have been to Tiaanamaat, to hear the Long Song and to do some shopping. So many aliens! Grandfather claimed to be able to name them all, but I swear he was making the names up. Anyway, I bought him a present from a bookstall - this 500-Year Diary! He wasn't at all grateful. He said it was a silly idea, writing down things that had happened only to find out that they had not happened at all, or that they had happened after all, but a long time ago. Well, I don't think it's silly. So I am going to keep this diary for him, recording all our journeys in the ship. He'll thank me one day.

I worry that Grandfather does not quite know how to operate the TARDIS. I have assured him that the principles are quite straightforward, even on such an antiquated model, but every time I try and help, he shoos me away with his hands, like I am a goose. I have met geese. They are an avian species native to the planet Earth. They were nesting on a beach. I have never been to the beach before - although I can quite see how it would be pleasant in the summer months. We always appear to be arriving in either the wrong place or the wrong time.

Grandfather insists that there is something the matter with the TARDIS, and repeatedly checks the Fault Locator. Secretly, I think all that is really wrong is his piloting, but I dare not quite mention this. He has been so very good to me, and we have never really ended up in any danger. Although, I will admit, life is more exciting than ever it was. We have sailed the metal seas of Venus, sung with the thought plants of Esto, got lost on Quinnis and won an election on the planet Dido.

SHOREDITCH POLICE STATIO[N]

MISSING PERSON REPORT
CONFIDENTIAL

CASE No. U-91

DATE 20.11.63   TIME 11.10 a.m[.]

INFORMATION TAKEN BY   P.C. Oswald

Full name: SUSAN FOREMAN

Home address: 76 Totters Lane,
Shoreditch, London EI

DESCRIPTION :-

Age: 15
Gender: Female
Height: 5' 2"

But, since then, we have seen a lot of Earth. An awful lot of Earth. Nothing but Earth for quite some time. Zeppelins and legionaries, and we have been locked up in the Tower of London (London is a giant, stinking city that we keep returning to), and met several kings. All of them have tried to execute us - which is a pattern that I hope we're not going to fall into.

We are currently back in London, in 1963. The TARDIS is parked in a junkyard while Grandfather overhauls the systems. He is being very secretive and mysterious about something and has told me not to start 'poking and prodding around' in the junkyard. I have decided to integrate myself with the people of this world. In order to do this, I shall enrol at a local academy.

I do not like school. It is most unlike the Academy I am used to. Human children mock each other constantly. They mock me when I get things wrong, they mock me when I get them right, they mock me when I say nothing at all, they mock me when I say too much.

It is, all in all, very hard being a 'teenager'. I do enjoy reading, although it is sometimes quite hard to distinguish a factual book from a fictional one. I am also trying to develop an ear for popular music. I have purchased a portable transistor radio (and have succeeded in keeping it from Grandfather's improving clutches). Grandfather, it transpires, is not a fan of 'popular beat combos' (apart from The Beatles). He has listed several composers of human music we really must go and hear instead. Once, of course, he has finished his overhaul.

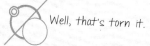

Well, that's torn it.

Shoreditch Cemeter[y]
November 1963

Dear Reverend,

I thought I should mention again the fr[esh] grave in the cemetery. It is still not occupied[. I] remember you asked for it to be dug a week or more back, but there's been no burial services since then a[nd] Mr Stewart has been asking whether he should ju[st] fill it up again? Well, truth to tell, his exact wor[ds] to me were: 'What am I meant to do with the gra[ve,] Verger, that's what I want to know?'

I am happy to report that the rest of the cemeter[y] remains extremely well-tended and in very goo[d] order indeed.

Yours sincerely

The good thing is that we survived the cavemen. Grandfather is in a bit of a state, to put it mildly. I love him dearly, but he's abducted two of my schoolteachers. It could have been worse - for a moment, I was worried that he might actually kill them. I've seen Grandfather cross before, but this was an actual rage. I think that Grandfather likes humans on his own terms - he likes to meet them (if they are historically important), but he does not care for it if they question or challenge him. (Come to think of it, he is none too keen on me doing that!)

Mr Chesterton and Miss Wright certainly stood up to him. They've responded to being abducted marvellously. I cannot quite see how this is going to work - he wouldn't let me have a pet, and yet he has dragged these two innocent people with us. I think Grandfather's plan was to take them on a single trip and give them a shock. It has all gone a bit wrong.

Simply put, he cannot get them home and they are not very impressed. I am not sure what he was hoping for from Mr Chesterton or Miss Wright (I suppose I should call them Ian and Barbara, but that is going to take some getting used to) but they have treated him with hostility and suspicion. Grandfather's behaviour is strange and upsetting - it is as if he is lacking a clear idea of what to do because events have got out of hand. Although that doesn't stop me from loving him dearly.

The problem is that we're lost. Any idea of a single trip before returning Ian and Barbara home seems to have fallen by the wayside. Our last two departures have been hasty, and the TARDIS systems need thoroughly recalibrating. The good news is that we have finally left Earth - but the planet we are on is strange indeed. We have landed in a fossilised forest on a dead world. I wanted to preserve a petrified flower, but it crumbled in my hand. We are on the edge of a great city - Grandfather is itching to explore, but Ian and Barbara just want to get home.

I have never been so frightened in all my life. The Daleks! What terrible creatures. Mr Chesterton and Grandfather formed an increasingly easy alliance to defeat them, and Barbara seemed to have quite a fancy for one of the Thals (dishy, that's what we'd say at Coal Hill School). But oh, those Daleks - just thinking about them makes my flesh creep. Thank goodness we've seen the last of them.

There's something in the ship! There's something in the ship!

FAST RETURN SWITCH

THE FIRST DOCTOR

Dear Mr Khan

Thank you so much for the gift of the backgammon set.

I have no idea quite how you knew I'd turn up here, but sir, I congratulate you. The man you entrusted with the gift (or rather, may I say, his grandson) tells me that you had also included some elephants, but these have sadly wandered off in the years that he has been awaiting my arrival. Rest assured, my dear sir, it is the thought that counts.

Your servant,
The Doctor

○ There wasn't anything in the ship, after all. I once travelled on the London Underground Northern Line. This is a very fancy name for the worst form of transport ever devised - a stinking metal tube crammed full of people and shot under the earth. The Northern Line, like the TARDIS, is very erratic, and when anything goes wrong (which happens frequently) tempers get frayed very quickly. You are stuck in a box with strangers, surrounded by darkness and your own fears. It sounds silly, but that's what happened to us. On the Northern Line it is often signal failure. For us, a switch became stuck and we turned on each other. We feel a little sheepish about it and are all making a determined effort to get along. Even Grandfather.

○ I am sorry I have not updated this for so long, but we have been locked out of the TARDIS. First by an explorer called Marco Polo - he took us on a wonderful journey along the Oriental Silk Road, in order to present the ship as a present to the mighty Kublai Khan - and then by an alien scientist called Arbitan.

Marco himself was a wonderful explorer - and, in many ways, just like Grandfather - capable of great heroism, but also with a cunning underneath all of his intelligence. Watching them spar with each other over long evenings in caravanserai, I feel I have come to know Grandfather better - he also seems calmer. It seems so long since we started our journeying that I cannot imagine life without him, Ian and Barbara.

Barely had we foiled a conspiracy at the court of Kublai Khan (he was ever so grateful) than we were on our way again - to Marinus. What a truly strange place - and horrid. Lethal plants, Voord, frozen soldiers. I've done my best to assure Ian and Barbara that it's not always like this. Whenever we land, I told them, we don't always get into danger. Grandfather chuckled to himself at that. Although he did end up having to defend Mr Chesterton on a murder charge. He did it very well - I think he's genuinely fond of Ian now. I can't help wondering if, a few weeks ago, he would just have left him behind!

▽ OBJECTIVE ▽
I, YARTEK, LEADER OF THE MIGHTY VOORD, SHALL WREST CONTROL OF THE CONSCIENCE MACHINE OF MARINUS FROM ITS CREATOR, ARBITAN.

▽ COMPLICATIONS ▽
THE MACHINE APPEARS TO REQUIRE FIVE MICRO-KEYS, WHICH HAVE BEEN SCATTERED ACROSS THE PLANET. FORTUNATELY, THEY HAVE NOT BEEN DISGUISED – IT WOULD PROBABLY TAKE A WHOLE YEAR TO FIND THEM IF THEY WERE.

▽ UNFORESEEN ADVANTAGES ▽
ARBITAN HAS BEEN FOOLISH ENOUGH TO DESPATCH ALL HIS FOLLOWERS AND EVEN HIS FAMILY TO RECOVER THE MICRO-KEYS. SO WE CAN JUST SIT HERE AND WAIT FOR THEM TO GET BACK.

The Travels of Marco Polo

Cathay

Karakorum

GOBI DESERT

Oasis

Shang-Tu

Himalayas

Great Wall of Cathay

Peking

Plain of Pamir

Tun-Huang

Su-Chow

Kan-Chow

Sinju

Cheng-Ting

Bamboo forest

Kashgar

Lan-Chow

Yarkand

Key
Towns

Yellow River

THE FIRST DOCTOR

Once I was content to spend the time here in the garden of peace like the others.

But he showed me that their minds were old. While his spirit and his heart remained young.

He was a gentle companion, and became most dear to me. My happiness outshone the sun. And I felt sure it might outlast it. It seemed that the gods were smiling favour through his eyes.

And I wished it always to be so. Oh, sweet-favoured man. He declared his love for me. And I acknowledged his gentle proposal and accepted my dear Doctor with all my heart.

It was the happiest day of my life. Yet then I lost all that was dear to my heart. I hope that he thinks of me.

YOU ARE CORDIALLY INVITED
TO THE WEDDING OF

LADY CAMECA
&
THE DOCTOR

INTERGALACTIC MINING COMPANY HEADQUARTERS   G-64-06-20

☐ Examination of data on board the craft shows high concentrations of Molybdenum reported on the surface of the planet named as the 'Sense-Sphere' by the Maitland expedition.

☐ The Maitland expedition also reports that the planet is inhabited, which would normally prevent extraction. Since, however, at least one member of that expedition has a history of psychosis, their stories of 'whispering ghosts' are unlikely to be believed. The only survivors of a previous expedition have also been declared insane, and I have taken the precaution of moving them to isolation for their own protection.

☐ Current extraction methods suggest we could send sub-orbital harvester ships to remove 71% of the Molybdenum through an open-cast approach, which, while having some impact on any indigenous structures, would not result in serious loss of life.

The more I find out about Earth's history, the less I care for it. Barbara kept saying that the Aztecs were a noble and civilised people, but they seemed barbaric. Nicely woven cloths and tall temples couldn't disguise that they were arrogant and bloodthirsty. Barbara has studied Aztec society and believed that if she could improve them by getting rid of their belief in human sacrifice she could save them from Cortez. In doing so, of course, she set herself up against Grandfather. 'You can't rewrite history, not one line,' he thundered at her. Of course, you can, but you have to be careful.

Barbara wasn't careful, and we were lucky to escape with our lives. I'm left worried - how is what we do in history any better, any more skilled than Barbara's attempts? What about the Daleks - before we arrived, they knew nothing of other worlds, or even of time travel...

We travel on reasonably unscathed. Mr Chesterton has even become quite the expert at the food machine, and regularly presents Grandfather with cups of hot chocolate. This seems to make Grandfather cross.

I shall miss the voices in my head. On the Sense-Sphere, I could almost hear what Barbara and Ian thought about each other, but now the minds of the humans are closed to me again. Grandfather seemed almost jealous of me, and I wish he wouldn't keep treating me like a child! However, the Sensorites have been a wonder to me. On the surface of it, their society is rigid and formalised, but in their minds, they have rich lives indeed. Yes, I do miss the voices in my head.

While trying to put Ian and Barbara back in their own time, we instead ended up in Grandfather's favourite period of human history - the French Revolution. He's told me so much about it, but it was horrible. Barbara and I spent much of it locked up in the Conciergerie, awaiting death by guillotine. Humanity has a genius for finding different ways of killing each other - this was their supposedly wonderful, humane invention: a giant blade which severs the head. In these last few days, I have seen so much blood and death. I'm hoping that, wherever the TARDIS lands us next, we'll have a peaceful time.

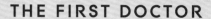

I am never, ever going near an ant again.

Oh, my dear Susan, I had no idea that you were keeping this diary. No, no idea at all. All these years that I have been taking care of you, you in return have been taking care of me, and yet we have kept such secrets from each other! I, perhaps, rather more than you, my dear. Yes, well, you are a young woman now and it is time for you to belong somewhere and to have proper roots of your own. I can only trust that young Cameron or Campbell or whatever the boy's name is will give you those roots and that you will live normally, as any young woman should do. You are still my grandchild and always will be, but your future does not lie with a silly old buffer like me. So I shall attempt to keep up this diary for you and, one day, I shall go back for you. Until then, there must be no regrets, no tears, no anxieties. Just go forward in all your beliefs, and prove to me that I am not mistaken in mine. Goodbye, Susan. Goodbye, my dear.

Daleks! Wherever I have travelled in time and space, I have met no deadlier adversary. It seems that we were not entirely rid of them after all. They dared to tamper with the forces of creation, and we dared to stop them!

REBELS OF LONDON.

THIS IS OUR LAST OFFER.

OUR FINAL WARNING.

LEAVE YOUR HIDING PLACES.

SHOW YOURSELVES IN THE OPEN STREETS.

YOU WILL BE FED AND WATERED.

WORK IS NEEDED FROM YOU BUT THE DALEKS OFFER YOU LIFE.

REBEL AGAINST US AND THE DALEKS WILL DESTROY LONDON COMPLETELY.

YOU WILL ALL DIE, THE MALES, THE FEMALES AND DESCENDANTS.

REBELS OF LONDON, COME OUT OF YOUR HIDING PLACES.

DALEKS OFFER YOU LIFE.

ASTRA FLIGHT 201: PLANET DIDO TO RESCUE
SHIP. PLANET DIDO TO
RESCUE SHIP. COME IN
PLEASE. OVER.

CAPTAIN: RESCUE SHIP TO PLANET
DIDO. RECEIVING YOU ON
STRENGTH TWO. OVER.

ASTRA FLIGHT 201: IS IT TRUE? HAVE YOU?
HAVE YOU LANDED? OVER.

CAPTAIN: LANDED? WE'RE STILL 69
FLYING HOURS AWAY.
WE'RE PROCEEDING ON A
NORMAL COURSE. WE SHALL—

ASTRA FLIGHT 201: BUT YOU. YOU CAN'T BE.
I MEAN...

CAPTAIN: NOW DON'T WORRY. WE'LL
BE THERE. TRY TO HOLD
ON JUST A BIT LONGER.
WE'LL CONTACT YOU FOR
DIRECTIONS IN 17 HOURS
FROM NOW. REPEAT.
17 HOURS. BREAKING
CONTACT NOW.

ASTRA FLIGHT 201: NO!

CAPTAIN: OVER AND OUT.

ASTRA FLIGHT 201: NO! DIDO TO RESCUE!
DIDO TO RESCUE!
69 HOURS AWAY? WHO'S
LANDED ON THE MOUNTAIN?

Dear Doctor

Well, we made it. We're home. I don't know if you'll ever get this letter, but I'm poking it through the letterbox in that junkyard on Totter's Lane. In case you should ever stop by to pick up your mail.

I'm writing to thank you. I know we've not always seen eye to eye. To you, we humans must be like disobedient, slightly intelligent dogs. Dogs with television and a strong sense of free will.

But to us – you're just as enigmatic – you're a creature from another time, another world. You find our ways strange and baffling, we find your morals and behaviour questionable.

You'll snap at us to not walk on the grass of history, but then you'll happily tear up the turf of alien worlds like Xeros. You'll deride us for caring, but you grieved for Susan when we left her behind in the 22nd century. Barbara and I were worried about you – heaven knows what you'd have done if we hadn't rescued Vicki from the clutches of old 'Koquillion'. She's a good girl, and she adores you – I hope you have many happy adventures together.

I pray you don't take her back to Vortis. All those giant ants and butterflies were too much for me. There's so much strangeness, so much evil in this universe. And plenty of it back home – as we've seen in Jaffa and in Rome. I would say our journeys together have given me hope for the future – despite knowing what the Daleks will do to London. But even then, you know, crawling among the ruins, we saw that humanity somehow kept going, despite it all.

Villa Flavius Guiscard

Set menu (4 persons)
Starter
Ants' eggs in
hibiscus honey

Main course
Breast of peacock,
with an orange and
juniper sauce
Garnished with larks'
tongues and baked
pomegranates

and not only this kingdom, its towns and fortresses, shall be yours, but also the Frankish kingdom. Our sister, the Princess Joanna, whose beauty is already spoken of wherever men of judgement and discernment are, is a fit match for one who not only ... so eminent a brother as the Sultan Saladi... but who also possesses an element of his ... Prince Saphadin, we beg you to prefer th... match and thus ... your brother...

Anyway, Barbara and I — well, we're delighted to be back. Despite everything you warned us about, that little Pepper-pot Time Machine worked a treat — got us home first go (although Barbara says I'm not to rub that in!). Amazing to think that when we originally met them, they didn't even believe in aliens and since then they've built spaceships, invaded the Earth, and made a time machine. Quite impressive little beggars — but I hope those Mechonoids put an end to them, as they've got it in for you.

We had some times, though, didn't we, Doctor? And I'll never be able to tell anybody that Richard the Lionheart made me Sir Ian of Jaffa! I hope that's it for us, though — you've shown us the excitements of the past, but I pray we'll have a boring future.

Both you and Susan have had your brushes with matrimony, but now, I rather think it's our turn.

Bon voyage,

Ian Chesterton

My dear fellow,

I'm sure you will excuse me but I didn't want to say goodbye, as you are obviously going to be busy for some time. Just in case you still have ideas about your master plan, I've taken precautions to stop your time meddling. Possibly one day in the future, when you've learnt your lesson, I shall return and release you.

The Doctor

6

Met Leonardo Da Vinci and discussed with him the principles of powered flight.

Put two hundred pounds in a London bank in 1968. Nipped forward two hundred years and collected a fortune in compound interest.

Latest plan proceeding very nicely indeed, if I do say so myself. The Vikings aren't a fun bunch. Try and get them excited and they'll just start drinking heavily and singing their awful poems about swords and blankets. (It really is very chilly here, had to turn on all three bars on the heater.) Now I've got the Vikings on side, though I can get on with wiping them out with bazookas. That'll save King Harold the bother of having to do it himself. Will he thank me? I doubt it, but the pleasure of seeing him beat the French will more than make up for it. Which reminds me – must remember to go steal the original Bayeux Tapestry before it gets wiped from history.

Finally managed to escape from 1066, having jury-rigged a replacement dimensional control from a toaster and a crystal set. Couldn't resist leaving behind some potatoes as a last little bit of mischief. Maybe the Doctor will land in the Middle Ages and wonder why he's being served chips. Ha!

GELM VM: NORMANNO RV M: DVCEM

Random Classics

**CRESSIDA
THE VICKIAD**

I am lost yet found in love.
My parents I have left behind
Lost in the burning sky above.
The people I came to trust
Have folded me in time.
The city I made brief home is dust.
My one hope is Troilus
Both survivors of the flames
We hold each other close.
I have lost my own words
And must learn his tongue
As mine can no longer be heard.
Truvium, city of wonder
Now but ash and captives,
Ransack and plunder.
Onto the wine-dark sea
We cast ahead our lives
Knowing that together we must be.

The Doctor! The! Doctor! THE DOCTOR!
If I never see him again as long as I live,
that'll be too soon. I hoped to trap him
on a planet of volcanoes, but you could boil the old
buzzard in lava and he'd still come out chuckling like a
pensioner at a bring-and-buy. Hot on his heels, I noticed
a large amount of Artron energy hanging around the
Great Pyramids in Ancient Egypt. Worth investigating –
either it's him or some long-lost Osiran artefact that's
gone on the blink. I could name about three species
who'd pay a pretty penny to get their claws on that.
But no. Not a bit of it. Purely in order to save my
own skin, of course, I had to enter into an alliance with
the Daleks. Honestly, the company that man keeps!
Naturally, I scarpered before they could shoot me in
the back. But I'll get him.

My dear fellow,

I'm sure you will excuse me
again for not saying goodbye,
but I sincerely hope I've taken
sufficient steps to ensure our
paths shall never cross again.

Bon voyage!
The Doctor

THE TRAVELLER FROM BEYOND TIME

HE WILL DIE SOON, AND HE WILL DIE ALONE.

USING INSTRUMENTS AND CHARTS, WE HAVE PLOTTED THE COURSE OF HIS SPACE-TIME SHIP FOR MANY LIGHT YEARS. WE HAVE CHARTED HIS VOYAGES FROM GALAXY TO GALAXY AND FROM AGE TO AGE. THOUGH WE KNOW HIM ONLY AS A RECORD IN OUR CHARTS OF SPACE AND TIME, THE WHOLE CITY LOOKS UPON HIM WITH ADMIRATION. FOR NOW IT IS CERTAIN. HE IS COMING HERE. IT WILL BE A GREAT MOMENT IN OUR HISTORY.

THE TRAVELLER FROM BEYOND TIME NOW THINKS HIMSELF A HERO. FOR HE HAS LEARNED THAT HE CANNOT WASH HIS HANDS CLEAN IN THE WATERS OF TIME. HE HAS LEARNED ABOUT LOSS. FIRST, HIS GRANDDAUGHTER LEFT HIM, THEN HIS FRIENDS, GOING HOME, OR VANISHING INTO HISTORY.

THE DOCTOR HAS MET ONE OF HIS OWN KIND – A PEOPLE HE HAS TRIED SO HARD TO FORGET ABOUT. THE MONK TAUGHT HIM THAT THERE ARE TIMES WHEN IT IS NOT WISE TO INTERFERE. HE ARRIVED ON A DYING PLANET AND HE CHOSE WHICH OF TWO RACES TO SAVE. IT IS A DECISION THAT ECHOES ACROSS HIS VOYAGES. IN THE TWILIGHT CITY OF PARIS, HE CHOSE TO ABANDON GOOD PEOPLE TO THEIR FATE.

THE TRAVELLER TOOK A YOUNG GIRL CALLED DODO TO A CRAFT IN THE FAR FUTURE. THE CHILD CARRIED WITH HER A VIRUS OF LASTING VALUE, CAPABLE OF WIPING OUT BOTH SPECIES ON BOARD. THE DOCTOR FOUND A CURE – BUT IN SO DOING CHANGED THE ORDER OF THAT SOCIETY, REDUCING HUMANITY TO A SLAVE RACE. THE DOCTOR AGAIN DECIDED WHICH SPECIES SHOULD LEAD.

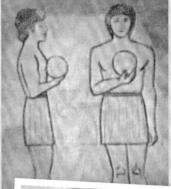

THE CELESTIAL TOYMAKER SHOWED THE DOCTOR THAT GODS ARE AT THEIR MOST DANGEROUS WHEN THEY ARE BORED. IT IS NO USE SIMPLY HAVING GREAT POWERS – THE TRUE VALUE IS IN KNOWING WHEN TO USE THEM.

HE IS BRINGING THE ASTRONAUT STEVEN TO US. IN SOME WAY, STEVEN IS AS IMPORTANT TO OUR WORLD AS THE TRAVELLER HIMSELF. WE CAN GIVE THE DOCTOR NO CLUE OF THIS. IF WE DID, THEN HE WOULD BECOME SUSPICIOUS OF OUR INTEREST IN STEVEN. INSTEAD, WHEN HE ARRIVES WE MUST HAIL THE TRAVELLER AS A GREAT SPECIALIST IN SPACE-TIME EXPLORATION. AND THEN, WHEN WE ACCORD HIM HONOURS, WE SHALL OFFER THE BLADE OF JUDGEMENT TO STEVEN. IF HE ACCEPTS IT, HE JOINS HIS PATH WITH OURS.

FOR THE PATH OF OUR FUTURE IS UNCERTAIN. OUR TWO CIVILISATIONS HAVE REACHED A CRISIS POINT. WHO SHALL BE SUPREME – THE ELDERS, OR THE SAVAGES? NO MAN EASILY GIVES UP THE MEANS WHICH GIVE HIM POWER. SOMETIMES THE BLADE MUST BE WIELDED BY ANOTHER. YET, SURELY, STEVEN CAN ONLY WIELD THE BLADE IN OUR FAVOUR?

HERE, OUR CALCULATIONS ARE INCONCLUSIVE. IN THIS STRANGE COMPLEX OF SPACE AND TIME ANYTHING CAN HAPPEN. WE DO NOT KNOW WHAT WILL HAPPEN WHEN THE TRAVELLER REACHES OUR CITY. WE CAN SEE A FUTURE WHERE THE DOCTOR IS SACRIFICED FOR OUR SURVIVAL; ANOTHER FUTURE WHERE HE LIVES ON AND LEAVES US; AND YET ANOTHER WHERE HE TRAVELS ON WITHOUT STEVEN. HIS WANDERINGS WILL TAKE HIM BACK TO THE PLANET EARTH, THE WORLD THAT HAS COME TO MEAN SO MUCH TO HIM. HE WILL HAVE A FINAL DECISION TO MAKE – WHETHER TO SAVE THAT PLANET, OR ITS TWIN. THE DOCTOR'S FLAME WILL BE LOW BY THE TIME OF THE FINAL VOYAGE, AND HIS STRUGGLES AGAINST THE PEOPLE OF MONDAS WILL SNUFF IT OUT. THERE REMAINS A SINGLE MYSTERY – ALTHOUGH HE WILL DIE, THE TRAVELLER'S JOURNEY IS FAR FROM BEING ALL OVER...

WANTED

TEVEN REGRETTE

WOTAN – The Super

By BERTIE GUNDY,
our SCIENCE CORRESPONDENT

PROFESSOR BRETT, the hero of the white heat of technology, is having a good day. I find him in his office at the top of the Post Office Tower. Leaning casually against WOTAN, the computer to end all computers, he tells me that the Great Switch On is really big news.

But what is the Great Switch On? 'Ah,' reveals Brett. 'Who better to ask than WOTAN himself?'

Oh yes, dear readers, WOTAN is a he. Brett leads me to a keyboard, where I type in the question 'What is the Great Switch On?' And, with a mighty spinning of tapes and clatter of punch-cards, the valve-operated fella that is the world's biggest brain sent forth the answer that I can pass on to you.

The Great Switch On is when all of the world's computers are linked together in a giant network. Via copper cable and microwave radiation, computers everywhere from NATO to Jodrell Bank will join WOTAN in thinking together. WOTAN may have a sinister name ('It stands for Will Operating Thought Analogue,' says Brett) but his intentions are benevolent.

'It will be a new age of philosophy,' says Brett. 'I have trained up WOTAN to do all humanity's thinking for us.'

But he's not just a brain-box. Brett shows me a picture of his cat. 'WOTAN can see this with an electronic eye and send Marmaduke onto every screen in Geneva instantaneously,' he explains. 'WOTAN can also assist in humanitarian crises. Call for food on a tele-printer at UNESCO, and WOTAN can activate a sophisticated distribution and shipping network, capable of delivering to the Amazon.'

He introduces his secretary Polly Wright, 25. 'Oh yes,' gushes the enthusiastic blonde. 'I do think WOTAN is marvellous. He can do everything! Why, he can type almost as quickly as me! I do hope the professor doesn't replace me with a machine!'

THE BALLAD OF CAPTAIN AVERY

They stripped the rings
From their fingers
And the flesh
From their bones
They sent those poor sailors
Down to Davy Jones

Good gracious!
Something is clearly amiss
with the translation mainframe.
Is this going to happen every
time we travel back in time?
Perhaps best avoided.

+ + + THE MONDAS CRYSTALS + + +

+ AS OUR PLANET JOURNEYS FURTHER FROM THE SUN, THE WORLD BECOMES COLDER AND THE SICKNESS SPREADS. IT IS FASCINATING TO LOOK THROUGH DOCUMENTS FROM ONLY A CENTURY OR SO AGO – WHEN WE STILL BELIEVED OUR PLANET FLAT, AND THAT THE SUN, MOON, DISC, AND STARS ALL SPAN AROUND US.

+ THEN, HUMBLINGLY, THE NOTION SPREAD THAT WE WERE SIMPLY ONE GLOBE AMONG MANY, PROCEEDING AROUND THE SUN IN STATELY PROCESSION. IT IS FASCINATING TO LOOK BACK ON THOSE OLD DOCUMENTS TO SEE HOW THEOLOGIANS SPECULATED THAT THE GODS WERE ANGRY AND WERE TAKING AWAY THE SKY. MEANWHILE, ASTRONOMERS AND SCIENTISTS WERE DEDUCING FROM THE CHANGING STARS THAT OUR ORBIT WAS ERRATIC, AND THAT, FOR SOME REASON, WE WERE BEING FLUNG OUT OF THE SOLAR SYSTEM.

+ THE CLERICS RAGED AND DEMANDED REPENTANCE, SACRIFICE AND APPEASEMENT. THE SCIENTISTS PLOTTED AND THOUGHT – THOUGHT OF WAYS TO DECELERATE OUR PLANET, OF WAYS TO ESCAPE IT, AND, EVENTUALLY, OF WAYS TO SURVIVE. DESPITE EVERYTHING, MONDAS HAS SURVIVED. SCIENCE HAS SHOWN US THE WAY – IT HAS DEVISED MEANS TO KEEP THE SPARK OF LIFE ALIVE, TO WARM THE SURFACE, TO COPE WITH AND WARD OFF THE SICKNESS. SCIENCE HAS SAVED MONDAS. WE WILL SURVIVE!

Computer!

Missing girl found in home of 'prominent figure'

DOROTHEA CHAPLET (17) who vanished several weeks ago from Barnes Common was today found in Hertfordshire. She has told police she has no memory of her experiences. The senior figure, who cannot be named as he is currently helping police with their enquiries, apparently told officers that the young lady was taken ill in London and it seemed easier to take her to his country estate than to a hospital.

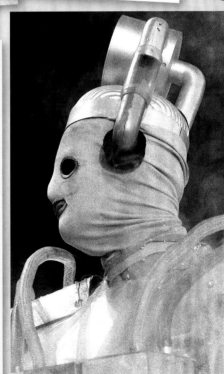

+ I BELIEVE OUR SOCIETY HAS TO OVERCOME THE ISSUES OF ASSIMILATION. AS DISEASE AND SICKNESS SPREADS, SO TOO DO THE NECESSARY SURGICAL ADAPTATIONS REQUIRED. IT CAN BE HARD FOR THE REST OF SOCIETY TO ADJUST TO THESE (SOMETIMES RADICALLY) ALTERED SURVIVORS.

+ I AM HOPING THAT, AS THE YEARS PASS, WE'LL COME TO GET USED TO CO-WORKERS WITH ARTIFICIAL EYES, LIMBS OR LUNGS – PARTLY THROUGH FORCE OF HABIT, AND PARTLY BECAUSE I HAZARD THAT THE PROCESSES USED WILL BECOME MORE GRACEFUL AND STREAMLINED. WE WILL SURVIVE.

+ I AM GROWING USED TO MY OWN ADAPTATIONS – NO LONGER A REPLACEMENT, BUT AN ENHANCEMENT. NO LONGER ARE WE DOOMED TO A BRIEF, TROGLODYTIC EXISTENCE BENEATH THE SURFACE OF THIS WORLD. OUR CYBERNETIC SCIENTISTS CAN NOW OFFER US ALL INCREASED LIFE SPANS, THE STRENGTH OF TEN, AND THE ABILITY TO BREATHE IN THE AIRLESS VACUUM OF SPACE. I CAN SEE MORE SHARPLY, BREATHE MORE EASILY, AND EVEN THINK MORE CLEARLY. OUR PLANET MAY BE DOOMED TO WANDER THE GALAXY, BUT SCIENCE HAS EQUIPPED BOTH MONDAS AND HER PEOPLE WITH ALL THE TOOLS WE NEED TO SURVIVE.

+ + + WE WILL SURVIVE + + + WE WILL SURVIVE + + + WE WILL SURVIVE + + +

The Story of Doctor Who
1963–1966

Aiming it at kids first was a masterstroke. Around teatime it's the children who decide what is seen on TV, not the parents. On the other hand, it is something mums and dads can watch as well without cringing.

William Hartnell

The best idea for a television programme ever was created in very humdrum surroundings. Doctor Who was devised by a working group in a BBC meeting room in 1963. They set out to create a whole new kind of programme – a science fiction serial for a family audience...

Envisaged is a 'loyalty programme', lasting at least 52 weeks, consisting of various dramatised S.F. stories, linked to form a continuous serial, using basically a few characters who continue through all the stories.

C.E. Webber, writer (Memo to Donald Wilson, BBC Head of Serials, 29 March 1963)

Each story, as far as possible, to use repeatable sets. It is expected that back projection will be available. A reasonable amount of film, which will probably be mostly studio shot for special effects. Certainly writers should not hesitate to call for any special effects to achieve the element of surprise essential in these stories, even though they are not sure how it would be done technically: leave it to the Effects people. Otherwise work to a very moderate budget.

C.E. Webber and Sydney Newman, BBC Head of Drama ('Dr. Who: General Notes on Background and Approach', 1963)

I had been working as a production assistant, and Sydney Newman phoned me one day out of the blue and asked me what I knew about children, and I said, 'Nothing.' And he said, 'Well, I want you to come in and meet Donald Wilson to see if you could produce this new series that we are thinking about for children.'

Verity Lambert, producer

The best thing I ever did on *Doctor Who* was to find Verity Lambert. She was gutsy and she used to fight and argue with me. Verity was a real pro and, whether she liked the script or not, she knew she had to make the script work, which is what any good producer does.

Sydney Newman

Verity Lambert had never actually produced a series. Newman backed up his gamble by appointing as associate producer Mervyn Pinfield, a TV pioneer, known for inventing an early autocue device, the Piniprompter.

I met her through being in the gallery at the time, from the early tests on the title sequence with Mervyn Pinfield. I immediately got on with her. She was a feisty, exciting person. She instilled a great passion into *Doctor Who*. It was her first big series, and she really, really loved it all.

Clive Doig, vision mixer

WILLIAM HARTNELL
was the First Doctor

I wanted the Doctor to have two sides to his personality, mainly to be able to be authoritative but also unpredictable. The Doctor was almost a grown-up child, and very much his own person. I had seen William Hartnell in two crucial things – he'd been in a long-running series called *The Army Game* where he played a very, very aggressive, hectoring sergeant major, and then I saw him in a film called *This Sporting Life*, where he played a sort of down-and-out talent scout, and he was quite pathetic and sad.

Verity Lambert

My agent said that the part was that of an eccentric old grandfather-cum-professor type who travels in space and time. Well, I wasn't that keen, but I agreed to meet the producer. Then, the moment this brilliant young producer started telling me about *Doctor Who*, I was hooked. I remember telling her, 'This is going to run for five years.'

William Hartnell

I was a real fan of Bill's – I thought he was a fantastic film actor. He brought that kind of deadly seriousness to *Doctor Who*. You couldn't mistake him. And yet, he always wanted to put in bits of comedy.

William Russell (Ian Chesterton)

My mental image of him is of an attitude he had: just standing there with one thumb sort of hooked to his lapel. If he knew what should be done then he came out with it.

Carole Ann Ford (Susan Foreman)

Billy really hit the essence of the character: the Doctor is a genius, but just a tad senile.

Richard Martin, director

I remember my eldest daughter as a baby being dangled on William Hartnell's knee and him tirading, for some reason, about steel being the problem of the world. Because he was a bit... kind of strange.

Clive Doig

Bill and I luckily developed a really good, strong relationship, and we did have this grandfatherly attitude from him. Quite

often I would have to say, 'Look, you know, Bill, I'm not actually 15, and you're not actually my grandfather, so don't talk to me as if you are.'

Carole Ann Ford

It was my job to laugh Bill out of his five or six tempers a day. And that's what I did, very happily, all the time I was there. I can't explain what he was like – he was a very charming creature in spite of his irascibility and those terrible teeth that he used to bare when he was angry. He said to me, 'When I was sent the script for *Doctor Who*, I decided this was my chance. I was going to make this mine, and I do make it mine. I make this show mine.' And that's why he insisted on everything being right. It was his reward after a lifetime of slogging away. So you could forgive him an awful lot because of that.

Maureen O'Brien (Vicki)

I got on very well with Bill. I mean, he was a very kind man who could be quite irascible. He really embraced the character – he believed in the character and he protected the character.

Verity Lambert

Mervyn Pinfield I liked very much. He had a very calm manner and he was a little bit more distinguished than you'd assume from his appearance – he looked like a secondary school master, but he was part of a very elite group of directors, who'd meet and discuss experimental television and what was to happen to television in the future. He was also the inventor of the first teleprompter autocue – but it had a very odd name like PrinkyPops!

William Russell

The series was devised as an ensemble show, with three characters accompanying the Doctor: his granddaughter, Susan, and her schoolteachers, Ian Chesterton and Barbara Wright...

I was the dashing action man. That was my little niche.

William Russell

I think the characters of Ian and Barbara were maternal and paternal, puzzled and irritated by the Doctor, but intrigued. They were both teachers, swept up into this cosmic whirlpool. The actors managed to retain that and make those characters interesting. When the TARDIS doors opened, those people had to come out and immediately go on some sort of childish exploration.

Richard Martin

Jacqueline Hill was a lot of fun. She had been a visiting actor in another series; it was very cliquey and she was made to feel very out of place. So she said, 'Let's make sure that to visiting actors we immediately embrace them into our little family.'

Carole Ann Ford

Jackie wasn't the sort of person you felt you could dismiss. There's a bit in *The Space Museum* where she's being gassed with someone and she goes down and then gets up and says, 'Come on, get a move on!' That was very Jackie. And the hair, the wonderful hair.

William Russell

Writer and actor Mark Gatiss on
AN UNEARTHLY CHILD

Imagine you know nothing about *Doctor Who*. You're sitting down to watch episode one of a new children's series one cold November night. The world is reeling from the assassination of President Kennedy the day before. The music begins, a throbbing beat accompanied by swirling patterns that writhe across the screen. A policeman shines his torch into a crowded junkyard, coming to rest on a battered police box. A familiar sight in 1963 London. But this one is humming. Like it's alive...

Ian and Barbara, two ordinary schoolteachers have a problem. One of their pupils, Susan Foreman, is different. When they discover the truth, it's beyond their wildest imaginings. Susan lives inside that police box. A bigger-on-the-inside machine called TARDIS that can move anywhere in Space and Time. At the helm, Susan's grandfather, a spiky, unpleasant old man called the Doctor...

It's hard to imagine the impact that *Doctor Who*'s arrival must have made fifty years ago. Originally entitled 'Nothing at the End of the Lane', there remains a poetry to the first episode, like the Doctor's 'One day we shall get back. Yes. One day, one day', recalled beautifully in *The Dalek Invasion of Earth* a year later as Susan leaves.

They say no one ever built a monument to a committee. But between them, Sydney Newman, Waris Hussein, Verity Lambert, David Whitaker, Anthony Coburn conspired to create something magical. There's a weary desperation as the schoolteachers come to terms with their situation and that their lives depend on this spooky teenager and the mysterious, unfriendly Doctor. The alien we will come to know and love is a very different character here. The Doctor, like us, is only at the beginning of a journey. It's still wonderful.

The character I was going to play was going to be very physical and immensely strong – along the lines of the *Avengers* girls. She was also going to have an extraordinary wardrobe designed by top designers. They decided to tone her down so that the teenagers could identify with her.

Carole Ann Ford

Susan had to be able to scream, so our auditions were quite bizarre because we did have to find out if people could do it. I mean, Carole Ann Ford could scream very, very well, as well

as acting very well. Susan wasn't stupid by any means, so I think the fact that she screamed when she saw things she didn't like was perfectly reasonable.

Verity Lambert

On 27 September 1963, the cameras rolled on An Unearthly Child, *the first episode of* Doctor Who...

Television is the highest form of drama, made almost impossible by electronics.

Sydney Newman

When I was assigned the job of directing the first ever episodes of *Doctor Who*, I was the youngest director in the BBC TV drama department. It was a daunting prospect. The BBC allocated us the antiquated facilities at its oldest studios at Lime Grove in which to create the ambitious script requirements. My task was to create adventure and

suspense involving a police telephone box which housed a large spaceship controlled by a mysterious being and his unearthly companion. These were the basic ingredients of what was to become one of the most iconic shows of all time and I am proud to have been a part of it.

Waris Hussein, director

So long as the camera script was good, and we were seeing the right people at the right time, and they didn't forget their lines, you could put the programme together as live, in the gallery. The very first programme didn't actually go out. We had to come back and do it again as so many things went wrong. It was a very crowded studio, and the equipment would be regarded as antiquated. It was a young team, who were all slightly inexperienced, so things could go wrong. In that first episode we had terrible difficulty keeping the TARDIS doors shut.

Clive Doig

Loving the programme but noticing the rough edges, Sydney Newman asked Verity Lambert to remount the first episode, and then press on with making Anthony Coburn's story of the TARDIS's arrival in the Stone Age. Doctor Who then debuted on BBC TV at about 5.15 on Saturday 23 November 1963...

The very first episode went out the day after Kennedy was assassinated, which was not the best day for it to go out, but actually in those days the BBC could be flexible with scheduling and they

scheduled the first episode to go out again the following week.

Verity Lambert

Verity Lambert had to fight hard to make the programme's second story – featuring a race of strange machines called the Daleks...

I definitely laid down the law – there should be no bug-eyed monsters. That's cheap science fiction. Then Verity came up with the Daleks, and I was so angry with her. I really ripped into her. I grew to love the Daleks like everybody else!

Sydney Newman

The row came when it was thought that the Daleks would drag the show down to being puerile rubbish. One of our prime intentions was to keep an educational slant to it, and Daleks were felt not to be in the right mould at all. Actually, that Dalek story was educational in a subtle way: it showed the dangers of war, pacifism and racial hatred. It contained many admirable and idealistic truths, and it was also a jolly good adventure story.

We were allowed to go ahead with *The Daleks*, simply because none of the other scripts had been finished. When it was shown, not very long after being recorded, we were, and I don't mean this to sound smug, proved quite right.

David Whitaker, script editor

Verity Lambert approached the Visual Effects Department at an early stage to see if they wanted to handle the series' visual effects work. They said they couldn't do it unless they had four more staff and an extra four thousand square foot of space. The powers that be weren't prepared to go along with that, so it was declared that the set designers would have to be their own visual effects designers.

Barry Newbery, designer

Our workload was doubled! Barry and I were both stuck with the situation, and neither of us knew what we were doing, quite honestly.

Raymond Cusick, designer

I think Raymond Cusick – sheer genius. The concept of the Daleks was good but the execution was spectacular.

Sydney Newman

I was very pleased with the first Daleks. Terry Nation only wrote that they were dynamic metal objects with a television eye, the rest Ray invented. The voices were brilliant. Peter Hawkins and David Graham were marvellous at this controlled hysteria: the Daleks had reduced themselves to a blob of jelly in a bit of tin. Their intelligence had become warped by the very nature of their confinement. And that fed their hatred of everything that was free.

Richard Martin

OPENING TITLES

I wanted something that looked different and sounded different, so I went to a composer called Ron Grainer and asked him if he would be interested in writing a melodic theme and using electronic music. He thought that was a fantastic challenge. The BBC had this department called the Radiophonic Workshop, and there was a wonderful woman there called Delia Derbyshire who did most of the music and a guy there called Brian Hodgson who did a lot of the effects, and

they just jumped at it because they'd never been let loose on anything where they could have so much input.

For the visuals, Mervin Pinfield had worked in an area of the BBC where they had been experimenting with different ways of looking at things. They had had a camera shooting down its own monitor and it had made these extraordinary shapes, and I said, 'Oh, this looks wonderful.'

Verity Lambert

I remember going down to the producer's run. We had the Dalek casings there, and everybody wanted to get in them, including me. I just thought, 'There's something happening here.' Once they started, the audience didn't take very long to find them and it was the start of catapulting *Doctor Who* onto the scene. I also discovered that my contemporaries were watching it – they would go to the pub on Saturday lunchtime and then they would come back and watch *Doctor Who*.

Verity Lambert

People would talk about it in the canteen, and that was always a good sign. I used to go to Verity's office and talk about what the ratings were, and so there was a different atmosphere – you were now working on a very successful show.

Clive Doig

Following the success of The Daleks, *the series was divided fairly evenly between futuristic alien worlds and explorations of Earth's history...*

Historical stories were definitely more fun. You could relate to the period. You didn't just have to look astonished and amazed, which tended to happen in the science fiction ones. I had a fair share of costume changes. Changes were always trouble – I once went on in a television play without any trousers on. Luckily, that never happened in *Doctor Who*.

William Russell

In Episode 2 of *Marco Polo*, we had to create a sandstorm in the corner of the studio. We achieved this by recording camera interference onto another camera monitor with a large fan off camera to give a violent wind effect. We shot the actors continuously with four cameras which took instructions from myself and my vision mixer in a control room separate from the studio floor. Music and sound effects were fed in simultaneously with the action in the studio. This is a far cry from the computer-generated images of today shot on a single camera with editing in post-production.

Waris Hussein

The television sensation of 1964 was the return of the Daleks. And they'd come to invade Earth...

The one we did where they invade London was so wonderful – there was such an immediacy to anybody who lived in London. I mean, I loved it.

Sydney Newman

I was passing Verity Lambert's office one day, and she said, 'Look at this mailbag full of letters all for the Daleks – they want more Daleks! And,' she said, 'BBC Enterprises are planning to make Dalek tea towels and Dalek soap on a rope. And I've heard there's going to be a feature film.'

Raymond Cusick

Carole Ann Ford had decided to leave the series, so Susan was left behind by the Doctor at the end of The Dalek Invasion of Earth...

Susan became the first girl to be married off. We knew nothing would part him from her, except the independent action of the Doctor himself. So it was decided that she would be given no alternative other than to go. In the process we created one of the most moving scenes ever to be written and recorded for the series.

David Whitaker

I hope to see you time and again on BBC screens in roles other than that of the 'waif from outer space' (what a title!)

Sydney Newman (letter to Carole Ann Ford, 28 October 1964)

I felt genuinely sad at not working with my lovely family. I was glad to be out of the series, though. I'd been offered some fantastic work whilst I was in it which I couldn't do. It was the usual actor's tale – as soon as you're in a job everybody wants you.

Carole Ann Ford

Actor Bernard Cribbins on

DALEKS' INVASION EARTH 2150 A.D.

It was one of those things that came through my agent. I'd worked with Peter Cushing in *She*, which we did in 1963, I think it was. So it may well be that Peter said, 'I know someone who can play that part.' We had a lot of fun making it at Shepperton Studios, which is near where I live, with the director Gordon Flemyng. He was a lovely man. He had a gruff Scottish voice and used to get angry when Peter and I got the giggles on set.

It was the first time I'd met the Daleks. I remember doing a scene where the guy in the lead Dalek was an Australian, Bob Jewell. He had his lines inside the Dalek and when he said, 'You will be exterminated' in an Australian accent, Peter and I got the giggles and Gordon got dreadfully cross with us.

Peter very often wore cotton gloves. He was a smoker but nicotine gave you bright yellow fingers on colour film. So he always wore gloves that he would take off before each take. He was a lovely man. He was a birdwatcher like me. When we were in Israel together, we had a contest to spot the most species each day.

Susan's replacement was Vicki, played by Maureen O'Brien...

The new girl was intended to be something of a waif and stray, someone basically for the Doctor to adopt in place of Susan and to carry on her role.

David Whitaker

Maureen managed to sustain it. She was enchanting and managed that 'Hey, what's out there?' feel.

Richard Martin

New script editor Dennis Spooner's take on Nero's Rome saw more comedy than ever before, as Vicki's first trip trapped the TARDIS crew in a lethal farce of slave traders and murderous emperors...

The Romans was great, but it was quite an exception. Billy liked comedy and was always wanting to put comedy in and was always being damped down by everybody. They accepted more comedy when Dennis came in – we rather welcomed him!

William Russell

The next serials were no less adventurous, with the TARDIS landing in a world of giant ants and flying butterfly-men, then in 12th-century Palestine, before 'jumping a time track' and giving the travellers a glimpse of their possible future... Then, with Dalekmania in full swing, the Daleks returned for their third appearance, pursuing the TARDIS through history in The Chase. *At the end of the story, companions Ian and Barbara left...*

William Russell and Jackie Hill were very supportive of Bill Hartnell, who by the end of *The Chase* didn't know if he was chased or chasing. He was a very tired man and already beginning to show signs of the illness which would eventually kill him. He found learning lines difficult. Billy and Jackie were able to support

him and never make him look foolish, and they did that with consummate love. They'd had a great time, but they'd also had an enormous weight holding the burden of that show, and they never, never sent it up.

Richard Martin

I felt a bit sensitive about Bill. I thought he'd be a bit upset and cross – and he was! The scene that takes place at the end of *The Chase* where he really gets angry, and you can see he is very angry, that was very much like what happened. It was difficult to explain to him that I felt I'd devoted enough time to being a swashbuckling action man.

William Russell

Peter Purves now joined the series as new companion Steven Taylor...

I cast him in a small part in *The Chase* at the top of the Empire State Building, and the moment Verity saw him she said, 'Who is that actor? When we get rid of Ian at the end, we need someone to take over...'

Richard Martin

Script editor Dennis Spooner moved on after The Chase, *with Verity Lambert departing a couple of stories later. Their replacements were Donald Tosh and John Wiles...*

I trailed Verity for a very long time and became a fly on the wall for six months or more. I learned how to cope with film requirements, design information, and all the other technical details. There always seemed to be an element of urgency (if not panic) in the air.

John Wiles, producer

Vicki was the next departure but, due to a slight miscommunication, it was almost as much of a shock to actor Maureen O'Brien as it was to viewers...

We went off on our six-week break. And when I came back I was expecting to find the next four scripts. And there weren't any scripts...

Maureen O'Brien

I know Bill Hartnell was furious. He really didn't want that to happen. I remember him saying, 'This is outrageous!'

Peter Purves (Steven Taylor)

THE TARDIS

The TARDIS was supposed to be a craft for one person, and with a central control panel all the controls could be close together and so easily accessible to that person. I had planned that when the TARDIS was operated the central column would rise and then slowly turn around. When the journey was finished, then the column would go down. The column was supposed to be a type of three-dimensional navigational instrument. The Doctor could look at it and see where the TARDIS was in space and time.

I wanted something that was timeless, something equally suited to Ancient Egypt and the far distant future. The walls were made from wood with the indents made from PVC. The walls were originally supposed to be translucent and were meant to pulsate when the TARDIS was working. The whole set was supposed to give the idea of tremendous power and efficiency.

Peter Brachacki, designer

The idea for the ship's police box exterior came from Anthony Coburn, writer of the first serial, while the BBC Radiophonic Workshop devised its very special sound effect...

I wanted a 'ripping' sound that was the tearing apart of time and space. So the idea came of running a key down a piano string to get this scraping, and I wanted things that were coming towards you and going away from you.

Brian Hodgson, BBC Radiophonic Workshop

Computer scientist Sir Tim Berners-Lee on
THE WAR MACHINES

I watched Episode 1 of *The War Machines* with enormous enjoyment. Even the signature tune still causes a childhood thrill of excitement for me, which I assume is the same for any British child, both when this episode was made and now decades later!

It was amusing to see that the machine in the storyline communicates over phone wires – sounding very like modems of the day – and also communicates with people with the same sounds. Although the theme of this episode is about Singularity of course – the technological creation of super-intelligence. It occurs to me how much we underestimated how long it would take to build machines that were able to do Artificial Intelligence like speech and vision, and how we may be overestimating how long it will take before we build something we cannot control... although... for an autonomous intelligent being which is out of control, how about a computer-run hedge fund company?!

Vicki's replacement was a handmaiden from ancient Troy, Katarina (Adrienne Hill) but, almost as soon as she joined, her days were numbered...

We suddenly realised the problems we'd have with someone from that far back in history. Everything would have to be explained to her. And it was going to be a nightmare. That was why she goes.

Donald Tosh, script editor

So Katarina became the first companion to die, in the fourth episode of a Dalek epic...

Well, Huw Weldon, then the BBC's Director General, ordered a long Dalek story. Twelve episodes no less! According to rumour, his mother liked the Daleks and was keen to see them on screen again.

Douglas Camfield, director

During The Daleks' Master Plan, *the Doctor and Steven were sometimes hunted, sometimes aided by first Bret Vyon and then Sara Kingdom. Bold space spies, they made very different honorary companions for this epic story. Though both characters died, the two actors would have long associations with Doctor Who...*

The director was Douglas Camfield. He interviewed me for the part of Richard the Lionheart, but Douglas remembered me for *The Daleks' Master Plan*. I was killed off in that one.

Nicholas Courtney (Bret Vyon)

Jeanie Marsh was a hugely experienced actress who was already building up a big reputation and she was absolutely terrific on screen. She was instrumental in that story working, but I don't think she'd have been an ideal permanent companion. I think she was too strong as an actress.

Peter Purves

One of the things I wanted to do was redefine our attitude to death on the screen. I'd always hated our offhand treatment of it when a puff of talcum powder and a rattle on the soundtrack ends a man's life. Donald Tosh and I were trying to shock, to surprise the viewer, who had come to depend on the predictability of the programme. Killing Sara seemed right at the time and fitted the context of the story.

John Wiles, producer

At the end of the next story, The Massacre, *a new companion entered the TARDIS. Dodo Chaplet was played by Jackie Lane...*

The Doctor was just becoming a crotchety old man, and we hoped that by giving him someone to be more grandparental about, it might soften some of the crotchetiness.

Donald Tosh

Part of Dodo's character was that the TARDIS is supposed to have this vast wardrobe which she would always raid and end up wearing totally the wrong clothes. I could really wear what I wanted. I was one of the very first people to wear a miniskirt on television.

Jackie Lane (Dodo Chaplet)

By now, illness was leaving William Hartnell feeling increasingly tired and finding it difficult to adjust to cast and crew changes...

The BBC have flatteringly said they'll keep it on as long as I'm willing to continue. But I want a change in conditions. It's not a question of money, the BBC pay me very well, though I work bloody hard for it. But you can never escape from the character – that's the agony of being Dr Who. I get a little agitated, and it makes me a little irritable with people. Once or twice I've put my foot down with a new director and told him, 'I know how to play Dr Who and I don't want you to intrude on it or alter it.'

William Hartnell

Bill was a great actor, but Bill was past the zenith of his skills. But he really took me under his wing and was very kind to me. I got on extremely well with Bill.

Peter Purves

While Hartnell remained with the show, Peter Purves was the next regular to depart...

The Savages was an excellent story to go out on, and I was left as King of the Planet.

Peter Purves

It was only a sandpit in Surrey. I never did get any glamorous locations.

Jackie Lane

New producer and script editor Innes Lloyd and Gerry Davis were planning even more changes. The War Machines *introduced two new companions, Polly Wright and Ben Jackson (Anneke Wills and Michael Craze). Halfway through the story, a hypnotised Dodo was quietly sent off to the countryside to recover – and Jackie Lane abruptly left...*

It is not an easy thing to work out an original way of writing a character out of a series. So having brought me back to the present time where I joined the TARDIS, it was logical that after all the adventures I would be glad to be home and to have it happen in the middle of a story was better than a sudden departure at the end. Whilst the cheeky Dodo appealed to the children, I know Innes wanted a little more glamour for wider appeal.

Jackie Lane

I don't remember anything about Dodo leaving. I hardly noticed she was gone. 'To hell with that,' I thought, 'I've got the role, and here I am!'

Anneke Wills (Polly Wright)

Peter Purves and William Russell before him had been a bit upmarket and they wanted to bring the series more into line with the Sixties. I think the producers wanted the girl in particular to represent Sixties fashion and appeal to an older market. They were completely disparate people: Polly was a bit more toffy than Ben. There was also quite a height difference, as we discovered at the first photo calls! I'm 5 foot 7 and Anneke Wills is 5 foot 10.

Michael Craze (Ben Jackson)

Innes Lloyd and Gerry Davis wanted to ensure the series' science fiction kept up with new ideas, so they brought in a 'scientific adviser', Kit Pedler. His first suggestion involved a supercomputer in London's newest landmark. His next introduced the Daleks' first real rivals as TV's most popular monsters...

I applied for a scientist with a creative mind who might be interested in joining me to explore possibilities in the science fiction area. Hence Kit Pedler – he had previously worked on medical programmes in my old department. From a medical man came the Cybermen.

Innes Lloyd, producer

The first Cybermen, they were astounding, Sandra Reid did the designs. I thought the early Cybermen were more frightening than the later ones, this peculiar thing like a skin stretched over and she forgot to do gloves, so the make-up lady silvered their hands, but this was brilliant. What concerned Kit Pedler was the mechanisation of medicine, the dehumanisation, and the idea we could have parts of our body that could be machines and, if you took that to the ultimate extreme, you could have a man who was cyber – a Cyber-man. That's where they were born.

Anneke Wills

With the Cybermen defeated at the end of The Tenth Planet, *the Doctor hurries back to the TARDIS and falls to the floor. As Ben and Polly watch, something very strange happens to him...*

I loved Bill Hartnell. I always thought Bill was simply tired of it. We certainly didn't want him to leave. We didn't want to end *Doctor Who*.

Sydney Newman

Bill had been in the role for a long time. He was getting on and he was getting tired. I remember taking him home after the party on his last night. I told him, 'Bill, now you can have a rest.' And he said, 'Yes, I'll be very pleased.'

Innes Lloyd

Mr Hartnell, God rest his soul, was a devil! He was a bit overpowering. I don't think he wanted to leave.

Michael Craze

Basically, I left *Dr Who* because we did not see eye to eye over the stories and too much evil entered into the spirit of the thing. *Dr Who* was always noted and spelled out to me as a children's programme, and I wanted it to stay as such, but I'm afraid the BBC had other ideas. So did I, so I left. I didn't willingly give up the part.

William Hartnell (letter to Ian McLachlan, 1968)

There was great speculation about his replacement. It was a very exciting time, really. There were so many names bandied about.

Michael Craze

I recall Hartnell saying to me, 'There's only one man in England who can take over, and that's Patrick Troughton!'

Innes Lloyd

Innes came in and said we're having a new actor, and the door opened and in walked Patrick Troughton.

Anneke Wills

Billy and I had to lie on the floor at either end of the set. With Edwina the floor manager, keeping everyone cheerful, it took nearly all day to perfect the scene and transmogrify Billy into me. It was a really historic moment, I suppose.

Patrick Troughton

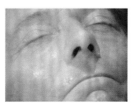

Dear me!
Well, I must say it's been a while. But I'm making a new start. I've turned over a new leaf, literally, you might say, so perhaps it's time I tried to keep this diary up to date again.

Things I've learned recently:

* Different body, different musical skills. I used to be good with a lyre, I think, but I can now play the recorder!

* The planet Vulcan contains swamps of mercury. Handy, should there be another incident with the fluid links.

* They spy on you with transistorised fruit on Vulcan. Suspicious lot.

* 'Lesterson listen' is extraordinarily hard to say. Try it for yourself. See? By the way, he didn't listen. Poor fellow.

* I'm currently travelling with Ben (a sailor, male) and Polly (a secretary, female). They are from mid(ish)-20th-century Earth (possibly). I can't quite remember how I met them, but hopefully it'll pop back into my head. Ben's the one on the right, I think. Ben and Polly don't quite trust me, not yet. But then again, I don't quite trust myself. These legs keep giving way. They're a bit short, and this hat is too long.

* Defeated the Daleks. ✓

VULCAN
EARTH EXAMINER
ACCORD EVERY ACCESS

On the whole, Atlantis contained rather more octopi than I would have either liked or expected.

NOTICE

TO **ALL RESIDENTS** OF **VULCAN**

THE **DALEKS** ARE YOUR **SERVANTS**

• • • •

THEY ARE HERE TO **HELP ALL MEMBERS OF THE COLONY**

• • • •

PLEASE TREAT THEM WITH **COURTESY AND RESPECT**

PLEASE NOTE For training purposes all conversations with them are monitored for sedition

ZAROFF VANISHES!

Governments around the world are stockpiling food supplies after the sudden disappearance of PROFESSOR HANS ZAROFF earlier this week. Zaroff, who leads the field in producing food from the sea, was reported missing earlier this week by his secretary, Miss Heidi von Herzog.

'He had been acting very strangely,' she told reporters gathered at a press conference. 'We had thought his troubles were over after the inquiry into the refinery accident completely cleared him. But the failure of the Zaroff Process clearly hung heavier on his mind than we had thought. Suddenly he stormed out of the house. We tried to prevent him, but he told us that none of us could stop him now.'

CONT p3

Oh my word, keeping up with this thing is quite impossible. I can see why I gave it up. What should I write about? The trip to the Moon? Or our excursion to Scotland in the 18th century, where we failed to meet anyone famous but did take on board a young Highlander called Jamie? No sooner had we dealt with Cybermen poisoning sugar on the Moonbase than the telepathic circuits warned us about the Macra. It really is just one thing after another. It's most unfair.

Examine EVERYTHING!

Shirts NEGATIVE
Trousers NEGATIVE
Jackets NEGATIVE
Boots NEGATIVE
Towels NEGATIVE
Soap NEGATIVE
Bread NEGATIVE
Milk NEGATIVE
Eggs NEGATIVE
Coffee NEGATIVE

SUGAR! YOU FOOL!!

Dear Simon,
Am having a wonderful
time in

THE SECOND DOCTOR

Seville

Dear Margot,
Am having a wonderful
time in Seville.
Chameleon Tours are
really satisfactory.
You really should give
them a try.

Best, Gerry

Completely Air-Conditioned — Cafe Ole Coffee
Shop — Castanet Lounge — Magnificent Matador
Supper Club — 500 feet of Private Ocean Beach
— 2 Pools, Kiddie Pool — Exciting Cabana Colony
and Play Area — Teen-Age Club.

7111   48437-C

Post Card

7117

Dear Sam,
Am having
a wonderful
time in rome.
Chameleon Tours
are really tops.
You really should
give them a try.
Love, Brian

POST CA

37437-C

The Doctor and his
associate have been located.
What do you require
me to do with them?
E. Waterfield

**Waterfield's
Antiquities**

Specialists in Victoriana ◆ 'As Good As New'
K. PERRY, ESQUIRE

Dear Father

How are you? I hope you are well and happily reunited with Mother. I miss you both terribly, but the Doctor has helped me to keep you both in mind. Sometimes, my new life with him and Jamie slows down, and then I remember you both and feel sad that you're gone. I've decided that, in these rare moments, I shall write you a letter. A letter that I know you'll never read. To begin with, I'll recount what's happened to me ever since you died. We stayed on the planet Skaro only until the Doctor had ensured the Daleks were defeated for ever.

The Doctor, it turns out, really does travel in that big blue box. It says 'police' on the outside, but on the inside is a remarkably large mansion which the Doctor says has been his home for a considerable number of years. He appears to wander in it endlessly, never settling down for long and we are always having adventures. To begin with, I rather hoped I would have a chance to pause and grieve for you, but frankly, we rarely even stop for long enough for me to catch my own breath.

LOGICAL ARCHAEOLOGY: IN PURSUIT OF THE ANCIENT THOUGHT PROCESSES OF THE CYBERMEN
BY ERIC KLIEG

THE ALEATORY THEORY OF PROBABILITY is also best ascribed as a con...
probability; and appeals mostly to empiricists. It is undoubtedly a mech...
unfamiliar to the Cybermen of Telos, whose operational substrates firml...
adherents to the logical theory of probability.

Aleatorists view probability as a feature of the natural world. Cybern...
natural world as a feature of probability. Anyone who has taken a mathe...
on statistics or probability theory has learned frequency probability. T...
theory of probability broadly defines probability as the frequency with which an outco...
long series of similar events. In order to apply the frequency interpretation of probabi...
sufficient data in order to arrive at a statistically valid and robust conclusion about the...
event in question.

The logical theory of probability defines probability in terms of a strict logical relation b...
evidence and hypothesis. The Cybermen progress through to synthesis by a rotational sorting set of function gates, rotating concepts against evidence until a smooth progression is achieved.

Thus if you take any progressive series it can be converted into binary notation. If you take the sum of the integrants, and express the result as a power series, then the indices show the basic binary blocks. Hence Six, cap, B four, if and only if, C is cap function of two F.

Nuts, but he'll do.
Kaftan

CALL TO ORDER The Chairman opened
the meeting at 2.30 p.m.
SECRETARY'S MINUTES Minutes of
August were approved.
TREASURER'S REPORT Dr Simeon gave
an excellent report.
CHAIRMAN'S REPORT Chairman Mervyn
Lincoln opened a discussion
concerning the putative whereabouts
of the SS Bernice.

Professor Travers went on to assure the
Committee that the body of evidence
accumulated over the years was undeniable:
the Abominable Snowman does exist.
Professor Walters interjected that,
given Professor Travers' certainty on the
matter, Professor Travers himself should
go to Tibet and look for the beast. The
Committee found this most amusing.
Professor Travers formally thanked
Walters for the suggestion, and indicated
that he might indeed take it seriously.

First we went to the planet Telos, which must be even further off
in space than Skaro. We met a party of space archaeologists,
who had travelled to this world to uncover the last remains
of creatures called the Cybermen — terrible metal giants.
They'd be frightening enough, but I gradually understood that
the Doctor and Jamie were letting slip (despite their best efforts
to protect me from the truth) that inside these automata were
actually living creatures, trapped in a sort of walking grave, a bit
like one of Miss Shelley's fantasies — only real. Luckily, the Doctor
defeated the Cybermen for ever as well.

Then we voyaged to Tibet! Imagine that, Papa. I've met
Buddhist Llamas and Yeti and been where only explorers
and adventurers like Professor Travers go. Oh, although
Professor Travers probably hasn't been born yet, but you'd
like him. Eventually — he's a bit of a grumpy old sort.
Anyway, he helped us in the end — you see, the Monastery
of Det-Sen had been taken over by this thing called the
Great Intelligence. At first it was just like a thought, but
then it was pouring out of the side of the mountain and
the Doctor had to work ever so hard to defeat it. It hadn't
just taken control of the monks, it had also made the Yeti.

For a brief period it also affected me, I'm afraid to say. I'm not sure you'd have been pleased, but the Doctor made it all go away.

He was sad, though. He'd been to the Monastery before — and borrowed a special bell from there called the Holy Ghanta. He was 300 years late returning it, so I dread to think what he's like with library books. When he'd last been there he was friends with the Abbott Padmashambhava, and the old Abbot was still there, kept alive by the Great Intelligence. When the Doctor banished it, it meant losing his friend. But the good thing is that the Great Intelligence has been defeated for ever.

BRITANNICUS BASE EUROPE

WORK POTENTIAL AND COMMUNITY VALUE OF 'THE DOCTOR'

HIGH INTELLIGENCE QUOTIENT BUT UNDISCIPLINED FOR OUR NEEDS

PRESENT EVALUATION

TO BE USED ON RESEARCH PROJECTS, BUT COULD BE OBSTRUCTIVE IN CERTAIN SITUATIONS. MORE INFORMATION NECESSARY FOR A FULL EVALUATION

Dearest Papa

May I confide a secret in you? I'm a little worried. It's probably nothing, but... well, you remember how I said that the Great Intelligence had been defeated for ever? It turns out that that might not have been strictly true. We went to London in the future. The proposed underground railway was everywhere — but it had been taken over by the yeti. The Great Intelligence had returned. Professor Travers was there too, and it was very dark and frightening. The Doctor was able to defeat the Great Intelligence, but, after it was all over, he admitted it wasn't gone for ever.

And so, Father, I'm wondering — if the Great Intelligence survived, when it was supposed to be gone for good, what about all those other creatures... The Ice Warriors, the Cybermen, the Daleks... are they also really defeated for ever?

Dear Father

Let me tell you about my new parents —
I have left the Doctor behind, you see. Maggie
and Frank. They are the kindest, most generous
people you could hope to meet. And they are, like
you, scientists carrying out investigations into
power sources. Whereas you and that dreadful
Mr Maxtible were working on the static power of
mirrors, the Harrises are working on exploiting
natural gas held under the sea bed.

They had, you see, disturbed some evil creature
under the sea, and this is what brought the Doctor
there (whenever we land, we end up in trouble, and
I refuse to accept the Doctor's assurances that
this is simply by accident). The creature — a
kind of prehistoric weed, was emerging and taking

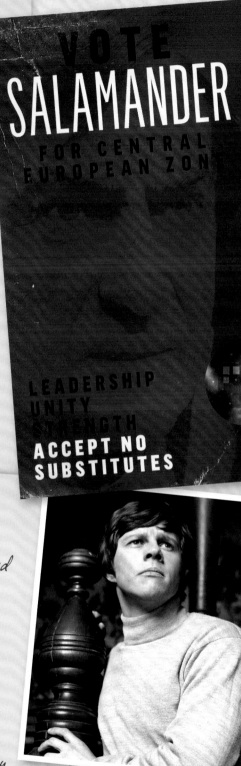

VOTE SALAMANDER
FOR CENTRAL
EUROPEAN ZONE

LEADERSHIP
UNITY
STRENGTH
ACCEPT NO
SUBSTITUTES

over people at the Gas Refinement Operation.
Soon it had Maggie in its power, and I had been
kidnapped. The Doctor and Jamie rescued me, and
between us we were able to defeat the monster,
using the sound of my screams to drive it away.

But I had decided that enough was enough. To
begin with it was all so much fun, and the
excitement almost stopped me dwelling on the
horrible loss of you. But suddenly I realised I
couldn't go on — every single trip, every single day
brought a new terror. Even the Doctor was not always

who he appeared to be — pretending to be a tyrant, or being possessed by the Great Intelligence!

Maggie and Frank offered me a stable home. Granted, it's quite bleak here, but I even like that a bit, too. It's quite nice opening the door every morning to find I'm in exactly the same dreary place I was last night. And even the emptiness has a certain beauty — the cold air, the birds, and the long empty beaches. It's a place for me to think, and I've a lot of thinking to catch up on.

The Doctor and Jamie go on alone. I do hope that they arrive safely. But I rather suspect they won't.

INTERNAL MEMORANDUM

U.N.I.T

Pleased to report tidying up of the Underground now complete. Many bodies now recovered, and LT looking to restore minimum service next week.

Only one body still reported missing, that of Rosemary Kizlet (8). The girl was left by her parents at Russell Square station during one of the earliest web attacks and has not been seen since. We had hoped to recover the body during the clearance work on the Underground, but there's no sign of it.

(Second Session)

Transcript of the Doctor's first trial

INQUISITOR: Doctor.

DOCTOR: Yes. What?

INQUISITOR: Were you listening?

DOCTOR: Of course I was. To every word. Why, what were you talking about?

INQUISITOR: Your fate has been decided. But before sentence is passed, we wish to hear more details about the places you have been to, and the adventures you have had.

DOCTOR: Really? My dear fellow, I've shown you the creatures I've fought. Do you want me to wheel them out again? Just give me control of that big screen thing again for a moment, and I'll have a jolly hard think.

INQUISITOR: No, Doctor. We were wondering if you would care to tell us a little more about your encounters with them. After all, we are well aware that a life form may look fearsome and actually be quite benevolent in nature. Why, look at us.

DOCTOR: Yes, yes. I do see your point. Look, is all this really necessary? Jamie and Zoe WILL be worried about me. Perhaps I could just nip out and reassure them that there's nothing for them—

INQUISITOR: They are also of interest to us. We would like to know that they have not been harmed.

DOCTOR: Of course they haven't! Just look at them.

INQUISITOR: We would like to be assured that their minds haven't been adversely affected by their experiences. It does seem a little worrying.

DOCTOR: What does?

INQUISITOR: To travel to such dangerous places, to be in a constant state of deadly peril, for people so young, so impressionable.

DOCTOR: I suppose they must seem quite young to you. But, by the standards of their species, they're both quite advanced, you know. I mean, if not exactly middle-aged then certainly grown-up. Well, just about.

INQUISITOR: But they are not the first, are they? Take, for example, Victoria Waterfield.

James Robert

ASSESSMENT

Very fit, mentally and physically. Breathing normal. Blood pressure suggests he's not been in space very long. Gamma globulins normal — no sign of fever he claims to have suffered.

PATIENT

John Smith (prob. pseudonym)

ASSESSMENT

Concussion. X-ray for fractures. Otherwise fit and healthy— Curious double

The Seventh Council under Director Malos initiated research which led to the development of atomic energy. The destructive capabilities of this were immediately apparent, and the Island of Death was used to test an explosive device, the results of which can be seen today. Thereafter all further research into this type of energy was prohibited, and the island was kept as both a museum and warning for future generations. ∎

EVERY THURSDAY

PRICE: ONE PENNY.

THE ENSIGN

MORE STORIES INSIDE

- ✦ Can Cyrano de Bergerac win his true love?
- ✦ Will the Phantom Piper claim the Last Highlander?
- ✦ Can plucky Tommy Space overcome The Men Of White Steel?
- ✦ Rapunzel gets herself in a right tangle with the Clockwork Soldiers.

TIME FOR ALL GOOD BOYS TO LOSE THEMSELVES IN A LAND OF FICTION

'REVEL OF THE REMOVE' AND THE TIGERS OF THE LOWER FIFTH FACE THEIR TOUGHEST MATCH YET –

WHEN UPPINGTON FIELD A TEAM OF ROBOTS!

'I SAY, REVEL,' REMARKED Pepper Percy as the charabanc pulled up ready to decant the opposing team for Saturday's deadly match, 'I wonder what those fiendish fellows of Uppington will have come up with this time?'

Revel of the Remove tied up a stray shoelace and permitted himself a tight smile. 'Oh, Pepper, I dare say that this time they'll play fair. We've beaten them 11-0 in every game of the season, and we've played a straight bat throughout. Maybe for once they'll have learned their lesson.'

No sooner had the Captain of the Upper XIV uttered this, than Tubby Lardson came puffing up, polishing off the last crusts of a sandwich from his tucker as he ran. 'I say chaps, have you seen what those blighters from Uppington have fielded against us for a team?'

Revel stood up, and laid a firm hand on his fat friend's wide shoulders. 'Well, Tubby, it can't be as bad as when they threw that team of Estonian Assassins at us, or the time when they bribed that team from the circus...'

But Pepper Percy's jaw had already dropped. 'Oh, I say!'

Tubby Lardson swallowed and nodded glumly.

'Good grief,' sighed Revel of the Remove. 'Those look like Robots. Is there nothing those blighters won't do?'

THE KARKUS — HE SPEAK... EVIL TREMBLE!

© Hourly Telepress

DOCTOR: Eh?

INQUISITOR: She travelled with you until recently.

DOCTOR: Have you been checking up on me? Infernal cheek.

INQUISITOR: Would you rather we concluded your trial without hearing all of your evidence, Doctor?

DOCTOR: Point taken.

INQUISITOR: She left you, did she not?

DOCTOR: The last I saw of her, she was on a beach, waving. Just before Jamie and I had that dreadful business with the Cybermen.

INQUISITOR: Why did she leave?

DOCTOR: Well, you'd have to ask her that. She'd met some lovely people, the Harrises and they were looking into gases and so on. Fascinating, really.

INQUISITOR: And not because she was too terrified to continue travelling with you? She had recently been orphaned.

DOCTOR: By the Daleks. And I'll have you know that I warned Zoe. When she came on board, I showed her my memories of that encounter. I don't abduct these people — they're my companions, my friends! Zoe stowed aboard and I tried to warn her of the things we'd see. But that didn't stop her. She had no home to go back to, and she'd just been so wonderfully clever with defeating the Cybermen. Very bright girl.. Of course, that got us into no end of trouble with the Dominators.

INQUISITOR: The Dominators?

DOCTOR: Oh, really, I've already told you. Big space bullies. Used their deadly robot Quarks to kill off anyone they thought was too clever — I had to pretend ever so hard to be as dull as a Wet Wednesday in.. Ah, I don't suppose you've ever been to Bognor Regis, have you?

INQUISITOR: We are aware of Bognor Regis.

DOCTOR: Splendid. Then you'll get the point. I had to pretend to be very stupid, or I'd be killed. Jamie didn't have nearly the same trouble.

INQUISITOR: The young man from the Scottish Highlands?

DOCTOR: Yes. Oh, the things he's seen. He's the bravest man I know, and a dear friend — why there's nothing he won't do. He came chasing into the Dynatrope after us, even though he wasn't a High Brain.

INQUISITOR: A High Brain?

DOCTOR: You see, the Krotons were quite the reverse of the Dominators. They valued intelligence — they harvested it. They'd turned a whole planet into a brain factory. Zoe couldn't resist showing off to them, and naturally they were rather impressed — she's very clever, you know. They wanted her to be a Companion of the Krotons. She'd help fly their craft with her mental power so they could continue on their journeying.

INQUISITOR: And you contend that this was quite unlike being one of your companions?

DOCTOR: I resent that! Zoe walked into danger, and I had to go after her. To keep her safe. And then Jamie came haring in after us, even though he didn't have the intelligence to survive their machines. Oh my word, it was quite a mess, but it ended up all right in the end.

INQUISITOR: But they would not have been in danger if you had not landed in the first place. If you had not interfered.

DOCTOR: Oh, I see where this is going — you'd rather I didn't land anywhere at all, or, if I did, that I never stuck my head outside the door. Perhaps I should have stayed in the Land of Fiction!

INQUISITOR: Explain?

DOCTOR: Oh yes, never got to the bottom of that one. Some sort of 'Other Realm'. They wanted to put me in charge of it. Can you imagine that, eh, stuck in one place for all eternity, never leaving, watching over countless other people's lives? What sort of a life is that?

INQUISITOR: Indeed. What happened when you escaped from the Land of Fiction?

DOCTOR: So there are some things you don't know, eh? Well, it's all a jumble, really. I know we landed on Earth. We've saved it a couple of times recently. Lovely, silly place, always getting itself into scrapes. Right now, I know how it feels. Anyway, it's learning to look after itself. After that tricky business with the Yeti, they've formed an organisation to defend it — headed up by the Brigadier. A lovely fellow. He's got helicopters and bazookas and all sorts of things that go whoosh! Bang!

INQUISITOR: Are the hand gestures really necessary?

DOCTOR: Well, you've never flown in a helicopter, have you? No, too much like fun. Dear Leonardo came up with the idea — must pop back at some point and tell him it worked. Marvellous things, zipping about in the air. We escaped from Tobias Vaughn hanging onto one.

INQUISITOR: Tobias Vaughn?

DOCTOR: Nasty piece of work. Very clever. In league with the Cybermen — they wanted to hypnotise and convert the human race and they'd started with Vaughn. Of course, he was planning on betraying them. I find people like that so interesting, don't you?

INQUISITOR: In what way?

DOCTOR: Keeping so many plates spinning. Building so many alliances, finding ways to betray each one. And, on top of that he was an electronics genius – but that wasn't.. I mean, it wasn't enough to be revered by the world, he also had to want to enslave them. I suppose – well, I suppose he can't really have liked people that much. In which case, why would you want to rule them? I don't understand. I meet so many people like that. And quite often they're really quite good company. It's as if they're born hungry, and no matter what they get, that's never enough. I feel sorry for them, really. Every time I meet one of them, I feel like telling them that I know how it'll end. They all want to live for ever, and none of them.. Anyway, where were we?

INQUISITOR: Saving the Earth.

DOCTOR: Ah yes. Poor Fewsham. He was quite the reverse. Oh, I'm sorry, I'm getting ahead of myself. He was a technician on the Moonbase. Now this one is really fiddly. You see, there came a point where (and don't go blaming me for this) but the people of Earth trapped themselves on their own planet. Instead of going out and exploring they stayed at home. They'd found a really convenient way of zipping around using matter transmission, and that contented them. Of course, it left them vulnerable, as it was all controlled from a relay station on the Moon, which was taken over by the Ice Warriors.

INQUISTOR: What did they want?

DOCTOR: To settle on the Earth. Everyone wants to live there. It really is like when you go on holiday somewhere and start imagining living there.

INQUISITOR: Does that happen to you?

DOCTOR: Well, not really. The great thing about the TARDIS is that, if I like somewhere, I can always go back there. Eventually. Hopefully. Anyway, Fewsham, that was it! If the Ice Warriors were to invade the Earth, they needed control of T-Mat and the only way they could get that was through Fewsham. He was terrified, so he did whatever he could to stay alive. I can't blame him, I suppose. I really can't. But he was as good as dead as soon as the Ice Warriors arrived. Poor chap.

INQUISITOR: And did this not stop you from trying to save him?

DOCTOR: No, I don't suppose it did. It's all too easy to say he was a weak man – but he'd just seen everyone else he knew wiped out. What was he supposed to do? Self-preservation, it's a very human instinct.

INQUISITOR: It clearly is not an instinct you share..

DOCTOR: No, I'm afraid not. I mean, I do hope I don't come across as foolhardy. In this case, the Earth was in trouble, and the easiest way to liberate it was for us to leap into a rocket and head for the Moonbase.

INQUISITOR: Us?

DOCTOR: Zoe, Jamie and me. Oh, don't look at me like that – Jamie's dealt with the Ice Warriors before and Zoe could have taken the T-Mat apart and put it back together again before the kettle boiled. Talking of which, I don't suppose you do tea here, do you?

INQUISITOR: And were you able to save the Earth?

DOCTOR: More than that, I got them interested in space exploration again. Put them back on track.

INQUISITOR: Are you sure they were off track?

DOCTOR: My dear fellow, you get an instinct for it after a while. A sense of when things aren't right. When there's been interference. I can't be everywhere at once, you know. So many terrible things are going on, all over the place. I'm bound to miss the odd one. Hadn't they just been invaded by the Daleks? I really do forget. It takes a planet time to get back on its feet after a thing like that.

INQUISITOR: Cybermen.. Ice Warriors, and now Daleks — this Earth is always under threat.

DOCTOR: Oh yes. It's a des-res.

INQUISITOR: We do not understand.

DOCTOR: Desirable Residence. Nice atmosphere, strategically handy, good plumbing, and, if there's not an R in the month, it can be quite balmy. I'd recommend it — for a visit. Not to invade.

INQUISITOR: We no longer have colonies. Just as we no longer interfere.

DOCTOR: Goodness me, you are harping on about that, aren't you? I've shown you that, if you know what you're doing, and you've a light touch, you can.. judiciously...

INQUISITOR: Interfere?

DOCTOR: Offer a helping hand. You really wouldn't understand, because you've never had a train set. They're marvellous things. You build a whole world in miniature — tunnels and platforms and hills and then you set these little trains whizzing around and around the track. And in theory it's a perfect bit of perpetual motion, but those toy trains are always coming off the track, wheels spinning in the air. And you don't need to do anything more than to reach over and set things right. That's all.

INQUISITOR: And the Earth is your model train set?

DOCTOR: Well, no. I mean, I am fond of it. And you've seen what the humans are like — you've had to ship enough of them home.

INQUISITOR: They are a race of warriors.

DOCTOR: Oh dear, aren't you meant to be observers? You really could look a little closer. Even in battle, they play. In the trenches, the two opposing sides stopped to play football. They lived in utter filth, under the command of generals hopelessly out of their depth, but do you know what — somehow, miraculously, amid all that squalor and slaughter, the postal system was marvellous. The mothers back home couldn't keep their sons alive, but they could send them cake. And oh, how those women baked. Humans really do learn how to make the best out of a bad lot. Exile one of them on a desert island and he'll build a hut and start making himself at home. Really extraordinary.

INQUISITOR: Indeed?

DOCTOR: Fascinating little planet. Once this whole mess is sorted out, I really must see a little more of it..

INQUISITOR: Your companions have reached their own time zones... They will both continue their lives as if nothing had happened.

DOCTOR: Yes, very efficient. Now then, what about me?

INQUISITOR: We have accepted your plea that there is evil in the universe that must be fought, and that you still have a part to play in that battle.

DOCTOR: What? You mean that you're going to let me go free?

INQUISITOR: Not entirely. We have noted your particular interest in the planet Earth. The frequency of your visits must have given you special knowledge of that world and its problems.

DOCTOR: Yes, I suppose that's true. Earth seems more vulnerable than others, yes.

INQUISITOR: For that reason, you will be sent back to that planet.

DOCTOR: Oh, good.

INQUISITOR: In exile.

DOCTOR: In exile?

INQUISITOR: You will be sent to Earth in the twentieth century, and will remain there for as long as we deem proper, and for that period the secret of the TARDIS will be taken from you.

DOCTOR: But you, you can't condemn me to exile on one primitive planet in one century in time! Besides, I'm known on the Earth. It might be very awkward for me.

INQUISITOR: Your appearance has changed before. It will change again..

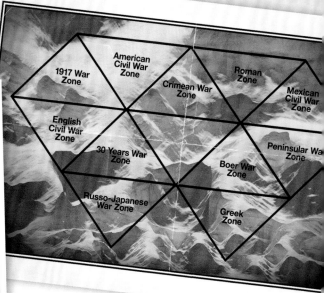

The Story of Doctor Who

1966–1969

A ware that the idea was to replace William Hartnell with another actor, I wrote the Doctor's part as sketchily as possible, so that it could be easily altered.

David Whitaker, writer

While the character of the new Doctor was still being fleshed out, the show's original script editor David Whitaker was writing a six-part story intended to reassure the viewers that this was very much still Doctor Who. *The new Doctor's first adventure saw the return of the Daleks...*

There was a first script, which was sort of written for Billy but which was written for, it struck me reading it, a very verbose, sort of autocratic Sherlock Holmes type who never stopped talking. And I thought, 'That's not going to do for me over three years every week.' So I said,

'No, I don't see the part like this, I see it really as a listener. I think this Doctor listens to everyone, tots it all up and then makes his own decision.' Then in comes Sydney Newman, and he starts talking about this cosmic hobo. And I leapt at it, what a good idea, and I said, 'A man like that would be more of a listener, wouldn't he?' and they said, 'Yes.'

Patrick Troughton

One change we have decided on is to drop the historical stories because we found they weren't very popular. This doesn't mean we won't use historical backgrounds, but we will not involve Doctor Who and his companions in events which cannot be changed because they really happened.

Innes Lloyd, producer

In The Highlanders, *the last purely*

historical story for many years, the Doctor was joined by an 18th-century Scotsman called Jamie...

Jamie was ideal because he could ask the questions the kids at home would ask, and the Doctor could explain. Jamie was wonderful to play. He was from 1746. He was a Highlander, Battle of Culloden. He'd never seen electric light, but he learnt quite quickly. He was very loyal, very tough. He was only supposed to be in four episodes, but halfway through I was asked to stay a bit longer. Innes Lloyd said, 'Now then Frazer, how do you fancy joining the old TARDIS crew for a while?' That was the way he put it.

Frazer Hines (Jamie)

We're often asked how we felt that there was a third person. We all got on well, there was no envy or jealousy. But

PATRICK TROUGHTON
was the Second Doctor

Our problem in choosing the new Doctor Who was very difficult, because we have decided to make considerable changes in the personality of the character. We believe we have found the man we wanted.

Sydney Newman, BBC Head of Drama

His hair is wild and his clothes look rather the worse for wear. Whereas at times he is a positive man of action at other times he deals with the situation like a skilled chess player, reasoning and planning his moves. After the first serial – the Daleks – we will introduce a love of disguises which will help and sometimes disconcert his friends. He is always suspicious of new places, things or people – he is the eternal fugitive with a horrifying fear of the past horrors he has endured.

BBC memo (1966)

He was an absolutely ideal choice. He was a distinguished character actor with a great many varied roles behind him. He was always in demand. Most importantly of all, I think, was that he had a leading actor's temperament. He was a father figure to the whole company and hence could embrace it and sweep it along with him.

Innes Lloyd

I thought it would be much more fun if we had a dangerous situation and a Doctor who just sat down and played his pipe. The companions would be screaming, 'My God, the water's coming up, what are we going to do!' and he continues playing and says, 'Well, I don't know, something will turn up.'

Gerry Davis, script editor

The atmosphere changed completely when Pat Troughton was cast. Pat, Anneke and I all used to socialise, and it became great fun to go into work.

Michael Craze (Ben Jackson)

He was eccentric though, very eccentric. He wore the same shoes throughout the three years. Hush Puppies. I'm sure he wasn't sponsored by them, but he wore them as Patrick in the rehearsal room, and as the Doctor as well. He had the same pair of shoes on, these Hush Puppies. So he was slightly eccentric, but great fun. And in the end we got telepathic, we could just look at each other and do whatever we wanted to do.

Frazer Hines

Patrick Troughton was a brilliant actor, to me, he was the Doctor and a real friend. I was very fond of Pat and the times we had together. We became very close.

Deborah Watling (Victoria Waterfield)

TROUGHTON *on* TROUGHTON

To begin with, I thought it would last about six weeks after Billy Hartnell had finished. However, my contribution lasted three years as it turned out. It was very hard work – nevertheless it was the happiest time of my professional life. *Doctor Who* gave me a chance to indulge my passion for dressing up and being able to have some sly fun as well as a bit of clowning.

Patrick Troughton

My original idea was to black up, wear a big turban and brass earrings with a big grey beard; doing it like *The Arabian Nights*. The idea was that no one would know who I was.

Patrick Troughton

The costume evolved. It was a ragged imitation of Billy Hartnell, only more way out. To begin with, I found myself playing it over the top, but the Head of Serials, Shaun Sutton, said, 'No, no, just do it in your head, old chap.' So I toned it down a bit after that, and it was warmer and a bit more successful.

Patrick Troughton

I never give interviews, never. Just tell them that I am that mystery man of television, Doctor Who. It is still magic, and I hope it stays that way.

Patrick Troughton

three companions is one too many, and I understand now why they decided to phase Mike out because his performance was becoming quite serious and heavy and Frazer was so child friendly with his kilt and Scots accent and sweet. So they felt they could keep Polly and Jamie and let Ben go.

Anneke Wills (Polly Wright)

He is a piper and the character must be that of a simple, but engaging Scot. He is cheerful, open, manly, flexible – more flexible in fact than Ben and Polly. When either Ben or Polly are pulling his leg, he reacts with a grin. The Doctor is a strange, loveable wee chap to Jamie. He is obviously some sort of genial wizard or magician. The Doctor enjoys Jamie as an oddity like himself. He knows he has an appreciative audience, and one that will laugh at his jokes. Jamie doesn't know how to treat Polly. He goes out of his way to look after her, but is often confused by her 1966 attitudes and appearance. Ben has complexes, Jamie has none. Ben is nervy, Jamie is calm. Ben is apt to take the mickey out of Jamie and is irritated when Jamie takes it good-humouredly.

BBC memo (28 November 1966)

Less than four months after The Tenth Planet, *the Cybermen made their first return, invading a 21st-century Moonbase...*

We thought we'd try and get to the Moon before Cape Canaveral!

Innes Lloyd

My basic premise for *Doctor Who* stories in that era of minuscule budgets was to forgo the usual dozen tatty sets in favour of one major set around which we could

concentrate all the money. This made a much more exciting and convincing central location for the drama.

Gerry Davis

The series now entered a confident and innovative period, inventing a range of monstrous species to menace humanity and terrify the audience...

I had my own 4-year-old daughter at home, and she was watching *The Macra Terror* with her father, and at the end of it she said, 'Dad, is Mummy coming home tonight?'

Anneke Wills

Innes Lloyd now decided to change the TARDIS crew. Three companions was proving just too many...

In *The Faceless Ones* was Pauline Collins, which was quite interesting as they were thinking Pauline and Frazer might go on. They had decided to let go of Ben, and they came to me and said, 'On you go with Jamie – are you up for it?' And I remember having to make a difficult decision and say I'll go with Michael, because I had a fear that if I stayed on, I'd become addicted to the lovely £60 a week, and it would be like *Coronation Street*, I'd be there for years! Also I wanted to support Mike, as I thought it was rather mean that they were making him leave. So I thought if Mike's going, I'll go. Pat was terribly sad. We were the ones who'd been with him from the beginning, so he

was very sad to see us leave, and we were sad to leave too.

Anneke Wills

I was not an obvious choice for a *Doctor Who* girl – a bit too regional, I gather – but the director fought for me and won. I loved my outfits, bloomers and all. I was offered a regular job on the show – somewhere between 12 and 15 episodes – but as much as I loved it, I'm a mover-on.

Pauline Collins

The fourth season ended with a seven-part Dalek adventure. Terry Nation was hoping to launch the Daleks in America, and so David Whitaker was asked to devise the Daleks' 'final end' in a civil war on Skaro...

We had an absolutely marvellous time in that battle sequence, and we even had two radio-controlled model Daleks. We had a giant Mother Dalek in the studio with a lot of hoses attached to it. We filled those up with all sorts of horrible mixtures, so that when they blew apart, the hoses swung through the air spewing filth. In those days we didn't have a model stage, and all those sequences were set up at Ealing. Compared with what was done in later years, it was fairly amateurish, but the great advantage was that it was on 35 mm film, so what we lost in being amateurish we gained in quality.

Michealjohn Harris, visual effects designer

The Doctor and Jamie rescued a young orphan from the Daleks – the very Victorian Victoria...

Innes Lloyd saw me as Alice in Wonderland and asked me to audition for the role of Polly. He then suggested I go away, learn more about theatre and try again in about a year's time. This I did, and was offered the role of Victoria Waterfield. I felt very strange coming into it as I did with the Daleks appearing in the same story. The dress I wore was so long it actually made me look a bit like a Dalek.

Deborah Watling

We had Marius Goring, Peter Barkworth, Peter Jeffrey, Michael Gough and a lot of such people. It's always a good idea, in this game, to get as much good talent as possible into things. We had extraordinarily fine designers, basically as good as anyone in the film business and yet they do it on peanuts and do five times as much. At that time one was thinking more of writers and actors. I should have thought of the directors too, but it was what was going to be up on the screen – who would be the faces, who would write the scripts. I took it for granted that the directors would do their jobs and that they would do as splendidly as they did.

Innes Lloyd

With Innes Lloyd wanting to move on, script editor Peter Bryant became joint producer, taking over completely with The Web of Fear *but starting on* The Tomb of the Cybermen, *with Victor Pemberton as his script editor...*

Innes knew I wanted to be a producer and by then I had a pretty solid background in the business. I had all the qualifications one needs to be a producer. I'd done it all. So Innes said, 'Yes, fine, sure.'

Peter Bryant, producer

I did suggest putting the dry ice into the tombs because when it was first done and the tombs were opened there wasn't enough atmosphere. I said something in the studio and it suddenly appeared on the screen. When I read it, I saw it almost as a kind of Frankenstein atmosphere with a touch of the Hammer horrors. I'd also just been to Egypt to see the tombs so I was very much into Egyptology.

Victor Pemberton, script editor

Since Victoria had only just lost her father, Pemberton inserted a small scene where the Doctor comforts her and reveals a little of his own background...

I just felt that occasionally there should be some sort of humanity in it. There should be some sort of relation to real life. I really don't think one should write things in for the sake of it. There was a family thing going on there, so I did write a scene which worked out quite well. I never thought you should write down to children. That's why I thought *Tomb of the Cybermen* could take a bit of adult writing.

Victor Pemberton

The comedy began to sneak in. Patrick and I were always looking for the humour of the show. So much so that when we did *The Tomb of the Cybermen*, that lovely thing that was not in the script, when we said, 'Come along, Victoria', and we grabbed each other's hands. It wasn't even in the rehearsals because we knew the director would cut it out.

Frazer Hines

With purely historical stories a thing of the past, the fifth season could concentrate wholeheartedly on monsters. Writers Mervyn Haisman and Henry Lincoln wrote an encounter between the Doctor and the Yeti

Writer Neil Gaiman on
THE TOMB OF THE CYBERMEN

The Tomb of the Cybermen is very much a favourite story and definitely one that I wanted to refer to in *Nightmare in Silver*. The things that I love most about it are the performances, from the humans and the Cybermen. Up until that point it had felt like the Cybermen were these strange, otherworldly things. When I was a small child watching *Doctor Who*, I remember Jamie being terrified in *The Moonbase* that they were ghosts – that a Cyberman was the Phantom Piper come to take him away. There was a weird level on which those Cybermen did feel kind of ghostly. They were weird, faceless shapes.

With *The Tomb of the Cybermen*, you felt that they were smart – suddenly, there was a huge intelligence going on. And you got fantastic performances out of big men in simple suits that covered their whole faces. You got a very small cast in a very small space experiencing a story where, essentially, you're never quite sure, apart from the Doctor, you never quite know who to trust – you're never quite sure who's been taken over by Cybermen, you're not sure whose motives for doing things are what. Then the Cybermen come in – there's that glorious sequence where they come out of their tomb and you realise that it's not a tomb, it's a fridge. They've been on ice and now they've come out.

and, along the way, created the sinister Great Intelligence...

I remember the costumes being terrible things to wear. Awful. And the trouble was that there was filming in North Wales, and the actors inside them couldn't see their feet. They had to have three people to help them through each sequence. The poor men kept falling down.

Michealjohn Harris

We began to get into terrible trouble for being too frightening. During *The Abominable Snowmen*, Wolfe Morris, who played the head monk, had to die, and his head was supposed to disintegrate. The visual effects people used a dummy head and poured some kind of acid over it and it slowly dissolved.

Deborah Watling

The next story introduced the Ice Warriors, another monster that would leave a lasting impression on the show. They were created by Brian Hayles...

Brian Hayles already had a certain reputation before he came to *Doctor Who*. He was very much an adventure writer and he did it very well. He knew how to put a good yarn together.

Victor Pemberton

The Ice Warriors were made out of fibreglass and the claws were rubber. Martin Baugh was the designer then and took a lot of publicity for them at the time in photos and press stories. We built about five in all of various sizes, including a midget, and we made the Ice Lord later on which was very similar.

Jack Lovell, costume designer

Innes Lloyd left after The Enemy of the World, *and Peter Bryant was joined by Derrick Sherwin...*

I wanted to do other things in Drama. Although at the start I was reluctant to do it, I enjoyed producing it very much and learnt a lot. They were a very good team to work with. *Doctor Who* hit a strange and compulsive note – part fantasy, part science-fiction, horror and not horror – a little something for all the family.

Innes Lloyd

Derrick Sherwin had written to Shaun Sutton, and Shaun had spoken to me about him. He said that there was this guy – an actor who'd done some writing as well – who wanted to come into the Beeb and work as a story editor and would I like to meet him? So I did, and I said OK. Shaun tried to encourage us to take people who possibly weren't getting

the beginnings or quite as much work as they should have been.

Peter Bryant

The Enemy of the World *saw the directorial debut of Barry Letts – an ex-actor who would later become the programme's producer...*

While we were making *Enemy of the World*, Patrick Troughton said, 'They've asked me to sign up for another year of *Doctor Who*, and I don't know what to do. This once-a-week pace is really killing me.' We were so pushed for time, I had to use doubles for the long shots of Patrick, Frazer and Debbie on film because they were in London recording while we were down on the south cost. It was a ludicrous situation. So I said to Patrick, 'Why don't you say you'll do another year, but then suggest that everybody would produce much better shows if they cut down the number of them and had gaps between each story to do the filming.' I think he went back and suggested this, but of course by this time the next season was already down on the schedules and it was too late. Nevertheless, the planners decided it was a good idea and set it up for the following season, with the connivance of Peter Bryant and Derrick Sherwin, with the idea of the Doctor being confined to Earth so they could make use of ordinary locations.

Barry Letts, director

The Web of Fear *saw the TARDIS land in the London Underground for a rematch with the Great Intelligence. The serial was a big hit – with its contemporary setting and frightening monsters, it paved the way for a major change in the series' format. It also featured the debut of another character who would play an important part in that new direction...*

Originally we planned to film in the Underground itself, and approached London Transport for their permission. They wanted the ridiculous sum of £200 an hour! So, with a lot of hard work, we built our own Underground in the studios, copying from the originals. After the serial had been broadcast, we received a letter from the Transport authorities saying that they were going to sue us for using their tunnels after all, and we hadn't been anywhere near them!

Douglas Camfield, director

I appeared in another Douglas Camfield story, *The Web of Fear*, with Patrick Troughton. The actor who was going to play, as he was then, Colonel Lethbridge-Stewart, was booked but couldn't do it. I was going to play a captain who was killed in that story, but Douglas rang me up and said, 'Do you mind playing the colonel rather than the captain?' And I said, 'It's a great promotion.' If it hadn't been for David Langton opting out of that part, my life would have been very different indeed.

Nicholas Courtney (Colonel Lethbridge-Stewart)

He came up with a terrific performance, it caught on, and the Colonel, later the Brigadier, was set for a long run...

Douglas Camfield

On set was Terrance Dicks, who had just accepted the post of assistant script editor, the start of a 45-year association with Doctor Who...

The first playback I attended was the last episode of *The Web of Fear*, which featured amiable droopy-drawered monsters called the Yeti, who looked like overweight teddy bears and made a noise exactly like a flushing lavatory when they roared.

Terrance Dicks, script editor

The next story, Fury from the Deep, *introduced another of the show's longest-running, most iconic objects...*

I actually thought the sonic screwdriver was a bad step, although I was partly instrumental in suggesting that was the way to undo bolts. The first time it was used, we were chatting about how the Doctor was going to escape this time, and we decided he'd get a screwdriver out and undo the lock on an inspection hatch. Then we realised that, in fact, screws are put in from the back to stop people taking the nuts out, so I said, 'I know what he does – he uses a sonic screwdriver!' It vibrated at the right interval, the screws turned around and it was a good visual effect, very easy to make, and we used that as a way to enable the Doctor to escape.

Michael E. Briant, director

Deborah Watling's Victoria stayed in 20th-century England at the end of Fury from the Deep, *and Wendy Padbury joined the TARDIS in* The Wheel in Space *as Zoe Heriot, a 21st-century teen genius with a photographic memory, martial arts moves, and some figure-hugging cat suits...*

Deborah Watling wanted to leave, she'd done a year and wanted to do other things, and she said she was fed up with screaming at monsters and stuff.

Frazer Hines

When I told Pat Troughton I was leaving, his face fell. I knew he was under a lot of pressure, and he looked at me and he said, 'I want to go now as well.'

Deborah Watling

I think probably Zoe managed quite well to fit in with the actual Sixties, because she did wear the miniskirt that was far too short and should never be allowed and the famous sparkly cat suits with zips up the front, which were a great hit. The background of Zoe was that she was this extraordinarily bright astrophysicist. There was nothing humble about Zoe. She gave the Doctor a run for his money with her brilliance. She had an eidetic memory. She could recall visions, images, things that had happened, so easily because that's the way she was made. She was able to outwit computers and she had a mathematical brain. She couldn't be more different to me, but it was a very interesting character to play.

Wendy Padbury (Zoe Heriot)

The sixth season's second story brought in another member of the production team who would go on to enjoy a long association with the show...

I'd been on the director's course and the head of serials, Shaun Sutton, called me into his office and asked me if I'd like to do a *Doctor Who: The Mind Robber*. I remember filming for that at two o'clock in the morning at a disused aerodrome south of Croydon, in order to shoot a scene with a unicorn. The unicorn was to be played by a pony, which we were

assured would be able to do all that was required, and would be white. When we arrived, we were horrified to see that it was actually a creamy brown. So in the middle of this aerodrome, in the dark, we had to paint the horse. Someone had some poster paint which covered half of it, somebody else had some blanco, and make-up turned out everything they had until the horse was in all sorts of different make-up. Then we tied a horn on its head and at last filmed it.

David Maloney, director

My favourite story is *The Mind Robber*, only because I thought it was incredibly innovative. I loved storybooks coming to life and storybook characters coming to life and forests of letters that, when you climb up them, are spelling words. I thought it was a very, very clever story and totally unlike any of the others.

Wendy Padbury

For the next story, The Invasion, *Nicholas Courtney's Lethbridge-Stewart was promoted to Brigadier and given a very special taskforce to lead, while Terrance Dicks became more closely involved...*

The idea of it happening on Earth with real people who were involved in everyday lives was a good one. So I invented UNIT and brought in some new characters.

Derrick Sherwin, producer

So UNIT was created, and I was promoted to Brigadier. Douglas Camfield liked me so much that they offered me a two-year contract. My first child had been born, so I was delighted.

Nicholas Courtney

Harry Melling, actor and Patrick Troughton's grandson, on
THE WAR GAMES

When I was young the fact that my granddad was the Doctor was something you could dish out to make yourself slightly more interesting – often to older people who would have known him. But I never really got into it. I mean, that's the most I've seen of him properly.

It's actually quite scary. Not the episode. I mean, I thought that was great, actually. Storytelling-wise it was really exciting, so simple. The set design at the end of Episode 10 is great. You can see they're cutting up the film and adding these layers of force field at particular moments. But that's part of the charm of it, isn't it? What I think is quite nice about *Doctor Who* is that the show is frightening, but there's a slight sense of tongue in cheek to it as well.

What was scary was seeing my granddad and all the things he was doing – when you see someone do things that make sense to you. The choices he made. Little moments like the hand wave to Zoe, as she leaves, little idiosyncratic things that tell huge stories. I think that's what was so scary about it – the fact that all of the things he did were things that are the things I immediately look out for when I see something or read a script. Which was bizarre.

What interests me as an actor is the quirkiness of characters and their bizarreness and trying to make sense of that. The more I see clips and pictures of my granddad, the closer I feel to him in his wackiness, his boldness... And – I hope this comes across the right way – I hadn't realised that I was fulfilling exactly the same things that excited him.

Derrick Sherwin wanted to leave *Doctor Who* to be script editor of another show. They offered me a three-month trial contract, and I thought I would try it. It could be an interesting experience. I signed up for three months and stayed there five years.

Terrance Dicks

The Invasion *was the last Cyberman story for several years, but a more recent alien menace was about to be resurrected in* The Seeds of Death...

The Ice Warriors were actually my favourite monster. I think there was something very, very eerie about them and their command and their voice. The Ice Warriors were the real deal as far as I was concerned. I could certainly sit in make-up and watch poor men have hours of scales all over their face, and still when it came to shoot a scene, be extremely scared. They absolutely worked for me – probably more than anything else I met during my period.

Wendy Padbury

The Seeds of Death *was preceded and succeeded by the first stories penned by another* Doctor Who *legend. Trainee script editor Terrance Dicks had made a discovery in the slush pile...*

I think I can claim to have found Robert Holmes as a *Doctor Who* writer. He wrote an outline for *The Krotons*, and they rejected it. Much later, Bob tried again, when he heard there was a new script editor, because it is very much a matter of individual taste. At that time I was still a sort of dogsbody and all unsolicited ideas were passed on to me. I read it, liked it, and I showed it to the producer. We already had all the stories we needed but they said if you like, you can develop it as a reserve. I got the four scripts in, then nobody really bothered about it.

Then they ran into script trouble, everything just went wrong, and everyone went around saying 'What are we going to do?' I said, 'Well, I do happen to have a four-part serial,' and they all seized upon it. The director, David Maloney, said it was fine, the other one was cancelled, and we did *The Krotons*.

Terrance Dicks

Holmes's second Doctor Who *script was the show's first space epic* – The Space Pirates *saw six weeks of ambitious model work...*

I designed all the spaceships from scratch and had them purpose-built by an outside contractor. The actual filming was done by a firm called Bowey Films. They had been working on *Thunderbirds* with Derek Meddings and they were specialists in that area.

Ian Scoones, visual effects designer

Now all Terrance Dicks had to do was finish off Season Six. Oh, and write out Patrick Troughton's Doctor...

Derrick Sherwin came up with the Time Lords. I've always given him credit for that. One day Derrick came into my office and said, 'Terrance, we need a ten-part *Doctor Who*, you've got to write it and we need it next week.' I'm exaggerating slightly but it was pretty much that,

because two other projects had collapsed – a six-parter and a four-parter. So they'd taken the decision to do one ten-parter. That just sort of landed in my lap. I immediately got in Malcolm Hulke, who had been my friend and mentor, because I knew I couldn't cope with it by myself. Mac and I wrote *The War Games* at great speed.

Terrance Dicks

As for *The War Games*, I was responsible for a lot of its conception. I remember sitting in this office with Terrance Dicks, Malcolm Hulke, and the producers. We came up with the idea of a very long serial but after that initial decision and the choice of theme, we still hadn't decided what theatres of war we'd go into. I went home and asked my young son what would be the periods of war he'd be most interested to look at. He said the

American Civil War, the First World War and the Roman invasion of Britain. These were the most romantic eras of war and that's why we chose them. Malcolm Hulke wrote it with Terrance Dicks. Malcolm was always a great influence on Terry. The last episode was the first Time Lord script. It was a whole new concept.

David Maloney

We got an important instruction to find a way of changing Patrick Troughton's appearance, but to leave it open. Patrick had said he didn't want to go on being Doctor Who and he wished to leave. No one had been selected so they wanted an open-ended serial. We then came up with the idea of Time Lords. A very complicated way of doing it, really, I suppose, but it gave a good few scenes.

Malcolm Hulke, writer

Three years was long enough. I didn't want to get typecast, and one had to get out while the going was good. Peter Bryant asked me way back how long and I said, 'Three years, no longer.'

Patrick Troughton

We were aware that Pat wanted to leave, of course. He had had a hard slog – don't forget we were doing about forty episodes a year in those days – and he was very, very tired. Eventually he decided that he had had enough. The Doctor had changed before, so we knew that we could change him again, and that's what we did.

Derrick Sherwin

That was three happy years of my life. It was wonderful. And I didn't want to leave, and Patrick didn't want to leave. But you know his wife was on to him. My agent said, 'You must do films now, you've done three years of television.'

Frazer Hines

We were asked to stay on, and Frazer and I decided it would be nicer to go with Pat. We didn't know who was coming in. I know it turned out to be Jon Pertwee, and we'd probably have had a lovely time, but I didn't think you could push your luck.

Wendy Padbury

When I'm asked if I have any anecdotes, I'm afraid to say that there are none that could be printed!

Patrick Troughton

GREYHOUND

A memoir by
Brigadier Sir Alistair Gordon Lethbridge-Stewart

It's strange writing something that you know no one will ever read. But I've come to the portion of these memoirs dealing directly with the Doctor. And how can I write about a man who does not exist? Someone is going to slap a D-Notice on these pages, so why bother? And yet, if I did not, I couldn't look him in the face. Any of them.

Memory is odd (says he, writing his memoirs) but in some ways my recollections of my years with UNIT's infuriating scientific adviser are sharper than my time in Peru, or even my recent visit to the Black Archive with Sarah Jane Smith (of whom, more anon, I'll bet).

I still have photographs of my earliest encounter – caught on Harold Chorley's camera dashing off into the Underground tunnels in pursuit of the Yeti and the Great Intelligence – and slap bang into a date with destiny and the Doctor. I genuinely thought he might be behind the Great Intelligence, and pretty much my first instinct was to arrest him. 'Don't be too hard on yourself, Lethbridge-Stewart,' he told me later. 'It's always happening to me. I'm used to it. The important thing is that we get on famously from here on in.'

He was a funny sort of fellow in those days – short and shabby chap, an air of having just saved the world with something he'd found down the back of the sofa. Yet you just had to meet him to trust him completely. After the Yeti do, UNIT was set up (see Chapter 5) and, when next we met, it was to expose Tobias Vaughn and deal with an army of Cybermen in the sewers.

Clearly, we had drawn attention to ourselves. Some while later, the Doctor's own people sentenced him to exile on Earth, I was able to make use of his services on a near-permanent basis. Mind you, it took some persuading that the mysterious stranger in the cottage hospital was really him – different face, you see.

We were in the middle of an invasion by the Autons at the time – killer space plastic. We'd already drafted in Dr Elizabeth Shaw from Cambridge to be our Scientific Adviser. She was a cool customer. You'd have thought the two of them would have resented each other, but they immediately ganged up against me. The Doctor wanted to leave Earth, while she… I don't know. I think each thought the other almost an intellectual equal and regarded me and my troops as clodhoppers at best.

It was mildly infuriating. The Doctor's always been a free agent, and rarely understood the amount of pressure from the higher-ups I had to deal with, even on a good day. The paperwork! Having to persuade a cottage hospital not to press charges over the theft of clothes and an extremely expensive vintage car. Having to create an identity for the Doctor, and, of course, buy him another car.

He blamed me dreadfully over the affair of the Silurians. His eyes were always on the big picture – he was ecstatic that he'd brokered peace with his lizards and that he'd cured a plague, but he'd not really realised the implications – a hostile alien species had tried to wipe us out with biological weapons and had taken control of a nuclear reactor. Politically, things couldn't have been worse. And, in the middle of it all, the Doctor's opening gambit was to suggest offering them some desert hotspot – as if those areas of the world weren't trouble enough already! The Doctor's a brilliant man, but the fellow had no grasp at all of the politics on the ground. My orders were, quite firmly, to blow their caves up and hang the consequences. I received them gladly. There's quite enough complexity in the world, and I admire certainties.

It was the same with those Martian fellows in the Recovery 7 affair. General Carrington was smart enough to know that the best way to win is to spread confusion and uncertainty. The 'Ambassadors' were, the Doctor assured me, an essentially peaceful species – and not even from Mars, apparently – but Carrington had muddied the waters by sending them out to kill some fairly high-profile figures. This almost guaranteed a forceful response – not one (the Doctor assured me) we stood any chance of winning. The General simply hated them so much that he wanted war. In that case I was able to help get the Doctor what he wanted.

We weren't quite so much in agreement over the Stahlman incident. You may remember all that talk about 'Free energy in our time' – that was all about the Stahlman Project, the idea of releasing energy by drilling into the Earth's crust. Instead it released an aggressive, ancient force. And – if it had gone any deeper, the drill would have brought about the end of the world. On that occasion what made it hard to take the Doctor seriously was that, in the middle of this crisis he went missing for days – worse, he came
back with an incredible story that he'd been in a parallel dimension. If there's one thing those up the chain of command don't care for, it's a seemingly work-shy eccentric proclaiming 'the End of the World Is Nigh'.

In a few minutes we shall know the answer to the question that has been occupying the minds of everyone here at Space Control since Mars Probe 7 took off on its return journey from the red planet nearly eight months ago. What has happened to astronauts Frank Michaels and Joe Lefee? Communications remained perfect on the long outward journey to the red planet and throughout the difficult landing. For a full twelve hours they sent back pictures and reports from the surface of Mars. Both then seemed in perfect health, then silence.

The world assumed that disaster had overtaken the mission. But when all hope was gone, radio astronomers at Cambridge reported that Mars Probe 7 had blasted off and was heading back to Earth.

You can see from the radar screen, that's the screen just to the left of Professor Cornish there, that the recovery capsule and Mars Probe 7 are on convergence. This is a tricky moment for controller Ralph Cornish and his team. The two craft will be linking up in a moment or two. And then we shall know the answer to the mystery that has baffled the world's scientists for seven months.

The Stahlman Process

EVERYTHING
YOU NEED
TO KNOW
BEFORE
INVESTING
IN A FUTURE
OF CHEAP
ENERGY
FOR ALL

STAHLMAN
SAVING
THE WORLD

ST. CEDD'S COLLEGE
NEWSLETTER

We're delighted that
Professor Elisabeth Shaw
has returned from sabbatical
and will be giving this
year's Fendelman Lecture,
entitled 'Making Genes Fit:
Mankind's Hidden History'.

It was around about that point that I realised the best option was to listen to the Doctor first and then try and smooth over Geneva afterwards. It wasn't always that straightforward – some department or other was always despatching an official to ask awkward questions and make notes. I tried to keep them as far away from the Doctor as possible – it was never going to end well – but the odd one or two always slipped through the net.

I have to admit that's rather what led to the appointment of Jo Grant. She was the niece of some mandarin or other, and she quite fancied being a spy, and could I see my way clear to… Well, Dr Shaw had just left, and I figured it would be handy having someone in the Doctor's laboratory making sure he didn't blow it up. Is it wrong of me to say that I enjoyed seeing his face when she arrived? He took me to one side after they'd met: 'It won't work, Brigadier. I'll have a properly qualified assistant or none at all.' But then, of course, the Nestenes tipped up again, and Jo Grant became a part of the furniture. A very small, very fashionable part of the furniture.

If the Doctor and Dr Shaw were allies, then he and Miss Grant were best friends. I'm not sure that, in those days, you'd say the Doctor and I were. As so often happens, our friendship blossomed after we stopped working together. I guess, at some level, he viewed me as his jailor. And, for all his brilliance, I saw him as the cause of the biggest paperwork headaches a man could have. I think, if he had have failed, and the world had ended, the paperwork would have continued.

****

Curiously, although I'm not permitted to write about the Doctor, I am allowed to write about the Master. He's one of the most famous villains of the last two centuries. (Good lord, have I really been around that long?) In my day, if he wasn't stealing missiles, he was in league with vampiric blobs, lizards, or, in one case, Old Nick himself. Recently, they tell me, he got to be Prime Minister without anybody realising. The infernal cheek of the man.

In my experience, most evil men are brutal and stupid. But the Master was charming, suave and clever. He had the most exquisite manners, something you could never accuse the Doctor of. Which goes to show you never can judge by appearances.

The Doctor, for example, was dressed like a showman. He liked to make an entrance, swirling more velvet than a music hall conjuror. The Master, by contrast, lurked in the background. If he wasn't wearing a disguise, he was just there, in the shadows, clad head-to-foot in black. This wasn't shyness – it was the reticence of a predator waiting to pounce.

Very few strangers warmed to the Doctor. The civil servants who managed to encounter him were left so ruffled their reports back recommended the immediate slashing of our funding. That's not to say the Doctor didn't have friends in high places. Turned out he belonged to a very exclusive club in Mayfair (claimed to have founded it shortly after the Restoration), where he'd hob-nob with all sorts of high-ups. If he wasn't in his lab, chances were he'd be heading off there. 'Ah, Lethbridge-Stewart, just off to sample the clarets with old Tubby Rowlands. Want me to put in a request for a new rocket launcher or anything? Only too happy to have a word in the right ear. Really must drag you along some time.' Of course he never did invite me along. But then again, we never ran out of rocket launchers.

It later turned out that the Master belonged to the same club, and contrived to ensure that the two of them never bumped into each other. He had a devilish sense of humour.

The Doctor wasn't just about fine wines in oak-panelled rooms. That makes him sound a snob – he was anything but! He loved a cup of strong, sweet army tea (made on a Bunsen burner), went ballroom dancing with Sgt Benton, and even popped along to a New Age Retreat with Mike Yates after his 'trouble'. That didn't stop him from being a fearsome namedropper, though. If there's one thing worse than being attacked by a dragon, it's being attacked by a dragon while being lectured about the favourite dishes of Chairman Mao.

'There's a time and a place for everything, Doctor,' I'd say to him.

'Is there, Brigadier, is there, though?' He'd reply, looking rueful.

He was a prisoner. Part of his showmanship was because he was as restless as a caged beast. He was stuck on Earth, unable to shoot off into space or backwards into time. And he saw the Master's frequent interventions as a game. I didn't – I was terrified, frankly. One false move and it would be the end of the world. Literally. It'd be World Wars III, IV, V and goodnight Vienna.

It did, at least, explain the Doctor's behaviour once he'd caught the Master. He was placed on trial (the secret trial was D-Noticed to the hilt, obviously), and would have been executed, but for the Doctor's passionate plea for mercy. He stood there and pleaded on behalf of his species for clemency towards someone who'd nearly wiped us out a dozen times. It wasn't a situation I could really understand (after all, the Doctor had plenty of bad words for his own people and the Master the rest of the time). He told me that 'taking life, any life, has to be wrong' – but there have been a fair few

PRODUCT RECALL

WARNING

If you have recently purchased or been given a **PLASTIC DAFFODIL**, either as part of a soap powder promotion or the Touring British Festival of Plastics Roadshow, you are urged to phone the following hotline:

01-123-800

NOTE: DO NOT APPROACH YOUR DAFFODIL

times when I've noticed him look the other way (from Azal to the occasional Ogron).

Anyway, the Doctor came up with an interesting suggestion. You know those Russian Dolls? Lift the lid off, and inside is a smaller replica? This was the form the Doctor's 'clemency' took – placing the Master in a remote prison, trapped on a single island, in a microscopic version of his own sentence. If it was a cruel irony, the Master appreciated the joke. He was always better than the Doctor at escaping.

For all his protests, the Doctor hung around after the Time Lords granted his freedom. That was quite an experience in itself. I remember how the day started – with equipment vanishing from around UNIT HQ. I knew that would probably be the last straw for Campbell, our long-suffering Scientific Stores Quartermaster. (About the only person to pierce his dourness was Miss Grant. She was so successful I nearly suggested the men adopt miniskirts before approaching him. Of course, I wouldn't suggest that now. It was in the days before I'd met Ms Smith and discovered Women's Lib.)

At first it was just some filing cabinets that went missing. Then it was a water dispenser and my new computer (practically the size of a house – amazing how much smaller these things have got). Next thing we knew, the Doctor himself had disappeared, only to be replaced by his previous self. Then, to cap it all, the whole of UNIT HQ had disappeared into another universe. (It's a longstanding joke by Sergeant Benton that I immediately assumed it to be Cromer, but I never said anything of the sort.)

One of the mercies of UNIT is that our HR department is in Geneva, which means that we were all back in our proper places before Geneva could even telex through a demand that the Doctor send through photos for a new staff pass. This time, the Doctors (three of 'em!) had saved the entire universe, and his own people, the Time Lords, gave him back his freedom to travel.

When he broke the news to me, I worried. Most people can be won over with a promotion or a rise, but not the Doctor (we paid him a salary, but I don't think he ever banked the cheques). I needn't have worried – the Doctor is a creature of

demands heeded and arrangements made for return of shipment. However, samples retained as per Acc831 in Roswell Containment Facility behind zero-balance dwarf star alloy. Thus, pleased to report that, while every other trace of Axonite has been removed from the planet, we still have sufficient stocks in order to investigate the material's alleged energy production and replicatory abilities.

habit, and, free to wander the universe, he and Miss Grant came home frequently. Although, she'd grown up fast, and he soon lost her to a rather dashing Welsh vegetarian hippy.

I have to say, the loss hit him hard. I'd never really wondered if the Doctor had feelings of a romantic nature. (Dr Shaw once speculated that the Doctor not only didn't speak our language, but had a whole range of alien emotions, some of which translated quite badly. I think she was trying to placate me after one of our more incendiary rows.)

The arrival of Ms Smith lifted him out of his slough. Or rather, I think she dragged him out of it and into several messes. By rights, after she lied her way onto UNIT premises, I probably should have had her arrested, but the two of them promptly went off into space.

By the time they came back, London had been taken over by dinosaurs as part of that Operation Golden Age malarkey. We had to cope without the Doctor for some time, and I have to say, we did... reasonably well. We needed his help to save us, however, which is the point at which he gave me a space-time telegraph, in order to summon him if we were in trouble.

I thanked him politely, but began making sure that UNIT were properly equipped to do without him. At a pinch. I was right to – over the next few months, he was around more sporadically (and in some new body or other), and I could sense he was getting restless.

I had an uncle in the navy, and he was just the same – always delighted to come home, always staring out the window wondering where he'd go next.

But, no matter where he goes, he always drops by from time to time. And there's always a glass put out for him. In case the Doctor comes to call.

INTERNAL MEMORANDUM

U.N.I.T

Eyes Only: Brigadier Lethbridge-Stewart

Re: THE MASTER

Regret to report unsatisfactory conclusion to Operation Gargled Rodeo: suspect was not, in fact, the Master. Foreign Office feels that personal letter of apology from UK head of UNIT may help assuage Spanish ambassador's distress.

THE THIRD DOCTOR

BBC 3

7.00 The Clangers
(rpt.)

7.10 Harold Chorley Goes... Underground
(rpt.)

8.00 News
Mid-evening summary
with Kenneth Kendall

8.08 Weather

8.10 The Passing Parade: Live from Devil's End
Alastair Fergus exclusively previews tonight's exciting archaeological dig.

8.15 FILM Dracula is Dead and Well and Living In London
BBC3 marks the greatest occult festival of the year bar Halloween with this supernatural blockbuster.

11.45 The Passing Parade: Live from Devil's End
Alastair Fergus is on the scene of the archaeological dig. Granted unprecedented access, and never afraid to get his fingers dirty, Alastair joins Professor Gilbert Horner as he uncovers what many say is an Anglo-Saxon burial mound, but some believe could well be the grave of the Devil himself...

12.30 Closedown

UNITED NATIONS INTELLIGENCE TASKFORCE

Dear Sir Reginald

I am writing to you to apologise both personally and on behalf of UNIT for the distress caused to you by the destruction of Auderly House. While you may rest assured that this was necessary for reasons of international security, I can also appreciate how personally upsetting you must find the loss of a house that has been in your family for two centuries.

I have personally detailed a squad to help with the salvage operation, and they report back that much of the wine cellar is unharmed.

I hope you have found the alternative conference facilities we have made available at UNIT HQ satisfactory and wish your peace conference every success.

I shall also be writing to the Prime Minister and the National Trust.

Yours sincerely

Brigadier Alistair Gordon Lethbridge-Stewart

The Curse of Aggedor

Mighty is Aggedor, fiercest of all the beasts of Peladon.
Young men hunt him to prove their courage.
His fur trims our royal garment. / His head is our royal emblem.
His soul is our protector. / His claw is our defender.
One day there shall come a darkness / The spirit of Aggedor will rise again
To warn and defend his royal master, King Peladon.
For at that day, on that hour / A stranger will appear in the land.
He shall bring peril to Peladon / Desolation to the throne
Ruin to the forests / And great tribulation to the kingdom.

62

COURT HEARING -- TOP SECRET AND CONFIDENTIAL

JUDGE: Counsel for the defence may now cross-examine the witness.

THE MASTER: Thank you, your honour.

THE DOCTOR: Of all the infernal... You don't mean to tell me he's defending himself?

THE MASTER: Sadly, yes. Sir Roderick met with a most unfortunate accident...

THE DOCTOR: Yes... I'm quite sure that he did.

THE MASTER: Would the court please make note of the witness's hostile attitude. The Doctor is a very old, and, may I say, a very dear acquaintance, but sometimes a little incautious and hot-headed in his choice of language.

THE DOCTOR: I am not hot-headed, you scoundrel.

THE MASTER: Do make a note of that.

THE DOCTOR: Now see here...

THE MASTER: I really think, Doctor, it may be best if you take a nice deep breath. I say this, speaking as a friend.

THE DOCTOR: I am no friend of yours!

THE MASTER: Indeed? The whole court has heard you give an impassioned speech asking for me to be shown clemency. Who but a friend would do that?

THE DOCTOR: A merciful man.

THE MASTER: A humane one?

THE DOCTOR: Yes.

THE MASTER: But it is these very humane humans of yours who wish to put me to death.

THE DOCTOR: Well... you've killed hundreds and tried to destroy their planet half a dozen times.

THE MASTER: I dispute that last statement. I really must protest. I have not tried to destroy this planet. I will admit I have, perhaps, encouraged regime change on several occasions.

(CONTD)

RECEIVED
29 JUN

BY: ----------

-- 2 --

THE DOCTOR: You admit it.

THE MASTER: The human race is not very advanced, is it Doctor? They still, for example, practise the death penalty.

THE DOCTOR: Yes...

THE MASTER: They regard all alien life as hostile and frequently wipe it out in their encounters with it.

THE DOCTOR: That is regrettable.

THE MASTER: You see, and, ladies and gentlemen of the court, please don't take this amiss, but as a species you're really not experienced enough. You are likely to misconstrue the actions of other species simply because you cannot yet comprehend them. You may perceive our actions as a threat when really they are a benevolent attempt to bring you advancement. Would you not agree, Doctor?

THE DOCTOR: I would not.

THE MASTER: So, when you brokered a peace treaty with the Silurians, what was the reaction of the human race?

THE DOCTOR: They, er, well, they blew them up.

THE MASTER: They destroyed an ancient civilisation? Dear me, hardly the action of an advanced species. Is it, Doctor?

THE DOCTOR: No. No, on that I must agree. But humanity is... well... I mean, for a Level 2 civilisation they're doing remarkably well.

THE MASTER: A Level 2 civilisation! Would you care to define a Level 2 civilisation?

THE DOCTOR: I'm not really sure I should.

THE MASTER: Come now, Doctor. You introduced it into evidence.

THE DOCTOR: Very well. A Level 2 civilisation is one that has discovered elementary space travel, hydrocarbons, antibiotics and the principles of nuclear fusion.

-- 3 --

THE MASTER: A capital definition. And what do most Level 2 civilisations do with the discovery of nuclear fusion?

THE DOCTOR: They build power stations.

THE MASTER: But what, would you say, is the principal use made of it by humanity?

THE DOCTOR: Oh, that's hardly fair. It's how humanity learns -- they find a thing and their first use is always...

THE MASTER: Yes, Doctor?

THE DOCTOR: In weapons. They make nuclear weapons.

THE MASTER: And how would such a development be viewed by, say, a Level 3 civilisation?

THE DOCTOR: As barbaric. But--

THE MASTER: Barbaric! And tell me Doctor. What level is our own race?

THE DOCTOR: Ah, ah, well, a Level 12 civilisation.

THE MASTER: So would you say you are more qualified to judge humanity's actions than they are?

THE DOCTOR: Er...

THE MASTER: I'll rephrase the question. Are they qualified to judge your actions?

THE DOCTOR: Certainly not.

THE MASTER: So are they qualified to judge me?

THE DOCTOR: Wait, no...

THE MASTER: All right. Let me put it to you. I stand here accused of being -- now, what is it, ah yes -- under article 18B of the Emergency Powers Act of being of 'hostile origin or association' and of committing 'acts prejudicial to public safety'. Doctor, I dispute these allegations, and you are going to help me prove them false.

THE DOCTOR: I have absolutely no intention of helping you.

THE MASTER: Since arriving on this planet, would you not agree that I have revolutionised the efficiency of the plastics manufacturing industry?

(CONTD)

-- 4 --

THE DOCTOR: Yes, but--

THE MASTER: Thank you. I'll admit my methods were aggressive -- but oh so human. And have I not also had remarkable results with the elimination of psychopathic tendencies in the criminal mind?

THE DOCTOR: Only by--

THE MASTER: I'm afraid it's a yes or no question.

THE DOCTOR: Yes, but--

THE MASTER: And, finally, did I not offer humanity a remarkable solution to its energy crisis?

THE DOCTOR: Fine, yes, fine. But in every case--

THE MASTER: I know, I know. My good intentions were rebuffed and misconstrued. Surely, however, even you can agree with my actions at Devil's End?

THE DOCTOR: Not in the slightest.

THE MASTER: Come now. Who better to sit in judgement on a Level 2 civilisation than its creator, Azal of the Daemons? We can both see the mess this species is in. You choose to do nothing. I tried, oh how I tried, and when that failed, I appealed to Azal, hoping he could shape and reform it. Instead, regrettably, he wrote the experiment off. Wasn't that what happened, Doctor?

THE DOCTOR: Well... yes. If it hadn't been for Miss Grant. You're leaving out your actions on Uxarieus, where you tried to take control of--

THE MASTER: Where I attempted peacefully to adjudicate on a dispute between worthy pioneers and a legitimate mining concern. But I'm fairly certain, Doctor, that events on other planets are outside the jurisdiction of this court, and should not be brought into play.

-- 5 --

THE DOCTOR: They prove that you want to play God.

THE MASTER: Merely to improve the existence of
               the common lot, I assure you. I am on
               this planet for its own good.

THE DOCTOR: If not the good of its population.

THE MASTER: Now, that is unfair, Doctor. I try my
               best. What more can anyone say? This
               whole proceeding, if you'll forgive
               me, your honour, is a little beside
               the point. Much as it troubles your
               conscience, Doctor, you really should
               let your Level 2 friends do what they
               want and execute me. No prison can
               hold me.

THE DOCTOR: You intend to escape?

THE MASTER: Oh, why bother? Someone will come
               for me. After the last war, both the
               Russians and the Americans snapped up
               Hitler's rocket designers. You have
               made me famous. I owe you a great
               debt, Doctor. The finest criminal mind
               on the planet. Didn't your friend the
               Brigadier have trouble avoiding my
               extradition to... well, let's start
               with Geneva, New York and Moscow.
               Correct?

THE DOCTOR: Yes.

THE MASTER: In fact, that's why this fine example
               of British justice is being beamed
               into the offices of every state leader
               around the world. Isn't it?

THE DOCTOR: You've certainly brought a lot of
               attention to yourself. You always
               were a conceited show-off.

THE MASTER: Thank you, Doctor. Tell me -- when
               you find a piece of alien weaponry
               lying about, what do you do with it?
               Do you hand it over to the Brigadier?

                                              (CONTD)

-- 5 --

-- 6 --

THE DOCTOR: Certainly not. I deactivated those little fusion mines you left for me. They could have blown up an entire county.

THE MASTER: Indeed. An amusing little toy. I can rig up something similar in a trice. I really must thank you for proving my point so neatly, Doctor. You really should have arranged for my deactivation when you had the chance. You've just reminded everyone watching that I am the most dangerous, most valuable weapon in the world. And I very much look forward to doing business with all of you. No further questions.

THE DOCTOR: Now see here--

THE MASTER: No further questions. Thank you.

In the time of the fifteenth emperor, death rained from the skies, causing much lamentation and consternation to the people of Draconia. A tenth of the population fell then a tenth of those remaining, until a stranger from the stars arrived at court.

◆ ◆ ◆ ◆ ◆

At first the soldiers named him a trickster or a fool and decided that he caused the sky-death. But this man, called Doctor, showed them a cure and saved the lives of many and, more importantly, the son of the emperor. For that he was accorded the honour of becoming a noble of Draconia. His title is THE·LORD·DOCTOR·OF·TARDIS.

THE LAMENT OF LATEP

THEN, THE DALEKS
VANQUISHED, THE BRAVE
WARRIOR MADE HIS
RETURN TO SKARO, TO THE
SANDS OF CONFLICT. BUT HE
CHOSE FOR HIS CONSORT
JOSEPHINE OF EARTH. YET SHE
DID SORE REGRET THAT SHE
WOULD NOT VOYAGE WITH HIM,
HAVING TO CARRY ON IN
HER TARDIS WITH HER OLD
FATHER THE DOCTOR.

8.00 Attenborough in the Amazon

(1 of 4) **David Attenborough**'s latest journey with the BBC Natural History Film-Making Unit takes him off the beaten track of the Amazon. This week, he's keeping up with the Joneses – a married couple trying to convert the world to eating the remarkable vegetables of the Borneo Basin. Will Mr Attenborough enjoy tucking into his Vegetarian Sunday Roast, and what of Sandy the Sand Beetle?

Oh, it's hopeless! Time travel? Medieval castles with potato-headed aliens in the great hall and potatoes in the kitchen? Who'd believe it anyway? Maybe write a novel?!

London Borough of Hammersmith & Chelsea

PUBLIC SAFETY NOTICE

DINOSAURS

BEWARE!

DINOSAUR ACTIVITY HAS BEEN REPORTED IN THIS AREA PLEASE KEEP BEHIND CORDONS

If you see a Dinosaur, please phone the Council DinoHotline

☎ 01-811-4949

8.00 Attenborough in the Amazon

(3 of 4) **David Attenborough's** latest journey with the BBC Natural History Film-Making Unit takes him off the beaten track of the Amazon. This week, he ventures to Darkest Peru and takes us on a tour of a remarkable city and a lost civilisation. Was ancient mankind really visited by flying-saucer people, and will Mr Attenborough make friends with a cockatoo?

POLICE CALL OFF HUNT FOR LOCAL MAN

LOCAL police have called off the search for missing businessman **REX LUPTON**, 54, who disappeared from a local meditation centre last week.

Mr Lupton retired from his post as Sales Director at Chatfield Electronics in 1972 after a 25-year career with the company. Chatfield Electronics had recently merged with Magpie Electricals and Mr Lupton was given a golden handshake. He tried to establish an independent sales consultancy, but without success.

FAILURE

Friends said that Mr Lupton blamed Magpie Electricals for the failure of his business. He was described as 'bitter' and 'resentful' and prone to 'extreme mood swings'. Lawyers speaking for his family said yesterday that Mr Lupton had attempted to find peace of mind by enrolling at a meditation centre run by Abbot K'Anpo Rinpoche, but that the Tibetan programme had not proved a success for him.

REX LUPTON: Bitter

A police spokesman denied any military involvement in the case, saying that reports of a series of high-speed chases involving Mr Lupton were 'a complete fabrication'.

and we're at our twenty-ninth native village. We haven't found our toadstool yet, and we're not likely to if I don't get rid of this crystal. You see, the Indian porters say it's bad magic. Like, it goes or they go.

So, Doctor, if you're away on a cheap daytrip to Mars, perhaps you could look after it for me, Brigadier? Or if you're away in Geneva, how about it, Mike? Or my lovely Sergeant Benton?

I must say I miss you all very much and the coffee's just about as filthy as UNIT tea, if that's possible. I must go now, or I'll miss the next cleft-stick to civilisation

My beautiful thief is broken.

He's no longer doing the in-out lung thing. Breathing. That's it.

Giant blue spiders of light crawl all over him. He needs to take one last breath but they are stopping him from going anywhere. And he is stopping me from going anywhere.

We are paused. Both Thief and I. It's so sad. And another thing. Big grey word.

Boring. Yes. I'm bored. I should take him home – but if I take him to the great orange place where nothing happens, that won't do. No. Stifling. Let's take him back to that little blue smudge that's always getting into trouble. Pop him down, throw him out and let him breathe again.

Such fun.

The Story of Doctor Who

1970–1974

What I want to do is to bring *Doctor Who* down to Earth. I want to mould the programme along the lines of the old *Quatermass* serials, which I found so compelling, with people with everyday lives coming up against the unknown.

Derrick Sherwin, producer

The seventh season saw the series change radically. The show was suddenly, vibrantly in colour. Each season was shorter – six months rather than ten. The Doctor was exiled by his own people, the Time Lords, to contemporary Earth, and actually got a job. Working as UNIT's scientific adviser, he was no longer saving the universe as a hobby, but as a profession...

I was a believer in having threats to Earth happen on Earth rather than us going off to unknown planets. The simile I always use is that it's more alarming coming home and seeing a Yeti sitting on your loo in Tooting Bec.

Jon Pertwee

The idea of UNIT worked very well because, when the Doctor was exiled to Earth, the idea of the Brigadier's army came in. I wanted some humanity and humour, apart from just barking orders. When I was in the army, I was only a private, but it gave me the chance to observe the officers. The good ones, like the Brigadier, were the ones you'd follow into battle. He was a very good foil for the Doctor. Barry Letts told me he rang up the War Office because he wanted some uniforms and they told him, 'That chap you've got playing the Brigadier, just like one of us!' He could be pompous, but I didn't want to play him as a twit.

Nicholas Courtney (The Brigadier)

Working alongside the Doctor and the Brigadier, new companion Professor

Elizabeth Shaw followed in Zoe Heriot's footsteps - she was a Cambridge academic who admired the Doctor as a colleague...

At the time I went for Liz Shaw, I sent them a leggy picture of me along with my details, hoping that this would sway their decision. I was called in to read and before long I was told that I had the part.

Caroline John (Liz Shaw)

The first threat faced by the Doctor and UNIT came from the Nestene Consciousness and its plastic Autons. Previous alien invasions had seen monsters parading round London landmarks. Now killer shop dummies were roaming suburban high streets...

It was about the time plastic was coming in, in a really big way – it was everywhere. As there was so much of the stuff around, I thought it would be effective to have an alien force that inhabited and used it. The Nestene itself I thought of as a plasticky, swirling mass, a glob of pure instinct which spawns the Autons. The Autons come from the word 'autonomous'

because, although they were formed from the Nestene element, they weren't a part of the host form. I started the show with a swarm of meteorites landing, because in *Doctor Who* it's very rare to actually see the alien land. As this was to be a season set on Earth, I thought it would be a good grab to open it with.

Robert Holmes, writer

Having cast the new Doctor and set up the new season, Peter Bryant and Derrick Sherwin were keen to move on as producers...

I was very surprised when I was asked to be producer. I'd left acting only a short time before when I was asked. At first I said, 'I don't want to be a producer; I left acting to be a director.' But Shaun Sutton, Head of Series and Serials at the time, said, 'Well, you don't have to give up directing, you can still direct something from time to time if it fits in.' And I said, 'Oh all right. On that basis, I'll do it for a year.' In fact, I did it for five years, and in many ways I've never left it.

Barry Letts, producer

The Third Doctor's stories quickly became increasingly engaged with contemporary issues – pollution, environment, apartheid and immigration...

Remember what politics refers to – 'the relationship between groups of people'. It doesn't necessarily mean Left and Right or Labour and Conservative, it's the relationships of groups of people, so really almost all *Doctor Who* stories are political. Even though the other people look like reptiles, they're still people. I'd say it's a very political show.

Malcolm Hulke, writer

The 1970s was a massive opening to all sorts of new things. People started to become aware of the planet and what we were doing to

JON PERTWEE
was the Third Doctor

The Doctor is fundamentally different from most science fiction heroes. He doesn't get everything right, he's not a superman, he does make mistakes. *Doctor Who* is different from every other science fiction story that's ever been put on the screen. The big difference is that you're dealing with real characters rather than science fiction excitement peopled by cardboard characters. Not only that, it's got a mythological element to it – the Doctor is a mythic character who is fighting the demons on behalf of the angels.

Barry Letts

Peter Bryant, who was then producer, saw Jon in *Carry On Cowboy* and he thought that underneath all the false whiskers there was a definite personality which could be brought out. Jon has this dashing flamboyant personality which came into his version of the character. Certain old film stars, like John Wayne, are always basically playing themselves. Playing the Doctor tends to be rather like that.

Terrance Dicks, script editor

Jon was a big contrast to Patrick – an imposing figure.

Christopher Barry, director

Jon Pertwee was wonderful. We were in a helicopter and we landed in this field and hundreds and hundreds of people came running towards us – it was kind of like being like being a rock star. It was kind of bizarre. I didn't quite get it at first, and Jon taught me how to do all of that. He had had an extraordinary career up to this point. He'd always been known as a comedian and I think this was a wonderful opportunity for him to prove that he could do other things. When I looked at Jon there was a feeling that he could be 2,000 years old, and I don't mean that in a rude way. He just had a look in his eyes – a great knowledge. He was also a tremendous adventurer – he skied, motorbikes, car racing, Jon did all those things. So there was a little bit of the Doctor in Jon, and I think he also brought

to it a tremendous warmth. I loved him so much. I really, really did.

Katy Manning (Jo Grant)

Jon was a very sensitive creature, a very vulnerable man. When he was first in rep, he told me his father didn't really approve of him going onto the stage, but he hoped that his father would come and see him. One night he saw his father in the audience, and he gave his best possible performance. Afterwards, he waited for his father to come round, but he didn't. When he next went home, he asked his father if he'd seen it. 'No, I didn't get a chance to.' Jon told me this, and when he told me, he had tears in his eyes. On the surface of it, you'd have said Jon was the most confident man in the world. He was egocentric. It seemed as though the world revolved around him – but in the nicest possible way. He wasn't a nasty man. You'd be having lunch and everybody was in there. You'd find Jon sitting in the corner, telling stories, and everyone was laughing, enthralled. If you got a little closer, you'd find out all the stories were about Jon Pertwee. In spite of that, he led the company well. He looked after people.

Barry Letts

PERTWEE *on* PERTWEE

I was doing *The Navy Lark* and one of my company said, 'Why don't you put yourself up for Doctor Who?' And I said 'Why? Is Pat Troughton leaving?' So I told my agent and was greeted by stony silence on the phone. 'I don't think it's a very good idea, but I'll try.' He phoned the producers and the producers received this suggestion with stony silence. He said, 'I had exactly the same reaction. Forget about it.' And they said, 'No, our jaws are hanging open. Your client's name has been on our shortlist for 18 months.'

Jon Pertwee

I suppose on reflection my Doctor was a kind of science fiction James Bond with a touch of the Renaissance Man. I was also a protective Doctor – my cloak was a bit symbolic of the mother hen!

Jon Pertwee

it. We've got this extraordinary world and we're behaving like tacky little children. *Doctor Who* was a great way of looking at all the issues of our planet, and yet it wasn't preaching. I think Barry Letts took a tremendous responsibility because he also cared deeply. People were discussing global warming, the poisoning of the oceans and all those kinds of things. Now we're seeing the results. And we were dealing with that on TV way back then.

Katy Manning

No, that's nonsense. The political element is read in later by critics and fans and people studying the stories. You can always find it if you're looking for it, but we never had a political agenda. People used to ask what my aims and ambitions were for the show. My aims and ambitions were that the BBC shouldn't have to show the test card at 6 p.m. on Saturdays – in other words, to get the show out. That's the first essential, having a transmissible show. The first thing was actually making a production. TV production in my day – and I don't suppose it's changed –was incredibly difficult. People don't realise the extent of the problem.

Terrance Dicks

I was asked to do something in caves. In science fiction there are only two stories – they come to us, or we go to them. I thought... what about... they come to us, but they've always been here. I described them as reptilian men in the script. It seemed to go down very well.

Malcolm Hulke

Barry insisted on my putting in that scene where the Doctor is angry and annoyed because the Silurians are killed. The Brigadier had just blown them up, and Barry felt that Jon should say the moral thing about a whole alien civilisation being destroyed.

Terrance Dicks

The story also introduced Bessie, the Doctor's vintage yellow car, another of the show's icons, which would reappear on and off through to 1989, as well as debuting a revolutionary new visual effect made possible by colour television...

Bessie was my idea. I escaped out of hospital in *Spearhead from Space* and stole an old Vauxhall 3098. At the end of the story, the Brigadier said, 'The owner wants it back, but I'll make sure you get something like it.'

Jon Pertwee

Colour Separation Overlay (CSO) is the biggest technical development in television in recent years. Although CSO can be used for faking-in backgrounds, it seems to work best when you want to have a framed view through something such as a window, the mouth of a cave, or an open doorway.

Malcolm Hulke (*Writing for Television*, 1974)

By the time he wrote his book, Hulke knew his CSO – his Doctor Who *stories featured ambitious effects, from a sea of giant maggots to dinosaurs roaming the streets of London. One of the most successful was also the first – when the Doctor looks through the mouth of a cave and sees a huge dinosaur. It was a period of experimentation and huge ambition...*

I had to learn to say no to directors. On *The Ambassadors of Death* – the second show I had anything to do with – Mike Ferguson, an excellent director, had loads of ideas.

There was a moment where a couple of men on motorbikes hijack a ground-to-air missile. He said, 'It's a bit tame, would you like me to soup it up a bit?' I said yes. He said, 'Well, we could have a helicopter for a start...' And he built it up, with whole teams of stuntmen, into a really lovely piece. And then I got the bills at the end, and I realised exactly how much we'd spent, and we couldn't afford it. Mike said, 'Listen, I'm just doing my job. It's my job to make the programme as good as possible. It's your job to stop me!'

Barry Letts

My favourite story was *Inferno*, a very good story, again directed by Douglas Camfield. Such fun for me to play the Brigadier and this rather fascist Brigade Leader with an eye-patch and a scar down one cheek.

Nicholas Courtney

I liked working with Douglas Camfield a lot, and the story which he was responsible for, *Inferno*, is probably my favourite piece of *Doctor Who*. He was thorough in the extreme, and treated the

Writer Nicholas Briggs on
INFERNO

I really love *Inferno*. I'm fond of all three of those Barry Letts seven-parters, because they feel very different from anything that came before or after. They're a unique little slice of the show, before Barry Letts and Terrance Dicks really worked out exactly what they wanted to do with the programme. *Inferno* stands out for me, because it's so atmospheric. The lack of what was to become the cosy incidental music of Dudley Simpson (whose music I do actually love) gives this a really bleak feel. And naturally, the whole alternative universe strand makes for a starkly unfriendly atmosphere. I love the fact that they simply generated more story to fill up the seven episodes by introducing that element, and it pays off nicely, with great performances all round. The actual central plot idea is startlingly simple and not entirely effectively thought through, but the sheer conviction with which the whole thing is told and carried out makes this a thoroughly entertaining curiosity piece that I return to again and again. Every time I watch it, I wonder, 'What if the whole Pertwee era had followed this template?' Although it's probably best that things turned out the way they did over the following years, *Inferno* works beautifully for me as a tantalising hint at a possible alternative 'future' path for *Doctor Who* at that time.

whole thing like a vast military operation which, considering our schedule, was probably a great thing in his favour. I was fond of the actual story, because it allowed me to do something a bit special with the character and to play the parallel world Liz with a great deal of sneering cynicism. She was very much the tough, cold professional soldier. Killing Nick Courtney was an added bonus which gave us all many a laugh, and which was very difficult to do with a straight face.

Caroline John

So, at the end of my first year, I had overspent quite considerably. I went to the Powers That Be, and I said, 'Look, it's always overspent. Why not just give me the money in the first place?' So they actually upped the budget – as at that time, there was loads of money at the BBC, because colour had started and people were getting colour licenses which were much more expensive than black and white licenses. Each year I managed to up the budget a bit, so what started out as quite a cheap programme ended up as quite an expensive one.

Barry Letts

The eighth season extended the UNIT 'family', with the Brigadier and Sergeant Benton joined by Captain Yates and Jo Grant, the Doctor's new assistant. So Liz Shaw went back to Cambridge...

Liz Shaw wasn't right for the part of the companion because this was the Doctor's show and the companion is always subsidiary. Since she was a super scientist in her own right, she didn't really need the Doctor to explain things to her. And the role of the companion is to have the Doctor explain what's going on, which Katy's character was ideal for. Jo Grant was really the answer to the Liz Shaw problem. She couldn't have been more opposite. She was sort of feather-headed and scatter-brained and cute. She was perfectly happy to waffle away while the Doctor did the strong dramatic stuff.

Terrance Dicks

Katy Manning was just a minx. And a very talented one, a girl with immense charm. If somebody wrote a scene for me where I had a motorcycle chase, Katy would get on the back and go with me, not

because she was brave but because she was a lunatic too.

Jon Pertwee

They wanted somebody very young because in the 1970s we were all kind of hip and groovy man and far out. How can I describe my clothes? Probably the most frightening thing in *Doctor Who*, really. I was climbing mountains in six-inch platforms, and I can actually do anything now in high heels.

Katy Manning

Barry was looking for a love interest for Katy Manning, because they now realised *Doctor Who* was appealing to young adults.

Richard Franklin (Captain Yates)

The season opener was Terror of the Autons, *which saw the Nestene's plastic army step out of the shop front and into the home...*

The elements in the story all came from plastic again. At the time there was a soap powder distributing plastic daffodils outside supermarkets, and I remembered all the warnings about children not being allowed near plastic bags. Then it all came together.

Robert Holmes

We had a plastic chair that swallowed someone up, and a troll doll that came to life and strangled people, and a telephone cord that tried to strangle the Doctor, and plastic daffodils that suffocated you. Really rather nasty. The Doctor and Jo Grant were being

driven away by a couple of policemen. The Doctor glanced at one of them and said, 'Can I see your warrant card?' and the policeman turned round, and the Doctor peeled his face off – and there was this blank face just staring. Eurgh! We had a letter from Scotland Yard, a very nice letter, saying, 'We do understand how you want to make your programmes sensational, but we work very hard to make children trust policemen, and then you go and put something like that on!' Someone wrote in one of the papers 'Why my children will never watch *Doctor Who* again.' Terrance says there were questions asked in the Houses of Parliament – I don't think there were, but there were certainly questions asked in the BBC.

Barry Letts

In 1974, I was sitting opposite Ronnie Marsh, the then Head of Serials, across acres of polished maple. He started telling me about the guidelines he felt the programme should follow. 'Two or three seasons ago,' he said, 'we had some clot who wrote the most dreadful script. It had faceless policemen in it and plastic armchairs that went about swallowing people. I might tell you, there were questions in the House. Mrs Whitehouse said we were turning the nation's children into bedwetters.' Could it be that he was referring to my *Terror of the Autons*? 'Tut, tut', I muttered, feeling the script editor's job slipping away. 'How awfully irresponsible.'

Robert Holmes

At the beginning of each season we used to want to find a show that would have something special about it. One of the things that came up in conversation was that the Doctor had often been compared to Sherlock Holmes. He's intellectual, he's superior, he can be a bit snappy and people can't keep up with him. And during that discussion I said, 'What he needs is a Moriarty.' Barry immediately said, 'That's a good idea. Let's do that, and I know who's going to play him.'

Terrance Dicks

I love playing villains. I am chosen by directors to play wicked men because I have a beard, a menacing chin and piercing eyes. I was thrilled to be offered the part of the Master. I enjoyed this chap who was really more than just a Moriarty to the Doctor, and I could tell from fan letters that I was the man they loved to hate. There were even one or two kids who complained that I wasn't wicked enough!

Roger Delgado (The Master)

There were two problems built in, neither of which we'd foreseen. One was that if at the end of every serial it turns out the Master's behind it, you rather lose the element of surprise! Also, if they're both so smart, how come the Doctor never catches him and he never manages to kill the Doctor? So that was a problem in story terms. So what we decided to do was not to have the Master in every story but to bring him back from time to time, so we could recapture that element of surprise.

Terrance Dicks

So we had *Colony in Space*, where the Doctor went off to have a space opera type adventure, but one which also had something to say about colonisation and the environment, because that's another thing that Terrance and I felt strongly: that the stories should be about something, that they should definitely have a point, and not just be an exciting story.

Barry Letts

With the show's viewing figures at their highest since the heights of Dalekmania, Season Eight went out with a bang...

If you want to bring real joy into the heart of any special effects specialist, ask him to make an explosion. Probably the best explosion on British television in recent times was when in the BBC's series *Doctor Who*, in a serial called *The Daemons*, they blew up a little country church. With meticulous care the BBC's Special Effects Department built a model which was an exact replica. This was so effective that the British Broadcasting Corporation received a number of letters from viewers angered by the destruction of this fine old country church.

Malcolm Hulke (*Writing for Television*)

The programme's ninth season saw the return of the Daleks after an absence of several years...

Barry Letts and I used to get something fairly dramatic for the opening show of the season. We were discussing the first story of that season, and although it was all right, we didn't think it was quite good enough to start off with. Barry suddenly suggested we made it a Dalek story, and that made the whole thing work because everybody was so pleased to see the Daleks back.

Terrance Dicks

The story tackled the thorny question of wibbly-wobbly timey-wimey paradoxes head-on, and came up with a practical solution...

In *Day of the Daleks*, the guerrillas were coming back from the future to the present day in repeated attempts to blow up a peace conference. While this was going on, the Doctor had gone ahead into the future to sort things out there, and so you had action going on in two places at the same time. Now why should these events be going on co-incidentally? Why if you travel forwards in time for a day and then come back, do you find a day has elapsed in your time too? It isn't necessary at all – you could come back the day before if you wanted, surely? This difficulty really got on top of us, and we eventually had Jo Grant say to the Doctor, 'Why don't we go back to the day before and get it right this time?' to which there is no real answer. So what the Doctor said was 'Ah well, that's the Blinovitch Limitation Effect', and when Jo said she didn't understand, the door opened and in came the guerrillas. So we never explained the Blinovitch Limitation Effect, but it provided us with a way out of time paradoxes.

Barry Letts

Barry and I both felt that for an opening story of the season it needed something more, and it came to our minds that the Daleks hadn't been back for a while. So we got the idea of making the Daleks the brains behind things – the villains behind the villain.

Terrance Dicks

Writer Robert Shearman on
CARNIVAL OF MONSTERS

The Jon Pertwee years are typified by two types of adventure. There's the Earth crisis story, where the Doctor saves our planet from invasion, and there's the space crisis story, where the Doctor saves the entire universe. They're big and noisy and great fun, and they're also just ever so slightly predictable.

And then there's *Carnival of Monsters*. Has there ever been a better title, one which seems to sum up what *Doctor Who* is about? But there's no invasion here, and this particular space opera has the volume turned down. It's the smallest-scale Pertwee story, a peculiar puzzle box in which the Doctor is reduced to microscopic size and aliens stand and watch his exploits on a television screen.

It's very clever, of course. There are jokes at the expense of the *Who* story formula, where characters literally run around in small circles repeating themselves. There's fun to be had poking fun at the special effects (Drashig is the best anagram for a *Doctor Who* monster ever!). But it's not mean-spirited. It's sweet and funny – the smaller scale allows a rapport between the Doctor and Jo that gets overwhelmed in some of their more grandiose adventures, and the aliens and humans alike that they encounter are at once both larger than life clowns and touchingly ordinary.

In the preceding story the Time Lords lifted the Doctor's exile and gave him the freedom once more to travel anywhere in time and space. What's perfect about *Carnival* is that by playing delicate and light it reminds us how extraordinarily imaginative *Doctor Who* can be, and that at its best no other programme has so much potential for wonder.

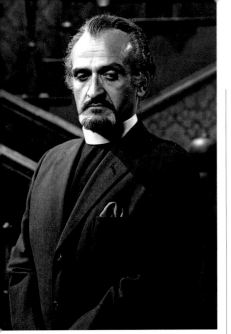

As Season Nine progressed, Letts and Dicks continued the gradual move away from the exiled-on-Earth format. The Sea Devils *revealed the Silurians' deep-sea cousins, while* The Mutants *and* The Time Monster *took the TARDIS to the planet Solos and the lost city of Atlantis. Then* The Curse of Peladon *revived another old enemy ...*

We brought the Ice Warriors back for the Peladon stories, giving them the twist in the first story that they appeared to be the villains, but they weren't. In the second story they said they weren't the villains, but they were!

Terrance Dicks

Barry Letts and Terrance Dicks came in and wanted to get away from the past, which I think was a very wise move. I was very surprised when they decided to bring the Ice Warriors back after a few years. If you followed the psychology of the Ice Warriors, they were still basically the same people. The Doctor accepted their help very reluctantly, because he knew they could turn nasty at the drop of a scale or something.

Brian Hayles, writer

Of all the scripts Dave Martin and I wrote for *Doctor Who, The Mutants* is the best... The monsters were terrific, really superbly done. It was part of the brief to involve the Time Lords and get away from Earth. The Doctor was a detective for the Time Lords, who would whizz him off to do jobs, though he didn't know what was involved.

Bob Baker, writer

After three years we both felt we'd run the gamut of ideas and wanted to do something else, but our boss said, 'You can't go! You're such a success.' And so we said, all right. As we left, Terrance said, 'This is the only prison where you get time on for good behaviour.'

Barry Letts

In December 1972, the programme's tenth season began...

I think I said, 'You know this ridiculous idea that the fans keep sending in, that all the Doctors meet each other? Suppose we actually do it?' Barry thought about it and said, 'Well, we can try. I'll talk to them.' He talked to Pat Troughton, who was very happy to do it, and he talked to William Hartnell, who was highly delighted. He said, 'Yes, I'd love to do it.' So Bob and Dave wrote the script with all three Doctors playing a more or less even part. And then Barry got a call from William Hartnell's wife saying, 'I've just learned with horror that you want him to appear in the show again. He can't. He's quite simply not well enough. His health won't stand it. You must just have got him on a good day.' So I came up with this idea of having his Doctor on a screen and commentating, but not really taking any active part, and then I built up Jon and Pat as the centre of the show.

It was all done in one day's filming. They drove him to the studio, filmed him against black drapes with prompt cards, did it line by line and he had the absolute minimum of effort. I think it worked, like many things that come out of a crisis, very well. And, of course, it has that lovely line of Bob and Dave's: 'You're my replacements, a dandy and a clown.'

Terrance Dicks

They wanted us all together and so I said, 'Yes, fine, great.' And it was fun, it was lovely. Especially having Billy Hartnell there, even though he was only on film, trapped in a sort of bubble. A bit ga-ga, poor lad, but it was lovely seeing him there. Jon Pertwee and I developed quite a rapport, shall we say.

Patrick Troughton

When the three came together it was lovely, although in one sense it was very sad. William Hartnell, by this point, was suffering enormously. But to watch Pat

Troughton and Jon Pertwee together – there was a little tiny edge of discomfort in the rehearsal period, and I got terrible giggles and was sent out of the rehearsal room, because they were both just a little bit terse with each other. Then they mellowed and started to float beautifully. It was a wonderful experience to work on that with them.

Katy Manning

Letts and Dicks were continuing to evolve the series. At the end of The Three Doctors, *the Time Lords lift the Doctor's sentence of exile. Most of the season was set far from Earth...*

Nowadays, we try to make *Doctor Who* as much for adults as for children. During the last four years it has developed to the point where nearly 60 per cent of its viewers are over the age of 15. *Carnival of Monsters* works very well on both levels – exciting for children, amusing and intriguing for adults. A line such as the one spoken by one of the rulers about dissatisfied serfs on Inter Minor, 'Give them a hygiene chamber and they'll store fossil fuel in it' will go right over the heads of anybody born since the war, but what a super line it is.

Barry Letts

My favourite monster of all time was the Drashig from *Carnival of Monsters* – a 40-foot serpent with a lovely radiophonic roar (which incidentally was made by playing a tape of a skid backwards). This monster was done in the same way as the Muppets – it was somebody's arm in a fearsome head shot in the Puppet Theatre at Television Centre and we ended up with these monsters that couldn't possibly be men in rubber suits. We later expanded on that – with giant maggots put into shot by Chromakey.

Barry Letts

Then came the Draconians, where one Draconian says to another, 'You can never tell from human faces what they're thinking. Very enigmatic.' They also wanted the Ogrons back. They're nice to write because they're so stupid. Not much dialogue.

Malcolm Hulke

The Ogrons or the Draconians had those marvellous masks where they let the human eye be seen, let the mouth be seen.

Therefore you get expression – eyes and mouth, it's where it all comes from with acting.

Jon Pertwee

The monsters I disliked the most were the Giant Maggots. I thought they were really nasty.

Nicholas Courtney

I think in my stories the baddies aren't really bad because they're doing what they think is right. I find it hard to imagine anyone as totally bad or totally inimical. A maggot that's just about to eat someone alive is in fact not necessarily a bad maggot, he's just maggoty. That's the way he is.

Malcolm Hulke

We did one story about the environment, *The Green Death*. I read the *Ecologist* magazine when they brought out one of the very first warnings to the world about fossil fuels and global warming, long before it became fashionable. I read this and said I could make a documentary about it, but Terrance said 'Why don't you make a *Doctor Who* about it?' So I got together with Bob Sloman and we wrote *The Green Death*, which was all about pollution and about a biological research establishment that was trying to find alternative ways of doing things.

Barry Letts

Somebody suggested Stewart Bevan. He came in and was absolutely perfect. When he'd read his stuff, he said, 'Actually, I have to tell you, I'm Katy's fiancée.' He got the part because he was a good actor, but I had to laugh. It would have been sad for Jon and Katy to be splitting up anyway, but with Stewart there it became almost like Stewart taking Katy from the show in real life as well as in the story. Some of the rehearsals became quite tense and everyone got quite weepy. But it was all there in the script – even down to having Jon drive off into the sunset.

Michael E Briant, director

New companion Sarah Jane Smith (Elisabeth Sladen) arrived in The Time Warrior, *for which Robert Holmes created another of* Doctor Who's *most popular monsters…*

They wanted to do a historical, which they hadn't attempted for some time.

John Barrowman and Carole E. Barrowman on
THE TIME WARRIOR

Perhaps, even back in the day, this story's special effects were sketchy[1] and some of the acting was, oh, just a wee bit stilted.[2] But we don't care. With a script from the show's prolific writer Robert Holmes, *The Time Warrior* remains one of our favourites in the original series. And here's why. The story contains a significant feminist first – the introduction of 'make your own coffee' Sarah Jane Smith (Elisabeth Sladen) as the Doctor's intellectually curious companion, and one of the best monster money-shots ever in the classic canon.[3][4]

Scientists are disappearing from UNIT without a trace. Naturally, the Doctor (Jon Pertwee) and the Brigadier (Nicholas Courtney) are trying to discover why. Taking advantage of the lockdown at UNIT, Sarah Jane marches into the room, introduces herself to the Doctor and to the television audience with only her name and her profession ('I'm a journalist')[5] and then she insinuates herself into the investigation and our hearts.

With what we now recognise as Sarah Jane's characteristic sarcasm (often directed gently toward the Doctor), smarts and fearlessness, she sneaks on board the TARDIS and travels back to Medieval England, where they must battle a rogue knight and a Sontaran warrior whose spaceship is in need of repair.

'Oh, Doctor,' says Sarah Jane early in the story, 'kindly don't be so patronising.' And snap, the Doctor's patriarchal stance towards the universe is challenged.

If watching Sarah Jane flex her feminist muscles isn't enough for you, then the monster money-shot right at the end of Part One will be. Until this moment in the story, Linx, the Sontaran, has remained disguised in full space armour. But, thinking he's alone, he steps into the castle courtyard, glances around, and, with his back to the camera, carefully lifts off his helmet. Then he slowly turns and stares directly at us.[6]

And, of course, he's every bit as horrible as you'd expect a Sontaran to be.[7] The camera steadies on his giant head for one, two beats and then… cue the music.

[1] JB: Mostly firecrackers, tinfoil and sparklers. [2] JB: Well, not everyone. [3] JB: Got chills just thinking about that scene. [4] CB: Not sure that means much. You can get 'chills' from a cup of coffee. [5] CB: I so wanted to be Sarah Jane from that exact moment. [6] CB: Such a brilliant shot. [7] JB: Such a massive mole-like head.

Now, I hate *Doctor Who* in history mode, because I think it's too whimsy and twee. So I compromised and offered them a story mixing science fiction with a kind of pseudo-history.

The Sontarans came after I'd been reading some heavy tome on war – it was terribly Teutonic and all about the Fatherland and so on.

Robert Holmes

I wanted Sarah Jane to have that kind of innocence that she never got over, that she would always fight for right, even if she made a fool of herself, because you have to as the assistant. You have to make a fool of yourself every week. I never had any problems screaming. I never felt that it demeaned my character or women because I scream a lot. If something frightens me, I let people know. I don't have a problem with this.

Elisabeth Sladen (Sarah Jane Smith)

Sarah Jane was sort of a concession to feminism. My view of the heroine is that her job is to be strapped to the railway line and scream until the Doctor comes and rescues her. But it was becoming clear that we couldn't get away with that

any more. So we decided on a strong, independent companion for the Doctor; and Sarah never was a companion, in the technical sense. She brought in a lot of new twists to work on and new ways to do stories.

Terrance Dicks

As the season went on, the Doctor took Sarah Jane to the planets Exxilon, Peladon and Metebelis Three. First, though, came a return to contemporary London...

For this one, I was given another instruction: the Special Effects department had found that they could show monsters wandering around contemporary London by various forms of trickery. So could I think of some reason why dinosaurs and so on might be wandering around London?

Malcolm Hulke

The dinosaurs we had in *Invasion of the Dinosaurs* were awful. They were so stiff. I was really rather cross at the time. I had various ideas of how they should be worked (with the neck of the Tyrannosaurus done just like the Drashigs in *Carnival of Monsters*), but we had some outside people making them, and they said, 'Oh, no, no, we know exactly how to do it.' By the time they were made, it was too late to change them. It's such a pity, as it's a lovely show and a very exciting story – if we'd had good dinosaurs it would have been one of the best we'd done.

Barry Letts

Roger Delgado had said, 'People keep not offering me jobs because they think

I'm tied up in *Doctor Who*. On the whole, I think I'd like to leave.' We were in the very early stages of planning a final story for the Master when a tragic accident happened.

Terrance Dicks

After we'd been doing it for about four years with Jon Pertwee, things had changed a bit. Poor Roger Delgado was killed in a car accident when he was filming in Turkey. Katy Manning had left. Lis Sladen came along and got along very well with Jon. We weren't doing so many UNIT stories. Jon started getting itchy feet. He said, 'The programme is changing, and I'm getting to the point where I think that I'm not getting offered work because people think that I'm going to be Doctor Who for ever.' We agreed that he'd do another season and then leave.

Barry Letts

Barry, who was very keen to go back to directing, said, 'Well, if Jon's going, I think I'll go too.' And I said, 'If you two are going, I shall have to go as well. I'm not going to stay behind as a sole relic of the old regime.' It would have been a very uncomfortable position. I'd worked with Barry for so long. I didn't think I could stand another producer or that another producer would stand me, possibly. So I went back to being freelance again.

Terrance Dicks

When I joined, I knew that Jon was leaving. Roger Delgado had died, Katy had left, and UNIT was being written out, and I suppose that was a moment. Jon wanted to go at that point. As the season got on, Jon was really sorry, as he didn't

realise we were going to get on so well. I know he didn't want to leave.

Elisabeth Sladen

I was very sad to go. I'd enjoyed myself for five years, very much. I would have liked to go on and do one more season, but I wasn't going to, not for the same money. I thought it was time they gave me a rise, and they didn't, so that was the end of that.

Jon Pertwee

The big thing was when we were going to do his last *Doctor Who*. He said to me, 'Have you been to the boat show? There's the most marvellous one-man hovercraft and we could get it into *Doctor Who*.' And I did and I thought, well, why don't we try and introduce all the things he'd like to have – so we had this famous chase, which started off in Bessie, which then went into the Whomobile, then he got into a one-man helicopter, and then he finished up in the hovercraft and a jet-propelled boat. And Jon had a whale of a time!

Barry Letts

I remember Jon regenerating into Tom Baker very well. Jon had to lie on the floor for a very long time. And then Tom. I was on my haunches all the time – it was rather tiring. Painful.

Nicholas Courtney

The last story was *Planet of the Spiders*, and Jon did something he had never done before. After each scene, he wouldn't mix with people, he would go and sign his fan mail. He actually had to start distancing himself before he left, and you didn't go and say anything because that was his choice. It wasn't very easy because when Jon's Doctor died there's Sarah Jane weeping and wailing over him, and I was sorry he was dying, and there's Tom, who came into the studio because he was filming *Robot* at the same time I was doing my last scenes with Jon. It was a case of 'How do you do? This is Tom, this is Lis and this is Jon.' There's Jon eyeing up Tom, and Tom's looking down at Jon. It was a very odd moment. And then I finished with Jon and I had to travel down that night and work with Tom, and you don't know if you're going to get on... You hope you are, and it was an absolute joy, but that was very different...

Elisabeth Sladen

Still need a title!

SARAH JANE SMITH: Are you recording, K-9?

K-9: Dictation mode activated, mistress.

SARAH JANE SMITH: Good. Then let's start at the very beginning. In the year 1980–

K-9: [Ahem]

SARAH JANE SMITH: What is it, K-9?

K-9: Factual inaccuracy detected.

SARAH JANE SMITH: Nonsense! It keeps it all sounding current. People want to read about aliens and the wonders I've seen, but if I bang on about the 1970s they'll just think flares and kipper ties and eurgh! It's hard to take an alien invasion seriously if you think they're all dressed as Showaddywaddy.

K-9: Query, define–

SARAH JANE SMITH: It doesn't matter. Nobody will ever care about the odd year here or there. It's not important. Let's start with Chapter One: 'Sarah Jane Smith and the Missing Scientists'.

N E R V A

GREETINGS, CITIZEN VOLUNTEER

This is the HIGH MINISTER speaking on behalf of the WORLD EXECUTIVE.

I salute you who are about to make the supreme sacrifice. In a few minutes, you will pass beyond life. In case there is any fear in your heart and doubt in your mind at this awesome moment, let me remind you that you take with you all our past. You carry the torch that has been handed down from generation to generation.

As our planet Earth falls into fire, many preparations have been made for this, the greatest exodus in our long history. Many times, the Earth has come under threat, but now the fires may be both swift and last for millennia.

On previous occasions the warning has been enough to let the entire population relocate temporarily. But this is too swift. Our only hope for survival is to place as many as we can into hibernation. You are one such lucky soul. If the process works, and we can only hope that it will, then humanity may some day continue…

MARS VENUS ROCKET RUN

★

Registered pilot

Signature of Licensee :

The Doctor

When I first infiltrated UNIT, I was simply a girl reporter on the hunt for some missing boffins. By pretending to be my Aunt Lavinia, the famous virologist, I was hoping that I'd get the inside story, but I had no idea the scoop I'd get would be a time scoop—

No, that's awful, isn't it? How do I explain that on my first day at UNIT I ended up in the Middle Ages on the run from an alien warrior? If I skip over that, then… Oh no, wait, then I'm fighting dinosaurs, then it's the Daleks, then it's one-eyed space things, and giant spiders. >>

SONTARAN G3
MILITARY ASSESSMENT SURVEY

FIELD MAJOR STYRE REPORTING FROM EARTH BASE.

There has been no intelligent life on this planet since the time of the solar flares 10,000 years ago. As we know, the Earth has not been repopulated. I have therefore carried out my instructions and lured a group of humans to the planet for testing. I ambushed a GalSec ship, and there were nine male survivors.

EXPERIMENT 1. Deprivation of O_2. Produced asphyxiation in less than three minutes. Conclusion: this species does not possess even a rudimentary respiratory bypass system.

EXPERIMENT 2. Removal of cerebral cortex. Termination instantaneous. Conclusion: No backup of brain function available to human species.

EXPERIMENT 3. Resistance of human tissue to chemical combustion reactions. Human skin has almost no resistance, burning and scarring quickly. More interestingly, the experiment had a rapid effect on the subject's mental state. The moron is of no further use to me.

EXPERIMENT 4. Immersion in the fluid H_2O produced asphyxiation in less than three minutes. Conclusion: this species has little resistance to immersion in liquids.

EXPERIMENT 5. Human resistance to fluid deprivation. Data: subject died after nine days, seven hours. Impairment of mental faculties, motor reflexes and physical coordination noted after only three days. Conclusion, dependence on fluid is a significant weakness which should be exploited in our attack.

EXPERIMENT 6. Self-preservation. Having captured the leader of the GalSec crew, it was a simple matter to convince him that his life would be spared if he betrayed his friends. I therefore released him. Using mighty Sontaran surveillance technology, I have since then been studying the free behaviour patterns of the remaining survivors.

Female number one, first assessment. Would appear to have no military justification. Offensive value therefore nil.

EXPERIMENT 7. Subject, female. Project: resistance to fear. Data: to follow.

EXPERIMENT 8. Compressibility test of human tissue: resistance to pressure on the human breast cage and muscular strength. Two human subjects will hold a gravity bar weighing a mere 40 pounds Earth weight over the lower thorax of a third subject. I will increase that weight to 200 pounds, then incrementally until they are unable to prevent it crushing their colleague. Data: to follow.

> SEND? YES / NO
> SEND? YES / NO
> SEND? YES / NO

SARAH JANE SMITH: And I'd have to explain about how the Doctor… Oh, how do I do that? Best leave him out. I want people to take this seriously, and if I start off by saying I worked with a man who can change his body and that he tried dressing up as a playing card… Oh, K-9, no one will believe me.

K-9: Negative. Time Lord physiognomy perfectly logical.

SARAH JANE SMITH: To you, obviously. But you're not Mr and Mrs Stephen Average of Tunbridge Wells. No! I've just made them up, K-9. It doesn't matter. My point is… Let's try again. It's chilly out here.

K-9: The temperature is normal for February in the United Kingdom.

SARAH JANE SMITH: I know. But brr! It's my fault. Sitting down outside the pub trying to write in this weather – what was I thinking? Come on, let's go for a… W.A.L.K.

K-9: This unit is capable of spelling.

SARAH JANE SMITH: And hopefully this unit is capable of tidying up all this into some kind of sense. So, anyway. Let's start again. Chapter One: 'Sarah Jane Smith and the Giant Robot'.

 You just have to look up into the night sky to see that there's a universe of wonders out there. But there are also many wonders all around us. And everyday objects tell a remarkable story. For instance, it was a crushed daisy that

MARK III TRAVEL MACHINE

BUY&SELL

FOR SALE,
one novelty
hat-stand.

Gold-plated.

**Genuine
Cyberman.**

told me that the creature that was attacking top–secret
military bases was actually an advanced robot.

At the time I was associated with a secret paramilitary
organisation who were involved in protecting civilisation as we
know it. Together we'd dealt with everything from a Doomsday
Cult that had convinced London it was under attack from
dinosaurs through to some New Agers who believed in
using crystals to pray to spider gods. But now UNIT were up
against science. >>

*Should we find another name?
Let's phone Alistair for a chat*

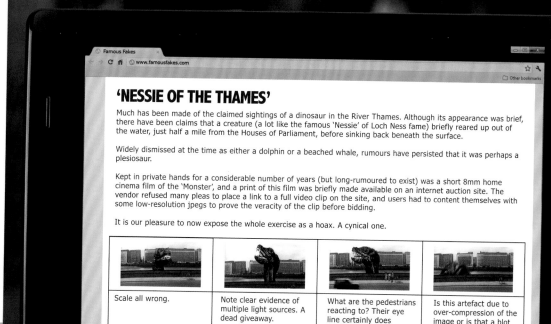

'NESSIE OF THE THAMES'

Much has been made of the claimed sightings of a dinosaur in the River Thames. Although its appearance was brief,
there have been claims that a creature (a lot like the famous 'Nessie' of Loch Ness fame) briefly reared up out of
the water, just half a mile from the Houses of Parliament, before sinking back beneath the surface.

Widely dismissed at the time as either a dolphin or a beached whale, rumours have persisted that it was perhaps a
plesiosaur.

Kept in private hands for a considerable number of years (but long-rumoured to exist) was a short 8mm home
cinema film of the 'Monster', and a print of this film was briefly made available on an internet auction site. The
vendor refused many pleas to place a link to a full video clip on the site, and users had to content themselves with
some low-resolution jpegs to prove the veracity of the clip before bidding.

It is our pleasure to now expose the whole exercise as a hoax. A cynical one.

Scale all wrong.	Note clear evidence of multiple light sources. A dead giveaway.	What are the pedestrians reacting to? Their eye line certainly does not match that of the 'monster'.	Is this artefact due to over-compression of the image or is that a blot on the 'sky'? Clearly a painted backdrop.

SARAH JANE SMITH: The Think Tank wasn't your average far-right bunch of blackshirts. They were very clever scientists with a car boot full of crazy ideas. We'd just got our first female Prime Minister, so it was thoroughly fashionable that Think Tank was run by Hilda Winters. She got a lot more coverage for her wacky opinions simply because of her gender, and it was the kind of thing that gave Women's Lib a bad name. (Mind you, for some reason, the press do love it if you look like a vicar's wife and sound like Lucretia Borgia.)

I was on to her because she looked dodgy. Call it female intuition but I knew at once that, beneath the tight smile and neat hair, Hilda Winters was as crazy as they come. Her plan was basically to take over the planet. She'd acquired a set of nuclear launch codes and was going to hold the governments of the world to ransom. And she got very close – she had all the right scientists in her power.

Actually, let's not, otherwise they'll assume I'm as drippy as Mike Yates on a wet Wednesday.

RANDOM MYSTERIES

SARAH JANE SMITH

THE OSIRIS CODE

We are not the first...

The Trial of the First Renegade

by Benncuiq IV of the Arcalian Chapter

The Battle done, the First Renegade was brought before the High Council. Not since the secession of Dronid had the High Council faced such a challenge to its authority.

President Pandak I faced the First Renegade and asked the Question of Singularity. 'Morbius, why?'

Initially, the Renegade's only answer was a sneer.

'I do feel you owe us some explanation,' Pandak prompted him gently.

The Renegade inclined his head slightly. 'You are statues,' he told them. 'You have sat still for so long, you have turned to stone, like the Weeping Angels of old. We are the most powerful race in the cosmos, we tread through infinity, and yet we do little more than sit on the side lines.

'On other worlds, people dream of immortality. Their lives are so short, they have to cram so much in, they ache at the thought of a wasted day. There's so much to be done, there's so much they'll never do, simply staying alive is exhausting. If you gave them another year, another week, another hour of life they'd find something to do with it. But we – we have immortality and we do nothing with it! Many of us never leave the Capitol, let alone the planet. We claim to be wise – but how can we be wise when we never live? What use is eternal life if you never once live?

'There is so much we could do,' the First Renegade thundered. 'Why, I've been to hundreds of worlds – from Solos to Kastria. And on every planet, they grapple with the same question: If there really were gods, why would they allow bad things to happen?

and her secret weapon was Professor Kettlewell. He it was, you see, who had built her the perfect weapon: the K1.

K-9: Query?

SARAH JANE SMITH: Oh, don't worry. Just your great, great grandfather. It was carrying out assassinations for Think Tank, but I – well, I formed a bond with it. I've always been good with robots, haven't I, K-9? And so, at the last minute, Miss Winters' nuclear winter was averted. *Gah!*

K-9: Mistress. I have a question. Was the Doctor-master involved at all?

SARAH JANE SMITH: Well, he helped. But I'm not going to big up his part. I haven't even mentioned Harry Sullivan or the Brig. Come on, Chapter Two: 'Sarah Jane Smith and the Ark in Space'. My next case took me into the far future. You see, I'd acquired a time machine and... >>

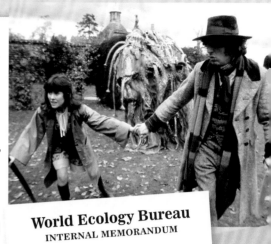

'We are the gods. We could stop everything bad from ever happening. But we choose not to. We simply watch. What a waste!'

President Pandak allowed himself a chuckle. 'That is the kind of argument I would expect to hear from a Time Tot, Morbius. But not from you! Why, you've taken our society to the brink for reasons that would amuse a tafelshrew. You know as well as I do, that we must stand still outside of Time. If we step into it, our every footprint will weigh upon reality until it falls apart. It is the curse of every Time Lord.'

The First Renegade laughed now. 'Are you sure, Pandak? Are you really sure? Has it ever been tried?'

'Rassilon strictly forbade—'

The Renegade interrupted him now. 'Rassilon? He skimmed creatures from existence like they were gobbets in stew. His greatest achievement? The Death Zone – a place where he made the two ends of eternity fight in one big paradox. You revere him as a great leader, but the slightest hint of dissent and he'd drop them in a time loop and—'

'I shall not listen to heresy!' countered Pandak, stilling the Renegade with the breath of the Time Winds.

When he was again able to speak, the Renegade continued. 'It is a point of view,' he sighed. 'I have shown you what can be done in the real world. I have raised an army. I have wrapped myself in history and it hasn't fallen apart. I have changed things. I have a legion of followers spread across the stars. I have shown them what a real god looks like.'

'And for that, you will be punished.'

The First Renegade nodded. 'Indeed. But think about what I've done. A myriad worlds now know what a Time Lord is. You can't undo that. And look closer to home. I've shown our people that it can be possible to leave this world, to wander in the Fourth Dimension. You can wipe me from time, but you can't kill an idea.'

The Masque of Mandragora

PERSONATED AT THE COURT AT SAN MARTINO,
ON THE ACCESSION OF PRINCE GIULIANO TO THE DUKEDOM

First, in front of the throne and assembled rulers, nobles and scholars were placed the ten entertainers, their form human, save that their faces were distorted and horrific, as partaking of some hellish travesty.

Before these, a figure in part leonine became conspicuous, the more so as, writhing his head, his golden visage seemed to sink forward and uncover a great glow.

Upon this signal, the ten entertainers were advanced in their purple robes, their own heads alight and with flames of hellfire let loose from their hands. The guests at court began to fall.

At once, Hieronymous – yet not in human form – began to speak, his voice dark and forebidding.

Hieronymous. Stop! Stop, brothers. The final sacrifice must be made in our temple. Bring the victims of Mandragora down.

Giuliano. The Brethren! We've been tricked, betrayed!

Hieronymous. Silence! Take them below.

Woman. The eclipse! Look, it's beginning.

Hieronymous. Now Mandragora swallows the Moon. Now, as it was written, the power of Mandragora will flood the Earth. Mandragora, we your servants welcome you. Bestow your power upon us that we may rule over the whole of your dominion.

Their hands linked upon an altar, the Brethren addressed the heavens in defiance of all good. And bolts of energy were returned to them from above, and the ten did fall upon the floor. A conjury! For their cloaks and masks were soon revealed as empty. Only Hieronymous remained standing, and he removed his mask.

Woman. Doctor!

Doctor. Well, I thought that was rather clever. A case of energy squared. It puts Mandragora back to square one. Well, don't just stand there, I'm in the market for congratulations. I wouldn't even say no to a salami sandwich.

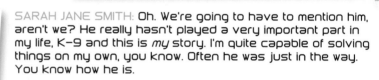

SARAH JANE SMITH: Oh. We're going to have to mention him, aren't we? He really hasn't played a very important part in my life, K-9 and this is *my* story. I'm quite capable of solving things on my own, you know. Often he was just in the way. You know how he is.

K-9: Memory banks of this unit suggest that the Doctor-master is of reasonably high intelligence, but minimal operational efficiency.

SARAH JANE SMITH: Good dog! Got it in one. When I first met him – the old one, he was like a favourite teacher. But the new one, he was like your older brother, home for the weekend and in a spot of bother. 'Oh, what now?' – that was always it, feeling happily cross as we jumped into Bessie, or the TARDIS crashed into an Egyptian god, or whatever.
  Sometimes, oh, you'd think he'd forget his head if it wasn't screwed on – at others, he seemed impossibly moral. We went back in time to try and wipe out the Daleks, and he thought twice about it. There was lovely Harry Sullivan on one side – now, if you'd handed him a detonator and told him to wipe out the Daleks, he'd have asked if that was enough dynamite. Not for Harry arguments about morality, causality or whatnot. Just 'fingers in ears, old girl' and BOOM. Aw, lovely Harry. But the Doctor stood there, thinking about obliterating the Daleks, and it was like he was standing on the edge of a cliff. Did he have the right to do it? Odd that – as if a Dalek would have paused for thought before zapping him! Was he really discussing it with us, or were we like his pets?

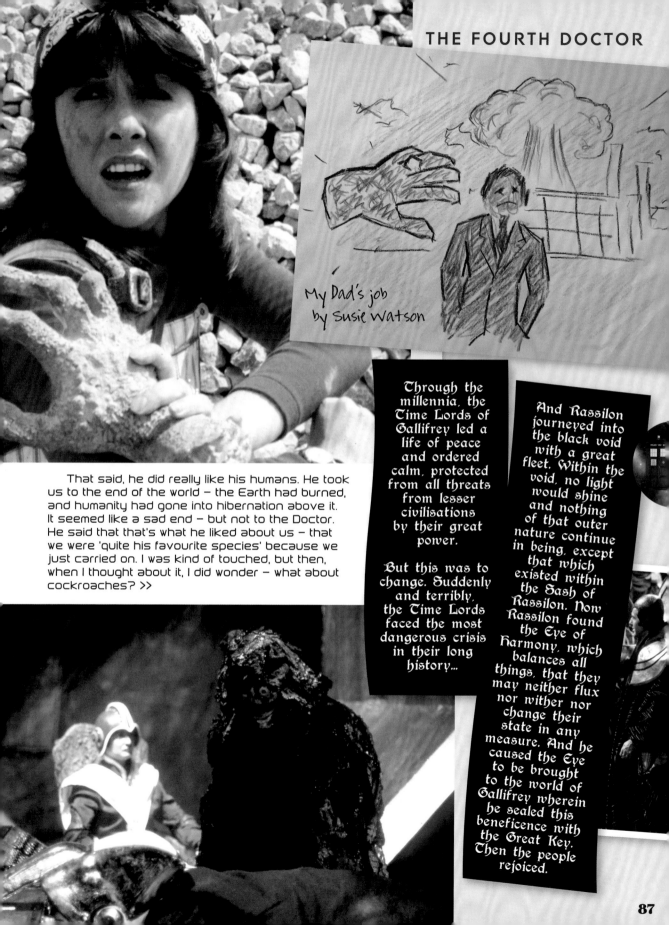

My Dad's job
by Susie Watson

That said, he did really like his humans. He took us to the end of the world – the Earth had burned, and humanity had gone into hibernation above it. It seemed like a sad end – but not to the Doctor. He said that that's what he liked about us – that we were 'quite his favourite species' because we just carried on. I was kind of touched, but then, when I thought about it, I did wonder – what about cockroaches? >>

Through the millennia, the Time Lords of Gallifrey led a life of peace and ordered calm, protected from all threats from lesser civilisations by their great power.

But this was to change. Suddenly and terribly, the Time Lords faced the most dangerous crisis in their long history...

And Rassilon journeyed into the black void with a great fleet. Within the void, no light would shine and nothing of that outer nature continue in being, except that which existed within the Sash of Rassilon. Now Rassilon found the Eye of Harmony, which balances all things, that they may neither flux nor wither nor change their state in any measure. And he caused the Eye to be brought to the world of Gallifrey wherein he sealed this beneficence with the Great Key. Then the people rejoiced.

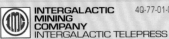

INTERGALACTIC MINING COMPANY
4Q-77-01-01
INTERGALACTIC TELEPRESS

☐ The Mordee Expedition continues to encounter difficulties. After the crash, communications were sporadic – the on-board technicians who had survived said that the crash was probably caused by the flight computer behaving erratically. Attempts to send software patches failed, since the computer (Xoan-1) was failing to install them correctly.

Meanwhile, the Survey Team were reporting extremely hazardous conditions. If the planet is rich in mineral deposits, extractions would have to contend with a variety of hostile flora and fauna, unless a lengthy process of complete terraforming were to be undertaken.

With the computer in its present state, the chances of the ship attempting a return journey – or even leaving the planet's surface – are negligible. Running a cost-benefits analysis of the expense of mounting a rescue expedition as against the profits from mining operations, it is recommended that we write this expedition off, and terminate all future communication.

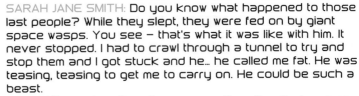

SARAH JANE SMITH: Do you know what happened to those last people? While they slept, they were fed on by giant space wasps. You see – that's what it was like with him. It never stopped. I had to crawl through a tunnel to try and stop them and I got stuck and he… he called me fat. He was teasing, teasing to get me to carry on. He could be such a beast.

And then, when the shoe was on the other foot, one row and…

K–9: Mistress?

SARAH JANE SMITH: Sorry, K–9. Daydreaming for a moment. Look how the sunlight is catching the glass of the garden centre. It's a nice day, you know. It's a lovely planet, worth saving.

And, after me, he went on saving it. It took some digging, but I found traces of him everywhere. There's a sketch by Leonardo of him. My heart stopped when I saw it in an exhibition. It was around the time they arranged that big tour, after there was all that hoo-ha, those rumours that the Mona Lisa had been stolen and was a fake. I looked into it, and of course, everyone was keeping shtum, and I thought, 'Oh ho, my girl, there's something in this.' And of course, there, at the heart of it, was the Doctor.

Then there was that diary they found kept by a Victorian pathologist they thought for a while might have been Jack the Ripper. A lot of people dismissed it as fiction. I mean, you would, wouldn't you – sinister Chinamen, killer dolls, and an oriental god feeding off young girls underneath a music hall. I mean, come on! But there he was – a mysterious Doctor, travelling with a girl he'd found floating down the Amazon in a hatbox.

K–9: Negative, hatbox. Correction: mistress Leela known to be a primitive native from the planet–

Laserson Probes

Need to punch a fist-sized hole through six-inch armour plate?

Need to take the crystals from a snowflake one-by-one?

Whatever your probe needs – choose Lasers

SARAH JANE SMITH: You knew her?

K-9: It is more accurate to say that data on her is held in the memory banks of this unit.

SARAH JANE SMITH: What was she like? In Professor Litefoot's account she comes across as some wild Boudicca.

K-9: Mistress Leela of the Sevateem was of above-average strength, skilled in hunting and fighting, and highly intelligent but uneducated. It was the Doctor–master's intention to 'bring her on'. >>

Tucked up at last, safe and well in my own home and enjoying one of Mrs Hudson's splendid cold collations, it is all too easy to discount the events of the last couple of days as a wild romance. If, that is, one ignores the broken windows and the dead Chinese in the flowerbed.

Can Mama and Papa's lacquered puzzle box really have been a time cabinet? Has London really been in the grip of deformed criminals from the future, passing themselves off as Oriental deities?

It all just seems so extraordinary. And yet, there is the evidence of my own eyes. And, of course, the evidence of my mortuary, which is now stuffed to overflowing with – as my new friend Henry would put it – Ceased Conjurors, Rusticated Rodents, Terminated Tong-Members, Juiced Jezebels, Deceased Dwarves, Perished Pigs and a One-Time Weng-Chiang.

It's all going to take a lot of explaining. There are going to be a lot of questions, and I'm not really sure I've any decent answers. I could find myself in a pickle hotter than anything even Mrs Hudson could cook up.

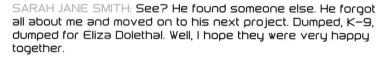

BI-AL FOUNDATION

NAME The Doctor

PLACE OF ORIGIN Gallifrey, Ireland, Earth

NEXT OF KIN Leela of the Sevateem

WARD Isolayshun, Level X4

TREATMENT Initial datalysis reveals patient is in self-induced cataleptic trance, and that he is not a member of the human race. He has two hearts and a symbiotic, self-renewing cell structure. Encephalographic test detects unidentified viral type infection with noetic characteristics, seated in the mind-brain interface and therefore having no ascertainable mass or structure.

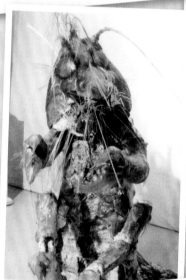

SARAH JANE SMITH: See? He found someone else. He forgot all about me and moved on to his next project. Dumped, K-9, dumped for Eliza Dolethal. Well, I hope they were very happy together.

K-9: They travelled together for some considerable time. Mistress Leela was of assistance to the Doctor-master on many occasions. A full list follows—

SARAH JANE SMITH: Oh, just pick the highlights, there's a good dog.

K-9: The Fendahl was a creature that fed on death. It had been planning a return to existence for twelve million years. It had altered the people of Earth at a genetic level in order to accomplish this goal.

SARAH JANE SMITH: That's like something out of *Chariots of the Gods*! Wow. I can see my name in gold leaf on the cover of that one. How did it end?

K-9: The Doctor-master blew up the Fendahl gestalt within Fetch Priory.

SARAH JANE SMITH: He does love blowing up a stately home. Well, make a note of that one. Another?

K-9: The Doctor-master and mistress Leela arrived on the planet Gallifrey. They were—

SARAH JANE SMITH: Gallifrey?

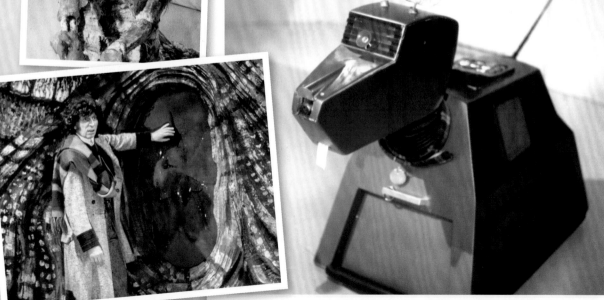

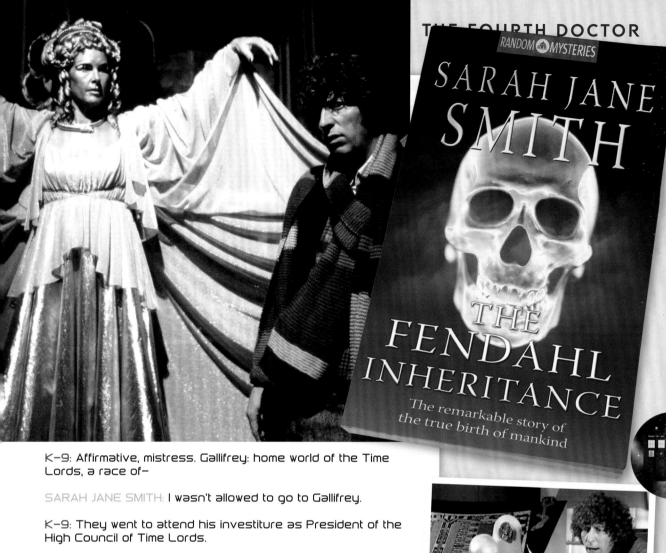

THE FOURTH DOCTOR

RANDOM MYSTERIES

SARAH JANE SMITH

THE FENDAHL INHERITANCE

The remarkable story of the true birth of mankind

K-9: Affirmative, mistress. Gallifrey: home world of the Time Lords, a race of—

SARAH JANE SMITH: I wasn't allowed to go to Gallifrey.

K-9: They went to attend his investiture as President of the High Council of Time Lords.

SARAH JANE SMITH: The what? No, K-9. It's fine. When did he become President?

K-9: On a previous visit. Immediately after he had deposited you on Earth. >>

THE DOCTOR

He has a long history of violence and of economic subversion.

He will not be sympathetic to the Company's business methods.

PRAISE THE COMPANY!

MEGROPOLIS

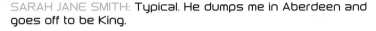

Our Darkest Hour?

by Benncuiq IV of the Arcalian Chapter

The Time Lords went to teach the Minyans of Minyos, but instead we learned a lesson from them. By then we were emerging from the Dark Days. The Great Citadel had arisen, we had mastery of time, and we had established the regenerative cycle. We were near immortal – barring accidents. And we stepped out into the universe.

The Minyans taught us to tread carefully.

When we arrived on Minyos we were greeted as gods. And, like any immature species, we responded well to flattery. We gave them medical and scientific aid, better communications, better weapons. We were, if not occupying their planet, then certainly improving it for them. We treated them as favoured children, and they grew up rapidly. All too rapidly.

Normally, when children grow up it is time for them to leave home. Instead, they asked us to leave Minyos. At gun point.

We retreated. Philosophically, perhaps it was time for the gods to move on – after all we had given them all the benefits we had to offer (apart from access to the Time Vortex – we weren't quite that foolish). We could watch from the side lines, proudly, as our children took their first steps into space.

Instead, to our horror, they went to war with themselves and split their planet in two.

From that point on, we vowed never to interfere again.

SARAH JANE SMITH: Typical. He dumps me in Aberdeen and goes off to be King.

K-9: His investiture was in fact a bluff. He was instead assisting the Vardans to invade Gallifrey.

SARAH JANE SMITH: He what?

K-9: Mistress, do you wish me to increase the volume of my speaker output?

SARAH JANE SMITH: No. I heard you. I just didn't understand.

K-9: Then please adjust the level of your attention, mistress. Please state if you wish me to simplify. The Doctor realised there was a plot by the Vardans to invade Gallifrey, and sought to assist them in order to defeat them.

SARAH JANE SMITH: The cunning devil.

K-9: However, the Vardans were the unwitting allies of a race who were waiting for their invasion to fail. Gallifrey was subsequently invaded by the Sontarans.

SARAH JANE SMITH: Linx?

K-9: No. The Sontaran invasion force was under the leadership of Commander Stor.

SARAH JANE SMITH: So, I didn't get to go to Gallifrey, I didn't get to see the Doctor made President, and I didn't get to help defeat the Sontarans?

K-9: Affirmative, mistress. >>

ORDER FOR THE RITES OF PRESIDENTIAL INVESTITURE

GOLD USHER: Honoured members of the Supreme Council, Cardinals, Time Lords, madam. We are here today to honour the will and the wisdom of Rassilon.

All stand. GOLD USHER strikes three times with his staff.

GOLD USHER: Is there anyone here to contest the candidate's right to the Sash of Rassilon?

Gold Usher strikes once.

GOLD USHER: Is there anyone here to contest the candidate's right to the Rod of Rassilon?

GOLD USHER strikes once.

GOLD USHER: Is there anyone here to contest the candidate's right to the Great Key of Rassilon?

GOLD USHER strikes once.

GOLD USHER: By custom, with wisdom, and for honour, I shall strike three times. Should no voice be heard by the third stroke, I will, duty-bound, invest the candidate as President of the Supreme Council of the Time Lords of Gallifrey.

GOLD USHER strikes three times.

GOLD USHER: It is my duty and privilege, having the consent of the Time Lords of Gallifrey, to invest you as President of the Supreme Council. Accept, therefore, the Sash of Rassilon.

THE CANDIDATE takes the Sash of Rassilon.

GOLD USHER: Accept, therefore, the Rod of Rassilon.

THE CANDIDATE takes the Rod of Rassilon.

GOLD USHER: Seek, therefore, to find the Great Key of Rassilon.

THE CANDIDATE acknowledges the Empty Cushion (of Rassilon).

GOLD USHER: Do you swear to uphold the laws of Gallifrey?

CANDIDATE: I swear.

GOLD USHER: Do you swear to follow in the wisdom of Rassilon?

CANDIDATE: I swear.

GOLD USHER: Do you swear to protect the law and the wisdom?

CANDIDATE: I swear.

The Circlet rises from the Panopticon floor. GOLD USHER takes it and walks behind THE CANDIDATE, who kneels.

GOLD USHER: I invest you Lord President of the Supreme Council. I wish you good fortune and strength. I give you the Matrix.

GOLD USHER places the circlet on THE PRESIDENT's head and moves away. THE PRESIDENT stands and all before him kneel.

THE KEY TO TIME (replica)

The Key to Time is a perfect cube, which maintains the equilibrium of time itself. It consists of six segments, and these segments are scattered and hidden throughout the cosmos. When they are assembled into the cube, they create a power which is too dangerous for any being to possess. There are times when the forces within the universe upset the balance to such an extent that it becomes necessary to stop everything – for a brief moment only – until the balance is restored. At such a time, these segments must be traced before the universe is plunged into eternal chaos.

(On loan from the Braxiatel Collection)

The Nine Travellers: Set in Stone?

A Puzzle of Archaeology Explained

by Professor Amelia Rumford

SARAH JANE SMITH: This Leela sounds quite something. What did she do for an encore?

K-9: Query 'encore'. Mistress Leela remained on Gallifrey. She married the Time Lord Andred.

SARAH JANE SMITH: Wait – they can get married? Ohh…

K-9: Mistress?

SARAH JANE SMITH: Back to the pub, K-9. That white wine may be horrible, but it's got my name on it.

[PAUSE]

Grendel: You Forgot Your Hat!

BEING A SHORT ACCOUNT BY SWORDMASTER ZADEK

OF THE DEFEAT AND DISGRACE OF COUNT GRENDEL OF GRACHT

and so, as Reynart, King of Tara, and the Lady Romana knelt before the Archimandrite under the malevolent gaze of the Count, it seemed that all was lost. For the Princess Strella. For the King. And for Tara.

IV

ch swordsmanship! I never thought I should e to see the day when anyone would beat unt Grendel of Gracht.

en the Doctor interrupted the Count's dish ceremony, Grendel was quick to w his sword – yet quicker to allow his y manservant to assault the Doctor. haps it was only the Archimandrite's timely vention at this moment that averted the tor's death.

del sneered, 'I shall give you a fencing before you die.'

octor, now armed, faced his opponent, ngs looked bad for him. He seemed to understanding of the rules of combat, on offered Grendel an open target. te seemed to rest in the hands of an nced peasant.

Yet, as the attacks and parries began, the

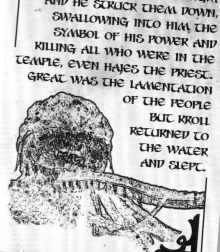

SARAH JANE SMITH: Where were we, K-9?

K-9: Query location. Query time period.

SARAH JANE SMITH: I mean… where were we in the story?

K-9: Mistress Leela and the original K-9 unit elected to remain on Gallifrey.

SARAH JANE SMITH: Yes – where did you spring from? Fancy some crisps? I'd kill for a packet of cheese and onion.

K-9: Syntax error. Logical extrapolation is that you were asking after my construction. My prototype was built by Professor Marius at the Centre for Alien Biomorphology, Bi-AI Foundation in the year 5000. The Mark I K-9 unit was able to offer the professor valuable assistance and advice until he decided to transfer ownership of it to the Doctor-master.

SARAH JANE SMITH: Maybe this Professor Marius just got fed up being told he was wrong all the time.

K-9: Negative. Stated reason was weight restriction on shuttle flights back to Earth.

SARAH JANE SMITH: Hmmm. >>

WHEN KROLL AWAKENED, HE SAW THAT THE PEOPLE WERE FAT AND INDOLENT, AND THEN KROLL BECAME ANGRY AND HE STRUCK THEM DOWN, SWALLOWING INTO HIM THE SYMBOL OF HIS POWER AND KILLING ALL WHO WERE IN THE TEMPLE, EVEN HAYES THE PRIEST. GREAT WAS THE LAMENTATION OF THE PEOPLE BUT KROLL RETURNED TO THE WATER AND SLEPT.

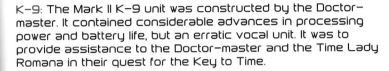

The Eternal War Transcripts Site

EPISODE 1789. Scene 27.

[The Astral Balcony]

(Recap. Alla and Betta are preparing for a tearful farewell. Everyone say hello to the Love Theme)

ALLA: Darling.
BETTA: Oh, my love.
ALLA: Don't go.
BETTA: I must.
ALLA: But you'll be killed!
BETTA: Perhaps.
ALLA: I can't bear it. I love you.
BETTA: There is a greater love. Men out there, young men, are dying for it. Dying so that Atrios might live. You must be strong. We must all be strong and play our parts until victory is won, evil vanquished, and peace restored. Then, and only then, my darling, can we love again. I must go. Kiss the children for me. Tell them their daddy will return before long.

(all transcripts are copyright by me, Karem of Atrios, and may not be reproduced elsewhere. No infringement is intended)

K-9: The Mark II K-9 unit was constructed by the Doctor-master. It contained considerable advances in processing power and battery life, but an erratic vocal unit. It was to provide assistance to the Doctor-master and the Time Lady Romana in their quest for the Key to Time.

SARAH JANE SMITH: So – what do I ask about first? The Time Lady or this Key thing?

K-9: The Key to Time was the most important object in creation. Ownership of it granted control over the balance between good and evil in the universe.

SARAH JANE SMITH: Yeah, right. Tell me about her instead. Hang on – 'Time *Lady*'? And you said Time Lords can get married! Did they–

K-9: The Lady Romanadvoratrelundar qualified from the Time Lord Academy with a Triple First. She was instructed by the White Guardian to assist the Doctor-master. The Doctor-master informed her that there were three rules for successful association with him–

SARAH JANE SMITH: No running, no jumping, no kissing?

K-9: Rule one, do exactly as the Doctor says. Rule two, stick close to the Doctor. Rule three, let the Doctor do all the talking.

SARAH JANE SMITH: That figures. How did she do?

The Movellan-Dalek War
by Benncuiq IV of the Arcalian Chapter

The war between the Daleks and the Movellans is a lesson, even for Gallifreyans, in stagnation. The Daleks had by this point evolved to the point at which they may as well have been robotic in nature. One theory put forward is that many of the mutant creatures inside the casings had by now endured millennia of torment, and were behaving increasingly erratically. Not only were Daleks beginning to make the occasional wrong decision, but worse, they were beginning to question orders.

It was thus decided by the Dalek Battle Computers to increase the conditioning of the mutants, overriding almost all organic personality and making them beings of pure, tightly controlled logic.

This was fine, in theory, up until the point at which the Daleks met an actual race of robots.

No one knows where the Movellans came from; indeed, they were as careful to obscure their own origins as the Daleks were to hide theirs – which made them the perfect match for each other. (Some have speculated that they may even have been of either Dalek or Time Lord

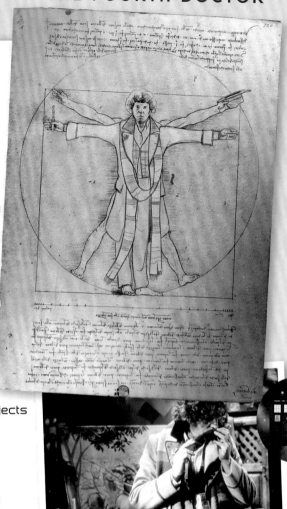

K-9: Her operational capability was of a quotient considerably higher than that of the Doctor. Her record for the minimum time taken to retrieve a segment of the Key to Time was 466 seconds. The Doctor-master was regrettably unable to come within twelve hours of that score.

SARAH JANE SMITH: She sounds a right barrel of laughs.

K-9: Query: container of involuntary mirth?

SARAH JANE SMITH: I mean, she sounds like she was thrilling.

K-9: Affirmative. The mistress Romana and I shared several most satisfactory interactions concerning subjects such as atomic weights, organic crystallography...

SARAH JANE SMITH: Oh, poor Doctor. »

manufacture!) They were a precision-engineered android race who could pass perfectly for humanoid. .

A race of robots pretending to be alive versus a race of living creatures pretending to be robots. Rather than sitting down to talk through this fascinating situation, their battle computers almost instantly locked both species into a long-lasting stalemate.

The Daleks of old would have sidestepped this immediately, possibly by entering into a short-lived, lethal alliance with the Movellans, using them to strategic advantage before exterminating them. Instead, the two space fleets hung motionless for centuries.

It is only thanks to a small unit (reporting to but independent from the Supreme Dalek) that a solution was found. A Dalek squad (battle-damaged and therefore unfit for proper duty) would report to Skaro and unearth their long-buried creator Davros. It was believed that his brain at least could be revived and the unconditioned unpredictability of Davros would give them the strategic advantage they had so long sought.

It was not to be...

K-9: Information: The mistress Romana's second regeneration was more compatible with the Doctor-master's character, and with only a 3.7 per cent loss in overall efficiency.

SARAH JANE SMITH: Oh, K-9, I'm so glad you're keeping score.

K-9: Recognition noted. Second mistress Romana proved highly capable. Assisted by this unit, she also reorganised the TARDIS wardrobe.

SARAH JANE SMITH: Oh, that wardrobe! It was like an explosion in Oxfam. I always ended up in the maddest things.

K-9: Mistress Romana's wardrobe rationalisation proved highly adequate.

SARAH JANE SMITH: Anything else I should know? Did she fix the kettle?

K-9: Affirmative. She also manufactured her own sonic screwdriver. It showed a modal 17.333 recurring per cent increase in operational capacity.

SARAH JANE SMITH: Lady Two-Shoes can't put a foot wrong. And let me guess – they're still larking about having wonderful adventures?

K-9: They travelled together for some considerable time before falling through a Charged Vacuum Emboîtement.

SARAH JANE SMITH: A what now?

K-9: A hole into another universe. There they discovered three other craft that had also become stranded. At the gateway between universes, mistress Romana elected to remain behind in order to free those remaining. The Mark II unit remained with her.

SARAH JANE SMITH: She turns up, borrows his clothes, steals his pet, then goes off to save an entire universe. Wow. Again, poor Doctor – I bet he was heartbroken. Hearts-broken. Is that right?

K-9: It was at approximately this point that the Doctor-master manufactured this unit for you. >>

Seth: Saviour of Aneth
by TEKA LARCHPUT

When Seth reached Skonnos on his voyage, he got from Soldeed, who Seth had shot, the famous staff and, having learned how to use it to make his way through the intricacies of the Complex, he slew the Nimon. Seth also staved in the remaining Skonnon ships, thus depriving them of the power to pursue. Sorak, the general of Skonnos, was expected to conquer all his competitors. But Anethans and Skonnons alike were filled with admiration for Seth's athletic prowess, when he conquered Sorak and disgraced him. Skonnos therefore gave back the Anethan youths to Seth, besides revoking Aneth's tribute to the fallen Skonnon Empire. Seth departed Skonnos in triumph with Teka and the Anethan youths.

THE LEISURE HIVE • VISITOR'S LOG.

Date	Name	Home world	Comments on your experience at the Leisure Hive
20-3-90	Mr Loman	Earth	Simply ripping time. Bet your Tachyon Recreation Generator is just showing old recordings though!
21-03-2290	Romana-dvoratre-lundar	Gallifrey	Some of your tachyonics solutions are really quite neat, especially the duration problem.
21-3-2290	Mrs Loman	Earth	You will be hearing from my solicitors.
21 March	Mr Stimson	Earth	I didn't want to come here in the first place.
21/3/90	Mr Hardin	Earth	I could stay here for ever...
21.03.2290	The Doctor	Gallifrey	I suddenly feel five hundred years younger
21. 03. 90	Clckclckh-weeeclkh-weee	Liaisici	Clkc clckhweeeclk hweeeedkclk ckckckl hweeeeeeee.

STARLINER TSS- 5

USER: FIRST DECIDER HALRIN LOGIN
>>>>>> BIOMETRICS VERIFIED

USERLOG BEGINS

SYSTEMFILES(SF):SECURE>
FIRSTDECIDER>ENT/00183174

We left Alzarius 15 day cycles ago, and our Starliner is travelling in the dark space between two planetary systems, onward towards our uncertain future. This is a dangerous undertaking, a leap into the unknown. We have left the world that was our home for generations, in hope rather than expectation that we will find a safer planet suitable for habitation. To date, the long-range scanners have detected no such likely planet.

The boy Adric has still not been found. Deciders' Decree 188 declares he is presumed absent from the Starliner, and is to be counted among the fallen.

I miss the fresh fruit of Alzarius, especially the grommelberries and the riverfruit, but the food synthesisers do well enough, and if that is my only complaint then it is no complaint at all.

We will prevail.

First Decider Halrin Login

ENDS

SARAH JANE SMITH: He could just have turned up and said sorry. Aberdeen, K-9. Aberdeen. Do you know how far that is from Croydon?

K-9: Approximate distance from Aberdeen Great Britain UK to Croydon Great Britain UK is 406 miles or 653.25 kilometres.

SARAH JANE SMITH: Exactly. One row. That's all. I just said I wanted a rest – a soak in a hot tub and a change of clothes. Could he do that? Oh no. Suddenly it's all 'Well, off you trot, I'm awa' to Gallifrey and I can't take you along. Chop chop.' I… I thought he died.

K-9: Affirmative.

SARAH JANE SMITH: What?

K-9: Probability of Doctor-master's death 83.57 per cent and increasing. This unit can foresee–

SARAH JANE SMITH: 'Foresee'?

STARLINER TSS- 5

USER: FIRST DECIDER HALRIN LOGIN
>>>>>> BIOMETRICS VERIFIED

USERLOG BEGINS

SYSTEMFILES(SF):SECURE>
FIRSTDECIDER>ENT/00282166

Twelve months out from Alzarius. We may have found our new home. The Science Unit tell me that the system we entered ten weeks ago has two planets orbiting its sun at a distance that may be conducive to supporting life. One looks very promising.

An exploratory landing party, to be led by Decider Haar, is being assembled. We have far more volunteers than places for what is a dangerous mission. I myself am frustrated that as First Decider I must remain with the citizens within our ship. I have personally briefed Lorana Haar and wished her well.

The citizens are continuing to adjust, but adjustment is what we're good at. We are not Marshmen; we are not Terradonians. We are our own people. Alzarians.

First Decider Halrin Login

ENDS

K-9: It can be read in the I-Ching.

SARAH JANE SMITH: Now you're having me on. That's not funny. Don't joke about him dying.

K-9: This unit is–

SARAH JANE SMITH: Is incapable of humour, oh, I know. Go on. What are you talking about?

K-9: The path is laid out. When the Doctor–master reassembled the Key to Time, one component was faulty. The rebalancing of the universe was imperfect, causing a rapid acceleration in the heat death of the universe. With entropy increasing exponentially, the excess energy has been funnelled out through a series of artificially constructed Charged Vacuum Emboîtements. But the last of these has now been closed. The universe is ending.

SARAH JANE SMITH: What? The stupid– >>

THE RECORD OF RASSILON

Then did Rassilon's fleet contend with the mighty Vampire army. So powerful were the bodies of these great creatures, and so fiercely did they cling to life, that they were impossible to kill, save by the use of bow ships.

Energy weapons were useless because the monsters absorbed and transmuted the energy using it to become stronger. Therefore Rassilon ordered the construction of bow ships. Swift vessels that fired a mighty bolt of steel that transfixed the monsters through the heart. For only if his heart be utterly destroyed will a vampire die.

The task seemed impossible, yet Rassilon was not afraid. And yet slain they all were, and to the last one, by the Lords of Time. The Lords of Time destroying them utterly. However, when the bodies were counted the King Vampire, mightiest and most malevolent of all, had vanished, even to his shadow, from time and space.

Hence it is the directive of Rassilon that any Time Lord who comes upon this enemy of our people and of all living things, shall use all his efforts to destroy him, even at the cost of his own life.

STARLINER TSS-5

USER: FIRST DECIDER HALRIN LOGIN
>>>>>> BIOMETRICS VERIFIED

USERLOG BEGINS

SYSTEMFILES(SF):SECURE>
FIRSTDECIDER>ENT/00343487

Planetfall plus 52 days.

For a while it looked as if we had made a dreadful mistake coming to this world. Decider Haar's party was attacked by a pack of feral creatures half an hour after stepping out from the Starliner into the local forestland. Four of her party were killed, and Haar herself was seriously injured.

Then we met the Haragi. A simple people, placid but good hunters, adept at fending off the wild creatures of the woods. They have a fascinating culture, based on an appreciation of the natural elements of their environment. We have befriended them, and Citizen Rysik has shown a particular aptitude for their language, and lives among the Haragi now and is my adviser on their customs.

They are fascinated by the Starliner, although they have so far been too afraid to accept our invitation to come inside. It seems they have difficulty processing something that is not a product of nature.

So we are neighbours, the Haragi and ourselves. And they are good neighbours.

The star maps that we carry have a name for this world: Oriana. A nice enough name. But by popular demand, now officially endorsed by Decider Decree 219, it has another.

New Alzarius.

First Decider Halrin Login

ENDS

K-9: The probability is that the Doctor will perceive the threat to all existence and intervene. The outcome will be satisfactory. For the universe.

SARAH JANE SMITH: Oh... Oh no! How long does he have?

K-9: Unknown. Stellar collapse is accelerating. This unit can no longer detect Metulla Orionsis.

SARAH JANE SMITH: I have no idea what that is, K-9. Tell me – is the Doctor still alive?

K-9: Uncertain, mistress.

[PAUSE]

K-9: Mistress. You have been silent for some time.

SARAH JANE SMITH: Yes. Sorry. The sun's setting. I wonder if it will rise again.

K-9: I have a message for you. Stored 'in time of need'.

SARAH JANE SMITH: I'm sorry?

K-9: The message reads:

> 'Hello Sarah! If you get this, then I rather fear I'm coming to the end of my scarf. The writing's been on the wall for some time, and it's been a wonderful, wonderful journey. But all good things... Well... I often thought of coming back for you, you know. But, what with one thing and the other, well, mostly the other... You've got your life to lead, and are probably off doing marvellous things. And I've taken up quite enough of your time – If I'd come back for you... well, perhaps you'd never have gone home. And Earth is such a lovely little planet. You asked me once why I liked humanity so much – well, it's because of people like you. You make the place worth saving. Live well, my Sarah Jane.'

Message ends... Mistress? The message has ended.

SARAH JANE SMITH: K-9... K-9 – re-engage dictation mode. We're starting again.

K-9: Yes, Mistress.

SARAH JANE SMITH: Chapter One. 'The Time Warrior'. The first time I met the Doctor I was disguised as my aunt and he asked me to make tea. It wasn't a great beginning, but it was a story that doesn't yet have an end...

K·9'S JOURNEYS EFFICIENCY QUOTIENT DATA EXTRACT

> THE HYDRAX: 73.78%
Highly satisfactory

> TARA: 63.89%
Some promising elements.

> PARIS: 0.15%
Disappointing after a promising start.

PHAROS PROJECT

Visitors Centre

We regret that the Visitors Centre and Gift Shop are currently closed for technical reasons.

Also, the lecture 'Bubble Memory – Forecasting the Future with Computers' scheduled for 5 March has been postponed due to unforeseen circumstances.

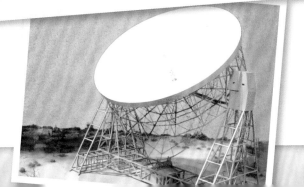

Dear Sir

I am writing to protest in the strongest terms at the actions of a group originating, we believe, from your establishment. A protest march is one thing, but a bunch of kids from the polytechnic running around claiming to be aliens and even making off with an ambulance is quite another. Shocking and shameful behaviour. If this is undergraduate humour then I fail to see the funny side.

Most disappointing of all is that some fool tutor even seemed to have joined in, and started clambering on the mast like a monkey. As luck would have it, he fell off, and gave our security guards quite a scare. It could all have ended very badly indeed - and serve him right - but CCTV footage confirms that he was soon up and on his feet, although not looking himself, as one eyewitness put it.

You have probably read in the press that this escapade has led to the termination of our contract with Group One Security Holdings. We were unable to accept assurances by GOSH that they would in future manage to deploy more than three or four security operatives at any one time.

But perhaps you would be good enough to inform your students - and your staff, for that matter - that they should not take these reports to mean that we are suddenly undefended. We are taking immediate steps to greatly expand our in-house Security Team. So any repeat performance will be met with considerably greater force and followed with swift legal action.

Yours sincerely

The Story of Doctor Who

1974–1981

The principal one I had to contend with was Elisabeth Sladen, who had been in it with Jon. Elisabeth Sladen was on to me in a flash. She adored my terrible jokes, you know. Elisabeth and I were always at one. Elisabeth could do whatever she wanted. Elisabeth was terribly good at that Pearl White stuff. She didn't get stroppy about the silliness of it. No one could touch her, you know, with her great wide eyes – cor, she was fantastic! She was absolutely fantastic.

Tom Baker

Tom always said I was very kind to him, but he's not difficult to be kind to. Lovely Ian Marter – who is no longer with us, sadly – played Harry Sullivan. He and Tom joined forces, so I just thought, 'Well, let the boys play and I can just wait...' Ian was far too clever to be an actor, really.

Elisabeth Sladen (Sarah Jane Smith)

They cast me before they knew anything about the new Doctor. I was brought in, in case the Doctor had been made much older and couldn't handle the physical side of the series. I would have been his strong arm – a sort of rough-and-ready action type. As it was, Tom didn't really need me there at all. Although Tom and I were coming into it and Lis was already there, we never had any problems at all. We all tried to work together as a team, which meant we were able to criticise one another and to go through an entire spectrum of suggestions, changes and compromises.

Ian Marter (Harry Sullivan)

I enjoyed that scene in *Robot* where Tom was trying to get my approval for what he should look like. Each time he came out of the TARDIS with a different outfit. I don't know who the costume designer was on that one, but he deserves a medal.

Nicholas Courtney (The Brigadier)

They had a wonderful designer who later became an Oscar winner, James Acheson. Jim had the idea that my costume should be vaguely Parisian-student – crazy and zany – and so he decided on a scarf. He bought a truck load of wool and sent it down to a woman called Begonia Pope. Jim said, 'Knit me a scarf for the new guy playing Doctor Who,' and she was thrilled to be working for the BBC. She was a fantastically speedy knitter. If there had been knitting in the Olympic Games, she would have been a gold medallist, she was prodigious. And Begonia used up all the wool. She just kept knitting. When we got there, you could hardly get in the room because of the scarf. Then they got me the hat, and away we went.

Tom Baker

Barry Letts saw in Tom Baker's Doctor, producing the first story then helping incoming producer Philip Hinchcliffe shape much of the twelfth season...

TOM BAKER
was the Fourth Doctor

I had to find another Doctor Who. A difficult problem. I had to find someone who was a character in his own right. I let it be known throughout the acting world that I was looking for a new Doctor, and I said, 'He should be a personality who is worth watching in his own right, and you're watching him even if he doesn't have much to do.' We got near when we had to make a decision, which had to be approved by Bill Slater, who'd just become the Head of Serials. I was discussing it with Bill, and he said, 'Have you ever heard of Tom Baker? Smashing actor.' I said, 'Well, what's he done?' 'Oh, you must have heard of *Nicholas and Alexandra* – he played Rasputin in that.' I said, 'Oh, well let's meet him.' This is my version of the story. Tom's is quite different!

Barry Letts, producer

I was working on a building site, absolutely out of work, having had a flirtation some years before with some big film. And I was terribly out of work, and I happened to write to somebody I knew at the BBC, Bill Slater, who that day, that very day he got my letter, had become the Head of Series and Serials. He'd been to a meeting to recast Doctor Who, and the producer said, 'Have you got any views about recasting?' And he said, 'No, I haven't.' And so he went home. And when he got home he was carrying his last letter of the day, which was from me, and his wife said, 'Do you know, he'd be a very good Doctor Who, I think.' So the next day, Bill said, 'What about Tom Baker?' And they said, 'We've never heard of him.' Lots of people hadn't heard of me. And he said, 'Well, there's a film he was in called *The Golden Voyage of Sinbad*.'

Tom Baker

Tom gave a marvellous performance as the villain, and I thought, 'We have found our Doctor Who.' I was always pleased that we'd found him. All the Doctors are one aspect of the same character, but Tom encapsulates this extraordinary wildness, this alien quality and yet he's intensely human at the same time.

Barry Letts

And that night the phone went, and it was Bill Slater. He said, 'Tom, will you come and see me tomorrow,' and when I got in there he said, 'Tom, we'd like you to play Doctor Who.' Then there was a delicious little catch. He said, 'Don't mention it to anyone for two weeks.'

I was working on this building site, and I couldn't tell them. They used to tease me and call me Sir Laurence, because they knew I was an actor and couldn't care less. At the end of the two weeks I had to say, 'Can I have the day off tomorrow?' And he said, 'Sure you can, certainly, Sir Laurence.' I said, 'I'm up for a job at the BBC.'

So off I went, down to the BBC at 10 o'clock in the morning, the photographers were there, and I was in the first edition of the *Evening Standard*, on the front page. It said, 'The New Doctor Who Tom Baker'. So the boys at the building site went down to get the first edition of the paper to look at the horses, and I was on the front page. This guy they'd been teasing for months, you know. And suddenly my whole life changed. And the next day I came back to the building site, they couldn't believe it.

Tom Baker

BAKER *on* BAKER

Doctor Who is like James Bond or Sherlock Holmes – they're not acting parts. The characters never develop. Doctor Who never learns anything. Doctor Who never suddenly becomes interested in women. Doctor Who is not greedy. Doctor Who is not even rude, really. So the fun of playing heroes is how within their utter predictability, you can be interesting or amusing or even, dare one say it, inspiring. It was a kind of idealised Tom Baker who was totally in control of the situation because I knew the lines.

Tom Baker

And when I became Doctor Who, of course, I didn't play Doctor Who, I *was* Doctor Who. There was no acting involved at all. The script, the silly scripts, the magical scripts, and poor old Tom Baker such as he was, absolutely coalesced. And all I had to do was say it, and everyone liked it.

Tom Baker

I didn't like watching it because when I watched it I used to keep thinking we should have done another take. I used to say to Philip, 'We should have done another take.' And he had no time. So what's the point of watching something that made you uneasy?

Tom Baker

Suddenly Tom Baker with all his inadequacies was adored by children, who saw me as a heroic figure.

Tom Baker

Children were always telling me how to avoid the Daleks. 'Doctor,' they'd say – you know the way children do, confidentially – 'why don't you run upstairs?' And I'd say, 'Wow.'

Tom Baker

There was definitely a buzz about it. It was my first job as a producer, and I had a very good team working with me. There was a sense of doing something very exciting and of communicating that excitement such that the programme became a focus of attention. It wasn't just another television programme any more, it was always in the public eye, and at the back of our minds we were always seeking new ways of keeping it there.

Philip Hinchcliffe, producer

Philip was so wonderfully tactful. He was very clever, a kind of comet. He'd take me aside and just mention little things and guide me. He was always there reassuring, always in my eye line. The only producer I didn't mind in my eye line because he mostly approved of what I was trying to do. And Philip was very quick on what was popular then. It went on and on and on, and it built and built, till the thing was really hitting huge, huge viewing figures.

Tom Baker

Philip took it into areas of horror films far more than I did. He was able to scare people far more than I did, because the world had moved on and people were more accepting. He was able to take on board the flavour of the programme – not to have gratuitous nastiness. He always made sure the scariness was absolutely part of the story.

Barry Letts

Robert Holmes had now replaced Terrance Dicks as script editor...

The two of us gelled! We immediately felt we wanted to make the series more exciting, and what we did with *The Ark in Space* was to take it into the realms of real science fiction. That point of view we then carried over into our treatment of other stories, including the ones that had been commissioned already. We pushed the design side to make it feel real and to make it constantly interesting to the eye. Then we pushed to beef up our monsters so they would be taken seriously, even in subsequent stories where we were using old favourites like the Sontarans and the Daleks.

Philip Hinchcliffe

I was very lucky when I handed over to Philip Hinchcliffe, as we had three

months working alongside each other. So when Terry Nation brought in a Dalek story, I said, 'It's all very well Terry, but you've sold us this Dalek story three times before... Why don't you show us the genesis of the Daleks?'

Barry Letts

Barry came up with the idea of calling it *Genesis of the Daleks* and having this Davros character who had actually invented the Daleks in his own image. This gave the story some scope.

Robert Holmes, script editor

Doctor Who is a very moral programme, there's a great morality in it, and it was taken very seriously by producers and directors. There's a particular instance in *Genesis of the Daleks*. We were getting to the point where 'You just have to touch these two wires together and the Daleks are gone, they've never happened.' And Tom just stopped and said, 'Look, I can't do it, there's something missing, do you realise how important a moment this is?'

Elisabeth Sladen

Just as I was going to destroy them, I suddenly paused and said, 'But have I the right? Have I the right?'

Tom Baker

At the time, heroes were really going out of fashion. Your hero could be a little bit more vulnerable, a little bit more complex. So our Doctor wasn't quite the same moral authority.

Philip Hinchcliffe

We were actually getting a great deal of stick from Mary Whitehouse, very unfairly. I think the kind of people who would be upset by *Doctor Who* would get upset about a cabbage rolling down the

stairs. You look at it as I looked at it then: at 6 o'clock, you knew you could run out to your parents if they weren't sitting there with you.

Elisabeth Sladen

We had a deliberate plan to raid the whole genre of science fiction in all its manifestations, from sword and sorcery to the gothic strain, but avoiding the Earthbound setting of a present-day Doctor fighting an invasion from space. All that had been done. Bob and I wanted to fertilise *Doctor Who* by borrowing from richer and more well-known themes from acknowledged classics.

Philip Hinchcliffe

Season 13's move away from Earth's present day meant the end, for many years, of UNIT and the loss of a companion...

How did it affect my career? It certainly pointed it in one direction! I got that one story, little did I think how long it would last. I hope people think I can play other things. It might have typecast me, it might not have. It's been very good to me.

Nicholas Courtney

My own unfulfilled wish was that Harry could have been blown up while trying to save Sarah Jane, or something on those lines – a genuinely heroic exit. I hadn't decided to go. Harry, the character (and that meant me too), was dropped from the series because he had finally outlived his usefulness and was simply getting in the way.

Ian Marter

As the 'gothic' era really got going, the show presented a run of memorable villains, and attracted some fine actors to bring them to life...

Solon [in *The Brain of Morbius*] was a sinister character – let's face it, anyone who's making a body has got to be sinister – but at the same time there were light points in it. One of the funniest lines was after the scene where we learn that he's looking for a head. The Doctor comes in through those doors, with the storm outside, and I just look at him and say, 'What a magnificent head.'

Philip Madoc (Solon)

You had all these amazing actors going, 'Oh! I'm in *Doctor Who*!' Everyone wanted to be on the *Doctor Who* table in the BBC canteen.

Elisabeth Sladen

Actors like Bernard Archard [Scarman in *Pyramids of Mars*] or Tony Beckley, who was in the one about the Krynoid. They were wonderful, because you know they weren't playing baddies, they were just playing characters who were misunderstood, and I was getting in the way. That's the way to play it.

Tom Baker

I believe the viewers want more horror, not less, and the children are among our most bloodthirsty clients. *Doctor Who* is a fantasy programme, a fairy tale even, and our efforts ought to be seen within that context. I reckon we trail a long way behind the Brothers Grimm.

Douglas Camfield, director

Doctor Who has turned into tea-time brutality for tots. My personal reaction to the sight of the Doctor being viciously throttled underwater is unimportant. What's important is the effect of such material – especially in a modern setting – upon the very young children still likely to be watching. Strangulation – by hand, by claw, by obscene vegetable matter – is the latest gimmick, sufficiently close-up so that they get the point. And, just for a little variety, show the children how to make a Molotov cocktail.

Mary Whitehouse, President of the National Viewers and Listeners Association

Despite these criticisms, Seasons 13 and 14 achieved record viewing figures, and not even the departure of the show's most popular companion at the end of The Hand of Fear *could dent Doctor Who's popularity...*

It was a terribly easy and wonderful relationship. It was Elisabeth who decided when she was going to go, because, when new people come into a fixed place, changes are inevitable. And she went.

Tom Baker

When we got the script for my last scene, it was so nebulous. It was so 'Oh, hi, had a nice time, bye, sorry to go', 'Off you go'... So we just rewrote it. Tom gave me a party when I left. He said, 'Why have you got to go?' then, 'I don't want another assistant...'

Elisabeth Sladen

For one story only, the Doctor (at Tom Baker's urging) was on his own...

Tom Baker was a very dominant actor, both physically and intellectually, so you did need to counter that. You really had to get a special actor to play against him in the villain's part. Bernard Horsfall I'd used before as Gulliver in *The Mind Robber*, and he was what I needed in *The Deadly Assassin* – big, tough and with range. I chose Peter Pratt as the Master because, apart from being a very well-known radio actor, he had a splendid voice.

David Maloney, director

Elisabeth was then replaced by Louise Jameson and that was an amazing change, because first of all Louise didn't have many clothes on. And I'd never seen Elisabeth's legs, you know. Suddenly I was confronted by this feral creature, so very well played by Louise. Louise was a leading lady, and she was powerful.

Tom Baker

Leela was following Sarah Jane, so they were going to go for something completely opposite – feisty and aggressive. Mind you, they had to take her clothes off to do it. They put her in a leather leotard. As far as I was concerned I was going into a kids' TV programme, and suddenly to turn into, for want of a better phrase, this sex symbol was extraordinary.

Louise Jameson (Leela)

Writer Paul Cornell on

HORROR OF FANG ROCK

Written in a rush, with minimal sets, effects and model work, it uses structure, dialogue and atmosphere to chill and entertain in equal measure. Our heroes and a terrific guest cast get stuck in a lighthouse with an alien who could be disguised as any one of them. It's a very economical story, where every beat of the plot and featured prop turns out to be significant later, and every single member of the guest cast comes to a sticky end. It's the best characterisation for Leela outside of her creator's scripts, as she crows over the death of the monster. And a famously unhappy shoot made Tom Baker more alien than ever, especially when set against Edwardian society. The script effortlessly moves, across four episodes, from temporal tourist excursion to paranoia to alien siege to saving the world from invasion, using only the slight materials at hand. This is *Doctor Who* at its absolute best.

I used to bundle Elisabeth ahead of me, and I would scrabble behind her. But now, with Louise, with very few clothes on, you know it would have been very immodest if I had been climbing in behind her.

Tom Baker

So, with Leela being a savage, her solution was to bang Janis thorns into everyone. I found this very bothering. I had become such a pacifist. I didn't want to even blow the monsters up. I wanted to have pepper guns to make them sneeze themselves into oblivion.

Tom Baker

Her other weapon was a knife. I was given this fantastic knife, and during *The Robots of Death* I had to hurl it into a robot. Instead of going anywhere near the robot, it went *swish* straight past the poor cameraman and nearly took his ear

off. After that episode, they took away my knife and I got a blunt one.

Louise Jameson

I wouldn't agree about pulling a knife on someone. I had to say, 'Take me to your leader or I'll cut your ears off,' or something daft like that. So I pulled out a jelly baby and I said, 'Take me to your leader or I'll kill him with this deadly jelly baby.'

Tom Baker

At the time, there were a lot of people at the BBC who were very worried about Mrs Whitehouse's general onslaught on the Corporation. But, at the same time, on my front, there were medical experts writing to me saying that *Doctor Who* was having beneficial effects on children, that it was helping children to crystallise what had previously been unarticulated

fears. In other words, if a child can actually pin its fears on something that is acted out, then although the child might be frightened during the battle of good versus evil, it gains a release and a removal of those fears when the Doctor is seen to win at the end.

Philip Hinchcliffe

Having completed three seasons, Philip Hinchcliffe was now moved to another BBC series, Target. *His successor was given a stiff mandate for Season 15...*

I was at this point being offered the job but with an absolutely clear dictate that the violence level had to come down, and the horror element with it! The moment I protested that this was what the audience for *Doctor Who* adored, I was shouted down. They wanted the horror out, but they also wanted *Doctor Who* not to be so much for the kiddies. We had to go back over all the stories we'd been commissioning and inventing among ourselves and take all the horror out, leaving us with a rather nasty hole – a vacuum. So, all we had left to fill it with was, predictably, the humour.

Graham Williams, producer

The main thing about Graham Williams was he introduced the character of K-9. K-9 was an immense success with the children. I personally hated it. Graham knew I didn't really like it. As the main actor in the piece, I knew perfectly well, it's all very well having this tin dog that talks but for a close two-shot you've got to get down on your knees. And I didn't want to have housemaid's knee as Doctor Who.

Tom Baker

Bob Baker and Dave Martin invented K-9 for *The Invisible Enemy* and, after all the agonies of his construction, he seemed too good just to be thrown away.

Graham Williams

The dog didn't function very well or we couldn't have it in the rehearsal room as it was still evolving. I mean, you couldn't run over a cigarette end – it would stop or fall over. The amazing thing was that John Leeson, who is a lovely imaginative actor, wouldn't stand at the side lines; he would get in there. John was there playing this part, you know, calling me 'Master'

Writer Andrew Smith on
THE RIBOS OPERATION

There are few worlds in *Doctor Who* so richly presented as the planet Ribos. We only see the city of Shur, but we learn a lot about Ribos's people, their culture and customs. We learn among other things that, although superficially civilised, this is a place whose population believe it is fought over by the Sun Gods and the Ice Gods, and that the lights seen in the night sky are ice crystals.

This is a story about a confidence trick, and the consequences when it goes wrong. Garron and Unstoffe are off-world conmen (Garron hails from Hackney Wick) who plan to inveigle the Graff Vynda-K, the embittered warmongering former emperor of Levithia, into buying the planet. Garron and Unstoffe come close to pulling it off. The rascals. We like 'em cos they're rogues and their 'mark', the Graff, is a nasty piece of work. He's so nasty he even looks the viewer in the eye

as he declares, 'No-one makes a fool of the Graff Vynda-K and lives!'

The other story being told here is the beginning of the Doctor's search for the Key to Time, given to him by the laconic White Guardian while sipping what looks like crème de menthe in an exotic fantasy landscape. With this mission comes a new companion, in the shape of Romana, a Time Lady. Very different from what had come before. Scriptwriter Robert Holmes gives them some sparkling dialogue to set up their relationship, including some nice putdowns from Romana.

The shining jewel among Ribos's riches is the scene between Unstoffe and Binro 'the Heretic', an original thinker tortured and ostracised for suggesting there may be other worlds apart from Ribos. It grips you completely. The pathos is accentuated because there is none of the humour that is liberally sprinkled throughout the rest of the story.

My agent rang me and told me they were casting a new kind of assistant. So he sent me to see Graham Williams. About three hundred applied for the part. It came down to six of us doing a screen test with Tom Baker. That was really wild.

Mary Tamm (Romana)

When approached about the producer's job, Graham Williams had suggested linking all the episodes of a season into one big adventure. Season 16 tried this out...

The Key to Time season was something I'd had at the back of my mind for a very long time, but it had been impossible to realise during my first year. I wanted something which had a bit more positive force to it. The concept itself was quite easy to get together, but I knew I needed stories which still could be self-sufficient in their own right.

Graham Williams

The second segment took the TARDIS to the pirate planet of Zanak. It was an ambitious script by a newcomer to TV...

I'd always wanted to write comedy sci-fi, ever since the early days of *Doctor Who* and Dan Dare in the *Eagle*. I sent the first episode of *Hitchhikers Guide to the Galaxy* in to *Doctor Who* – hoping that they would then want me to write for the show.

Douglas Adams, writer

I picked it up and read it and thought, 'Now, here's a guy who obviously has a very lively imagination. He could be very valuable and give us a whole new dimension in *Doctor Who*.' I was very taken with him. Ideas were sparking off in all directions. The problem was harnessing him to the format, because he had a tendency to go off in his own directions. In the end it worked extremely well.

Anthony Read

The original idea was just the basic concept of a hollow planet. Graham was interested in space pirates, so we just married the two. The original storyline was of a planet being mined by the Time Lords. The plot was so complicated, I remember reading a synopsis of it to Graham, after which he sank into his chair, mumbling that now he knew how Stanley Kubrick felt.

Douglas Adams

and looking up at me and doing all sorts of funny things to make us laugh.

Tom Baker

Robert Holmes was keen to move on, after more than four years as script editor. He signed off with a satirical swipe at taxation and BBC bureaucracy...

It was just so wittily written, and it was supposed to be Bob Holmes's farewell to the BBC, so there's all these kinds of little jokes in there, like the P45 route. I'm not quite sure how he got away with all of it.

Louise Jameson

It was very much against my preference that Bob Holmes left, because in my estimation he is one of the greatest assets the series can have, not only in the ideas he had, which were smashing, but in his ability to step into the breach when scripts fell down and do it all himself – which took an enormous load off my shoulders.

Graham Williams

Holmes's successor was Anthony Read...

We agreed I would run alongside Bob Holmes because there was so much to learn about the background of it. There's so much history attached to the series that one needed to be able to pick up all the background stuff first. We were concerned to keep the humorous side up. Not to send the programme up, but simply because this was good storytelling and Tom Baker had an enormous capacity

for humour without losing the thread of things.

Anthony Read, script editor

Closing Season 15, The Invasion of Time *took the Doctor back to Gallifrey, apparently aiding and abetting an alien invasion. It featured a journey to the centre of the TARDIS, the surprise return of an old monster, and the abrupt departure of Leela...*

We needed something fresh to come in, but without having the time to set up something completely new the Sontarans were a useful sort of adversary. A good monster that had worked in the past.

Anthony Read

I was quite sad at the way Leela left the series – you know, falling in love with the Time Lord guard. It would have been much more interesting to have her have some fantastic adventure, or even dying.

Louise Jameson

Louise was replaced by Mary Tamm, who was incredibly glamorous in the style of a 1940s star – you know, with boas and a fan. And Mary was so terribly funny.

Tom Baker

The idea was to have an equal. This was the idea, to give the Doctor somebody who wasn't just a push-around, somebody who could come back at him.

Anthony Read

At the end of Season 16, Mary Tamm left the show, but her departure wasn't the end for Romana. The Armageddon Factor *was a six-part epic in which the Doctor and Romana end an interstellar war, reset the universe and save a young princess, played by Lalla Ward...*

I'd said to Graham Williams when I accepted the part, 'You have to know, I'm only going to do the one year,' and he'd said, 'Yes, yes, fine,' hoping, I suspect, that I'd change my mind. And sure enough, when the time came and I said this is my last story, he said how much they wanted me to stay on. The character had been highly popular with the viewers, and I think to try and persuade me into doing extra time, I didn't get a proper leaving scene.

Mary Tamm

Mike Hayes, who directed it, had seen me in something and just offered me the part of Princess Astra. It was incredibly enjoyable and I liked Mary very much, we got on very well. Graham Williams was absolutely lovely. Tom, I got on terribly well with. He was sort of impressed with me because I could beat him at the *Times* crossword. In the end, we finished the serial, and that was the end of that, and I went off. And then Graham Williams rang me up and asked me to come in and see him, and said, would I be interested in playing Romana? And I said, 'Well, yeah, why not?'

Lalla Ward (Princess Astra / Romana)

With the departure of Anthony Read, Graham Williams's final season as producer required a new script editor...

The result of *The Pirate Planet*, of course, was my job as script editor, which Graham offered me in the bar at Television Centre. I had always been a fan of *Doctor Who* and had wanted to write for it, and now I find that I'm script editor! It is such a heavy workload.

Douglas Adams

I think his stamp was enormous. He brought wit to it. He brought huge intelligence to it. He brought his own inimitable style to it. I don't know how much he worked on and actually edited other people's scripts, but I suspect quite a lot. You can recognise Douglas-isms all over the place.

Lalla Ward

Actor Nicola Bryant on
FULL CIRCLE

I guess it could be every fan's dream to sit and watch an episode of *Doctor Who* with a live DVD commentary in their front room. It was my first New Year's Eve in my new home, and I decided to invite some friends over. I had two friends (Andrews Forbes and Smith) who shared memories of working together on a *Doctor Who* story. The story in question was *Full Circle*. I had never seen it before, but I knew it was one of my stepson's favourites. Andrew Smith wrote it, and Andrew Forbes played Omril, the man who bashed the Doctor on the head with a space hammer.

I was relieved I enjoyed *Full Circle* so much, as sitting with the writer and *not* finding it very good would have proved rather embarrassing! For a cerebral script with a lot of complex ideas about evolution, inertia and procrastination, it was truly exciting with lots of dramatic moments and three really good cliff-hangers. I have to say Omril's chest, though a little salt and pepper these days, is still as thick and hairy as when its owner chased the riverfruit thieves across the wilds of Alzarius. Although he didn't have many lines, I enjoyed the way he kept popping up, looking suitably moody about being stuck on a broken spaceship.

Writing and chest hair aside, what impressed me the most was how good their monsters were. As an arachnophobe, I found the giant spiders hatching out of the fruit extremely disconcerting. The swamp monsters emerging from the water brought me right back to my own early, vivid memories of watching *Doctor Who* as a child, being terrified by the invasion of the Sea Devils. The chill factor was high.

I would heartily recommend sitting down to watch this timeless story, although I cannot guarantee that your DVD commentary will be quite as lively as mine.

I've only ever seen tapes of Lalla's *Doctor Who* episodes, and I very much enjoyed them. They were done at a time when Douglas Adams wrote the scripts; therefore they were witty – which is exactly the right word for his writing.

They demonstrate an intelligence and fascination with the comic aspects of science. And some of the ideas of science can be comic if you pursue them as he did.

Richard Dawkins (Mr Lalla Ward)

Graham got on with everybody. He was an intelligent, gentle, good man. So it would have been impossible for anyone not to get on with Graham. I think Douglas was the inventive, bright, energetic creator, in a way that Graham wouldn't have wanted to be. He was just getting on with being the producer.

Lalla Ward

If anything can go wrong, it will. You find yourself in the cutting process, or in the studio, or in post-production, trying to save some disaster or other. We've written around situations, cast around situations, we've dropped or picked up scenes. Because *Doctor Who* becomes a way of life, you expect problems, rather than being surprised by them. If there aren't any problems you worry about what's gone wrong.

Graham Williams

Graham was then replaced by John Nathan-Turner. He obviously wanted to get his mark on it and so things began to develop. The tempo of the music was changed. That had nothing to do with me. I didn't see it myself, but he could do whatever he liked. Gradually, more people came into it. Several young people came into it who had strict views about whether the narrative could be shared in several strands, cos you can't have people standing around.

Tom Baker

I had three years as production unit manager before I took over as producer in November 1979, so I had a really good grounding in the finances of the show, of the kind of day-to-day problems that can arise, as well as working with Tom.

John Nathan-Turner, producer

Nathan-Turner's changes for Season 18 were sweeping: revamped theme music, new logo and opening titles, electronic incidental music, a new costume for the Doctor, computerised special effects, and the phasing out of K-9, as well as the casting of a new Master and the expansion of the TARDIS crew. But bigger changes were just round the corner...

That was around the time that I began to realise that perhaps I was past it. The new people with the power – John Nathan-Turner and his script editor, and his choice of companions.

Tom Baker

The idea was that the eccentric and unpredictable Doctor would arrive at a real planet which had real rules and a real economy and a real history, however bizarre. It was all to be rational and understandable, the only element of fantasy being the Doctor himself.

Christopher H. Bidmead, script editor

I can only tell you that I felt very privileged to be given the part of the Master and follow such a wonderful performer as

Roger Delgado. I didn't know it was going to be as important as it turned out to be. The thing to do is not to try to copy people, no matter what you thought of the way I did it, I think it might have been not very successful if I'd tried to be a pale imitation of Roger.

Anthony Ainley (The Master)

I remember very clearly my journey on the Tube the morning of the first day and sitting there, I have never been so frightened and excited in my life. And I remember arriving at the read-through and Tom was late, so we were all sitting around the table waiting for the read-through to begin, and he stalked in, in his mac, his brown mac, and I was physically shaking. It was extraordinary. Extraordinarily frightening, a very surreal first day.

Matthew Waterhouse (Adric)

Nyssa was quite different. She came from this planet where everyone was very polite. She was of high birth, she had a stepmother and a very loving father, and it all goes pear-shaped for Nyssa because the Master takes over her father's body. It's very tragic for her, and I think that's one of the things that forces her to join the Doctor because she has a score to settle.

Sarah Sutton (Nyssa)

There were 100 people up for it. John Nathan-Turner looked me up and down and asked how tall I was. Quick as a flash, I replied in my best Australian accent, 'I'm five feet two, the minimum height for an airline hostess in Australia. I thought about being one once, so I checked it out.' I don't think he believed me, but I got the job!

Janet Fielding (Tegan Jovanka)

I knew K-9 was going to be run down for the next few stories, and John Nathan-Turned asked me if I'd like to see him out, to do the job right. And I said yes, I would.

John Leeson (K-9)

I really don't think that this rather gentle, little, technologically infantile, sweet, melodrama-story, could have gone on being what it had been. I think John had to change it. It didn't make it comfortable for me to going on doing it having been part of the old regime.

Lalla Ward

So anyway one thing led to another and I thought, 'Well, it's time I gave someone else a go.' I'm sorry if I went on too long, but I couldn't wrench myself away. When I offered my resignation, I was quite astounded at how swiftly it was accepted. Well, I can't blame them. I can't blame them.

Tom Baker

THE FIFTH DOCTOR

WHEN IT WAS FUN

DR SONG: So how did you meet him?

TEGAN JOVANKA: It was all my Auntie Vanessa's fault. When I turned up on her doorstep, she looked me up and down and laughed. 'An air hostess? My girl, how a temper like yours is going to cope with smiling sweetly at drunk businessmen, I'll never know.'

I shrugged it off, but it nagged away at me. Was I really doing the right thing? I needed something to do and this seemed like a glamorous something to do. And, when you got chatting to the other trainees it sounded all right – London, Sydney, Tokyo and the New York stopover. Even better, the thought of bagging some Prince Charming of a pilot with all the skies at his command. Who doesn't love a man in uniform?

As it turned out, I got my man in uniform, but it was cricket whites. I guess that's an example of how it all went wrong.

I never did get to that first day at work. It had all seemed so certain, so mapped out for me. Instead I wandered into a blue box on a frosty bypass. The TARDIS. It was many things, but it certainly wasn't a jumbo jet. At first it was just an unscheduled detour – but what a detour it was – saving the universe. Then it all got out of hand.

DR SONG: Rule 1 – everything always gets out of hand with the Doctor. What went wrong this time?

Tegan Jovanka: The Doctor fell off a radio telescope. He didn't die – no, he regenerated, grew a whole new body out of the broken bits, and someone had to look after him. He needed a grown-up to help him. Looking back on it now, I'm all 'Girl, what were you thinking?' but all he had with him was a couple of kids, so a mouthy 20-year-old from Brisvegas was the nearest the Doctor was going to get to a responsible adult.

The Doctor had been reborn – as in, gone from wise old grandfather time to a newborn babe. Someone had to take charge. Nyssa (great girl and all that) looked on the verge of panic, and Adric just wandered off. It was all a mad blur – getting the Doctor back to the TARDIS, getting it off the planet, finding him pottering the corridors, dragging him to the Zero Room, finding out the Master had flung us back to the Big Bang... and all the time, this nagging nag-nag-nag at the back of my head: 'Tegan, you are going to be *really* late for work.'

DR SONG: ...?

TEGAN JOVANKA: Stop that. I can see what you're thinking. But when a Jovanka gets an idea in her head it stays there. My parents were going to be farmers, desert or no desert. And I'd decided I was going to be an air hostess and, crazy idea or not, I was going to be an air hostess. So yeah, it was all

TARDIS index file

REGENERATIVE FAILURE

A rare occurrence on Gallifrey, and almost unknown outside the Capitol. Commonly triggered if the regenerative state is achieved off-world and outside a time capsule. Immediate physical relocation to a Zero Environment is strongly recommended.

Ambient complexity is the cause of many of these failures of regeneration. Some real locations are known to have properties similar to Zero environments and, in some cases, are eminently more effective.

Classic Plainness as exemplified by regions like Dwellings of Simplicity. For Dwellings of Simplicity, see Castrovalva.

THIS ARTICLE IS A STUB

very well for the Doctor to say he couldn't steer the thing, or that we had to stop some giant frog from turning the human race into microchips, but the important thing was — I was going to be an air hostess.

As my dad used to say, it didn't matter if you were no good at it, it was important that you had a fair shout at it. And I wasn't getting a go. It's why I kept putting on the uniform — reminding the Doctor, reminding myself, that I had a job to get to. Once we'd saved the world one more time.

It had all been a bit of a shock, so I needed something to fall back on. We were a ship full of odds and sods. Adric —

he was one of those kids that expects to get praise just cos he's clever at maths (back home we'd have dangled him out of a tree till he got good at sport). Still, he'd lost his brother and was trapped in the wrong universe.

But Nyssa sure won the orphan sweepstake — the Master had killed her whole family, her whole world, her entire star system, and he was now flying around wearing her father's body. How she got up in

ANCIENT CHINESE PROVERB

Traditional: 天高皇帝遠

Simplified: 天高皇帝遠

Transliteration (pinyin):
Tiān gāo huángdì yuǎn

Meaning:
The sky is big and the emperor is far away.

the morning without being so full of pills she rattled, I'll never know.

The Master had only killed my lovely Auntie Vanessa. He didn't even do it for any reason – just for kicks – and the only time I got to grieve for her was during a quiet hour on a plastic chair in a corridor at an observatory, when I was supposed to be working through the night helping the Master build a supercomputer, with only instant coffee from a drinks machine to keep me awake.

As I said – after that, we were all a bunch of misshapes out of breath. Even the Doctor looked like he needed a sit-down. All of a sudden he was a very old man poured into a young body. I think he had trouble taking himself seriously. All that knowledge of space and time at his command, and he felt he had to pop on a pair of specs to show when he was being smart.

But we just got on with it, staggering from Castrovalva to Monarch's ship, doing the Charleston, starting the Great Fire of London... All the time, I kept putting on my uniform, doing my make-up to Air Australia standards and reminding everyone that I really should get back to work.

It changed a bit on the Kinda world. While Nyssa was enjoying some well-earned kip, my mind was occupied. The Mara just turned up and said, 'You need a rest too, sport. It's all getting a bit hectic. You take a back seat and I'll drive.'

Of course, that's not how it turned out. The Mara had been waiting outside existence for a long time, looking for someone run down, scared, and out of their depth. I guess I was the ideal target. (There's

Aristophanes
The Frogs

Aboriginal Proverb
After rain comes the toad.

Will the world end on Wednesday?

by Our Correspondent

ACCORDING to the Ancient Mayan calendar, the world ends on 4 March 1981, with the Coming of the Great Frog.

Some believers cite recent political unrest and solar flares. Astronomers even point to recent unusual stellar activity and a dramatic increase in background radiation as proof that the ancient Mayans knew the end of the world is nigh.

The Mayan Calendar is commonly seen as a series of complicated and interconnected wheels (or Bak'tun), each one smaller than the last. One such calendar has recently come to prominence among scholars of the apocalypse. The outer Bak'tun on this calendar goes back to 35,000 years ago. The next circle 8,000 years. The next 4,000 years, and the final ring begins 2,500 years ago. At the centre of one of these circles is a carving of what many have taken to be a giant frog or toad. And, according to Professor Jon Kipling of the University of South Minnesota, the Coming of the Great Frog is in four days' time.

At noon, to be precise.

DOME SAFETY PROTOCOL

IN NO CIRCUMSTANCES SHOULD ANY MEMBER OF THE PARTY LEAVE THE DOME WITHOUT A TOTAL SURVIVAL SUIT.

IF SURVIVAL INSIDE A TSS PROVES IMPOSSIBLE THEN THE FOLLOWING EMERGENCY PROTOCOLS MUST BE ADHERED TO:

1) IF A MEMBER OF THE LP/SURVEY/T FAILS TO MEET SCHEDULED REPORTING INTERFACES, THEN DESIGNATED SR SECURITY WILL INSTITUTE AN OFFICIAL AROUND-THE-CLOCK ALERT.

2) THE TAKING OF NATIVES AS HOSTAGES IS STANDARD PROCEDURE AT THIS POINT.

3) IF FURTHER MEMBERS OF THE LP/SURVEY/T FAIL TO REPORT, THEN PUNITIVE ACTION MAY BE TAKEN AGAINST NATIVE HOSTAGES AS WARRANTED UNTIL ALL MEMBERS OF THE LP/SURVEY/T ARE ACCOUNTED FOR.

4) ON NO ACCOUNT SHOULD ANY LOCAL FLORAL OR FAUNA BE HANDLED OR BROUGHT INTO THE DOME.

a dodgy parable here for career women, but I don't run one of those centres for executive stress management, so there's a blessing for us all right there.)

Suddenly I was alone and scared and literally out of my mind. The whole experience was horrible – I did dreadful things. But also... it was kind of liberating. Suddenly I wondered if I really had got my priorities right.

If that was a nudge in the right direction, I got a massive shove when Adric died. Sounds terrible to say it, but he'd been at his worst that day. Sulking round the TARDIS, saying how little he fitted in and how much he wanted to get home and I thought, 'Bless you, Tegan, is that how much of a pain you seem?' I realised how much time the Doctor spent getting it in the neck from us. (I'm not including Nyssa. She wouldn't complain about a British Rail sandwich.) I decided he deserved a break.

Turns out, I gave him his break on the wrong day. We spent it being hunted through caves by killer androids. Then we were having gun battles on a spaceship with Cybermen. So many people died, and then Adric fell back through time, crashing into the Earth.

It all happened so suddenly – the freighter was there on the screen, then it was gone. I remember screaming at the Doctor, ordering him to fly the TARDIS back there and rescue him. This was a man, remember, who couldn't even get to Terminal One and I was asking him to change history while flying the TARDIS like he was one of the Red Arrows. Instead, he promptly landed us at Heathrow.

KINDA PROVERB

Wheel turns
It is all beginning again.
History is. Time is.
The great wheel rolls down the hill
Gathering speed through the centuries.
The wheel crushes everything in its path.
Unstoppable until once again.
The Wheel turns, civilisations arise,
Wheel turns, civilisations fall.
Wherever the wheel turns, there is
suffering, delusion and death.
Wheel turns.
It all begins again, with a
killing. It doesn't end.
That ends as it has always done, in
chaos and despair.
It ends as it begins, in the darkness
It is the Mara who now turns the wheel.
It is the Mara who dance
To the music of our despair.
Our suffering is the Mara's delight.
Our madness the Mara's meat and drink.
And now the Mara turns the wheel of life.
It ends as it begins
Wheel turns

Being an account of the true hiftory of

THE GREAT FIRE

which did lately confume

LONDON

and many people thereof.

With divers explanations of the involfment of
GIANT LIZZARDS, the tragical account of a SILVER MAN,
and containing the remarkable cure of a DEADLY PLAGUE,
as given by one who saw it all,

Richard Mace, esq

Actor and Gentleman

He claims it was an accident. I wonder if it was the universe having a massive laugh at us. Look, why am I telling you all this? I've never talked to anybody about any of it. I don't even know who you are. I think you should leave.

DR SONG: We've been through this, haven't we, sweetie. Think about it and you'll remember.

TEGAN JOVANKA: You're... you're a fr— You know the Doctor, don't you?

DR SONG: Oh, I know the Doctor.

TEGAN JOVANKA: And you... you need me to help you to...

DR SONG: To help him, that's right. So – Heathrow? He finally got you home...

TEGAN JOVANKA: It wasn't that straightforward. The Master was involved – this is the kind of man who couldn't uncork a tin of corned beef without putting on a disguise and then hypnotising a cow into opening the can. But, I'd always wanted to fly on Concorde and now I got the chance – only to prehistoric Earth.

DR SONG: Oh, sounds ghastly. I've always wanted to go to Planet One – the oldest planet in the universe. It's got a cliff of pure diamond, and on the cliff there's writing. Letters fifty feet high. A message from the dawn of time. And no one knows what it says. What's prehistoric Earth got? Soup and dinosaurs.

TEGAN JOVANKA: Shows how much you know. Actually, there were a couple of Concordes, a crashed spaceship, some blobby things and the last of the Xeraphin. But you know the Doctor – Master defeated, Xeraphin sent home, and everyone back to Heathrow in time for tea. I just sort of wandered away – just to get my bearings, really. I was finally back where I'd wanted to be. All right, I was probably a few days late and would get some funny looks when I wandered into the crew room, but I'd got where I was supposed to be. Heathrow. I could finally be an air stewardess.

I looked around at it all – at the bright signs for Sydney and Hong Kong with New York stopovers, and I looked at all the people... thousands and thousands of stressed people with luggage and queues and screaming brats and duty free, all running about five

THE MISSING CONCORDE

What happened to Speedbird Concorde 192?

Here's a transcript of the last communication from the doomed flight.

SC: Good afternoon, London. Speedbird Concorde one nine two.

ATC: Speedbird Concorde one nine two. You are cleared to descend to flight level three seven zero.

SC: Roger. Clear to three seven zero.

ATC: Speedbird Concorde one nine two, you are cleared to continue descent to two eight zero. Speedbird Concorde one nine two, will you acknowledge, please?

ATC: Speedbird Concorde one nine two, will you acknowledge?

SC: Speedbird Concorde one nine-

ATC: Speedbird Concorde one nine two, will you acknowledge, please? Speedbird Concorde one nine two, will you acknowledge, please? I have total RT breakdown on Speedbird Concorde one nine two. I don't believe it. She's approaching London but the trace is becoming intermittent. Emergency. We have lost contact with Concorde Golf Victor Foxtrot.

Search this blog

Links

Alex's Secrets

Bob's Blacklist

Climate Central

Conspiracy Today

Deep Secrets Forum

Disenfranchised

Dinosaurs in London

Electronic Barriers

End the Conspiracy

Pharos First Contact?

Guy Crayford – hero?

Latest missing scientists

Mona Lisa - fake?

Nunton cover-up

'Think-Tank'

minutes behind schedule to catch a plane that was probably delayed... I looked around at it all, and – massive light-bulb moment. I realised that I didn't really want to be an air stewardess after all. Sudden change of plan. I ran to tell the Doctor.

And he'd gone.

DR SONG: Rabbits.

TEGAN JOVANKA: Are you trying to be funny? Turned out, Air Australia didn't much want me to be an air stewardess either – something to do with turning up for my first day several months late and in tears. So, I ditched the uniform and carried on travelling. With the TARDIS it was spaceship one moment and horse and cart the next, but I made do with back-packing my way across Europe.

Which is when all the coincidences started. Of course my cousin would be in Amsterdam. It just so happened that Colin was bivouacking right next to a huge space curtain called the Arc of Infinity, which was being swished open by an old enemy of the Doctor's who had decided to borrow his body – it was all a bit complicated, but let's just say it wasn't long before I was back aboard the TARDIS.

But something was nagging at the back of my mind – it was a bit convenient how I'd been brought back aboard. I thought I got the answer when we next landed and the Mara tore through me like an undercooked rissole.

Greetings from Amsterdam

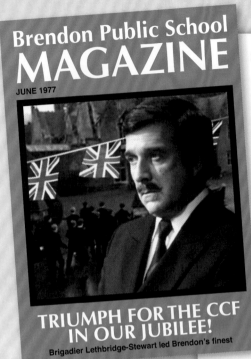

Brendon Public School
MAGAZINE
JUNE 1977

TRIUMPH FOR THE CCF IN OUR JUBILEE!
Brigadier Lethbridge-Stewart led Brendon's finest

November 1983   Brendan School Magazine 3

Vale: The Brig
by the Headmaster

It is with great sadness I must report that the Brigadier is moving on at the end of term, back to his soldiering. He has revolutionised the Maths department and marshalled the...

DR SONG: Like a what?!

TEGAN JOVANKA: Look, do you want to hear about this or not? This time the Mara had dragged us back to its birthplace and wanted to make a permanent comeback. The Doctor defeated it. Now, this is the thing about the guy – anyone else, you'd expect would go at it, all guns blazing. Not the Doctor. He came to the big showdown... to the Mara, holding my body and an entire civilisation hostage. The Doctor just came to talk to it. And, when that didn't work, he thought it to death.

Thing is, he hated killing it. And he hated the pain it caused me. Remember the end of that space film where the heroes blow up thousands of people then dance round a bonfire with some koalas? That was not the Doctor's style. He wasn't a gloater. He just looked grim.

It took us a while to realise that our travels were being manipulated by something greater than the Mara. Turned out, the universe is run by two great stuffed bird gods – the Black and White Guardians. Once, long ago, the Doctor had annoyed the Black Guardian, and now he was taking revenge. So – how do you reckon some mighty power that's got it in for the Doctor might go about assassinating him?

DR SONG: Do tell.

TEGAN JOVANKA: He went and found a child. Turlough. Seriously, get hold of a schoolkid, put the frighteners on him, then rely on him to kill the Doctor. Mad, isn't it? I could tell Turlough was a

Sick?
Diseased?
Dying?
DON'T WORRY WE'LL TAKE HER ON

TERMINUS INCORPORATED

Giving her one last chance

wrong 'un, but the Doctor and Nyssa seemed more than happy to welcome on board a mysterious orphan. Funny thing about being an Aussie; even now, you catch people eyeing you up, wondering what kind of crime your ancestors did and whether they've left anything valuable on display. So it seems a bit wrong of me to say this, but you could tell Turlough was a schemer just by looking at him – his eyes were all shifty.

One of Tegan's rules for life, when figuring out someone – if you're dangling over a cliff, would they come and rescue you? The Doctor and Nyssa would be fighting for the job. Adric – well, he'd explain to you how he could help you up with the use of a rope and pulley, then get all cross cos he couldn't find a rope. Even the Master, on a good day, might give you a hand – but no, not Turlough. He'd sit down and watch you fall. While sketching it.

When Nyssa left us (to cure a space plague, which let's face it is a fax from the Department of No Surprises – it was either going to be that or run a space dolphin sanctuary), Turlough and me were alone with each other, which was in no way awkward. For one thing, right, he was really a grown-up alien dressed as a schoolboy. Weird. For another, he was all over the Doctor. Frankly, I wasn't surprised to learn that he was working for the Black Guardian – what was surprising was that the Doctor had kind of thought so all along.

I was all for dropping him at Intergalactic

You are cordially invited to take part in

THE RACE FOR ENLIGHTENMENT

Boats assemble in the orbit of Woman Wept

Newport Pagnell, but the Doctor was convinced Turlough was actually 'a good egg'. Out loud, I agreed with him, but I always made sure he wasn't left alone in the console room. With the silverware.

I was starting to realise that what made the Doctor so much fun was that, for all his cucumber-sandwiches-with-the-crusts-off geniality, he had no safety catch. No light ever came on saying 'Fasten your seatbelts'. He'd just go anywhere, talk to anyone. Invite everyone back to his. I've known Aussie house-shares like that in Shepherd's Bush, and believe me, it never ends well.

Even Turlough thought it was a bit odd when the Doctor invited the Master's pet robot on board. It kind of made me wonder – I mean, clearly, the Doctor adored travelling with Nyssa – but Adric, Turlough and Kamelion? I mean, really? It was at this point I decided to be a bit nicer to him. Did he really need friends that badly? After all, for all the danger, and being flatmates with a psychopath and a killer robot, it was the most fun I'd ever have in my life.

We went to the Eye of Orion and, for a brief moment, it all

seemed good. Then we ended up on the Doctor's home
planet of Gallifrey — their President had gone mad
and summoned all the Doctor's past lives to the
Death Zone. I got to spend time with the original
Doctor — and I suddenly realised how ancient, how
different my Doctor was. I'd got so used to the
ever-eager, slightly lost boy, so it was a bit of
a shock to see that he was born as an old man and
was ageing backwards. Does that make sense?

DR SONG: Well... So you've met — what — three
Doctors?

TEGAN JOVANKA: Five! There was also a dashing
Doctor and a crumpled Doctor — but, with my
luck, I got to spend time with the grumpy
one. And pretty devious he was too — he
was more than able to outwit the Master,
and it was the old codger who helped
defeat the President... but, all that
said, the first Doctor looked at my
Doctor... well, it was a bit like someone
coming back for a poke round a house
they've sold off long ago, and not quite
approving of the new kitchen.

   He'd also had a granddaughter back then
— another surprise. She seemed quite a
plucky old bird — but then again, the whole
thing was a bit like a family reunion.
Where most of the guests were the same
person. I know it sounds bizarre, but it

THE [logo] TIMES

We won't fade away

THE   RETIREMENT
yesterday of Brigadier
Lethbridge-Stewart was a
historic moment, although
few will understand the
significance – or even have
heard – of the Brigadier.
Yet   this   mysterious,
self-effacing   figure   is
regarded as one of the
most important soldiers of
the 20th century. Working
with the UN, he's revered
in this country – but not as
a bureaucrat.
   To look at him, you
wouldn't exactly assume

he is an enigma. In his
working life he has been
sighted everywhere from
Loch Ness to an English
public school. He played
a part in two evacuations
of London. Yet exactly
what the Brigadier does
has remained a mystery for
several decades. And, with
his retirement, all that we
know is that, whatever he
did, he does it no longer.
In a brief, self-effacing
speech, he did remark that
he intended to keep up his
garden.

Lullabies for Time Tots

by Benncuiq III

Who unto Rassilon's Tower
would go

Must choose – Above,
Between, Below

Who unto Rassilon's Tower
would go

Must fight with those he
used to know

Who unto Rassilon's Tower
would dare

Must dance across the
deadly square

If Rassilon's Tower
you will step in

Then you must choose
– to lose or win

all seemed jolly enough, and kind of gave me hope for the future.

Thing is, everyone has bad days. And after that, I had a run of bad days that were off the scale. We got shot at by spy satellites in the future, we ended up stopping a world war, and the Doctor killed off a race of lizards. As if that wasn't enough, we found my uncle had been kidnapped by people working for an ancient alien Devil living in a church...

SIR CHARLES
INVITES ALL OF
LITTLE HODCOMBE
TO TAKE PART IN
**WAR
GAMES**
IN HONOUR OF
**THE QUEEN OF
THE MAY**

The Doctor took us to the end of the universe – I think he
figured it'd be peaceful there, but instead the TARDIS was
destroyed by a race of giant earwigs intent on dismantling
the last humans for spare parts. And then, just as we left
Frontios, we got pulled into a Dalek time corridor.

You've never met a Dalek, have you? I can just tell.
It's the way you're still sat there, rather than
running screaming out the window. They wanted to
conquer the Earth. They started by wiping out
everyone I met. By the end it got so mad that
the Doctor... the Doctor, a nice humane man who
slumped when he destroyed the Silurians... the
Doctor slaughtered the Daleks. He didn't stop
until all the Daleks on Earth were dead. And he
did it without a qualm – he didn't pause, sigh,
or have second thoughts – he was positively
breezy, and all ready to move on. Job done.

But I'd seen so many good people die, wiped out
by these dreadful creatures. It had been a long,
horrible day. The Doctor didn't seem to notice
– he was simply glad I was alive. That'd do fine,
come along Tegan, scoot me into the TARDIS and

27

EURO FLU CLAIMS ANOTHER VICTIM

ANOTHER senior politician became the latest victim of the so-called 'Euro Flu'. Sir Reginald Styles collapsed in front of concerned colleagues while hosting trade talks in Geneva.

Friends said that Sir Reginald had seemed suddenly confused, with slurred speech – the classic symptom of a mysterious disease which is spreading through the upper political echelons with no sign of a cause or a cure.

move on. But... I just couldn't. I looked at that blue door hanging invitingly open and I shuddered. What would be next? I needed a break. A rest. And I was scared – it was like the Doctor was changing. And I ran away.

It had all got too much for me, and I didn't know what I wanted to do. There's a song by The Clash – you know – 'Should I stay or should I go now? If I stay there will be trouble...' There. That'll be in your head for the rest of the day now. Job done.

But it sums up how I felt. Confused, sad, desperate. I know it sounds lame, but I had concussion, it had been a really, really long day, and I'd seen a lot of death. In my work now, I'll see people say, 'The stress, Tegan, the stress is really killing me, I tell you.' And I'll smile. Cos they don't know anything. And even after all these years, I know I ran away, out into the rain.

DR SONG: Did you have a plan? Any idea what you were going to do next?

TEGAN JOVANKA: No. Perhaps I expected the Doctor to come running after me. It's what any human man would do, if he cared. But he didn't. Perhaps that settled it. Perhaps it didn't. And I stood there, in the rain, looking out at the grey river, the grey sky, the grey buildings... home of a sort... and I wondered if I hadn't made a terrible mistake. I ran back into the warehouse... and as I ran in, I heard, for the last time ever, the sound of the TARDIS, fading away for good.

  Brave heart, Doctor.

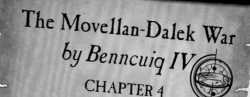

The Movellan-Dalek War
by Benncuiq IV
CHAPTER 4

The war between the Daleks and the Movellans continued for a further 90 years after the failure of the Skaro Gambit. With Davros imprisoned by the humans, the Daleks fought on by themselves, thinking to maintain the stalemate.

But in the intervening 90 years, the Movellans had themselves advanced still further, and their Battle Computers were finally able to come up with a new solution. As the Movellans were non-organic, it was easy for them to experiment with a virus that would eat organic matter. (Indeed, such a compound already existed in the Dalek laboratories on Spiridon, leading one to infer that the Movellans may have helped

themselves.) Not (for the moment) wishing to wipe out all life in the universe, the Movellans gradually refined the virus until it became a very efficient consumer of Kaled tissue. They then unleashed it.

The Daleks lost a war for the only time in their long history. The Supreme Dalek sought out their creator and pressed him into service again – to override their conditioning and cure the virus. By this time, however, Davros was no longer content with playing a subservient role to his creations. History will show that the Supreme Dalek would have done better to have left well alone.

Lanzarote

POST CARD

Janine —

Well, Peri's gone. The selfish brat vanished without a trace. I did all I could to stop her, but no, she had to go on the run. And, of course, she made a scene – some nudists thought they saw a girl drowning. We've had the local policia out, and work's been hellish these last few days. But, like a bad penny, she'll turn up.

Howard

JANINE BROWN FOSTER

256 EAST LOMBARD ST

FELL'S POINT

BALTIMORE 21231

MARYLAND

UNITED STATES

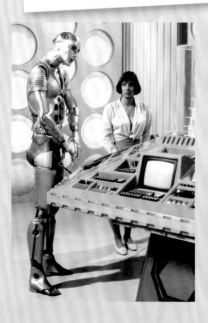

SIRIUS CONGLOMERATE

Minutes of Meeting of 17 March 28

CALL TO ORDER

The Vice Chairman opened the meeting at 8.15 a.m. and extended the Conglomerate's welcome to the new Chairman, Krau Timmin.

EMERGENCY STATEMENT

All mining and military operations on Androzani Minor have now ceased, with no survivors. The casualties are known to include:

CONGLOMERATE

MORGUS

MILITARY

GENERAL CHELLAK

MAJOR SALATEEN

CRIMINALS

SHARAZ JEK

STOTZ (GUNRUNNER)

KRELPER (GUNRUNNER)

DOCTOR (GUNRUNNER)

PERI (GUNRUNNER)

CHAIRMAN'S REPORT

Chairman Krau Timmin addressed the Committee on the Conglomerate's immediate future in the wake of the disgrace and death of ex-Chairman Morgus and the loss of all Spectrox-mining facilities on Androzani Minor.

She reported that examination of Morgus's assets on other worlds in the Sirius system has already begun, with those assets now seized by the Conglomerate. One potential source of new income has already been identified - the harvesting of trees on ▮▮▮▮▮▮▮▮▮▮▮▮.

Krau Timmin explained that this particular species of tree appears to be in some way sentient. Naturally, the exploitation of 'intelligent wood' could be highly lucrative if farmed and harvested intensively. Equally, it is vital that the Conglomerate's interest and the very existence of these 'Tree forms' both be shielded from public or political knowledge. If people knew they were eating their dinner off a 'living' dining table, there might well be considerable consumer resistance.

The Committee agreed to proceed.

The Committee agreed to extend the Conglomerate's condolences to the late President's family and to the people of Androzani Major in general, following the unfortunate death of the President.

The Committee agreed to extend the Conglomerate's condolences to the late Chairman Morgus's family.

The Committee also agreed to retract the Conglomerate's condolences to the late Chairman Morgus's family.

The Story of Doctor Who

1981–1984

John Nathan-Turner transformed *Doctor Who*. The urban myth, which may be true, is that he was given *Doctor Who* because he promised he would make it for less money than anybody else. Apparently the job was offered to other people and they said, 'We can't make it for that.' And John said, 'I can,' and he did.

Mark Strickson (Turlough)

John Nathan-Turner was brilliant at getting the show publicity. He was extraordinary, keeping the programme incredibly high profile, even though the viewing figures were actually not that great. The thing about *Doctor Who* was everyone knew it was on Saturday teatime, but over the years viewing figures just dropped off. During my time they moved it to midweek, and there was a huge outcry. In fact, the viewing figures went up massively when it was moved to midweek, although it didn't seem right.

Saturday is perfect because that's where it should be. Because that is *Doctor Who* time, and it still is.

Peter Davison

When I was doing *Doctor Who*, we had three different companions. There was Janet, Matthew and myself, and I think actually it was a very crowded TARDIS. Probably a bit too crowded. I think it must have been a nightmare for scriptwriters because we all had to be given something to do, we all had to be split up at some point, and someone had to get lost or get into trouble. Janet was always very strong and very up for sorting things out, and I was much more standing in the background doing as I was told. And Matthew was quite new to television.

Sarah Sutton (Nyssa)

With four people on board the TARDIS, you can have two storylines going and

you can have plenty of dialogue. Or you can have four storylines, with the regulars speaking only to non-regulars. It's a very useful device but, like everything, after a time it begins to bore. Keeping four characters on the air throughout the story can be a difficult responsibility.

John Nathan-Turner, producer

We were sent off to do different things in different stories. In one story, I had a headache for about three episodes and went to lie down in the TARDIS. I think that was so that Janet could have a better go at playing Tegan.

Sarah Sutton

I always thought of Tegan as Lucy in space – the *Peanuts* character. She was quite vociferous and she was quite argumentative and assertive, although not particularly smart. She was very cranky and she got annoyed with the Doctor easily, and she had that sort of fishwife

PETER DAVISON
was the Fifth Doctor

I had worked with him for three years when I was production assistant on *All Creatures Great and Small*. He really was my first choice for the Doctor. So I rang him at home and just said, 'How would you like to be the next *Doctor Who*?'

John Nathan-Turner

And it's like everything stands still because it's so bizarre. He offered to take me to lunch. And this is a BBC producer, so I thought, 'He must be serious if he's taking me for lunch.'

Peter Davison

Peter provided a complete contrast to Tom. Peter helped take the show in a new direction and, with all the problems such a transition created, we couldn't have had a better person.

John Nathan-Turner

I suggested my costume should be loosely based on a cricketing outfit. John decided on a more designed look, so he came up with this rather strange idea of a Victorian cricketing outfit with sort of nice stripy trousers and a nice beige jacket... I was a vision of beige, really, and I thought it was really silly until I saw Colin Baker's outfit.

Peter Davison

What I remember most about Peter was his wonderful cool quality. You know, things can get very fraught making a series like *Doctor Who* – running out of time, sets needing changing, all that sort of thing. But Peter was always cool – his youthful appearance belied an enormous professionalism. You always felt that if you had to say to Peter that everything had to be changed – could he do all his moves backwards and even speak his dialogue backwards – he would just do it.

John Nathan-Turner

John came to me and said, 'We've had this great idea. We think you should wear a stick of celery on your lapel.' I went, 'Yeah, great. Why?' And he went, 'We don't know, we just thought it would be a good conversation piece.' And I said, 'That'll be fine, as long as you explain why

I'm wearing it before I leave the series.' And so we got to the very last story and I said, 'You still haven't explained why I'm wearing this stick of celery.' So they went away and they came up with this new scene which explains why I'm wearing the celery.

Peter Davison

I think that the vulnerability of Peter's Doctor came from a couple of sources. There's a vulnerability in a younger person that isn't there in an older person. Also there was clearly a decision to show him as much more emotionally engaged. And therefore he is bound to be more vulnerable.

Janet Fielding (Tegan Jovanka)

I just liked that idea that the Doctor was doing the best he possibly could. It also struck me when I used to watch the programme that at the moment when the story starts if he just left then it'd be far the best thing to do. I mean he created many more problems than he solved, actually, but that was part of the way he was. He did his best.

Peter Davison

I suppose I felt, really, that I was too young. In retrospect, and from the point of view of today and the present series of *Doctor Who*, I don't seem at all young. It's hard almost to remember that's how I felt. But nevertheless I came after Hartnell, Troughton, Pertwee – Tom was a little younger – but I was by far the youngest.

Peter Davison

I mostly used the first two Doctors as my influences, so it was a kind of cross between the grumpy old man and the comical sort of clown-like figure of Patrick Troughton. I was very aware that Tom had done it for seven years, and there were a lot of children out there who would only ever have remembered Tom. I had a kind of advantage in that I was known on television, but that also could be a disadvantage – I'd been playing a vet, not a Time Lord. They asked these kids on *Pebble Mill* how they thought I should play the part, and one little boy said, 'I think you should be like Tristan but brave,' which is really what I used as my 'keynote' for the performance – 'Tristan but brave'.

Peter Davison

You do have to work out who you are. I probably must have some kind of personality! But I'd never been aware of using it to play a part. All I really had was the character I'd developed playing Tristan. That wasn't really quite me; although it had facets of me. But really that was just something I came up with in the course of playing *All Creatures*. So I largely used that as a basis and then just hoped that a character would develop along the way.

Peter Davison

element to her character. The Doctor exasperated her, and I liked the fact there was that humour that came from teasing Tegan. There's an affection there between the Doctor and Tegan, but he enjoys teasing her.

Janet Fielding

The Fifth Doctor's TARDIS is full of life and energy, these are people who like each other and are fond of each other, but it is also friction. They are people who have been thrown together, they are not actual friends.

Matthew Waterhouse (Adric)

My favourite companion of my time was Nyssa because she did the job that she was meant to do and did it very well – she was meant to be a bright and intelligent

woman, but still her basic job really was to say, 'Help me Doctor, save me.' And there's nothing wrong with that.

Peter Davison

Tegan and Nyssa are very different characters, but they got on very well and they were very fond of each other. Nyssa's an understanding character, she's very tolerant and forbearing, and she embodies all the virtues that Tegan lacks. Tegan, on the other hand, has got that get up and go – she's got a directness which is a characteristic that people think of as being very Australian anyway.

Janet Fielding

Season 19 opened with Castrovalva, *in which the newly regenerated Doctor faces a*

series of attacks from the recently revived Master...

Anthony Ainley, was the son of a very famous actor, Henry Ainley. He had this way of playing him which was terribly, terribly urbane. The Master was the face of seductive evil.

Janet Fielding

I think Anthony Ainley did enjoy the disguises, because he thought of himself as coming very much from the stage. In fact, I think he probably encouraged them. It was a bit of a trend, though. You had to suspend your disbelief that he wasn't recognisable as the Master, when really he was.

Peter Davison

As the season continued, Nathan-Turner secured guest appearances from a series of high-profile actors...

The rehearsals were enormous fun because, while you didn't have the costume, you were aware that, say, Stratford Johns was playing a big frog. You had to get that side of things out of the way before you turned up at the studio. I was going to say we didn't have a big enough budget, but I just think we didn't have the technology you have now. For a lot of the time, it was just very heavy rubber suits.

Peter Davison

At the time I was trying hard to break the typecasting because I was known everywhere as the fellow who'd played Charlie Barlow in *Z Cars*. Right after came this part as a power-mad frog in *Doctor Who*. It was great fun to do, a bit over the top. I thought even then that Peter Davison made a good Doctor – such a change from all the others.

Stratford Johns (Monarch)

Things like *Kinda* were written by people who you felt had a kind of passion for the genre and had used its incredible scope to write something that was a little more thoughtful. Richard Todd was great – it was nice to have a star of British cinema in one of my *Doctor Who* stories. And it was nice for Janet to get a stab at playing something meatier than just asking, 'Why are we here, Doctor?'

Peter Davison

Writer Marc Platt on KINDA

There's no other *Doctor Who* story quite like *Kinda*. It's strange and playful, rich in character, and carries an elaborate mystical subtext, planted deep in Buddhist belief. Best of all, amid all the dark suggestion and corruption, is *Kinda*'s innocence. Christopher Bailey came to writing *Doctor Who* with barely any knowledge of the series. He had none of the luggage that '*Who*-experienced' writers carry. Bailey's writing is an unfettered ride of the imagination that most of the rest of us wouldn't have even dared! Other stories have mystical undercurrents, but here the mysticism is given full rein. Kinda is about time and no time at all. It's about innocence and experience, dreams and reality, wisdom and insanity, the male and the female. Tegan's nightmare is in a direct line from the darker moments of Lewis Carroll's Alice. And the whole tale is set in an exotic jungled Eden.

The demon Mara isn't really a

monster; it's the darkness inside us and how the characters in the story react to its release. Each goes on a journey of self-discovery – even the Doctor, who discovers his inner Holy Fool. Go to Bali and it's like a Kinda theme park – an earthy, innocent, flower-bedecked dreamscape balanced against the hard facts of reality. The demons of the imagination are everywhere you turn.

Kinda also boasts the sort of cast that writers dream about. They promptly turn in a mix of understated and bravura performances, crowned by Simon Rouse's Hindle – a strong contender for Best *Doctor Who* Madman Ever. And the Mara snake is a fantasy creature, born out of the imagination. So how real does it need to be? Actually it is pretty naff, yet even here, the ideas win hands down over the studio-bound execution. Given the rest of this extraordinary story – who really cares?

You were constantly trying to find things to anchor your performance on to. I mean nobody teaches at drama school how to do possession by snake. In *The Visitation*, Tegan's looking forward to getting back to Heathrow, and she's very upset when she doesn't, but of course she would feel responsible for what happened to her aunt and she would at some level blame the Doctor. I was very conscious when I was playing those scenes that Tegan would have been deeply, deeply upset by what had happened. Her beloved aunt is dead and it's because she was drawn into this world which she's now part of, and when she's looking forward to going back to her old life, it is to a life of innocence.

Janet Fielding

I just love the idea that mysteries in history were actually caused by the Doctor. In my time, the Doctor started the Great Fire of London and wiped out the dinosaurs. I just hope that no kids actually wrote that down in their exams.

Peter Davison

The Visitation, written by incoming script editor Eric Saward, demolished more than London...

We got rid of the sonic screwdriver. We destroyed it. We decided it would be best to blow it up. Which meant he did have to rely on his wits. And safety pins.

Peter Davison

I delivered *The Visitation* script in January 1981. Chris Bidmead had left the previous December and Antony Root filled in for about three months. I saw Antony about the script as it needed to be tightened. I was then paid the second half of the fee and I sat back thinking, 'Oh well, perhaps I'll get asked again one day.' Then one day I had a phone call from John Nathan-Turner, quite out of the blue, asking me if I would come in for a chat.

Eric Saward, script editor

Saward also wrote Earthshock, which brought back an old enemy, killed a companion and featured an unusual guest star...

I played Captain Briggs with a rather nice red wig and leather gear and was told to 'Warp Drive' – which I must say rather baffled me, but not the other members of the cast. We were being pursued by Cybermen which seemed to be very important to the episode. They were all told when to die and fall over.

Beryl Reid

We had decided the story was going to be a Cyberman one. I had quite good memories of them and John invited me to write it. I wanted a very fast-paced story that had thriller elements. I always thought the Cybermen worked well when they're confined in a claustrophobic atmosphere.

Eric Saward

I loved the idea in my incarnation of the Cybermen that you could just see the face through the Perspex mask. You got a real sense that there was some kind of being in there, actually inside that outfit, on the life-support thing. And we had David Banks as the chief Cyberman, and I thought he was very good as well.

Peter Davison

GEORGIA MOFFETT
on Doctor Who

I don't actually remember the first time I was made aware of *Doctor Who*. It's sewn into the fabric of my life so deeply that there has never been a point when it didn't exist for me. My childhood was scattered with *Who*. We had a Dalek weather vane that sat pride of place in the lounge. I was given an Easter egg with a Dalek pointing its gun at the Fifth Doctor's crotch, and I could often be found cooking in my play kitchen with a piece of felt celery. TARDIS money boxes, key rings, telephones, endless mugs and even a *Who*-wallpapered hallway could be found in our house. Oh, and my dad; my dad, who would stand outside my primary school and watch me run in with my dear friend Lucy Baker, with her dad Colin standing beside him. Even if that didn't rip a hole in the fabric of space and time, I was aware that it was an unlikely coincidence. I went to many conventions, often hiding behind Dad, but observing this weird and wonderful world that was loved by so many. At 7 years old, we were set a homework assignment, a project on a topic of our choice. While my friends chose Barbie, Trolls, Hollywood and Disney, I chose *Doctor Who*. It was the thing I seemed to know the most about.

But to this day, the awful thing is that I haven't seen an episode from the Fifth Doctor's run – or any of the classic *Who* – in its entirety. (Sshhh...) Many years later, I excitedly started watching when my having kids coincided with the relaunch in 2005. Now, nearly three decades after my *Who*-filled life began, I sit in my house with my children's *Doctor Who* figures, duvet covers, much shinier TARDIS money boxes and more magazines and DVDs than any human could possibly have time to look at!

Oh, and their dad of course...

I was asked to include the departure of Adric. John and I had discussed this at some length and strangely we came to a joint conclusion that he should be killed off. It was for dramatic impact; it had been quite some time since a companion had died and, because Adric was stubborn, difficult, cocky even, I decided that it wouldn't be a bad idea if he spent the last part of the story struggling to do something that had already been pre-ordained, and that his action, although heroic, was really for nothing.

Eric Saward

We had too many companions in the TARDIS, and one of them had to go. Risky idea, that they would kill off a companion.

Peter Davison

It didn't much appeal to Matthew Waterhouse who played Adric, I have to say. He wasn't too keen on the idea of dying, although it was a heroic death. We kept telling him it was a very heroic death because he was trying to save Earth, but of course, in the end, totally futile, because he just wiped out the dinosaurs.

Peter Davison

The decision he makes when he runs aboard that ship attempting to stop it crashing towards the Earth is a very difficult one to read. It is heroic, it is an attempt to save many, many, many people, but it is also somebody who has given up. As a heroic act, of course, it fails. But he does create the conditions which create the human race. So it is a hugely heroic act, a great a generous kind act, but it is also coloured by a sort of melancholy.

Matthew Waterhouse

It was very dramatic. The closing credits went up in silence, which I don't think had ever been done before.

Sarah Sutton

The Doctor
PETER DAVISON

Writer Marc Platt on
SNAKEDANCE

Faced with writing the sequel to the darkly dazzling *Kinda*, Christopher Bailey steers clear of a return to the forests of Deva Loka. Instead, he takes the most important element of the first story, Tegan's internal struggle with the Mara, and transposes it to an entirely opposite world. The innocent parable-like Eden of the Kinda is swapped for the crumbling heart of the Manussan Empire, a place where greed and decadence are an everyday staple – Manussa is a Buddhist word for a man.

Christopher Bailey is a great builder of complex new worlds. On Manussa, the people have risen above their spirituality. They have forgotten their dark past and have, in modern parlance, dumbed themselves down. Manussa is bright and colourfully beguiling. Its heritage is a thing to be marketed and sold. Instant gratification rules and only a few remember the old, more meaningful ways. But the undercurrents are there. For Manussa is where the Mara was born and once ruled and, when unleashed, it treats the place like a playground. One of the great aspects of the Mara is its humour in mocking the humans whose minds it was born from.

As in *Kinda*, there are great guest characters here with a depth which is reminiscent of *I, Claudius*. In particular, the relationship between Lon, the Federator's bored son and his doting mother, Tanha, is beautifully framed. Christopher Bailey's writing has relaxed; he's more at home with the regular characters. The story feels more traditional, yet it's still innovative, still shedding fresh light and dark on our heroes' foibles. And it's so much fun. Peter Davison's Doctor, so earnest and determined, seems like a madman in his warnings of potential disaster; even more, because this 'alien' world is so recognisable to us. Janet Fielding has never been better as Tegan: defensively stroppy, cruelly mocking, sexy and vulnerable.

The tawdry culture of Manussa is exemplified by its colourful street markets, airy rooms, stylised caves and the trappings of carnival. Design, music and production all pull happily in the same direction. It all feels absolutely right. Even the snake, at its final emergence, takes on a menace appropriate for the world it seeks to dominate.

When the show returned for its 20th season, Nathan-Turner decided that each story should feature some element from the programme's past. And, as it turned out, someone from the programme's future...

When we were filming *Arc of Infinity* in Amsterdam, I was playing two parts – the other being Omega. Once he turned into me, he started to decay. I had to cross Dam Square which is in the middle of Amsterdam, wearing horrific make-up – a mixture of rice crispies and glue and all sorts of things fixed down one side of my face. It must have been quite terrifying to those people – who, of course, had no idea

we were making a film. It wasn't easy for me, either, having to dodge the cars and trams as well.

Peter Davison

I guested in three episodes of *Doctor Who* when Peter Davison played the Doctor. I played Maxil, who was chief of security on Gallifrey, and I got to shoot the Doctor. Many people suggested that that was my audition for the part – if you zap the incumbent, you get to be the next one!

Colin Baker

My two Mara stories, *Kinda* and *Snakedance*, were just great, interesting stories. We had such a wonderful cast. It was Martin Clunes's first telly; Collete O'Neill was fabulous. It's a really good script, that Chris Bailey script, and it was wonderful to do it. The Mara was a kind of *spiritus mundi* of evil. It was the collective evil unconscious of another race and it was channelled via various shamans, and Tegan would break that control, allowing the Mara to escape, so there were images of circularity and containment always within the stories. When that evil managed to break the circle of containment it would channel its way in to your-subconscious... to what end I was never sure. That's the interesting thing about evil – what's evil going to do? What's evil really want? What makes evil?

Janet Fielding

I went back to visit the Brigadier who is now a teacher I think, and then UNIT came into it in some shape or form, and also a younger Brigadier. Nicholas Courtney was playing himself twice, and then we had to stop him meeting him otherwise he would explode. Poor Nicholas.

Peter Davison

Also joining in Mawdryn Undead *was a new companion, Turlough...*

And then they introduced Turlough, who was trying to kill me the entire time.

Peter Davison

I came in before I worked on the programme to watch it being filmed and I was petrified how quickly they were working. I mean it was finish a scene, production manager goes, 'OK, on we go, on to the next scene!' and voom, you were running and you did the next scene whilst they were setting up another. It was quite frightening.

Mark Strickson

Mark Strickson was wonderful – he learnt so quickly. He felt himself into the part and gave the same enthusiasm and attention to detail.

Peter Moffatt, director

When he first came in, Turlough was obviously trying to kill the Doctor, but he was only trying to kill the Doctor because the Black Guardian wanted him to... I

hope that you can see that Turlough had, not necessarily a nice side, but a good side to him. I decided to travel in the TARDIS with the Doctor and learn from him.

Mark Strickson

Turlough joined in Mawdryn Undead, *while Nyssa left at the end of* Terminus...

Costumes are a bit of an issue really with *Doctor Who* girls. We were always complaining that we didn't get enough costume changes. I started off with a very nice sort of fairy outfit and then I went into trousers and I believe the BBC got quite a few letters saying 'where have Sarah's legs gone?' which is why I then went back into a skirt. And in the last episode I had a very, very nice suede skirt and jacket outfit with very pretty underwear underneath and someone decided it might be a nice idea for everyone to see it before I left, so that's why I ended up in my underwear for the last episode.

Sarah Sutton

It was a rather bizarre thing. She got a bit hot and took off all her clothes. I think that stemmed from John Nathan-Turner getting a letter of complaint at the end of my first season that the companions were too covered up. And so to make them into unashamedly sexual objects he had them remove most of their clothes! Anything that would result in a couple more viewers.

Peter Davison

The King's Demons *introduced one of the TARDIS's stranger occupants...*

It was rather weird sitting in rehearsals. I was amazed because they brought

Kamelion in and stood it in a corner. Then I realised I could hear my voice apparently coming out of it. I actually played two parts in *The King's Demons* – the evil King John and Kamelion's voice – although they were really one and the same. Originally, Kamelion wasn't meant to go with the Doctor and the others in the TARDIS, he was supposed to go off with the Master, but the producer and his team liked the idea of this robot companion and rewrote it so that it went into the TARDIS.

Gerald Flood (Kamelion)

Kamelion seemed like a great idea at the time. They decided to have a companion that was a robot, and they came to me and said, 'Look we've got this fantastic new thing, it's a robot, and we just programme it and when you speak it will speak its lines.' And it never worked. It only ever moved from the waist up. It couldn't walk, because it was a mechanical robot, we're talking 1983. And so we put it in one of the back rooms of the TARDIS and forgot about it.

Peter Davison

Industrial action brought Season 20 to a premature close, but the anniversary celebrations continued...

Longleat was the first big British convention, and we all went, and they had as many people from the show as they possibly could. It was manic. There were thousands of people there. I don't think anyone expected it at all, and then we realised actually what the programme was meaning to the fans. And how many fans there were. It was a chaotic weekend, but such fun.

Sarah Sutton

I can't remember who it was that organised Longleat but they were warned that they were severely underestimating the number of people who would turn up. I think they just didn't believe us. I remember John coming to me and saying, 'They only think there's going to be a 1,000 people there.' So when we got down there and there were just these absurd queues, I spent an awful lot of time just walking up and down. These people had come along and some of them weren't going to get in. We organised a thing almost like a parade, but in reverse, with me walking along the queue and saying hello to everyone.

Peter Davison

The convention at Longleat reunited all the surviving Doctors, something that the subsequent TV special, The Five Doctors, *wouldn't quite manage...*

Eric Saward phoned me up at a convention in New Orleans and said, 'We would like you to write the 20th-anniversary special.'

Terrance Dicks, writer

John Nathan-Turner saw my likeness to William Hartnell when I played Nebrox in *Blake's 7*, and he asked me to play it! I admired William Hartnell a great deal and I tried to play the part as he would have done. I understand that William's widow, Heather, approved of the choice. I remembered his approach to the role very well, but decided it would be stupid to try and mimic him so I hoped I split the difference between his performance – his personality and mine, just adding a few of his more familiar mannerisms.

Richard Hurndall (The First Doctor)

It was wonderful, I fell into it at once! There's only one thing I regret and that is that I didn't quite get the hair right. Because my make-up lady, fifteen years ago, used to lift it with sort of curlers, you know, so it was fairly high. And I forgot this time. So although the length and so on was right – it was my own hair, it wasn't a wig, although it looked like a wig, I know – it wasn't quite the same. If I do it again, I'll lift it up a bit more.

Patrick Troughton

You'd imagine it would be very difficult to pick up a style of acting after ten years. I came back to do *The Five Doctors* with Lis Sladen and we were sent up on top of a mountain in Wales where we froze to death...

Jon Pertwee

Eric Saward turned up and told me Tom Baker wasn't going to do it. Obviously he played a big part in it, so I immediately said, 'Have you got any footage? Otherwise, we can't call it *The Five Doctors*.' Eric said, 'Well, there's this stuff from *Shada*.' I said, 'Well, give me somewhere I can get him captured, see

him later, and I'll trap him in a time loop for the whole story.' And so you have the lovely bit on the river with Tom and Lalla on the punt. I think that's one of the best things in the show and I didn't write a word of it. It's all *Shada*. But again, very often out of a crisis, something better will come than you'd originally planned.

Terrance Dicks

John Nathan-Turner feared that there would be too many egos flying about on the set. So he kept us apart a bit. It was a bit of a shame that we didn't have more than one final climactic scene together.

Peter Davison

The Five Doctors *also featured assorted companions, the Time Lords, the Master, a Dalek, a Yeti and the Cybermen, and Season 21 continued in the same vein, bringing back the Silurians, the Sea Devils, the Daleks and their creator...*

One thing I liked about Davros, which is why I brought him back, was you could give him straight dialogue. He is evil, he

is ambitious, he is vicious, but he can be funny too.

Eric Saward

When you first see a Dalek, it's extraordinary, because when you rehearse the Daleks are basically cut-off versions and there are little men sitting in them without the top on. But when the top goes on, suddenly it all changes. Suddenly it's actually rather frightening. Suddenly it just clicks in your brain.

Mark Strickson

They got into such trouble for that Dalek story because there's two policemen at the end who walk away, and of course they're Dalek duplicates. Questions raised in the House of Parliament, you know, 'Kids won't feel confident to go up to bobbies and ask for directions or ask for help' and all that kind of stuff...

Janet Fielding

By now, the series was gearing up for another change of Doctor. Before that happened, Tegan, Turlough and Kamelion made way for Perpugilliam Brown...

Tegan was emotionally battered by all that she'd seen. There's nothing said about where Tegan intends on going. She's back on Earth, she's in the Butlers Wharf building near Tower Bridge. A friend of mine currently owns the flat actually, which is very strange because sometimes I've stayed with her when I'm up in London.

Janet Fielding

I started in a bikini because my character was on holiday in Lanzarote, but it seemed like I never really got dressed! I moved from filming in Lanzarote in October, which was very pleasant, to wearing the same outfit in Poole in Dorset in November, which resulted in frost bite and pneumonia, and that was only my second story.

Nicola Bryant

John thought it was good for the show to have a couple of prestige foreign trips. We'd had, in my second season, Amsterdam, so he came up with idea of Lanzarote. There was one fantastic scene where Nicola jumps off the boat and is meant to be rescued by Turlough, who runs in the water to pick her up. But the

moment she jumped in the water and started going, 'Help! Help!' about a dozen naked German sunbathers – for some reason we were filming on a nudist beach – dived into the water and swam out to save her.

Peter Davison

When I got the job, lots of my friends were like, 'Aw, Peter Davison!' They all had schoolgirl crushes on him. I really liked the relationship that Peri and the Fifth Doctor had, and I thought the chemistry worked really well. There was this hint, which I'd sort of worked out with John Nathan-Turner, that her father has been dead quite a long time, and she's thinking about what he looked like when she was 10, and there's something about the Fifth Doctor that reminds her of her father. And so I played that extra connection between the two of them.

Nicola Bryant

The last story I did was the best story. *The Caves of Androzani* – everything just worked with it. I always loved the cliff-hangers. In one, I was shot by a firing squad, and even I thought, 'How am I going to get out of this?' Everything came together right in that story.

Peter Davison

The Caves of Androzani was certainly an above-average script, but I think Graeme

Harper had a great deal to do with the impact of the story. Robert Holmes's script was lifted by Harper's direction and the whole thing came together.

Eric Saward

I thought *The Caves of Androzani* was brilliant! It had a lot of action, good characters and a good story to offer to a good class of actor. I mean, it was so good. It all came off the page so easily and I was very excited about doing it.

Graeme Harper, director

When I started work on my second story, I didn't realise how lucky I was. *The Caves of Androzani* is a very special story, but to me it was like a classic fairy tale – you had the beast, you had the baddies, the gun-runners, you had the elements to fight, you had everything that comes into a classic story. And when I got to the final scenes, and read that our hero is now risking his life to go and get the only possible remedy for his companion, I thought this was really exciting. When I got to the final pages to discover there's only enough serum left for one person to survive and the fact that he gives this to Peri – I think it was a fantastic ending for Peter Davison. It was a beautiful, brave and lovely performance and I think possibly one of his best performances.

Nicola Bryant

Anyway, I'd saved Peri's life, and the only sad thing from my point of view was that I was acting my heart out on the floor, lying on the floor, about to change into Colin Baker, God forbid. And I'm acting my heart out to Peri. And then, when you see it back, all you can see is Nicola Bryant's cleavage.

Peter Davison

I hummed and hawed for a long time. I had set myself three years, not knowing how I would feel at the end of those three years. It was touch and go – I almost did a fourth year. If I'd been offered *Doctor Who* when I was, say, fifty, then I would have gone on for many, many years. The fact of the matter is that I was still fairly young.

Peter Davison

I just felt that I'd enjoyed my three years and that it was time to move on and do other things.

Peter Davison

THE DARK SCROLLS OF THE
VALEYARD

I could do it all so much better than him. He is little-more than a perambulating Pierrot, a do-nothing jackanapes decked out in trumpery. But take away that coat, and the petty posturing, and really he is a very small man indeed. A little grey stain on the universe I could scratch out with my thumb.

I am a daring impossibility summoned into existence by people even greyer than him. They gathered together in a room that never was and built a man who would never be.

When a Time Lord dies, they say he leaves a scar across existence. All their little interventions and alterations drawn into a single pucker across space and time. In most cases, it is a carefully tempered schism. But, for the Doctor, the end of his days is a big crack in causality. Big enough to reach into and pluck out a great, daring impossibility from before the end.

Me. When you take every dark thought the Doctor has ever had and strip it of moral qualms, then you get me.

I am the Valeyard. I am the summation of the Doctor's daring without his hesitation. I am ambition without regret. And I could do it all so much better than him.

SUNDAY 6 JANUARY, 1986

4

■ AS A SIXTH BANK IS ROBBED, WE ASK
Who are the 'Lytton Gang'?

It takes a lot to rock London's criminal underworld, but one man has shaken it to its foundations. The enigmatic 'Lytton' has come from nowhere, executing a series of daring heists on financial institutions. While it's widespread knowledge that this mysterious figure is behind these raids, nobody knows who he is. The police are baffled, Interpol deny all knowledge. Senior figures at New Scotland Yard refuse to speculate openly that he may be from behind the Iron Curtain. ▶

TARDIS INDEX FILE

MIASIMIA GORIA

While many have laid claim to the sobriquet 'the planet that never sleeps', there is only one place in the universe where this is literally true – the world known as Miasimia Goria. A planet where, for three centuries now, not a single member of the population has slept. Once a race of graceful poets, the 'Restless Ones' now exist in a state of constant warfare and brutality. Many outside agencies have tried to help, but the baffling disease appears to be without cure.

TUB

If the Doctor knew what the Rani had done, why didn't he do anything about it? What was he doing, playing with trains?

– River x

Is YOUR governor doing a good job?
YES/NO
VOTE NOW *

* Voting is compulsory and will cost no more than 1 work credit. Multiple voting will be met with extreme punishment.

Failure to vote can result in enforced surgery.

· VOTE ·

YES

NO

LAS CADENAS
BARIO SANTA CRUZ, SEVILLE

YOUR BILL:

LOBSTER ×3
CLAMS ×7
BRAISED SQUID ×2
SQUID AU MARIE ×2
BRAINS IN WHITE SAUCE ×4
SUCKLING PIGS ×2
HAM W/ FIGS ×1
STEAK IN BLUE SAUCE ×8
FAMILY PAELLA ×1
PIGEON BREASTS ×12
RIOJA, BTL ×12

TOTAL   81,600 PESETAS

That's the offer placed on the table. His own people are tired of him – of his dash and stupidity, that he always gets away with it. They are going to put the Doctor on trial, and they want me to prosecute him. If I succeed, then my reward is existence. I shall inherit his remaining lives.

What, you may well ask, is in it for them? It was almost my first thought (beyond working out in three heartsbeats how to escape their chamber leaving them all dead). The answer is simple. Or rather, the answer is simplicity.

The Time Lords have grown tired of the Doctor's complexity. They like their rebels to be straightforward. Would-be gods with overweening arrogance and a desire for ultimate supremacy. And then there's him. He arrives – perhaps to save a planet, perhaps to have tea. And then he moves

quietly on – billions of lives saved, or two whole scones consumed. It is all water off a duck's back to him. And it's infuriating to the Time Lords. Not once has he saved a world and turned around and said, 'It's mine now.' Not even when he saved Gallifrey from Borusa.

I really believe that was the last straw. They offered him the Presidency. Gallifrey held up its hands and said, 'All right then, you win.' And he ran away. Again. If you ask me, it was an idiotic move by all concerned – perhaps they were hoping that he would succumb, and that custom could stale his infinite variety. And he, the man who wouldn't be king, scampered off to continue playing the fool... Oh, I could have done so much with the Presidency. But no, off he went.

Well he would, obviously. Know your enemy. Know yourself.

So, I am to pick through his current incarnation. I hazard I am in luck. His sixth time stream is quite promising. I can make him look very bad indeed (with a few alterations). But, in actual fact, if you look at all he's done with this body – stripped of the bluster and braggadocio, it's a tale of sound and fury signifying really very little.

IS THIS THE LOCH NESS MONSTER?

POST CARD

Hey Mike!

Look at this! A space-time postcard! The Doctor swears that this will arrive back at UNIT HQ shortly before we left! While you're reading this over your cocoa, the Doctor and I are having an adventure in outer space!

We're on the planet Karfel, catching up with one of the Doctor's old friends, Professor Megelen. He's ever so dashing and took a fancy to me, but it seems he's gone a little potty and started experimenting on the local cattle (horrid things called Morlox).

Anyway, it was all getting out of hand, with killer cows on the one side and a lovesick mad scientist on the other. Luckily the Doctor called on some more old friends to save the day. Thank heavens for the Bandrils! Sweethearts!

Lots of love, Jo xxxxx

CAPTAIN MIKE YATES
UNIT HQ
THE PRIORY

EARTH
THE SOLAR SYSTEM!!!!

Most of his landings have seen him do no more than any Time Lord would. For all his protestations to the contrary, he is frequently a smug onlooker to events. The violence-based economy on Varos may well have collapsed anyway. The people of Necros would have sent for the Daleks without the Doctor's help.

Many of his triumphs have been puny. A few peasants saved from madness. A citadel unbombed. A fragile alliance between Androgum and Sontaran defeated.

It's only been interesting when he's got his hands dirty. Thanks to him, Cyber-history is now a tangled mess hanging by a thread – and didn't he have fun, gripping that gun in his hands and blasting away? A little voice inside him told him, 'This is how it really feels to be a hero.' A dark little whisper. My voice.

I'm inside him. Just waiting to bubble to the surface. After his regeneration he was weak and, for a few seconds, the chance to be a god seized him. He could have snuffed out his companion so easily. When later the Androgum inheritance coursed through his veins, I was its fellow traveller. Such violence, such mayhem. Such achievement.

He could do so much more if he was just a little more daring. A little less hampered. A few more guts. He is more Time Lord than renegade, although he would be the last to admit it.

Why, look at what happens when he stumbles on a real mystery. He discovers that the Earth is home to a Gallifreyan secret so terrible the Time Lords plucked the planet out, burning it across the stars and rechristening it Ravolox. A crime so monstrous that any true champion of Earth

would be storming the Capitol with a fleet of War TARDISes. But not him. No. He decides to investigate further. Then closes the door behind him and moves on.

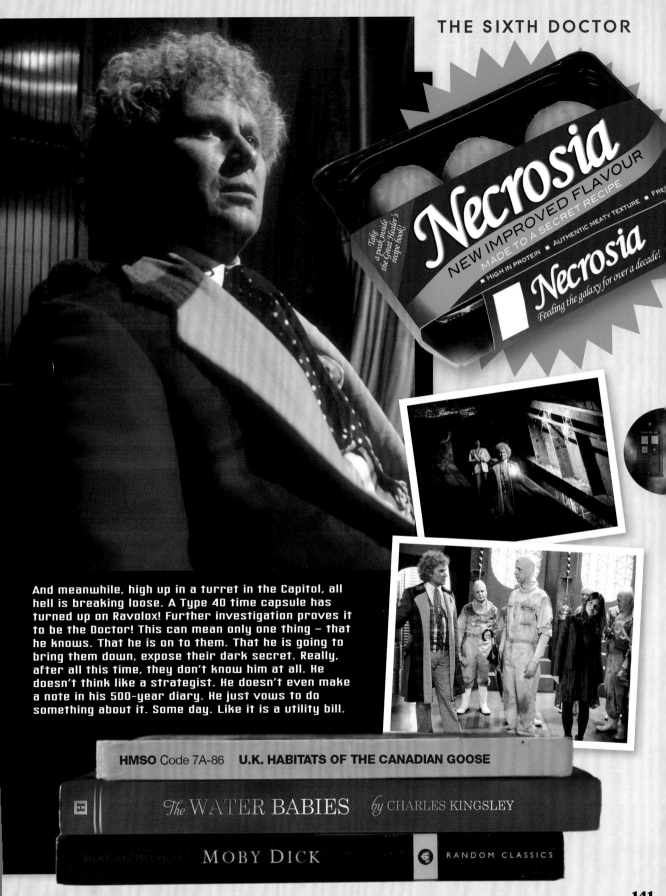

Necrosia

NEW IMPROVED FLAVOUR

MADE TO A SECRET RECIPE

Take a peak inside the Great Healer's recipe book!

• HIGH IN PROTEIN • AUTHENTIC MEATY TEXTURE • FRE

Necrosia

Feeding the galaxy for over a decade!

And meanwhile, high up in a turret in the Capitol, all hell is breaking loose. A Type 40 time capsule has turned up on Ravolox! Further investigation proves it to be the Doctor! This can mean only one thing – that he knows. That he is on to them. That he is going to bring them down, expose their dark secret. Really, after all this time, they don't know him at all. He doesn't think like a strategist. He doesn't even make a note in his 500-year diary. He just vows to do something about it. Some day. Like it is a utility bill.

HMSO Code 7A-86   **U.K. HABITATS OF THE CANADIAN GOOSE**

The WATER BABIES *by* CHARLES KINGSLEY

HERMAN MELVILLE   MOBY DICK   RANDOM CLASSICS

141

The Annals of the Warlords of Thordon

VROOMNIK! VROOMNIK!
Mighty battle is joined
Thoros Beta send more beams that kill!
Crush the skulls and bathe
Bathe in the blood of the weak
Drink the milk of their brains
And make shoes from their spines
Marry their daughters and
LET BATTLE
LET BATTLE BE JOINED
The Krontep warriors shall subdue the
massed hordes of the Tonkonp Empire.
Blood. Death. Terror. Kill.

PERPUGILLIAM BROWN
&
LORD YRCARNOS, Warrior King of the Krontep

invite you to share the beginning of our new life together
when we exchange marriage vows

on the Day Of Six Deaths at half after four o'clock
in the Hall of Blood and Skulls

VROOMNIK!

And, as the Celestial Intervention Agency and the High Council marshal their forces against him, the Doctor just potters on. He has trivial warlords to overthrow on Thoros Beta. At the back of his head, of course, he is wondering what the business on Ravolox was all about. But there's so much else to see and do. He'll get round to it some day.

What the Doctor does not realise is that he has finally run out of time. Oh, it has all been a delight to arrange. This Doctor is such a whirl of blunder and bluster that it is easy to reach into the Matrix and make him look bad. And, while I'm there, to construct a few traps. After all, the Time Lords want me to be a real renegade – why should I not wipe the whole lot of them out? It's little more than they'd expect.

It's curious that I can imagine destroying all Gallifrey with so little compunction. It's almost as if, at some point in his future he will... But no. He wouldn't. He couldn't. It's simply that he doesn't perceive the pattern of our own history – all powerful Time Lords go mad, from Rassilon to Borusa. He just doesn't have the imagination to see it.

But I do. I shall wipe them all out. And then I shall close the door behind me and move on. No more half measures or patchwork solutions. No more Daleks. No more Cybermen.

The Fall of the High Council
by Benncuiq IV

That the Andromedans had been able to penetrate the Matrix, repository of all Time Lord knowledge, was crisis enough; that they had removed such sensitive material was seen as catastrophic, for Gallifrey and for the universe. But the countermeasures the High Council adopted proved senselessly destructive, on a scale none foresaw.

Tracing the breach in the Matrix to the planet Earth, the High Council took the near-unprecedented step of ordering the use of a Magnetron to draw the Earth and its entire constellation billions of miles across space, renaming the planet Ravalox. By any reckoning, this was a criminal act – an enormity made worse by the resultant fireball which ravaged the planet and all but extinguished life. A few lone voices on the High Council argued that even the Daleks would establish an atmospheric shell to hold in air and heat, should they

THE SIXTH DOCTOR

With them out of the way, his precious humans can get on with rampaging across the universe like vermin. Well, they would, if I let them get away with it.

As I said, I shall be so much better at it all than the Doctor.

DATELINE 22.11.2986

IS 'TONKER' TRAVERS THE WORST SPACESHIP CAPTAIN IN HISTORY? A SPECIAL REPORT

WE ALL REMEMBER WHAT HAPPENED TO CAPTAIN TRAVERS A FEW YEARS BACK — A WEB OF MAYHEM AND INTRIGUE THAT NEARLY COST HIM HIS SHIP AND THE LIVES OF ALL ABOARD. SOMEBODY UP THERE MUST LIKE HIM, THOUGH, BECAUSE THEY MADE HIM A COMMODORE AND GAVE HIM A NEW SHIP — THE HYPERION III.

AND GUESS WHAT?

THEY DON'T WANT YOU TO KNOW, BUT OLD TONKER'S BEEN AT IT AGAIN. A SIMPLE TRIP — MOGAR TO EARTH, A FULL COMPLEMENT OF PASSENGERS, A FEW POT PLANTS AND A CARGO OF METAL ORES.

WHAT COULD GO WRONG? WE'VE BEEN POKING AROUND, AND WE'VE FOUND OUT. CLICK ON THE LINKS BELOW FOR THE FULL STORY!

- COMMUNICATIONS OFFICER ATTACKED AND DRUGGED!
- MAYDAY CALL FAKED!
- BREAK-IN AT HYDROPONICS CENTRE!
- THEFT OF BOTANICAL SAMPLES!
- PASSENGER LOST IN WASTE-DISPOSAL UNIT AND EJECTED INTO SPACE!
- COMMUNICATIONS OFFICER ELECTROCUTED AND KILLED!
- SECURITY GUARD ABDUCTED AND KILLED!
- SHIP'S COURSE ALTERED TO PASS CLOSE TO A BLACK HOLE!
- MOGARIAN PASSENGER POISONED!
- DEAD MOGARIAN PASSENGER UNCOVERED AS HUMAN UNDERCOVER INVESTIGATOR!
- PASSENGER HELD HOSTAGE!
- PASSENGER ASSAULTED!
- PASSENGER ABDUCTED AND EATEN!
- SECURITY GUARD ASSAULTED!
- SHIP STEERED INTO THE BLACK HOLE BY HIJACKER!
- HIJACKER GASSED TO DEATH!
- MUTINY — LED BY THE CHIEF SECURITY OFFICER!
- MOGARIAN PASSENGERS MURDERED!
- MORE PASSENGERS KILLED!
- ENTIRE STOCK OF POT PLANTS DESTROYED!

SO — COME ON, TONKER! ISN'T IT TIME TO HAND IN YOUR COMMODORE'S BADGE?

HAVE YOUR SAY

SHOULD TONKER GO?

YES / NO

ever attempt such a grand folly. This was of little consequence to the majority of the High Council. All that mattered was that Gallifreyan secrets were saved.

The crime went unrecognised and unpunished for several centuries, however, until the Doctor visited Ravalox. The High Council, aware of what he might uncover, panicked. They established contact with – or perhaps even brought into being – an amalgamation of the darker sides of the Doctor's nature, somewhere between his penultimate and final incarnations. They made a deal with this 'Valeyard' to manufacture and manipulate evidence against the Doctor; in return for the successful prosecution of the Doctor, the Valeyard was promised the remainder of the Doctor's regenerations.

When these squalid machinations were uncovered, the High Council was swiftly deposed. Yet, with insurrectionists running amok on Gallifrey and another renegade – the Master – waiting on the side lines to take control, Gallifrey began a swift collapse into chaos.

The restoration of law and order was to be a long and arduous process.

Carrot juice

Serves 2

INGREDIENTS

3 carrots
A small piece of ginger
500ml freshly squeeze

PREPARATION

For best results, chil

The Story of Doctor Who

1984–1986

I was only slightly involved in *The Caves of Androzani*, because I just turned up on the studio day and did it. Peter and I didn't have much time to discuss the role. After the recording, I went home, walked in to where my wife was watching television, and said, 'I am the Doctor.' She looked at me and said, 'Oh, yes. Could you take the rubbish out, please?'

Colin Baker

Colin Baker's brief debut at the climax of The Caves of Androzani *was followed just six days later by* The Twin Dilemma *– a tale of talented twins and a giant slug that wanted to rule the universe...*

The Twin Dilemma is a very traditional *Doctor Who* story – ranting maniac defeated by Doctor. When all is said and done, we wanted a simplistic story in order for the audience to concentrate on the new Doctor.

John Nathan-Turner, producer

Somehow, Colin never had any doubts. It just seemed to go right. He's very outgoing and dominant, yet he can be calm, quiet and gentle. There were no real birth pangs; it all came from those initial rehearsals.

Peter Moffatt, director

When Peter arrived after Tom, they decided that the regeneration process would make him exhausted and helpless and weak, and he had to be looked after by his three companions at the time for the first couple of episodes. In a neat contrast with that regeneration, they would have me hyper, so that for a couple of episodes I would be rushing around like some manic, selfish monster who had been unsettled by his regeneration.

Colin Baker

I just didn't want him to behave in an obvious, sentimental, approachable way. I wanted him to be a little bit unapproachable. He could get extremely angry about something – a build-up followed by a sudden explosion, so that the rage might seem to be about one thing when it was actually about something that had happened two episodes ago. Now, John liked this idea, and in the end he pushed it further than probably I would have had the courage to do, by making the Doctor so unapproachable in my first story. You had to wait for four episodes before finding out if this person had anything remotely likeable in him, and I think that was very brave, especially as it was the end of a season. I like that kind of bravery in television. It's all too easy to play it safe all the time.

Colin Baker

In 1985, Doctor Who *returned to Saturdays but, instead of 26 episodes lasting 25 minutes, the season comprised 13 episodes of 45 minutes. Made for a later, more adult timeslot, Season 22 was shown earlier than intended, which was to have serious consequences...*

COLIN BAKER
was the Sixth Doctor

I got to know Colin during the time he played Maxil, a Gallifreyan guard captain, in *Arc of Infinity*. Then we met up again later when we were invited to the wedding reception of my assistant floor manager, Lynn Richards, with whom Colin and his wife Marion had become very friendly. The *Doctor Who* crowd were sitting together on the grass, having a good time, and for the whole afternoon, Colin kept us thoroughly entertained. Even though I wasn't actively looking for a new Doctor then, I thought that if he could hold the attention of fifteen hard-bitten show business professionals for hours, then he could do the same with a television audience.

John Nathan-Turner

John Nathan-Turner and I were having a sneaky drink at a pub one day when Peter Davison came in quite by chance, and we had to make up stories. He knew he was going, but John didn't want anyone knowing who was taking over until the right moment. So I had to pretend I was there for another purpose: 'I come to clean the windows.' It's tough as an actor.

Colin Baker

I want to continue the tradition of making him as quirky and as eccentric as possible; to inject a little acid humour occasionally, perhaps. I think what the producers try to do with *Doctor Who* is to use as much of the actor's own personality as possible, because it's such a high-density rehearsal and performance rate that you don't have time to go out on a limb.

Colin Baker

From Peri's point of view, when the Sixth Doctor appears, there is no other word really than shock. Peri is in a state of shock because she's just sort of seen this metamorphosis, this transformation, the regeneration of the Doctor, which is not what you would expect. And then to have this quite brash and egocentric Doctor turn up – after a Doctor who's just basically died to save his companion – is completely disarming for Peri, but I think in terms of drama fantastic.

Nicola Bryant (Peri Brown)

John Nathan-Turner said, 'What kind of costume do you fancy?' and I set about describing pretty much what Christopher Eccleston got years later. There was a brief pause and he said, 'No, I think he should be totally tasteless.' Pat Godfrey, who was the designer, had apparently put together lots of 'tasteless' designs but, of course, being a designer she couldn't be totally tasteless. So they were colourful but rather attractive. So in the end she got so fed up with being told that's not tasteless enough, she went, 'Oh, something like this then!' So that's what I ended up with. The plus was that I was on the inside looking out.

Colin Baker

I did keep saying that I wanted to change the costume, but it's a large expense, unfortunately. John liked it as it was and so was not prepared to waste money, as he saw it. They did let me have new waistcoats and ties, just in order to make the timescale clear. I had a different tie and cat button in each of the different time zones.

Colin Baker

During the time I was playing the Doctor, Mary Whitehouse was at her strongest in terms of her effect on public attitudes, and that was when the programme was under fire about the violence.

Colin Baker

I think *Vengeance on Varos* was the nearest I got to a stand-out story, in that it was very different. That was the one that got all the criticism in Britain. It was violent and it was dark and it was gloomy.

Colin Baker

I woke up one morning with the idea for what eventually became *Vengeance on Varos*. I wondered what the entertainment business of the future would be. Then I wondered how a prison planet would develop, and the two ideas collided. I began to get the idea that the original officers of the prison planet had become the ruling elite, and that the original prisoners and their descendants had become the masses who would need to be entertained by violence. The National Viewers and Listeners Association have an extremely naive conception of entertainment, of developing drama, and this is the sort of show that catches them out. What we're actually doing, in a way, is arguing on their side, but are they intelligent enough to see it? They should be, because it's there, but then you need a sophisticated response, and you have to have shows like this, so people's critical faculties can spot what is gratuitous and what is there for a purpose, almost a moral purpose.

Philip Martin, writer

Mary Whitehouse had said that *Doctor Who* was violent. BBC One Controller Michael Grade picked up on that and said, 'We need more humour and less violence,' which fed the perception that *Doctor Who* was violent. But I don't think my Doctor was any more or less violent than any other Doctor. The famous thing about me pushing people into acid baths – not at all, they were trying to push me into an acid bath and I dodged out of the way. I think what people objected to was the flip comment afterwards.

Colin Baker

The Mark of the Rani resurrected the Master again, and introduced another Gallifreyan renegade...

I would have liked to have done more stories with the Master. It is the battle of equals. They are both Time Lords. The Master was peripheral in the Rani story.

Colin Baker

The Rani does not have a sense of humour. At all. She thinks she does, but it's a cruel sense of humour. She was supposed to have been at school with the Doctor and been determined to oust him. She's sort of had a go at it, but nobody can. He's invincible.

Kate O'Mara (The Rani)

Having had such a good time on The Five Doctors, *Patrick Troughton was keen to make another return...*

I had the joy of working with Patrick Troughton on *The Two Doctors*. I was slightly daunted, even though I knew him, to be working with the Doctor that I revered, because he made the job easy for the rest of us. He instantly made me feel at ease and that I, in his opinion, was a worthy inheritor of the mantle. I said to him, 'I'm a bit daunted working with you,' and he said, 'Oh, don't be daft.'

Colin Baker

The season ended with a return for the Daleks, in a grimly comic tale of body-snatching in a funeral home...

You have to have a Dalek story, and I was delighted when I did. The vision of these things gliding across the floor, they had castors on the bottom, like an armchair in your house. As anyone who has wheeled a supermarket trolley would know, they do tend to have minds of their own.

Colin Baker

Actor Dan Starkey on
THE TWO DOCTORS

One big difference between the 'classic' series and its modern incarnation is a greater willingness to show death on screen. *The Two Doctors* is quite exceptional in this, not just in its body count, but in the sheer grisly relish with which it depicts various characters' demises: there are at least three graphic stabbings; the story's villainess tastes the Doctor's blood, still warm as she scrapes it off the floor; an old lady is karate-chopped to death by a vicious alien chef whose motivation throughout the story is to get his first taste of human flesh; and the Doctor suffocates this aspirant cannibal with a cyanide-soaked hanky. The senior Sontaran is betrayed by his allies and suffers a prolonged three-fold death: he's gassed by acid vapour, then fried by a sabotaged time machine, before finally limping in agony to his spacecraft only to be blown to pieces by a concealed bomb. His severed leg is then brought in, dripping with green blood. As violent demises go, Strax would no doubt heartily approve!

These Sontarans are quite physically different from their predecessors, and really quite tall. Sartorially they stand out too, their armour having acquired a spangly sheen. I don't envy the actors wearing those costumes under the heat of the Andalusian sun, nor their prosthetics, which look heavier and less flexible than the ones I wear. I've been in danger of overheating in my Sontaran suit on a rainy location shoot in Llantrisant, so I can't imagine how it must have been for them in Spain.

When I watched this story at the age of 7, the Sontarans were imprinted on my mind as one of the top tier of the Doctor's enemies; little did I realise, that one day I would be donning that collar and potato-head myself for some glorious warfare of my own!

The story was scripted to end with the Doctor promising to take Peri to Blackpool. He very nearly never took her anywhere ever again...

DR WHO IS AXED IN A BBC PLOT

The Sun

When I was running BBC One, the show was really creaky and groany, and it was as if the people who were making it had never been to the cinema and seen *Close Encounters* or *ET* or *Star Wars*, and the production values, once you'd seen those movies, didn't stack up any more. And I cancelled it.

Michael Grade, Controller BBC One

We had never had any comment from Head of Drama Jonathan Powell concerning the scripts. Not one word of criticism, nothing at all. We were then cancelled and told we were doing it wrong. My supposition is that it was some kind of political argy-bargy going on within the BBC.

Eric Saward, script editor

I remember when we started we were actually opposite *The A-Team*, and there you had all these guns firing, all these people just dying. They had a very high death count, and it didn't seem to register.

Nicola Bryant

SAVE DOCTOR WHO!

Daily Star

Doctor Who will be on the air in 1986, as it is in 1985 ... Instead of running in January 1986, we shall wait until the start of the Autumn schedule, and then *Doctor Who* will be a strong item in the mix. We are also going back to the old tradition and have 25-minute programmes ... I am confident that *Doctor Who* has a great future on BBC1.

Bill Cotton, Managing Director of BBC Television

We then had to decide what we were going to do with 14 episodes, and the general conclusion was the trial sequence. We were on trial ourselves, so why not reflect it in the programme?

Eric Saward

The trial has a great many twists. The three stories are all very different stories, and there are also interconnections in them. There are lots of layers, and it's very, very complicated.

Colin Baker

There was a surprising and shocking ending to Part 8...

I was very sad when I heard Nicola Bryant was going. She was asked if she wanted to die or go so she could come back. She said, 'No, kill me off, I want an opportunity for a good bit of acting.' She certainly got it, her body was taken over by a malevolent slug creature. There's a moment when she sits up with her shaven head... It was a very dramatic end.

Colin Baker

I said, 'It just needs to be as dramatic as you dare make it.' A mind transplant, losing Peri altogether, is about as dramatic as you could get. It was then rejigged later on... I had no idea I was going to end up married to Brian Blessed!

Nicola Bryant

After Peri, along came Mel. Anyone who knows Bonnie Langford knows that she is a ball of energy and enthusiasm and acting. The grass does not grow under her feet and the same was true of Mel. It was considered a good idea to make her a fitness freak who is obsessed with the idea of the Doctor being overweight.

Colin Baker

You know I was a computer programmer who never went near a computer!

Bonnie Langford (Melanie Bush)

Robert Holmes, who had been due to write the last two episodes of the Trial *season, sadly died after handing in Part 13. The death of his friend hit script editor Eric Saward hard...*

We delivered the scripts for Parts 9–12 and there was this great silence, so we phoned the office and the next thing we heard was that Eric had left the BBC. Bob Holmes had died – we didn't know him, but Eric was very upset and emotional about it. Bob had written only about twelve minutes of the last episode before his death.

Pip and Jane Baker, writers

Pip and Jane Baker then had to write a new version of the last episode over a weekend, and I thought they did it brilliantly. I think Parts 13 and 14 were the best; the characters of Glitz, Popplewick and the Valeyard were wonderful.

Colin Baker

I suppose I was naive when, before the season went out, I said, 'I'm so confident of the new season that I think the future of *Doctor Who* is secure.' I even thought my own job was secure, because the 'buzz' when we were doing each separate story was really good.

Colin Baker

The edict was passed down at the end of my final season that I should be replaced, and John Nathan-Turner rang me up and said the programme was coming back, but that Michael Grade wanted a new Doctor. So I asked to meet Jonathan Powell and said, 'Why are you sacking me?' 'Oh no, we are not sacking you. We're just not renewing your contract.'

Nice distinction there.

Colin Baker

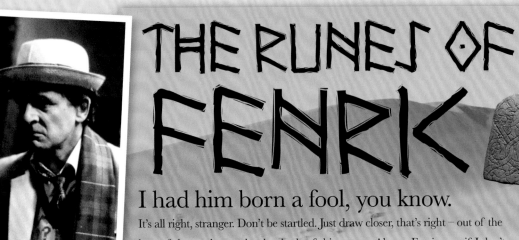

THE RUNES OF FENRIC

I had him born a fool, you know.

It's all right, stranger. Don't be startled. Just draw closer, that's right – out of the heat of the market, under the shade of this canvas. Ah yes. Forgive me if I don't get up. This body is weak. Come closer, and listen to my story. I would like to tell it, and I have so little time.

We were talking of fools, were we not? I shall tell you how I turned a hero into a fool. The Doctor – the greatest hero of them all. I could see him in the distance, shimmering like a mirage in the dunes as he headed through time towards me. And I tell you, I didn't like the look of him one bit.

I cast the bones in the sand, and I arranged things thus. For I knew that, one day, we should do battle in the desert, and I wished to be at an advantage when we played our little contest. Yes, yes, all right, so I cheated. You think me not nice – but, stranger, I could have had him killed. Instead, I arranged for an accident – one that shook him into a new body.

The bones fell in my favour, and he emerged a baffled innocent. I'd taken a champion of time and I'd made him a hapless imbecile. And yet, somehow, still he escaped from the Citadel of Lakertya. Ah well, I figured, something dreadful would happen to him eventually. It was just a matter of pushing a few pieces into place and waiting. I am good at waiting.

He travelled on. He thought himself victorious, but every journey was simply another step across the board. Closer to me. Stupid fool.

He kept on escaping, and I became worried. The bones kept up their song – that he would defeat me. But surely not… not like this?

I turned a few of his squares into traps. I'll admit that. Paradise Towers, that was me. Tollport-G715, that was me as well. I shook the bones, and of course, he just happened to win a competition, bringing him back to Earth, to the 1950s, so close to me. And then, before I could reach out for him, he moved on again…

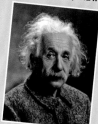

INSTITUTE FOR ADVANCED STUDY AT PRINCETON, NEW JERSEY

We regret to announce that today's lecture 'A Complete Refutation of the Accepted Theory of Quantum Physics' by Professor Albert Einstein has regrettably been cancelled for personal reasons

EXPERIMENT 953/7D-19870907-28

AIM
To construct and deploy a Time Manipulator to introduce order to creation by redirecting evolution wherever it has taken a wrong turn.

HYPOTHESIS
A cerebral mass capable of dominating and controlling time anywhere in the cosmos will give me the ability to change the order of creation.

METHOD
(1) Abduct scientific genii from all of time and space, but mostly from Earth's first couple of millennia. And the Doctor, of course. His knowledge of temporal mechanics will be invaluable.
(2) Establish a base on the planet Lakertya, and channel the mental processes of the genii to form a single giant super-brain.
(3) Programme the super-brain to discover the formula for a lightweight equivalent to Strange Matter (Loyhargil).
(4) Load synthesised Loyhargil into a rocket and blast it at an asteroid of Strange Matter.
(5) The resultant explosion will send off a blast of gamma rays equivalent to a supernova, as well as producing Helium 2. The Helium 2 will fuse with the upper zones of the Lakertyan atmosphere to form a shell of chronons.
(6) In the same millisecond, the hothouse effect of the gamma rays will cause the primate functions of the brain to go into chain reaction, multiplying until the gap between shell and planet is filled. This will turn the planet Lakertya into a Time Manipulator.

RESULTS

THAT CURSED DOCTOR! EVEN IN HIS RIDICULOUS NEW BODY, HE REMAINS AN INSUFFERABLE PRATTLING IMBECILE!!!

CONCLUSION
I shall pickle him in time like a gherkin in a jar!

If the Fool was going to carry on his charmed life, then I needed control of his moves. I could see his course across the board, leading him to Iceworld. I'd had enough of the honest Bishop who travelled the board with him, Melanie Bush. I had her captured by my black Rook, Sabalom Glitz. I pulled time apart, moving one of my Wolves into place. I put the girl, Dorothy, on the board, in Iceworld. She attracted his attention, and he took her with him, thinking her his Pawn. The Pawn was now driving the King into position. And, if you'll forgive a mixed metaphor while I am eulogising, I had played my Ace.

The Doctor's eyes were on the future of the universe. He didn't see the Darkness clouding the eyes of the girl at his side. He didn't spot the traps I had lain. Her weaknesses should have told him that there was something black in that girl's childhood. True, he set out to examine her demons. For instance, her simple fear of clowns (ironic, given that she travelled with one) led them to a circus. Even then, the show was a mask for a bid by ancient gods to reclaim existence. I am not beyond dropping him the odd clue.

He set out to educate her. And, all the while, she unwittingly drew him further into my gambit. As he played for her, he showed her his real tactics – he destroyed the entire Dalek home world, blew up the Cyber-fleet and overthrew a whole world in a night…

If this was a fool, I thought, then he was quite a formidable fool. My relish for our final confrontation had gone a little stale. If I had my time over again, perhaps I would have shaped events differently. Perhaps, I should have made Ratcliffe ruler of a new British Empire. Maybe he and Herr de Flores could have plunged Europe into Armageddon.

But instead, I picked Lady Peinforte as my Black Queen. A 17th-century alchemist and sorceress who had tangled with the Doctor before. Surely, I thought, she was a worthy opponent to defeat him? I whispered words in her ear, told her who he really was, and how to defeat him – and then I allowed the witch to think she could ride the back of time, pushing her into the future in time for the return of the Nemesis statue.

In the event, Peinforte was a most unsatisfactory Wolf, and the Doctor shrugged off her accusations. Do not think me angry – no, no, not at all. I had lost my Black Queen, so I merely changed my strategy, concentrated on shaping the Pawn Ace to my will.

I could see him clearly now – no longer shimmering in the distance, but instead drawing sharp and close. And, if I felt a chill, I did not show it. Surely, I could defeat this fool – why, others had managed it – why not I?

COAL HILL SCHOOL

one, two,
buckle my shoe
three, four,
shut the door

it gets dark here early. i like that. i keep asking them when there will be lessons. but they say there will be no lessons. not for a while. they just leave me to sit and sing.

five, six,
pick up sticks
seven, eight,
lay them straight

the numbers never stop. so many numbers. over and over. i ask what they mean. but they tell me that they do not mean anything. i hear the numbers even in my dreams. sometimes it is my voice. sometimes it is another voice. a voice as old as rust.

i wonder how i came to be here. everyone is very kind. but the memory is not coming back. they will not tell me the date. they say dig and delve the numbers would confuse me. i tell them that no, i am quite good with numbers now. i wonder what happened to me. something must have happened to me.

nine, ten,
a big, fat hen
eleven, twelve,

COAL HILL SCHOOL

thirteen, fourteen,
maids a-courting
fifteen, sixteen,
maids in the kitchen

my last clear memory is of school. it was not like here. coal hill school was very loud. it was not normal. not at the end. first those two teachers ran away. then they found that girl had gone missing. the odd girl. i was in detention with her once. she looked right through me.

then one day, i stayed late. i was going to see the headmaster. but i cannot remember seeing him. they say he has gone missing too now. they ask me if i know. but i do not. i ask to see mummy or daddy. but they say not today. maybe tomorrow. it is never today.

seventeen, eighteen,
maids a-waiting
nineteen, twenty,
my plate's empty

The Life and Conduct of Lady Peinforte

Lady Peinforte, of Windsor, was a woman of eminent learning, and held up among her peers and gentryfolk for her wisdome.

But she was, in faith, little liked in the neighbourhood, and many tongues did wag about her after the strange and sudden death of Sir Roger Peinforte left her a widower of some estate. Her riches allowed her to pursue her studies almost entirely, devoting herself to questionable magicks and dark inkantations, although none dared bring the accusation to account against her, for fear of the forces she held at her command. It is said that, for some time, a silver statue of herself (whom she hight 'Nemesis') did walk the grounds of her estate, its touch lethal, and that this statue did hold court with her for some time, until Lady Peinforte was visited by a wandering physician, after which milady's Nemesis was heard of no more.

Few would sup at her table. Twas not unknown for guests not to make it to the last course alive, although some were tempted due to the high abilities of her cook. One such family to keep acquaintance with her were the Remingtons of Remington Grange. So impressed were they by the viands pressed upon them that Dorothea Remington took it upon herself to offer the cook a position at Remington Grange. On hearing of the desertion of her cook, Lady Peinforte did take herself into a high rage, vowing that little good would come of it. Dorothea died before the year's end after a long illness. Twas said her sufferings could be heard even into the nearby woods, where some villagers swore they could see Lady Peinforte, practising with her bow and laughing.

Some years later, the Dark Lady vanished. Many wondered whether Satan had claimed her for his own. but, after some absence, her manservant, one Richard Maynarde returned, saying they had both been on a pilgrimage, and that Her Ladyship had seen herself clearly before being carried up into the heavens.

Although many did scoff at his account, it was held certayn true that she had provided well for Maynarde in her will. and he did continue as manager of her estate until he was carried away on the 2nd day of November. 1657. aged 51.

"THIS COUNTRY FOUGHT FOR THE WRONG CAUSE IN THE LAST WAR."

If you desire a COLOUR for your neighbour – vote Charles grover If you are already burdened with one

VOTE RATCLIFFE
for Shoreditch on 8th October 1959
Britain's All Right When It's All White

THE PSYCHIC CIRCUS

THE GREATEST SHOW IN THE GALAXY

GABRIEL CHASE

Location: Perivale , Greater London

The House: Originally intended as a hunting lodge, Gabriel Chase was built by Sir Gabriel Pritchard in the 17th century. It was home to the Pritchard family until the late 19th century and lays claim to at least four separate ghostly manifestations.

The house's reputation as a haunting hot spot stems from the early 1880s when Sir Gabriel's great grandson, the big game hunter and astronomer of note, Sir George Pritchard, disappeared in uncertain circumstances. Shortly afterwards, his wife, Lady Margaret and their daughter Gwendoline, also vanished.

The house remained shuttered and locked for many years. Local villagers refused to go near the building, claiming it had bad 'atmospheres'. In the 1920s, an exorcism was attempted, but the attendant priest was said to have fled the building in a state of terror. He declared that he had seen a fiery angel with piercing eyes and wings like thunder. He also insisted that the contents of his phial of holy water had turned to the consistency of soup and tried to attack him. He ended his days, beset, he said, by the cries of wild animals, in an asylum in Sussex. The ghostly manifestations of the house include the sound of jangling keys, which heralds the appearance of a gaunt woman in black, and a girl in a midnight blue dress, who runs along the corridors laughing. These are thought to be the abandoned mother and daughter. Also sighted have been a policeman in full Victorian uniform, who haunts the pantry, and a crusty dog-collared clergyman, who squats in the rafters of the upper rooms emitting ape-like whoops. A marble statue, said to represent Lady Margaret and Gwendoline, was recovered and now resides in the Victoria and Albert Museum. (*Viewable by appointment only*.)

By the 1980s, the long abandoned house was frequented by local youth. In 1983, it was burned to the ground in an act of vandalism. More recently, the local Council's attempts to bulldoze the site were abandoned after workmen reported dangerous subsidence due to underground workings and infestations of aggressive insect life more akin to the tropics than Middlesex. The discovery of several colonies of non-indigenous beetles and butterflies has resulted in the site being declared of Special Scientific Interest. This ensures that it, along with the burnt out ruin of Gabriel Chase, will remain conserved for the foreseeable future.

How to get there: Take the London Underground (*Central Line*) to Perivale Station. 10 minutes' walk south across the local playing fields (*another area with a reputation for unexplained manifestations*), cross Western Avenue and turn left at the Golf Club.

 Perivale   10 mins

In another dimension, they called him Merlin, and Queen Morgaine sealed him in the ice for ever. I took it as a good omen. If the time came, if they could do it, then I could defeat the Fool.

I laid a final trap for him. Poor Ace. She was a most nimble pawn. When she was a child, it was the easiest of things to arrange – a hurt friendship here, petrol through a letterbox there… and so Dorothy went to a ruined house and she sensed an evil. Just another memory that she recounted one evening in the TARDIS. And, thinking himself clever, the Fool listened, and took her back there.

Again, he fell into my trap – into a confrontation with Light, an ancient spirit imprisoned under Gabriel Chase, a creature which sought to stop change and impose its own order on creation. Light may not have been a god, but he was fairly close to one in power. Surely, this time, I had the Fool?

And yet, somehow, infuriatingly, he knocked Light aside. I was amazed he escaped – but, even that defeat had a savour of Victory to it. The Doctor had set out to show Ace that there were no ogres, demons or old gods… and yet… what else had he shown her that he was? A man who burns stars, defeats immortals; who is, in fact, Merlin? What else is a god? Oh, Doctor, what have you set yourself up as in Dorothy's eyes? You Fool.

Her unshakable faith in him is the last piece in the puzzle, and the real game is now ready to begin. I have tried to put it off. You can see that I have. But, if it cannot be avoided, and I must play fair, then my Wolves are all ready for him.

It is a game that began long, long ago – when I encountered that lonely old man in the desert, he suggested we sit down and carve pieces from the bones of the dead and play a game of Chess for the world. The Doctor thought himself so clever, sealing me in the flask for eternity, but, for a creature such as myself, it has been so easy to reach out and shape the entirety of the world.

I caused that flask to be bought and sold down the Road of Silk. I caused that merchant ship to be assailed by Vikings, and those Vikings to bring the flask to England and seal it beneath the church. I summoned my Wolves from across the globe and across the generations and gathered them around that church. All paths led them back to Maiden's Point. While the flask rested, the

The Imprisonment of Merlin

'Now sey than what ye will,' seide Merlin.
'I will,' quod she, 'ye teche me that I myght
enclose a place by art in soche wise that never
myght be undon.' 'Madame,' seide Merlin, 'that shall I
well do.'

Than he began to devise the crafte unto hir, and she it
wrote all that he seide;

And so thei sojourned togeder longe tyme till it fill on a
day that thei wente thourgh the frozen caves most depe.
And Merlin leide his heed till he fill on slepe.

And whan she felt that he was on slepe, she aroos
softly and began hir enchauntementez soche as Merlin
hadde hir taught.

He dide awake. And than he loked aboute hym, and
hym semed he was in the frozen cave enclosed and that
enchantment never myght be undon. Ne never after com
Merlin oute of that fortresse.

***

Whan Sir Gawein herde the voyce that hadde hym
cleped by his right name, he ansuerde and seide, 'Who is
that, in the name of God, that to me doth speke?'

'My lorde Sir Gawein,' quod Merlin, 'me shull ye never
se; Ne fro hens may I not come oute, ne never I shall
come oute.'

'How is that, swete frende,' quod Gawein, 'that ye be
in this maner withholden, that be the wisest man of the
worlde?'

'Nay, but the moste fole,' quod Merlin. 'And therfore,
now returne and grete wele the Kynge Arthur and telle
how it is with me; I beseche yow to God that kepe the
Kynge Arthur and the reame of Logres as for the best
peple of the worlde.'

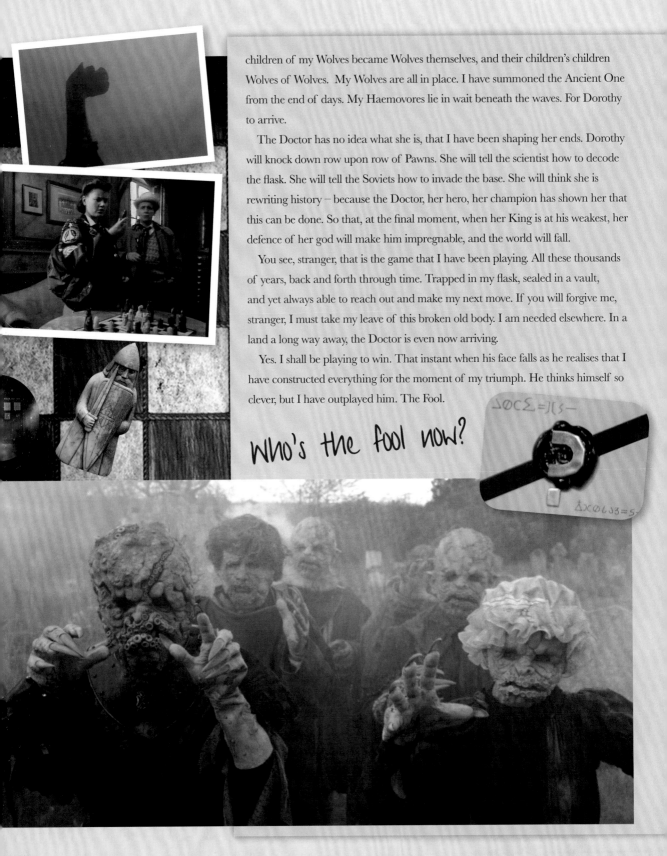

children of my Wolves became Wolves themselves, and their children's children Wolves of Wolves. My Wolves are all in place. I have summoned the Ancient One from the end of days. My Haemovores lie in wait beneath the waves. For Dorothy to arrive.

The Doctor has no idea what she is, that I have been shaping her ends. Dorothy will knock down row upon row of Pawns. She will tell the scientist how to decode the flask. She will tell the Soviets how to invade the base. She will think she is rewriting history – because the Doctor, her hero, her champion has shown her that this can be done. So that, at the final moment, when her King is at his weakest, her defence of her god will make him impregnable, and the world will fall.

You see, stranger, that is the game that I have been playing. All these thousands of years, back and forth through time. Trapped in my flask, sealed in a vault, and yet always able to reach out and make my next move. If you will forgive me, stranger, I must take my leave of this broken old body. I am needed elsewhere. In a land a long way away, the Doctor is even now arriving.

Yes. I shall be playing to win. That instant when his face falls as he realises that I have constructed everything for the moment of my triumph. He thinks himself so clever, but I have outplayed him. The Fool.

Who's the fool now?

A Short Treatise on Dalek Justice
by Benncuiq IV

To many Time Lords, it is something of a curiosity that the Daleks have a Parliament. The idea that this chamber is presided over by a Dalek Prime Minister seems equally anomalous – but the sheer absurdity of the idea is what makes it so very Dalek.

It is commonly believed that the Daleks have no sense of humour, but it can be argued that they have a highly developed sense of irony. The Daleks regularly enter into alliances which always end with the extermination and betrayal of the non-Dalek party. The Daleks employ slave labour in order to achieve a task less efficiently than if it were done by a Dalek. And, the biggest irony of all is that the Daleks have a Parliament, a debating chamber where nothing is ever debated, only agreed to in total chanting uniformity by every Dalek.

Since the days of the Dalek Empire, for a Dalek to question an order was to incur instant death. This is pretty much the definition of the Dalek legal system. The arrogance of the Dalek belief in themselves as supreme beings makes the idea of Dalek justice a laughable irony, unless you are on the receiving end of it – they are right and you are wrong.

The only Time Lord ever brought before the Dalek Parliament was the Master. Their case against him was obscure. There are rumours they were dissatisfied with the lacklustre results of his attempts to cause war between Earth and Draconia. If that was the case, however, it seems odd that they waited so many centuries (in the Master's timeline) before dealing with him.[1]

Quite why the Daleks chose to put him on trial rather than order summary execution is also puzzling. The only conclusion I can reach is that they wished to make a point. They had, after all, managed to resurrect their home world after its destruction by the Hand of Omega. They were aware of our attempts to interfere in their genesis. Perhaps they wished to show Gallifrey that they considered themselves not merely our equals but our superiors. Certainly, the trial itself was extremely perfunctory, even by Dalek standards. The full transcript ran to a word count of two: 'Exterminate' and 'Exterminate'.

Interestingly, one other theory was floated post mortem – that the entire exercise was a trap. The Daleks didn't really give a fig about the Master, but used his execution as a massive lure for the Predator of the Daleks. The two of them were in it together – the Daleks wanted him dead, the Master wanted his body. Indeed, looked at in that way, the whole thing was indeed an obvious trap. And the one thing the Doctor has never been able to resist is a trap...

[1] By this point, remember, the Master's attempts to prolong his life had left him barely Gallifreyan; having spent several hundred years occupying the body of a Trakenite, he eventually succumbed to the mental and physical influences of a sentient planet and its indigenous felines. This biological corruption may, it seems, have saved his life when the Daleks caught up with him.

THE EIGHTH DOCTOR

It was on the planet Skaro that my old enemy the Master was finally put on trial. They say he listened calmly as his list of evil crimes was read and sentence passed. Then he made his last, and I thought somewhat curious, request. He demanded that I, the Doctor, a rival Time Lord, should take his remains back to our home planet, Gallifrey.

It was a request they should never have granted.

Did the Daleks think they were laying a trap for me? They may be brilliant and ruthless enough to restore an entire world, but they still suffer from the same old drawback — that dependency on rationality and logic. And I always do the unexpected, unless, of course, they're expecting the unexpected. Then I do the expected. And they weren't expecting that. A Time Lord has thirteen lives, and the Master had used all of his, but rules never meant much to him. So I stowed his remains safely away for the voyage back, because even in death I couldn't trust him. In all my travels through space and time, and nearing the end of my seventh life, I was finally beginning to realise that you could never be too careful. And having begun to realise that, I promptly forgot all about it. Which was careless of me. Oh well.

So... what happened next? To be honest, it's all a bit hazy — I think I've been suffering from post-regenerative amnesia, but I can't quite recall. I remember a Timing Malfunction diverting the TARDIS to Humanian-era Earth. China, or possibly America. I know I was shot. (And there's an irony. All those years plotting and calculating and staying one step ahead of the enemy, then I walk into the middle of a gunfight. Wasn't expecting that, was I?)

Anyway, it was only three little bullets — I just had to regenerate. But I wasn't expecting a bunch of well-meaning humans to start poking around in my insides, leaving bits of primitive wiring in my cardiovascular system. Lovely people, humans, mostly, but very bad at listening. And I'm fairly certain I must have been shouting at them to stop what they were doing.

So the next thing I really remember is a pair of unfamiliar feet running around in a new pair of shoes, and memories of home and family that hadn't surfaced in centuries. Oh, and Dr Grace Holloway. I'm a little worried she may have taken that kiss the wrong way. She had troubles of her own. As the 20th century drew to a close, her boyfriend Brian had moved out. Humans are wonderful creatures — finding a removal firm that would work over New Year was pretty amazing. No wonder his shoes fitted perfectly.

The great thing about regeneration is how much life it gives you. I was bursting with it. I'd never felt more alive — whereas the Master had just swapped one dead body for another. Humans are quite my favourite species, but they're just not designed to contain a Time Lord — so the Master needed to find a new host pretty quickly. His best bet was me — and he was so desperate to survive that he was prepared to suck the entire planet Earth into the Eye of Harmony.

I did try to save him. As he fell into the Eye of Harmony, I offered the Master my hand...

We said our goodbyes, Grace and I. Funnily enough, I could foretell the futures of everyone else I met — but not hers. I can't say whether she went back to the remarkable Brian, or ever set out to go looking for the guy with two hearts...

So now it's just me and this sentimental old TARDIS, off on our travels again. I'm feeling quite hopeful, quite positive. When I found this old diary, it reminded me how it all started — how I set out to explore and to wonder. That's my mission again now: to learn. No more Cybermen, no more Autons, no more Sontarans, no more bad old Daleks or mad old Time Lords. No more war.

As the year 1999 comes to a close, strange natural phenomena have been reported — and not just in San Fran! Since early this evening, Bay Area tides have risen to levels that break all records for this time of year. Flood warnings have gone out along the Napa and Russian rivers, and — believe it or not — in Hawaii it has even started snowing.

You may be wondering what this has to do with the millennium? Well, scientists say that the freak conditions are due to very slight fluctuations in the Earth's gravitational pull. Fluctuations that apparently only happen once every thousand years.

Our cameras in Hawaii may be showing snow-fights on the beaches of paradise, but where will most fashionable San Franciscans be going tonight to ring in the new year? Rumour has it they'll all be going to see a clock getting started.

And you know, it isn't just any old clock. It happens to be the most accurate atomic clock in the world, and it's right here in the Institute of Technological Advancement and Research in Downtown San Francisco. If you want to have a happy new year, don't go away.

The Story of Doctor Who

1987-2003

If I told you that the next programme for the winter season stars Brenda Bruce, Elizabeth Spriggs, Judy Cornwall, Clive Merrison, Richard Briers, Hugh Lloyd, Stubby Kaye, Ken Dodd, Don Henderson and Edward Peel, you would probably think it was one of Shaun Sutton's Theatre Night Specials. But you would be wrong – it's *Doctor Who*!

Jonathan Powell, Controller BBC1

The new script editor Andrew Cartmel and I saw eye to eye. We got together and discussed every season and met the writers, and we discussed the journey the Doctor was going to make. John Nathan-Turner was pretty much hands-off at that point – all very encouraging behind the scenes that we should get on with it, and so that's what we did.

Sylvester McCoy

John asked me, 'If there's one thing you could do with the show, what would it be?' And I said, 'Overthrow the government,' because I was young and I didn't like the way things were going at the time. John said, 'Well, you can't do that. The most you can do on *Doctor Who* is say that people with purple and green skin are all equal.' Which we then proceeded to do.

Andrew Cartmel, script editor

The twenty-fourth season faced an immediate challenge...

I didn't want to do a regeneration scene. It was nine months from the time that I was given the heave-ho, it was very public, and I just wanted to go away and forget the whole thing. I didn't see why I should go back, and that didn't suit some of the fans, and it was inconvenient for the BBC, but it was an inconvenience of their own making.

Colin Baker

We were well into the story when we were shown a video of Sylvester – we had to find a way of (a) regenerating the Doctor, and (b) finding a character for him. John

asked for a pre-credit teaser. All of us felt we couldn't go straight into the story. If we had to regenerate in this way, we needed to start with it, then have a full stop and then start the story. You couldn't open with Sylvester's titles otherwise, it would have looked silly.

Pip and Jane Baker, writers

That was quite interesting wearing Colin's costume, literally. I'm the one Doctor who's played two Doctors, numbers Six and Seven. They put me in Colin Baker's costume and they lost me for three days. They put a curly blond wig on my head and I looked like Harpo Marx. So they laid me on the floor and that was me being Colin and then a hairy hand came in and turned me over, and as it turned me over so my faces goes 'zoooooo' and that is where you see the transformation and I become me.

Sylvester McCoy

Bonnie Langford helped bridge the changeover of Doctors really well. She established a very good relationship with Sylvester. I know there are those who love Bonnie or hate her, but to my mind that is the mark of somebody who is making an

impact. I think she has been very good for *Doctor Who*.

John Nathan-Turner, producer

Mel was Bonnie. Brilliant Bonnie Langford. She was Colin's companion. She was big and wore flashy costumes and she had to try and upstage or equal Colin's costume. So that was interesting, to try and make it work out. What was great about having Bonnie there was I was a new boy, and she was an old friend. We did a year on a musical on Drury Lane. It was great to have a friend on the set. So she kind of helped me a lot that way.

Sylvester McCoy

Kate O'Mara's Rani was just glorious to work with, and in that first story it was hilariously funny because she had to pretend to be Bonnie Langford, or Mel. She was really good at doing Bonnie when Bonnie wasn't there, but she was very self-conscious about doing her when she was there, so it was fun to watch that.

Sylvester McCoy

Time and the Rani was fun because we had Kate who was hilarious. I love her. She used to make me do the lines and then she'd copy me. It was the most hysterical thing.

Bonnie Langford (Melanie Bush)

Bonnie Langford is a dear friend of mine, I like her very much indeed, and to have to try to impersonate her was not easy, because she's about as different from me as it's possible to be. They gave me a costume that exactly resembled hers, a wig that looked like her hair then, masses of red curls, but of course what I had to do was to try to imitate her voice and her personality, her walk, so I had to do a sort of bouncy, very bouncy sort of gait.

Kate O'Mara (The Rani)

As Season 24 continued, the show attracted a range of notable guest stars...

In *Paradise Towers*, there were Brenda Bruce and Lizzy Spriggs and Judy

SYLVESTER McCOY
was the Seventh Doctor

I had endless lists of possible Doctors. I also got a lot of calls from actors' agents. It really is a plum job. One of these calls was from Sylvester McCoy's agent who suggested I went to see him at the National Theatre in *The Pied Piper*. I was very impressed with his performance and decided to meet him.

There is a wonderful, natural eccentric quality about Sylvester. There is a sort of disjointed way that he speaks – the gestures are never quite in the right place at the right moment. I found myself riveted and quite happy to go on listening to him.

Well, I would have been quite happy to have booked him then and there, but my head of department asked me to spread my net a little wider and do a few screen tests with other actors.

Anyhow, I did some screen tests with Sylvester and some other actors and, with no disrespect to the others, Sylvester was the Doctor I was looking for. I had always envisioned a Troughtonesque quality and here it was. I also wanted someone who was much smaller than Colin Baker.

John Nathan-Turner

He goes through quite a story arc from when he first started to when we ended with Survival. He even had a darker costume. He started off with this light jacket doing funny tricks – playing his spoons and all that, and then by the end he had his much darker brown jacket and he was really quite manipulative.

Sophie Aldred (Ace)

McCOY *on* McCOY

I didn't have a sonic screwdriver. I had an umbrella.

Sylvester McCoy

My Doctor, well, he's kind of Chaplinesque in many ways. Buster Keaton, mixed with something rather darker, more mysterious. He didn't start off fully formed. He came out of the womb, the TARDIS, a more comedic character. I wasn't given much guidance really, which was great in a way, because I had to find my own feet.

Sylvester McCoy

In my first season, I suddenly realised the potential of another journey I could go on with the Doctor, and it took a little time to turn around, because scripts had already been written for the next series, and it was like turning around the Titanic. By the time I got to my third season, the Doctor I wanted to create had arrived. He was darker, more mysterious – I wanted him to be mysterious, because the first Doctor was a mystery.

Sylvester McCoy

I stipulated immediately that my Doctor would not win by violent means. He must solve the problem by intellect, by guile, by humour, or by letting his companion blow them up. I lived through the time when Harold Wilson managed to solve the Rhodesian problem, not by invading, but by actually getting these people and putting them on a boat and letting them talk to each other and not letting them off until they had peace. My Doctor was like that.

Sylvester McCoy

Another thing I wanted to do, especially at the beginning, was to try and bring bits of each Doctor before me into it. Sometimes you read it and think, 'Oh, that's a Jon Pertwee line' or 'Oh, that's a Colin Baker line', especially in the first one where there's a lot of Colin Baker lines because that had been written for him, and then I took over.

Sylvester McCoy

Cornwall, fantastic people. So it was a great room to be in, it was always fun to go up to the canteen at lunchtime. All the turns would be talking to each other about being in *Doctor Who*. There was this great sort of cachet, but at the same time there was an element of something fun to be in.

Bonnie Langford

It was a fascinating experience, if a bit of a macabre one. Certainly it was a change from my usual roles, playing a kind of fascist dictator complete with Hitler moustache who feeds people to his monster!

Richard Briers (Chief Caretaker)

I remember *Delta and the Bannerman*, Stubby Kaye suddenly turns up. I was like, 'Oh my god!' That was fun. Hugh Lloyd was in it. Ken Dodd was at the last day of shooting. And I have to say I've never seen so many people on set in the middle of the night, just because Ken was coming. It was fascinating, they all wanted to come and see Ken entertain the crew. He was brilliant.

Bonnie Langford

The season ended with Dragonfire, *a treasure hunt in space that introduced a lost girl called Ace...*

Ace is a tomboy, she's very feisty, she comes from the outskirts of London, a council estate in Perivale, in West London, and she was just a really realistic character for the time. I was 24, playing 16, but I absolutely knew that she had to wear Doc Martens. When I was a kid, I never understood why the assistant would take off with the Doctor, go out into what she knew was going to be an alien landscape

with lots of rocks and hills and holes, and be wearing high-heeled shoes. It was actually my idea for the bomber jacket with the badges and the safety pins and all that, because I'd seen girls wearing them in very trendy clubs and there was a picture of them in *The Face* magazine that I particularly remembered.

Ace was based on three real girls. Three real 16-year-olds, with whom Ian Briggs, who wrote *Dragonfire*, had been working at the theatre in Ealing. They came to the first studio day and it was great. I was given my thumbs up from these three girls. So Ace was one of the first companions who had a really realistic back-story. She wasn't just a journalist or a computer programmer, she actually did have a life before the Doctor.

Sophie Aldred

When I got a new companion, I said, 'Listen, we don't want a screaming companion.' I wanted a more equal footing. And also, I'm incredibly lazy – as *Doctor Who* you have to learn an amazing amount of gobbledegook, and I, in my canny little mind, thought I could use Sophie, playing Ace, as a means to put some of that onto her. So I reduced my gobbledegook and increased hers.

Sylvester McCoy

At the end of Dragonfire, *Mel suddenly announces that she's leaving the TARDIS to run a space supermarket with Tony Selby's Sabalom Glitz...*

I didn't know I was meant to stay. It was only towards the end of that story that John said, 'So, are you actually leaving?' And I said, 'Well, I thought I was here for two series, and that's coming to an end

isn't it?' Nobody actually turned around and said, 'We would like you to stay or not like you to stay.' I enjoyed my time there, but it was only meant to be – for me – that long. The only thing I said was 'Could you just not kill me off or give me a brain transplant. I don't want to wear a bald cap as I can't be doing with going to make-up for that long.' I think I just went off to a supermarket, didn't I? I just went shopping!

Bonnie Langford

The show now moved into its silver anniversary year...

Working on the series at the time was an absolute joy. It was my first ever TV work and so I was so lucky to be plunged in at the deep end. It was real proper BBC drama the way they used to do it. It was multi-camera in the studio with very experienced crews. We had really brilliant people who would come back again and again because they loved it. I was meeting people who were saying, 'Oh, when we worked with Tom...' It seemed to me such a sensible way of working and such a sense of community.

Sophie Aldred

Remembrance of the Daleks *saw the Doctor returning to the site of his first adventure – Shoreditch in late 1963. Waiting for him were more Daleks than the programme had ever seen before...*

I didn't really feel I was a true Doctor until I'd stood up against the Daleks. We were filming under Waterloo Station, and the IRA were pretty active around Britain around that time. There was a great battle going on between two races of Daleks. The pyrotechnic boys from the BBC were blowing things up underneath this arch, and it was suddenly on the news that the IRA had set a bomb off under Waterloo Station. It was just chaos – ambulances,

fire engines, police came rushing to the area. I was standing on the road there was smoke everywhere, I saw this ambulance first, behind it a fire engine, all the noise – flashing lights screaming down the road and then suddenly the ambulance stopped. The driver's jaw dropped to his chest because out of the smoke came three Daleks. He couldn't believe it.

Sylvester McCoy

I think the seminal moment of my whole career as Ace was when I got to beat up a Dalek with a baseball bat. Nobody else has ever done that and I hope they never do because I think that's probably going on my tombstone... It's just the coolest thing ever to have done, isn't it?

Sophie Aldred

There was a lot of racial tension then, and it was so important to come out and confront it face on, the madness and the badness of it. That's what we did in *Remembrance of the Daleks*. There was a beautiful scene written in that about sugar, and how the westerners' sweet tooth kind of created slavery.

Sylvester McCoy

The next story was a three-parter about a strange world where the ruler, Helen A, had outlawed unhappiness...

I didn't see the story as a satire on Thatcherism, but the character was a take on Mrs Thatcher, absolutely.

Andrew Cartmel

Having revived the Daleks and the Cybermen for the 25th anniversary, Nathan-Turner and Cartmel decided to bring back a couple of other names from the show's earliest days for the start of Season 26...

The Brigadier was supposed to be killed off in that story. John Nathan-Turner said, 'Do you mind if we kill him off?' and I said, 'No, he's been around a long time. Give me a good send-off.' But the way the script then developed, my death might have gone unnoticed, so they kept me alive!

Nicholas Courtney (The Brigadier)

I was so pleased to do another one, playing a wicked queen. I got to be very wicked but actually very intelligent

and rounded, as characters go. I'm very grateful for that.

Jean Marsh (Morgaine)

The next serial made the audience sit up and pay attention, with critics praising a complicated story of Victorian evildoings and dastardly Darwinism...

Ghost Light was set in Victorian times. It was in a way the best studio one, I think, because the BBC are very good at building Victorian buildings in a studio. I still don't quite know what it was completely about. No one seems to know really, but it was great making it and they were very well-written scenes. That was a really interesting journey that the Doctor was on, as was Ace his companion. It was more about Ace's journey.

Sylvester McCoy

We had a story arc. It was very much based on the Doctor and Ace's relationship and the fact that the Doctor needed Ace to work something out, which was a precursor of the modern Doctor. The story arc that we came in on was this young girl who gets blown up to this ice world in a time storm. And then Andrew Carmel had this wizard plan that actually this was going to be explained in a later story. And he brought back Ian Briggs to write another story, *The Curse of Fenric*, which explained why she'd been blown up in this time storm and that it was all to do with Fenric. This was a sort of long-term plan that the Doctor was trying

Writer Tom MacRae on THE HAPPINESS PATROL

The Happiness Patrol made me cry. It was the first time *Doctor Who* had ever done that. I'd been thrilled before. Breathless with excitement before. Gripped with tension at a cliff-hanger mixed with frustration I'd have to wait a week to see what happened before. Once or twice, I'd even been scared. But *The Happiness Patrol* was the first time *Doctor Who* had made me cry. It was that bit, right at the end, when Helen A's horrid mini-dog-beast Fifi died, and Helen A started sobbing, and suddenly this vile little puppet that I'd loved to hate for the last three weeks... well, suddenly it felt real to me. Fifi's death felt real. And Helen A's emotion – and the emotional lesson it taught her; that true happiness must be contrasted with true sadness to be true – it just got me, somewhere in the pit of my chest where usually my instinct to hide behind the sofa was housed, except tears, rather than fears came out. That was the measure of the show: it could make you laugh, make you cry, make you scared, make you care and generally make you feel. And it had a psychotic Bertie Bassett that drowned you in custard. Which clearly is what television was invented for.

to solve. There were also the Hand of Omega and the Nemesis statue, and this suggestion that the Doctor had been part of a triumvirate of Time Lords...

Sophie Aldred

The later stories, were not only about each individual story but also about Ace's journey, and Ace's education. The way my Doctor did it was to become very manipulative. The Doctor seemed to know what was going to happen. He was playing this three-dimensional chess game but he knew who was going to win it. That was cool. But also there was a cruelty in there too, towards Ace.

He believed it was for her own good, and that one day she would thank him for it. So that was kind of an interesting journey, being woven into the various stories through those last episodes that we did. It was quite interesting for all of us.

Sylvester McCoy

Season 26 closed with Anthony Ainley's return as the Master in Survival, *which unexpectedly turned out to be the last story of* Doctor Who's *original run...*

At the time we didn't know that *Survival* was going to be the last story because in the wonderful world of television you always film everything completely back to front and out of order. So we actually filmed *Ghost Light* last. John Nathan-Turner was clinging on to *Doctor Who*, his great love that he'd been with for such a long time, and probably if he'd gone then *Doctor Who* would have gone earlier.

Sophie Aldred

The BBC was getting a bit bored of *Doctor Who* because in order to get on you've got to make a name for yourself, and to make a name you need a new programme. You can't make a name out of something that has already made a name for someone else, so what do you do – you get rid of it and make a new programme. Jonathan Powell moved up and took over BBC One, and he was the one who actually shut it down.

Sylvester McCoy

Script editor Gary Russell on
GHOST LIGHT

Ghost Light was a curious beast. Its biggest claim to fame was that it was the very last *Doctor Who* adventure made by the BBC in its 'classic series' phase (though not the last shown; that's *Survival*). But it's a real template for what was to come more than fifteen years later when the show came back. It tells a tight, contained story, with larger-than-life grotesques populating its narrative, all of them providing an important part of the overall mystery for the Doctor and Ace to solve. There's nothing thrown away here: every line, every moment, every camera pan screamed out its relevance and importance to the story. No, you couldn't go off and do the ironing, or casually glance down at the newspaper to see what time *Bergerac* was on, because you'd miss something. The joy of *Ghost Light* was that it held the attention so much, the viewer never needed to look away.

Take a spooky house, monsters in the basement, a Neanderthal butler, a man who sheds his skin on a regular basis, and a couple of ladies who think nothing of chloroforming a clergyman and sticking him in a bell jar – and

mix. Marc Platt's script is layered but not obfuscating, and could happily have starred Matt Smith and Jenna Coleman, because it smacks of modernity and intelligence, of whimsy and pastiche, everything modern Doctor Who does so well.

Perhaps *Doctor Who* in the 1980s should have taken a few more chances, risked a few more moments to make stories like this – a story that wears its studio-boundness on its sleeve and flashes a big neon sign that yells 'We didn't need a million-dollar budget to make this, we just needed good dialogue, good actors, good design and one hundred per cent of conviction from those involved.' Basically, everything *Doctor Who* has had in spades since 2005.

Today, *Ghost Light* is a story that everyone involved in still remains incredibly proud of. Quite right too. It's a marvellous achievement that disproves the tawdry idea that *Doctor Who* was staid, boring and on its last legs in 1989. If *Ghost Light* is any kind of indication, classic *Doctor Who* could easily have run another few years. It certainly deserved to.

The very last speech that we had of our tenure was as we walked off through a bush in a quarry somewhere in Dorset. We didn't actually know that was going to be the final scene. Andrew Cartmel wrote that final scene, and it's the most beautiful speech, it sort of sums up *Doctor Who* in a moment, and it makes me emotional even now to think of it. It was a really fitting tribute to our time on *Doctor Who*.

Sophie Aldred

'There are worlds out there where the sky is burning, where the sea's asleep, and the rivers dream. People made of smoke, and cities made of song. Somewhere there's danger, somewhere there's injustice, and somewhere else the tea's getting cold. Come on, Ace, we've got work to do...'

Survival, Part Three

What very few people knew in 1989 was that there were already moves afoot to rework the series as a well-funded UK-US co-production. Negotiations were complex and protracted and, in the meantime, the Doctor's exploits continued in multiple forms, beginning in 1989 with a theatrical outing – The Ultimate Adventure...

The performance had to be enlarged for a live audience. It couldn't be played down in the way I do on television. We had a short rehearsal period really, so we had to get the script right before we went to rehearsals. The writer Terrance Dicks and I have worked closely for years, so that presented no problem.

Jon Pertwee

Jon Pertwee had been playing the part for ten weeks before I took over, and Terrance Dicks wrote it specifically with Jon in mind. So he sent me a copy of the script and asked me what kind of changes I thought I'd want. There were very few changes. Basically, the Doctor is the Doctor.

Colin Baker

By that stage, we'd already decided that we were going to go ahead and do original fiction. It would carry on from where the television series left off. We basically designed the *New Adventures* to start from where Survival left off.

**Peter Darvill-Evans, editor,
Virgin Publishing's New Adventures**

We were stuck with a licensed magazine that no longer had a TV show to sell off, so at that point we had to make the most of what was out there. One of the things I did was bring in new writers on the comic strip.

John Freeman, editor, Doctor Who Magazine

I knew right from the outset that I would throw it open. We recruited a band of talented writers, many of whom have gone on to have something to do with the new television series – Paul Cornell... Gareth Roberts... Mark Gatiss...

Peter Darvill-Evans

Shada went into the studio in 1979 after one week's location filming, but after only two studio recording sessions had been completed an industrial strike meant that the subsequent recording

Writer David Roden on
DIMENSIONS IN TIME

I love *Dimensions In Time*. I don't actually think it's particularly good, and there's a lot in it that I'm deeply embarrassed about... but it raised a huge amount of money for charity, and I'm very proud of that. I have some of the fondest memories of working on that show. It was a real honour to work with five of the Doctors – to meet childhood heroes, and not be disappointed by the real people playing them. They were all wonderful, and the companions, too. It was a once in a lifetime event, so I feel deeply privileged to have been asked by JNT to get involved.

And my involvement was as simple as that. John Nathan-Turner phoned me up at home asked if I'd like to write this 30th-anniversary *Children in Need* story. I said yes immediately, and set to work trying to come up with half-decent ideas. Originally it was one episode, and then BBC Entertainment offered to pay for a second episode if we showed it during *Noel's House Party*. The original script was just the Seventh Doctor and the Brigadier holed up in a derelict church fighting Cybermen; then I was asked to add the other Doctors; then asked to add *EastEnders* elements; then I was asked to remove the *EastEnders* elements; then I rewrote it to feature the Celestial Toymaker and Doctors 3 to 7; then *EastEnders* was back in, so another rewrite; and another rewrite; and on it went... Companions were in, and then out, then back in, then not available on the day we needed them to film the scenes with their Doctor, so everything became jumbled. Then Sylvester wasn't available on the days we were filming in Albert Square, so we could only have him on the Friday for filming which meant he only appeared in the Greenwich sequences. The story did make some sense once...

The whole thing was utterly driven by JNT's enthusiasm. It simply would not have happened without him. When JNT asked if the Doctors would come back and do this episode for free, they all leapt at the chance. Yes, it was all JNT – he was a man of big ideas, and sometimes those ideas made no logical sense at all, but you could never fault him for having ambition and passion and drive. And everybody loved him – we'd all have done anything for him.

These German techno geeks had been developing this 3D filming technique using something called the Pulfrich effect. It worked because the brain takes slightly longer to process darker images than lighter ones – but the effect only really works with constant movement within the picture. So, everything had to be written with characters going somewhere – either running or walking, but always moving. You can't film drama like that. It's loopy! It becomes about the cameras and the effect, not the story. I clearly remember the cameraman shouting at an actor to move so that the effect would work. Well, he'd picked on Tom Baker. And of all the actors to pick on, Tom wasn't a man to hold his tongue. I can't actually repeat what Tom said...

The filming was by and large an absolutely wonderful experience. I remember Sylvester McCoy and Louise Jameson getting on like a house on fire. And he and Sophie Aldred suddenly falling straight back into the old routine. And filming a sequence with Jon Pertwee and Nick Courtney driving Bessie towards this massive UNIT helicopter, and as they started the long drive towards their 'mark' the builders working on the roof of a nearby building started singing the *Who* theme tune – it was magic.

sessions were lost. BBC Home Video have announced plans to release the story, using the existing material with new linking narration supplied by Tom Baker to complete the tale. Many sequences have had specially commissioned visual effects, sound effects and music.

Doctor Who Magazine (1992)

Coming across the BBC airwaves at the moment is the first brand new *Doctor Who* adventure made by the BBC in nearly four years. *The Paradise of Death* reunites the Third Doctor, Sarah Jane Smith and the Brigadier in a battle against the rapacious Parakon Corporation.

Doctor Who Magazine (1993)

The series' 30th anniversary was also marked with prime-time repeats accompanied by short pieces complementing a full-scale documentary, as well as a unique TV crossover for 1993's Children in Need appeal...

The idea of *30 Years in the TARDIS* was to celebrate *Doctor Who*. It was a chance to wallow in all the richness and diversity the programme had presented.

Kevin Jon Davies, director

The BBC Radio 2 *Doctor Who* adventure *The Ghosts of N-Space* has been assigned a broadcast date. The six-part serial – starring Jon Pertwee as the Third Doctor, Nicholas Courtney and Elisabeth Sladen as Sarah Jane Smith – will begin transmission in March 1996.

Doctor Who Magazine

And then, on 10 January 1996, came a long-awaited announcement – Doctor Who was coming back, Sylvester McCoy would briefly reprise his role, and...

PAUL McGANN
was the Eighth Doctor

I played the Doctor for about six weeks, seventeen years ago. The film was coolly received but probably played a part in ensuring the show's eventual revival.

My own part's later regeneration owed more to the magic of radio than it did to iconic TV. In 1995, I was invited to go on tape by the casting director John Hubbard. He told me that producer Philip Segal (may his tribe increase) had caught my recent turn as the priest in the BBC's *The Hanging Gale* and had seen shades of Time Lord in the long hair and Victorian garb. My brother Mark was also called in, so I suspect Phil secretly couldn't tell us apart. We'd heard it rumoured that the Doctor might be staging a comeback, perhaps even in an American guise, but Mark and me had had little reason to think either of us might be seen for the role. Names like Eric Idle and Rowan Atkinson had been mentioned which, on the face of it, at least made sense. Phil had other ideas, though, and soon set about persuading me to do it. It took a while, though in truth my doubts were never a match for his enthusiasm.

We shot in Vancouver in 1996 during winter, mostly at night. We shared a city hotel with the *X Files* crew, who were doing the same. As well as being an agreeable place to work in, Vancouver had the added appeal of being far enough away to deter network execs from showing up much. Phil kept such distractions to a minimum and the atmosphere on set, for the most part, mirrored his own relaxed good humour. Being the sole Brits in the cast meant that, between us, Sylvester McCoy and me had the only working knowledge of *Doctor Who*. My own was minimal, but enough to fill in the gaps for Daphne Ashbrook, who was born the year the show had started but had never even heard of it.

Though it would later be known as 'The Movie', we were, of course, making a television pilot, and we knew it. Despite discussing the possibility of local schools taking our children for the next five years or eyeing up family houses in the bay, we privately accepted the probability that the shoot would be a one-off.

I think the critical reaction to the film was generally fair. It might have failed in its function but its ambition was acknowledged, even applauded. Perhaps, in the end, the dual demands of instructing the ignorant on one side of the pond while satisfying the enlightened on the other meant that it had risked doing neither, and succeeded.

Paul McGann

Devising the story was not easy. Fox had serious concerns about using monsters that might confuse the broad American audience... The ultimate conclusion was that the script would centre on a story that brought the audience to the centre of the Doctor's mythology. It would introduce a new Doctor and not feature creatures that were too 'out there'.

Philip Segal, executive producer

Philip wanted something set in contemporary America so that we could introduce the Doctor to a new audience. I thought that sounded great. The new Doctor is very British in his nature and ways. He's just as much of an eccentric as he ever was and still just as ingenious. I didn't have to make big changes but changes enough to make everyone feel confident about saying goodbye to $5 million.

Matthew Jacobs, writer

Paul McGann brings a freshness to the role. He's a good actor and he's got a great sense of humour. He's also sexy which, I think, is a first for the Doctor.

Matthew Jacobs

Fox had never heard of Paul McGann and they were sure their audience hadn't either. We finally got over this hurdle by promising that we would put a 'name' in the role of the Master. We finally settled on Eric Roberts.

Philip Segal

Eric Roberts was the nicest guy to work with. There was a great theme running through Chang Lee and the Master – a sort of father/son thing. Eric and I thought that it was a powerful basis for Chang

Lee's reaction to the Master's eventual betrayal.

Yee Jee Tso, actor

Broadcast in May 1996, the movie was a big success in the UK, but the USA was not persuaded. TV Doctor Who *dematerialised for another nine years, bar a one-off* Comic Relief *appearance in 1999, though the print adventures continued and were soon complemented by a run of brand new stories featuring classic Doctors in a new medium...*

Although *Doctor Who* had been in comic-strip form right back to the 1960s, to put a *Doctor Who* comic strip inside *Radio Times* meant the strip was having its biggest audience ever.

Gary Russell, comic-strip writer, Radio Times

Paul McGann and the TV movie gave the opportunity to develop our own on-going saga. We set up these big story arcs to run through the Eighth Doctor saga.

Alan Barnes, comic-strip writer, Doctor Who Magazine

BBC Books became the publisher of *Doctor Who* original fiction. They built very much on what Virgin had done, they continued with two ranges of books, one that told new stories about past Doctors and another which continued the Eighth Doctor.

Justin Richards, editor, BBC Books

Knowing I was a *Doctor Who* fan, *Comic Relief* figured they could get me to do what I thought would be a two-minute sketch, which turned into 20 minutes! The point of these spoofs is they always have to be affectionate. We cast it quite authentically, with a bunch of people you absolutely could picture playing the Doctor: Rowan

Atkinson, Hugh Grant, Richard E. Grant, Jim Broadbent and Joanna Lumley. It was a very successful evening, and the biggest-rated item on it was the *Doctor Who* sketches. Every time it switched to *Doctor Who* that night on *Comic Relief*, the audience went up to ten million.

Steven Moffat, writer

We had been doing other sci-fi audio dramas and then, out of the blue, we were asked to go in for a meeting, and they said, 'We've heard what you do and we quite like it – how would you like to have the licence to do *Doctor Who* on CD?' Our first one came out in 1999, and we've been bashing away at it ever since.

Gary Russell, producer, Big Finish

One of the first websites the BBC had was a *Doctor Who* one. When I took it over in 2000, it was run by an ex-nun who didn't own a television and thought Jon Pertwee was still Doctor Who. Due to the fans, it was incredibly successful, beaten only by News, Sport and *EastEnders*. We did webcasts, photonovels and ebooks. But it wasn't loved by the BBC. Every year our budget was cut, and in 2003 we were told, 'Ah well, *Doctor Who*, there's only another couple of years left in it...'

James Goss, website producer

By 2003, Doctor Who *was among the most multimedia franchises in the universe. But with its 40th anniversary approaching, it seemed its only televised appearance would be in the form of a new documentary...*

Word has reached *DWM* of plans for a new documentary celebrating 40 years of *Doctor Who*. It is tentatively intended for broadcast on BBC1 near the anniversary in November.

Doctor Who Magazine

But by the time The Story of Doctor Who *was broadcast in late 2003, there'd already been some incredible news...*

Doctor Who, one of the BBC's best-loved and most enduring characters, is set to return to BBC One, it was confirmed last night by Lorraine Heggessey, Controller of BBC One. Heggessey said that all rights issues regarding *Doctor Who* have been resolved and that she has green-lit scripts from award-winning writer Russell T Davies.

BBC Press Office, 26 September 2003

I want to talk of happy days. But my pen won't let me. I fill page after page with memories so distant and yet so close than I can smell them.

I can see myself laughing forever in a giant balloon with a girl who is so bright and clever.

Sometimes, if I turn my head just a little to one side, the girl isn't there. Like she never was. Instead my hand is gripped. It's a wet and slippery grip, a cross between tentacle and paw. You'd think such a hand owned by a nightmare creature, but its tall piscine mouth laughs, laughs with row after row of shark's teeth. She calls me by name and tugs me and we fall from the balloon into the oceans. Oceans that flow with anger and with metal.

A third calls out my name, a girl so easy to forget. She stands by the school gates and she waits for adventures. We fall, all three, and we are scared, but somehow we are excited.

But all three of us have endless times without even meeting, our fun overlapping. We are torn between friends and fears. I see death sliding towards us in the shape of a man of shining crystal; I see a woman with a goldfish bowl for a head; I see a bleeding skull. Our days go on, wrapped around each other.

Every time I run the tap to shave, I see the water spiralling away down the sink, and I think of we three, flying above that tumble, laughing in a balloon.

Other friends come and go. An old friend with a high collar and a high eyebrow laughs as we run through cloisters looking for brains. Her little tin dog follows behind connecting us. Both of them so familiar, and yet so lost to me. If I stroke the dog it vanishes beneath my touch, as though eaten away by time itself.

I run on, run on towards a city by the sea. The city of a thousand lights and the cries of a crowd jubilant into the night. I run faster and faster to the city because a friend lives there. I am running to save her, but she is dead in burning metal, and no matter how fast she runs I cannot catch her falling star.

That smell continues. That smell of dead steel. It's like it waits over the page.

I know what is over the page. I turn it and smoke

the journey continues.

My ears are big, my smile is bigger. I wear leather, hot against my skin as the shop behind me burns, cold on a night when lights search the sky, and slick with rain as I run through the streets looking for the girl, the girl who devours time.

But something is missing.

It is like there is a figure beyond time. One who decides how things are now, not how they were. Not a writer. A rewriter.

I stop a moment. I turn the page of this journal back. And flip it forward. And back again.

It is like when you are reading a book and the story jumps. The big bad wolf has eaten the little pigs, the children are suddenly grown up. You read on, joining up two broken sentences. And it flows on, gaps filled in by mind and thought and thoughtlessness. The story carries on and soon that little jump is forgotten.

But I pause, and I flip the pages of my journal backwards and forwards, forwards and backwards. From happy jumbled days to a woman made of skin and a smile.

There is something missing. Something that waits between the tick and the tock. An idea that bides its time. Somewhere between the old unending and the new beginning is a broken sentence.

I thumb the page itself. The edge of the page. When you cut a cloth with scissors, what is torn asunder — if the fabric is reassembled is it the same thickness, or is there something missing from the frayed edge? What is lost? Nothing more than a molecule.

But whole worlds live in atoms.

I thumb the page edge. It is, I notice, thicker than its fellows. Two pages have become joined together. Not through accident, I now realise. They have been glued. Half of one sentence and half of another have been stuck together. If I hold the paper up to the light I can see writing and drawings lost in between. Trapped stories. Things I have pulled from my mind to the page. Knowledge found then lost. Things I cannot put a name to.

But there is still plenty in this tired old head of mine. Still lots to come out. So perhaps, after all, it does not matter.

THE NINTH DOCTOR

→→→ SATURDAY, MARCH 26, 2005

For Rose

I still can't believe she's gone. I can't believe she's just vanished with that *Thing*. It's been nearly three weeks, and there's no sign of her. And here's me still looking out for big blue boxes. Maybe I've just gone crazy. Who could blame me?

I guess that's it – she's gone for good. But Jackie's not giving up. Oh no. Her little princess wouldn't just wander off, would she? So who's it gotta be? Me. Yeah right. Cos I'm the sort of bloke who'll murder his girlfriend then sit around watching telly till the police turn up. Three times I've been taken in. I told them – they should be talking to Jackie about the stuff she keeps putting through my letterbox.

Posted by **A Friend** at **3:46PM** 💬 **0 comments** ✉ 💬 **Links to this post**

→→→ TUESDAY, MARCH 29, 2005

Who is he?

He thinks he's so cool. All leather jacket and boots and big ears and shaved head. He might think I'm dumb, but I ain't thick. First thing I did was check my internet history and there it was – Rose had been searching for him and she found that dodgy website – **"Doctor Who?"**, run by that bloke Clive. I went back to that street to see him. Turned out he had been killed by those plastic things so I had to pretend I'd known him. His wife was nice, said I could take all the mad stuff from his shed. And that's when I found out how far all this goes. We are living in a completely different world and NOBODY has even noticed.

The cops keep going through my computer, so now I'm using internet cafes and keeping everything on disks. Clive was right. Dig deep enough on the internet and there's his name. The Doctor. Followed by a list of the dead. Everywhere. Krakatoa. The Titanic. JFK. He even worked for some secret army fighting Bog Monsters, years back. Every disaster, every mystery, he's been there. Maybe he's even making it all happen?

I miss her. And I'm scared.

Posted by **A Friend** at **10:26PM** 💬 **0 comments** ✉

APPEAL FOR ASSISTANCE

CAN YOU HELP?

Rose Tyler has been missing from her home on the Powell Estate since 6th March 2005.

Rose is described as 19 years old, 5' 4" in height, *slim* build with shoulder-length blonde hair.

Anyone with information regarding Rose should contact 0207 946000.

Have you seen Rose Tyler ?

Do you have any information?

Please call the information line on

0207 946000

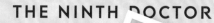

THE CORPORATION
INSURANCE CLAIM FORM

- IMPORTANT INFORMATION

Please complete all sections and return to us within 30 days. We will assess your returned claim form within 24 hours of receipt. Knowingly giving false or misleading information about an Insurance Claim is a criminal office under Peace Treaty 5.4/cup/16. If you have any questions about this claim form please contact the Corporation.

PERSONAL DETAILS

TITLE		OFFICE USE ONLY
FULL NAME	Lute and Coffa	
ADDRESS	The Forest of Cheem	
CLAIM NUMBER	02042005/1900-45a1	
DATE CLAIM FORM ISSUED	5.5/apple/26	

- INCIDENT DETAILS
- DESCRIPTION OF INCIDENT

Please provide as much detail as possible regarding your claim. Failure to provide detailed information may result in a delay in dealing with your claim or your claim being rejected.

Jabe of the Forest of Cheem perished in flames while preventing the destruction of Platform One during Earthdeath after a deliberate act of sabotage by the Lady Cassandra O'Brien Dot Delta Seventeen. With all safety syst...
gone, sun filters down...

THE CORPORATION
INSURANCE CLAIM FORM

- IMPORTANT INFORMATION

Please complete all sections and return to us within 30 days. We will assess your returned claim form within 24 hours of receipt. Knowingly giving false or misleading information about an Insurance Claim is a criminal office under Peace Treaty 5.4/cup/16. If you have any questions about this claim form please contact the Corporation.

PERSONAL DETAILS

TITLE		OFFICE USE ONLY
FULL NAME	Class 55	
ADDRESS	University of Rago Rago Five Six Rago	
CLAIM NUMBER	02042005/1900-45d4	
...ISSUED	5.5/apple/26	

...ease complete all sections and recui... ...im is a criminal of receipt. Knowingly giving false or misleading information about an Insuran... cup/16. If you have any questions about this claim form please contact the Corporation.

PERSONAL DETAILS

TITLE	The brothers Hop Pyleen	OFFICE ...
FULL NAME	Rex Vox Jax	
ADDRESS	02042005/1900-45c3	
CLAIM NUMBER	5.5/apple/26	
DATE CLAIM FORM ISSUED		

- INCIDENT DETAILS
- DESCRIPTION OF INCIDENT

Please provide as much detail as possible regarding your claim. Failure to provide detailed inf... dealing with your claim or your claim being rejected.

THE CORPORATION
INSURANCE CLAIM FORM

- IMPORTANT INFORMATION

Please complete all sections and return to us within 30 days. We will assess your retur... receipt. Knowingly giving false or misleading information about an Insurance Claim is a cr... cup/16. If you have any questions about this claim form please contact the Corporation.

PERSONAL DETAILS

TITLE		OF...
FULL NAME	Jolco and Jolco	
ADDRESS	Balhoon	
CLAIM NUMBER	02042005/1900-45b2	
DATE CLAIM FORM ISSUED	5.5/apple/26	

- INCIDENT DETAILS
- DESCRIPTION OF INCIDENT

Please provide as much detail as possible regarding your claim. Failure to provide detailed information may result in a delay in dealing with your claim or your claim being rejected.

The Moxx of Balhoon was reduced to ashes and dust on Platform One during Earthdeath after a deliberate act of sabotage by the Lady Cassandra O'Brien Dot Delta Seventeen. With all safety systems disabled, force fields gone, sun filters down and planet Earth about to explode, Platform One was...

→→→ FRIDAY, APRIL 1, 2005

Conspiracy

So how come there was never anything on the telly or in the papers? How can people get eaten by wheelie bins and shot by shop window dummies and it's not even on the News? It's got to be the Government, hasn't it? They've known about aliens for years. They've just kept us in the dark. Or maybe they're in on it. Maybe a big tub of Alien Gloop can't get itself under London without a bit of official help?

There must be people out there who could come forward and tell the truth.

Posted by **A Friend** at **3:58PM** ✉ **0 comments** ✉ 🗨 **Links to this post**

→→→ SATURDAY, APRIL 9, 2005

What the - ?

THE LIFE OF CHARLES DICKENS

the story. His final fancy for *The Mystery of Edwin Drood* was expressed in a letter in early October. "What should you think of the idea of the story continuing in this way?—Two people, a man and a woman—Mr Gabriel, a medium, and Mrs Plumchute, a false practitioner, both in residence at a spiritualist hotel." This was laid aside; but it left a marked trace on the story's conclusion as afterwards designed, in the position of Edwin Drood. I first heard of the later design in a letter dated "Sunday the 2nd of January 1870", in which he spoke of the change that had occurred to him for the new tale. "I laid aside the fancy I told you of, and have a very curious and new idea for my new story. Not an easily communicable idea, but a very strong one, though difficult to work. Mr Sneed, an undertaker, discovers that his parlour maid is possessed of some sixth sense. Together the pair witness an unholy rising from the dead, precipitated by a force of creatures composed entirely of gas. Edwin Drood's killer is not the boy's uncle—he is, in fact, not of this Earth." The climax of the story, I learnt immediately afterward, was to be that of the "blue elementals" and their quest to pass into our realm through some great deception; the originality of which was to consist in the authenticity of the parlour maid's mystical powers. The last chapters were to be written in the morgue of the funeral parlour.

465

This should be impossible. But who'd fake a photograph of Rose and *him* in Victorian Cardiff??

Posted by **A Friend** at **6:03AM** ✉ **0 comments** ✉ 🗨 **Links to this post**

Big Ben destroyed as a UFO crash lands in Central London.

LONDON UFO CRASH

The military are on the lookout for more spaceships. Until then, all flights in North American air space have been grounded.

And look at that, your very own spaceship ready to eat.

A body of some sort has been found inside the wreckage of the spacecraft.

Mystery still surrounds the whereabouts of the Prime Minister.

→→→ FRIDAY, JUNE 3, 2005

Missing Rose

Jackie's put up more posters round the estate. I feel a bit sorry for her now. But how can I tell her where Rose went? At least she's stopped accusing me and the police are leaving me alone. Taken in for questioning and released without charge FIVE TIMES! But they don't have a body, they don't have any evidence — how could they?

Posted by **A Friend** at **6:03AM** 💬 **0 comments** ✉ 🔗 **Links to this post**

Our inspectors have searched the above our heads and they have fo massive weapons of destructio

171

→→→ MONDAY, SEPTEMBER 5, 2005

Miracle?

I reckon Rose and *him* were in London in the Blitz. I've found this weird story about kids in gas masks terrorising the East End and some brilliant doctor finding a miracle cure for all his patients. That's got to be *him*, hasn't it? So maybe he's not that bad?

Posted by **A Friend** at **10:18AM** 💬 **0 comments** ✉ 🔗 **Links to this post**

→→→ SUNDAY, JANUARY 1, 2006

A New Life

They're never coming back, are they?

Time to move on. Eat chips. Go to work. Sleep. Have my lovely beans on toast and pretend there's nothing weird Out There. Bye Rose.

Posted by **A Friend** at **12:01AM** 💬 **0 comments** ✉ 🔗 **Links to this post**

SACRAMENTO POLICE DEPARTMENT
INFORMATION BULLETIN

CRIME/INCIDENT	LOCATION OF OCCURRENCE	DATE/TIME	CRIME/INCIDENT
164 RS	Greenhaven, Sacramento	05/02/12@0155hrs	164 RS
SUBMITTED BY	APPROVED BY	DATE SUBMITTED	DATE CANCEL
CSO Morris #1690	Sgt. J. Barnes	05/07/12	

THIS BULLETIN IS AUTHORIZED FOR PUBLIC DISSEMINATION

In the early hours of the second of May, officers were called to a disturbance at Riverside Blvd. on the South involving a vagrant. Observers described the unnamed male as 'a homeless brainless junkie'. When cautioned by officers, the man refused to cooperate, and simply repeated 'Don't you know who I am?' several times.

We need your help in identifying this man. Please report all previous sightings and any knowledge of his identity or origin. To report suspicious activity or persons or to report a crime, call the Police Department non-emergency number at **396-8602. For crimes in progress call 9-1-1.**

Looks a bit like Henry Van Statten. Get outta here!

→→→ TUESDAY, MARCH 7, 2006

We're just idiots

Blimey. Rose and the Doctor come back and the whole world changes again. Aliens and spaceships and dead politicians, all in public. They can't deny it now, can they? Oh, that's right – they can.

Great big green things with claws, stinking and wet and disgusting, pretending to be policemen. Big Ben in pieces. 10 Downing Street blown apart. Course it was all a hoax.

I've met the Slitheen and I helped the Doctor to beat them. So I guess I'm one of the good guys after all. And I guess that means the Doctor must be too. We saved the world.

Even Rose's mum's being nice to me. Jackie came round with loads of tubs of shepherd's pie, said I needed feeding up. Just when we thought Rose was back, her and the Doctor swan off again. Jackie asked him 'What if something happens to you and Rose is left all alone standing on some moon a million light years away?' You know what he said?

Nothing.

Peter & Jacqueline

Our wedding invitation

→→→ THURSDAY, JUNE 8, 2006

Don't forget to vote

Think I'll be voting for Harriet Jones. The Doctor seemed quite keen on her. Us good guys have to stick together.

(That girl in the shop, Rob Delaney's sister, I think she fancies me.)

Posted by **A Friend** at **12:01AM** 💬 **0 comments** ✉ 💬 **Links to this post**

→→→ THURSDAY, SEPTEMBER 7, 2006

Cardiff

Things I've learned this week:

1. Rose doesn't care about me, it's always going to be the Doctor. Never me.

2. I can't go out with Trisha because I'm going to spend the rest of my life waiting for Rose.

3. Rose is really boring when she's going on about TARDIS this TARDIS that. "Ooh Mickey, the Doctor took me to see the end of the world. And did I tell you about the Darlek?" Yeah yeah.

4. I really hate the Slitheen.

5. I've never met an American before. I don't like Americans either.

Posted by **A Friend** at **2:06PM** 💬 **0 comments** ✉ 💬 **Links to this post**

PROJECT TITLE: THE BLAIDD DRWG PROJECT/ PROSIECT Y BLAIDD DRWG

The BLAIDD DRWG project
Prosiect Y BLAIDD DRWG

APPOINTED ENGINEERS	PROJECT COMMISSIONED BY: **CARDIFF** City Authority
Butetown Construction	**CARDIFF** City Authority Awdurdod Dinas CAERDYDD
	263/801

Western Mail
NATIONAL NEWSPAPER OF WALES PAPUR CENEDLAETHOL CYMRU   www.icwales.co.uk   ◆◆ 40p

THE WONDER DIET
Find out what Kale can do for you

HOSPITAL WAITING LISTS
Wales still

Western Mail
NATIONAL NEWSPAPER OF WALES PAPUR CENEDLAETHOL CYMRU   www.icwales.co.uk   ◆◆ 40p

The Lady Mayor Vanishes

Blaidd Drwg future in doubt
by Cathy Salt

POLICE HAVE APPEALED for anyone with information on the whereabouts of Mrs Margaret Blaine, Cardiff's newly invested Mayor, to come forward as soon as possible. It is understood that additional officers have been drafted in from nearby forces to assist in the extensive search. Mayor Blaine, 56, had earlier hosted a launch party for the

Blaidd Drwg nuclear project planned for central Cardiff. While in development, the project has been affected by a series of unfortunate accidents, including the death of its architect. Fears were expressed last night that Mrs Blaine may have become the latest victim of the "curse" of Blaidd Drwg.

But members of the public and protesters against Blaidd Drwg are already suggesting that the project should be suspended – and Cardiff Castle reprieved – until it is known what has happened to the city's Mayor.

Mayor Blaine – The Last Interview? by Cathy Salt – see centre pages

Callers to Abigail Crowe's popular *Dark Talk* radio phone-in show were mostly hostile, with Owen Harper calling Blaine "obviously deranged" and her backing for a nuclear power station in the heart of Cardiff "bonkers".

A spokesman for the Mayor's office, Idris Hopper, told the *Western Mail* that Mrs Blaine (cont'd p.2

HOUSE PRICES ROCKET
...as celebs buy in the Bay

The BLAIDD DRWG project
Prosiect Y BLAIDD

→→→ THURSDAY, OCTOBER 19, 2006

Parting

Rose said: "The Doctor showed me a better way of living your life. That you don't just give up. You don't just let things happen. You make a stand. You say no. You have the guts to do what's right when everyone else just runs away."

Rose said: "There's nothing left for me here."

So I helped her go back to him. He sent her home to Jackie and me cos he knew she'd die if she stayed with him to fight the Daleks. He sent her home to live her life.

But I helped her go back to him.

AM 💬 **0 comments** ✉ 💬 **Links to this post**

▶ Job Opportunities

Controller

Location: The Game Station
Industry: Broadcasting
Level: Senior executive
Contract: Extremely permanent
Hours: Full time
Salary: Benefits to be agreed

This position would suit a female aged four to five years with no strong family ties. Applicants should be good with numbers. Applicants demonstrating any tendency to independent thought may be exterminated.

Apply: Bad Wolf Corporation, Game Station, Sol 3 orbital

Director of Programmes

Location: The Game Station
Industry: Broadcasting
Level: Executive
Contract: Probably temporary
Hours: Full time
Salary: To be agreed

We currently run a hundred different game shows, broadcasting to all households on planet Earth. We are always looking for experienced and dynamic individuals to ensure the effective delivery and sustainability of our current work, and when appropriate, to identify and create new programme models. Monitoring of contestants is a major part of the job, but people skills are unnecessary since all game-show participation is compulsory.

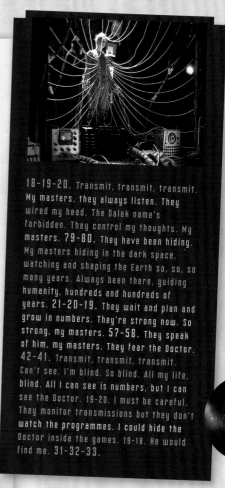

18-19-20. Transmit, transmit, transmit.
My masters, they always listen. They
wired my head. The Dalek name's
forbidden. They control my thoughts. My
masters. 79-80. They have been hiding.
My masters hiding in the dark space,
watching and shaping the Earth so, so, so
many years. Always been there, guiding
humanity, hundreds and hundreds of
years. 21-20-19. They wait and plan and
grow in numbers. They're strong now. So
strong, my masters. 57-58. They speak
of him, my masters. They fear the Doctor.
42-41. Transmit, transmit, transmit.
Can't see. I'm blind. So blind. All my life,
blind. All I can see is numbers, but I can
see the Doctor. 19-20. I must be careful.
They monitor transmissions but they don't
watch the programmes. I could hide the
Doctor inside the games. 19-18. He would
find me. 31-32-33.

→→→ TUESDAY, NOVEMBER 7, 2006

Pete Tyler

I'm round Jackie's all the time now. Help out around the flat — loads of things go wrong, but I reckon she just wants a bit of company. She does my dinner on a Sunday, talks about Rose all afternoon, yap yap yap. Today she asked me round again and she was quiet for once. Turns out it's the anniversary of Rose's dad getting knocked down. We drank Amaretto and she showed me photos of him, told me all about him. The driver stopped, waited for the police. It wasn't his fault. For some reason, Pete just ran out. People say there was this girl, and she sat with Pete while he was dying. She held his hand. Then she was gone. Nobody ever found out who she was.

But it was Rose. She told Jackie. The Doctor took her back to watch their wedding and then took her to be with Pete when he died. Rose said "That's how good the Doctor is."

Is that good? I don't know any more. Months ago, we talked, him and me. He said I could go with them and look out for Rose. And I said no, because I was scared of their life. It's just too much, I couldn't do it. But he didn't say his life was dangerous. He said *he* was dangerous. He gave me a disk with a virus on it that would destroy every mention of him online. "I would cease to exist."

Maybe it's time I used it?

Posted by **A Friend** at **11:42PM** **0 comments** **Links to this post**

The Story of Doctor Who

2003-2005

I think everybody has a memory of *Doctor Who* going right back to the early days of black and white, and being completely petrified and hiding behind the sofa. It was a fixture of the Saturday night schedule for so long and in so many people's lives, and it has never been recreated. And we kept saying, 'What we need is another thing like *Doctor Who*.' And then we suddenly thought, 'Well, actually, what we need is *Doctor Who*.'

Lorraine Heggessey, Controller, BBC One

It was my first meeting with Jane Tranter, the Drama commissioner, and she just came out with it and said, 'How would you feel about bringing back *Doctor Who*?'

Julie Gardner, Head of Drama, BBC Wales

Then all I had to do was find the right person to make it – and there was only one name. I'd never worked with Russell T Davies, but I knew his work very well,

and I had no hesitation asking him. He has terrific humanity, a brilliant sense of comedy, and is naturally witty, warm and irreverent. He has a very modern sensibility as a writer, and yet the themes of his stories are universal. And he is a terrific craftsman.

Jane Tranter, Controller, Drama Commissioning

When I walked into our first meeting, Jane just smiled and said, 'Off you go, if you want to.' It was confirmed as going out at seven o'clock, right from the word go, and that's the genius of it: not eight o'clock, not six o'clock, so we knew exactly where we were pitching it. Forty-five minutes was perfect, too – it's the perfect time for modern drama.

Russell T Davies, writer and executive producer

The most difficult thing about reviving the show was just people's expectations. Like any drama, you try to get the best scripts and the best talent attached, and the best

cast and crew, and you try to keep focus, and with something as big as this there were so many distractions. And you just have to keep plugging away at the script and what you're making, and just try to make the best drama you can.

Julie Gardner

It was daunting, but daunting in a good way. I love a challenge, and this has been a hell of a challenge – right from the word go, really.

Phil Collinson, producer

As soon as the show's return was announced, press interest was huge, with much discussion focusing on how scary the new series would be and which elements of the classic series would be retained...

Simply a Time Lord, with a human – that really classic combination. A police box, that's bigger on the inside than on the outside, the noise the TARDIS makes

CHRISTOPHER ECCLESTON

was the Ninth Doctor

We just wanted someone who would be a brilliant actor and who would surprise the audience and not be a predictable choice.

Julie Gardner

I would never have approached Chris in a million years, I don't think. I wouldn't have thought he'd have been interested.

Russell T Davies

I approached Russell. I read that he was going to do it and emailed him and said, 'When you draw up an audition list, put my name on it.' Because I'm a fan of his writing – I've worked with him on *The Second Coming*, I love *Bob and Rose*, I love *Mine All Mine*, I love *Queer as Folk* most of all, I think. It kind of changed television. So – easy. Which is crazy in a way because it is a big deal, I now realise! But I really didn't think, I didn't consider that. I just wanted to work with Russell.

Christopher Eccleston

Russell, Julie, Chris and I met up in Manchester, and had a talk about him coming and making *Doctor Who*. We were quite straightforward about what a challenge we knew it was going to be for any actor to take on, but we obviously didn't scare him and he was still up for it, so then we talked about a screen test.

Phil Collinson

He was absolutely wonderful; he had that balance of intensity and presence and emotion. It started to feel very real when he was there.

Julie Gardner

In lots of ways, Christopher Eccleston was by no means the most obvious choice, but as soon as we saw him audition, he played it in such an interesting way, and you thought, 'He's got real credibility, he's an incredible actor with real range, and he is going to bring out some hidden depths to Doctor Who.'

Lorraine Heggessey

Chris, as one of our finest actors, brings so much new to the part, and, for a whole generation of kids watching, there's going to be a completely new Doctor who's going to be absolutely theirs; that generation will own him.

Russell T Davies

I rather wrote him like he'd been in *The Second Coming*, and that seemed to work. Because I had that in my head, the Doctor of Russell's scripts sounded like Chris to me before he'd actually been cast, and I remember saying so in a production meeting, which must have made people wonder.

Paul Cornell

ECCLESTON *on* ECCLESTON

It's kind of the closest I've been to playing myself, in a way. It's like a version of me as a child, the way I felt about the world and everything that was in it, which we kind of, as we grow older, we possibly box in and change, but it's as close to myself as I've played it, I feel. And I based a lot on Russell, in a way... I kind of borrowed some of Russell's speed of thought and pace, and it's his words, really.

Christopher Eccleston

It's great, all the profile you get, but it's a difficult thing to do; you're the motor for every scene, you have to deliver a lot of pseudo-scientific jargon and give it some charisma and wit. I just think it's a fantastic series, and I'm proud to be part of it.

Christopher Eccleston

I think I've given quite a flamboyant performance, really. I wanted the flamboyance and the eccentricity to be in the performance – I wanted to see if I could convince you that he was an alien with the performance. And I think if I'd had a flamboyant costume as well you would've needed a circus tent, really, to contain me. I am different from all the previous Doctors, there is a line between all of them in that they speak in received pronunciation. I think it's good that we say to kids actually, people who sound like me can also be heroic and very intelligent. It's a good message to send, really.

Christopher Eccleston

when it takes off, and the theme tune. And the sonic screwdriver. Those are the basic principles. And the concept, the concept is the most fundamental thing to keep. They land somewhere, they have an adventure, they escape and save the world. Good concept.

Russell T Davies

It's a balance. We knew that we were going after that family audience, dads and mums watching with kids, and we wanted to be as scary as we could while also being really responsible so we don't leave kids in terror, but we want to scare them during the 45 minutes.

Julie Gardner

If you're 8 years old and you're sitting there watching this, then you don't want to bring a whole load of baggage from the past – this is a new start. I thought Paul McGann was brilliant and a fantastic Doctor and sadly didn't get enough of a chance. But we never even approached him, right from the very first script – we were going to start from new. And if you're a fan, you can go and make up a story in your head about how Paul McGann became Chris Eccleston!

Russell T Davies

I don't think Russell could have done anything but build on it because he was so interested and embroiled in all the *Doctor Who* folklore.

Jane Tranter

It felt important for the first series to get writers who knew the language, the shorthand of the original series. Not in a fannish way, but people who would understand when I said to them they could use the sonic screwdriver, but not to save the world.

Russell T Davies

The biggest challenge was the whole notion of how to create a living, breathing new television series, rather than a kind of faithful recreation of the past.

Mark Gatiss, writer

It wasn't the industry we know today. At first, it felt quite small and marginal, a long shot. The decor on the corridors of BBC Wales was all about local services then. I grew to loathe the child's voice in the lifts that yelled out the number of the floor it was stopping at. I think my introduction to making the show there was in such small increments that I never really had an enormous 'wow' moment until broadcast night. It felt like there was something deliberate about that, for all of us, we were afraid to count our chickens.

Paul Cornell, writer

Christopher Eccleston's casting was announced in April 2004, and press attention promptly turned to who might play the Doctor's new companion, Rose Tyler. For once, the press speculation was well founded...

It is fair to say that from the minute she came through the door we all knew we'd found our Rose, but we couldn't quite believe it. I think we saw about forty different girls over three days, but we kept coming back to Billie Piper.

Phil Collinson

I think Billie is a terrific actress. She was in *The Canterbury Tales* on the BBC last year and she is just one of those people who lights up the screen, has a natural presence, great warmth and I think she'll

---

Script editor Donald Tosh on
THE END OF THE WORLD

Back in the mid-1960s, when John Wiles and I were steering the good ship *Who*, he had been obsessed with the idea of a huge spaceship leaving doomed Earth at the end of its natural life in order to colonise a 'sympathetic planet'. Just before we finished, we produced *The Ark* with the writer Paul Erickson. This then wildly ambitious story was duly watched by the second-lowest viewing figures of our time. That was unfortunate, but perhaps it seemed to fall between several stools while trying to reach out into a new era. In 2005, however, in the second story under the splendid, reviving hands of Russell T Davies and his colleagues (plus a budget that we couldn't have dreamt of!) and the use of some marvellous technology that we might have dreamt of but wasn't available then, along comes *The End of The World*.

I have loved the 'new' *Doctor Who* stories. They are full of excitement, fun and humour and a nice, fine, black edge. I don't know if the 8-year-olds still watch it from behind the sofa – probably not; 8-year-olds are much older than they were back in the 1960s – but I have watched it and cheered

the Doctor(s) and his companions on, as they have saved the world or saved something worth saving on their space and time related journeys.

The End of The World is special not only because of all those aliens, which reminded me of the space parliament in *The Daleks' Master Plan*, but also because it produced a gloriously dotty, evil villainess in Cassandra (so wonderfully voiced by Zoë Wanamaker). She is wicked in the same vein that Mavic Chen was wicked back in the 1960s and, long after we have forgotten some of the ins and outs of the story, we find we can recall gestures or lines by these splendid creatures and feel again that frisson of alarm coupled with a smile.

Christopher Eccleston is on top form, his Doctor showing that laconic objectivity, and a toughness with the humane touch. Billie Piper proves what an excellent actress she is, with her display of a huge range of reactions to what appears to be Armageddon. All in all, *The End of The World*, beautifully scripted and directed, takes us by the hand and shows us the ultimate end, so that then the programme can go back in time and fill in all the gaps for many seasons yet to come.

give *Doctor Who* a run for its money as well. So in the same way that Chris will be a modern Doctor Who, Billie is very much a modern Doctor Who's assistant.

Lorraine Heggessey

I think we were well cast... we were very cleverly put together. We had a great time. It was hard, we didn't know each other, we were thrown together for eight months, six days a week, fourteen to sixteen hours a day. Both with our careers on the line in a way: hers at the beginning; mine in the middle. And I think we did really, really well.

Christopher Eccleston

They're on a par with one another, more like partners, and the audience sees everything through Rose's eyes. She's human, the Doctor's an alien, and she's experiencing all these alien situations throughout the series. At times, the whole thing is slightly overwhelming for her, but she can cope with it and match the Doctor. He is constantly challenging her, trying to broaden her horizons, and she's trying to show him how to be more in touch with human emotions.

Billie Piper (Rose Tyler)

Doctor Who's always been a hero, and there's been no heroine there for 8- to 12-year-old girls or women watching the programme, and we've now got one. Billie carries the series with me. A man

and a woman do this thing together, and she, well, she's a heroine. She saves his life in the first episode, teaches him huge emotional lessons, as does he. And Billie pulled it off.

Christopher Eccleston

The series is a great balance between science fiction, which can be a bit detached, and real, genuine emotions. I don't think I would have done it if it was strictly sci-fi, as much as I've enjoyed being chased by monsters! I get my biggest buzz from working opposite Christopher when Rose and the Doctor are having 'domestic' conversations. If Rose had been older she might not have gone off in the first place with this strange man who calls himself the Doctor and abandoned the life she knows. But when we first see her she's so bored and

looking for excitement. She feels trapped and doesn't want the kind of mundane life she's living. But then she meets this guy who totally shakes up her world.

Billie Piper

You've got the freedom to go anywhere in time and space, and that is wonderful and liberating. It can also get annoying, because it means there's no anchor, there's no connection to the people watching, which is a very, very important thing. And you're only going to do that by constantly bringing Rose back to Earth.

Russell T Davies

Jackie was totally real, an ordinary mum waiting for her daughter, not knowing where she'd been for a year, so anything could have happened to her.

Camille Coduri (Jackie Tyler)

Camille was instantly Jackie. I think if you put her and Billie together, they look alike. With Camille, we just laughed from the first time she opened her mouth.

Phil Collinson

There's implications of someone disappearing. I think they kept her coming back to show how it affected her mother and her boyfriend.

Noel Clarke (Mickey Smith)

Noel Clarke was the only person who read the audition scripts with enough lightness. Everyone else delivered Mickey as a very hard, a very angry character. What Noel did was to make it sparkle. I knew then that we could eventually make Mickey stronger, and put him aboard the TARDIS as a full-time companion in the second series.

Russell T Davies

The first production block for Series One began in Cardiff and London in July 2004, comprising Episodes 4 and 5, Aliens of London *and* World War Three, *and the series opener,* Rose...

Look how much of this show is defined by Mickey Smith. Rose is meant to be the everyman, the companion, the touchstone by which we measure everything – but *Rose* uses Mickey as an equal and opposite insight. I don't remember doing that deliberately, but it works.

Russell T Davies

181

The first few episodes had to introduce the show's icons to a massive new audience, while remaining faithful to the original series...

Our design team chose to keep a lot of the iconography of the inside of the TARDIS; I mean, they had a completely free hand but actually I think they loved the old one as much as everyone else did, and they've updated it.

Russell T Davies

The brief I gave was that you don't build a TARDIS, you grow one – a phrase that actually turned up in a script, but I'm not sure whether I got the line from Russell or vice versa. I wanted to be able to say to the public that the TARDIS had changed so much because it was nine hundred years old; it had developed; it's organic.

Edward Thomas, production designer

The ambitious first production block featured invasions by Slitheen and Autons, with lots of stunts, practical effects and explosions. The availability of computer-generated imagery (CGI) had transformed the show's possibilities...

At the first tone meeting in Cardiff, we were all preparing for the fact that in four weeks we would be filming with Autons and Slitheen. We had more experience than anyone else of how to make a big lumbering creature – we also knew that when a script required a Slitheen to run down a corridor, a man in a rubber suit, who can't see anything in front of him and

has a ten-kilo animatronic head on, isn't going to do it very well. So we suggested The Mill did it as CGI. Sometimes the Slitheen were men in suits, but the running was CGI.

Neill Gorton, Millennium FX

At one point, we looked seriously at building the entire frontage of Number 10 and Number 11 Downing Street and blowing them to pieces but costs started to spiral... In the end, we built a one-third-scale model of the door, and shot that being blown out, against black. The Mill were then able to composite that over the plate photography of the Downing Street set.

Mike Tucker, Model Unit

The lady who did the Additional Dialogue Recording phoned me, saying, 'You're doing a Nestene voice.' I said, 'What's that like?' and she said, 'Oh, Russell said you'd know.' I went in to Air Studios and stood in front of an enormous screen, doing a lot of snarling and burping. They had several lines they wanted me to say: one featured the word 'Doctor', one was 'Time Lord'...

Nicholas Briggs (Nestene voice)

The Nestene's words would prove key to the story of the Ninth Doctor...

The Doctor's journey through this series is one of having to come to terms with what's happened to his people and what's happened to his planet, and the profound sense of loss and possibly guilt and loneliness that he feels. Talking to Chris about what it's like to feel that lonely was a key to making those scenes soulful and truthful.

Euros Lyn, director

When I first read a scene description that said, 'The Earth blows up,' I always knew that it was possible, but the question was – how? Episode 2 involves a huge amount of CGI; there's something in the region of about 220 CGI shots. When we stage the scenes, obviously those elements aren't there. The camera's moving around, following something that doesn't exist. All the actors are there, their eyelines looking at things that aren't there. And then when you cut it together in the first picture cut, they're still absent, so you're looking at something that's half-finished. And it stays half-finished until the very last moment of post-production, so there's a huge leap of faith that you have to make...

Euros Lyn

Flying Daleks. How marvellous is that? When I was young and watching the Daleks, I never sat there thinking they couldn't go upstairs because I knew they could. It hadn't been seen on television, but there were comic strips and books, those marvellous old strips with Daleks flying about on their little hoverbout things. But I wanted them to fly independently, to be able to just rise up, gracefully.

Russell T Davies

My favourite alien is the Dalek. Because of the psychology that goes on between the Daleks and the Doctor. They know more than you all do about the Doctor's history and they use it on him. It's not so much the suckers and the lasers for me, with the Daleks, it's the insight they have about the Doctor's history and personal and emotion history.

Christopher Eccleston

The most exciting moments writing *Dalek* were when I got to challenge all those lazy ways the Daleks had been mocked over the years. It was getting to use the sink plunger! It was getting them flying upstairs! And, most of all, it was that bit when the Dalek breaks its chains and can stop play-acting, when it can exult

in its own power once more. 'The Daleks survive in me!'

Robert Shearman, writer

When I started writing *Father's Day*, I think I initially overcompensated, with a bit of cultural cringe, and wrote something that didn't feel enough like *Doctor Who*. I, and I think a few of the others, also wrote for a very cheaply made show, when actually we had a bit of money. It was quite a pleasure to discover that the baby hadn't been thrown out with the bathwater, and that this was indeed going to feel quite a lot like old-school *Doctor Who*.

Paul Cornell

Whatever I wrote had to be stitched into the visuals of the time. It's the Blitz and it's terrible with London being bombed, but Russell felt that there's an iconography and a terribly romantic mood to that period. And of course gas masks look creepy. I saw a little picture of a boy in a gas mask that looked so scary because there is nothing more symptomatic of a world gone wrong than a child in a gas mask.

Steven Moffat, writer

I remember writing this and thinking, 'What is the most jeopardy I can get Rose

into within five or six minutes?' I figured hanging from a barrage balloon during the London Blitz, wearing a Union Jack, has got to be uncomfortable.

Steven Moffat

Steven Moffat's The Empty Child *also introduced a new – and long-running – companion, Captain Jack Harkness...*

I play an intergalactic, 51st-century Time Agent, who hooks up with the Doctor and Rose and becomes the male assistant. If it were a swimming pool, he never just tests

the water; he jumps in head first rather than feet first, and that's what I like about him – he acts spontaneously.

John Barrowman (Captain Jack Harkness)

I was given four hundred provisos. Jack had to be a military man, heroic and dashing, good with guns. And, although it wasn't a big part of the brief, he was pansexual. I also knew that he was on board specifically because there was going to be a grand battle in the last episode and they needed to have a soldier around to do the soldiery bits. The idea of him being this kind of intergalactic con-man was mine.

Steven Moffat

Before Captain Jack's entrance in The Empty Child, *Series One had pulled off its own con-trick at the end of* Dalek, *seeming to introduce a new companion called Adam Mitchell...*

We have someone who is just like a child in a sweetshop: he has no responsibility; he is totally self-motivated, and he's clever and informed in a way that Rose isn't... Leaving Adam with doors in his head is a comedic punctuation to *The Long Game*, and in a sense he's got what he wanted – he wanted to be ahead of the game, he wanted to be more advanced, but was too greedy, and now he's got doors in his head! Let that be a lesson! The Doctor and

Rose are a team, and Adam just didn't live up to the Doctor's expectations.

Helen Raynor, script editor

Adam was played by Bruno Langley, one of a number of high-profile guest stars the new series quickly attracted. Several of them became recurring characters in later series, sometimes in very unusual ways...

Episode 2 included an entire CG character, the Lady Cassandra – a tricky sequence to cut when you haven't got anybody there at all, and what they shot on set didn't even have Zoë Wanamaker playing the part. So what we did, once Zoë was cast, she did the voice as if she was doing it for an animated sequence, and we filmed her in a studio. And we took her mouth area as a pattern for the animation we applied.

John Richards, video editor

Simon Callow responded to the whole idea of Charles Dickens as this weary man, seeing fantastical things. I really love the séance when he's watching as the Tribune of the Gelth appear, and you completely believe what he's seeing; his eyes are full of wonder.

Mark Gatiss

I really have been sworn to secrecy on that project... But let's just say that I will be using that famous black door at No 10 Downing Street.

Penelope Wilton (Harriet Jones, MP for Flydale North)

So much of *Father's Day* is down to Shaun Dingwall as Pete Tyler – he can make the most ordinary man seem to be someone you want to love. It takes real acting talent to make someone seem so ordinary and yet so important.

Helen Raynor

In rehearsals for *World War Three*, I read in for Chris for an afternoon. I'd never met Annette Badland before, but we did that scene where Margaret Slitheen reveals the evil plan to the Doctor... and she scared the pants off me! Right there and then I began to think ahead and saw a nice gap in Episode 11...

Russell T Davies

When we first discussed *Boom Town*, it was supposed to be utterly effects-less. It was going so well until Russell decided he wanted an earthquake in Cardiff!

Julie Gardner

Sixth Doctor Colin Baker on
THE EMPTY CHILD *and*
THE DOCTOR DANCES

The day after the brilliantly titled *The Empty Child* first aired, I visited a local primary school and was delighted (if that's the right word) to see children wandering around the playground intoning eerily, 'Are you my mummy?' The chilling image of the forlorn gas-masked figure of a child seeking its mother had clearly made an impression that served to propel younger viewers back behind the sofa where we all know they belong.

This story achieved what Roald Dahl always contrived to do so well. The fear factor was neatly racked up to the very point where parents might begin to be a bit concerned for their little ones, forgetting the huge part that fear can play in stimulating imagination and enabling developing minds to work their way through some of the more difficult bits of what it can be to be a human being.

The second episode of this two-parter has another inspired title that uplifts and excites in the same way as the first part's title chills and menaces. The

denouement of the story brings about the best single line I can recall from *Doctor Who* – a line that in this age of mission statements could easily be inscribed somewhere in the TARDIS 'pour encourager les autres': 'And everybody lives, Rose! Everybody lives! I need more days like this,' the Doctor says before showing us his moves. I must confess to feeling a shiver of recognition and joy down to the base of my spine when Christopher Eccleston spoke those words and I realised how neatly they described for me what the Doctor is all about.

And then of course there was Captain Jack and the sonic screwdriver exchange with the Doctor. That made me laugh a lot.

It did not escape this viewer either that the title of the first episode paid silent homage (intended?) to the first ever outing for the Doctor in 1963 entitled *An Unearthly Child*. I think that 'empty' manages to neatly trump 'unearthly' and elegantly raised the stakes for a new generation of viewers.

I loved the script, which wasn't as technically challenging as the others: a Slitheen on a toilet in Cardiff, and an earthquake. It was more of a character piece, less about monsters. I loved the stuff with the Doctor and Margaret in the restaurant... *Boom Town* was a lot easier, despite the fact that we used a lot of public locations around Cardiff Bay.

Joe Ahearne, director

We've managed to film in places that a normal drama series would never be able to do. The police have been fantastic at closing roads for us. We closed one of the main roads in the centre of Cardiff on a Wednesday night, and the police said to me, 'This is *Doctor Who*; you wouldn't be able to do this if it wasn't, but we'll help you.' Cardiff's wonderful to film in because it has everything, and we've done everything with it: we've turned Cardiff into London; we've filmed in neo-classical buildings and turned them into space stations...

Phil Collinson

The Daleks returned in force for the series finale, a two-part epic in which Rose Tyler saved the world but lost the Doctor – a carefully planned surprise exit for

```
126   INT. TARDIS - DAY 126
      ROSE, on the floor, blinks, awakes, confused.
      WIDE SHOT, as she stands. The room swaying a little, the
      Rotor rising and falling, the Doctor slamming levers, happy.
      The two of them together, just like the old days.

                    THE DOCTOR
          Where d'you fancy next? How about
          Barcelona? Not the city Barcelona, the
          planet Barcelona, you'd love it.
          Fantastic place, they've got dogs with
          no noses, imagine how many times a day
          you end up saying that joke. And it's
          still funny!

                    ROSE
          … but what happened?

                    THE DOCTOR
          Don't you remember?

                    ROSE
          It's like… there was this singing.

                    THE DOCTOR
          That's right, I sang a song and the
          Daleks ran away!

                    ROSE
          No, but what happened?

                    THE DOCTOR
          No, but what happens next? I promised
          you the universe, and that's what
          we're gonna see. Next stop, Barcelona!
          Or somewhere, anywhere, I don't care,
          we can go anywhere and do anything.

      He glances down. On the scanner: an image of Rose, alien
      letters scrolling up and down. And the words:

      ROSE TYLER. TIME DAMAGE. LIFEFORM DYING.

      The Doctor gives her a lovely smile.

                    THE DOCTOR
          And we've got the rest of our lives
          to do it!

      And Rose smiles too, trusting him completely.
                                        CUT TO:

127   EXT. FX SHOT 127
      The TARDIS tumbles away, into the Vortex, smaller and
      smaller, gone…

      END OF EPISODE THIRTEEN
```

Christopher Eccleston that ultimately fell victim to intense tabloid interest in the show...

We weren't just doing the regeneration – we also recorded a fake scene where Rose is supposedly dying from Time Vortex damage. The plan was to put that into the edit then replace it at the last moment before broadcast. It would have been great if the episode had gone out in June and all the press had reviewed the dummy ending. Then people would have been hit between the eyes with the regeneration.

Joe Ahearne

The central problem is that the BBC is a public service broadcaster, so we are Not Allowed to Lie – and we end up craven and apologetic. That's why the leak about Christopher Eccleston leaving could not be plugged. Once asked by *The Mirror*, Jane Tranter could not deny it. Even though it ruined the surprise cliffhanger to Series One.

Russell T Davies

Series One launched on 26 March 2005, with Rose *watched by almost 11 million UK viewers. Some of whom had seen it a fair number of times already...*

I wish I'd kept count. The crucial thing is the edit, where you might watch it 15 times or so. Or 20, or 25. Which means, in total... maybe 50 times? We actually had a screening in France where I fell asleep, that's when I knew I'd reached my limit. Though I'd love to see it again now!

Russell T Davies

It hit me, watching *Rose*, that this show is exactly what I wanted it to be – and it is, in its first 45 minutes, exactly what it is now. It has never fundamentally changed. There has been no mission creep since 2005, no timidity, no reversals. There has been development and exploration, but no wandering. It's a powerful template, still at work today.

Russell T Davies

We took time to get the schedule to work, as every new drama does. You just don't have 'Downton Confidential' or 'Call the Midwife Magazine' to tell you what goes on

behind the scenes with every other drama ever made. And the production team itself likes telling funny stories and anecdotes, so we beef up the stresses, to make a good yarn. But it's nonsense. We shot every day, we achieved the page count, we found the money, we transmitted exactly what I'd written, and the show got on air on time, exactly as planned. That's a production triumph.

Russell T Davies

If people remember me just for this, I'd be happy to be remembered, really.

Christopher Eccleston

The most important thing about *Doctor Who* isn't that I left but that I did it. Those 13 episodes were a real success and I'm proud of the work. I'm very proud of what we did with it.

Christopher Eccleston

It was a great part. I loved playing him. I loved connecting with that audience. Because I've always acted for adults and then, suddenly, you're acting for children, who are far more tasteful: it's either good, or it's bad.

Christopher Eccleston

I'm hugely grateful to the children who to this day come up and talk to me about the show.

Christopher Eccleston

I've loved taking part in the basic essence and message of the series, which is: it's a short life – seize it and live it as fully as you can, care for others, be respectful of all other life forms, regardless of colour or creed. And to be part of that has been fantastic.

Christopher Eccleston

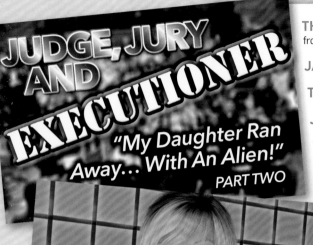

JUDGE, JURY AND EXECUTIONER

"My Daughter Ran Away… With An Alien!" PART TWO

"My daughter ran away with an alien"

JACKIE TYLER

THE HOST: Welcome back. Before the break, we were hearing from Jackie—

JACKIE: Hello, yes.

THE HOST: Jackie, you were telling us how your daughter, Rose—

JACKIE: Rose, yes.

THE HOST: Can you not do that, please? How your daughter, Rose, ran away with an alien called the Doctor! Now, the next 18 months were awful for you, but things got even worse when you found yourself helping her go back to him.

JACKIE: I did, yes. Well, me and Mickey.

AUDIENCE: Oooh! Shame!

THE HOST: But things got even stranger when Rose came home for Christmas and brought the Doctor with her… Can you tell us what happened?

JACKIE: Well, I'd done all the presents under the tree, nothing flashy, you know, but I did get something for Rose, just in case she came back, nice new red top, because that old one was full of holes. And she did come back. That spaceship of his, crashing in the Estate, knocking over all the bins.

THE HOST: That's the Doctor's TARDIS. And Mickey's Rose's boyfriend?

JACKIE: Well, he was until that Doctor came along. Then he wasn't good enough for her no more, poor lamb. Then it turned out she'd left him not for one alien but for two! Suddenly we had a whole new Doctor – there's this complete stranger lying in the street with my Rose saying, 'That's him, that's the Doctor.' She comes swanning back, cool as you like, all 'Oh, his blood's top secret, he's got two hearts, he can change his face…'

THE HOST: It must have been very difficult to accept him?

JACKIE: Didn't have any choice, did I? Put him in Rose's room, give him a bed, well, he's sick, you've got to help, haven't you? I was just glad to have her back. Mind you, she was a bit, you know, thinking she's better than everyone else cos she's saved the world and she's met the Prime Minister. But life goes on, doesn't it? It's not all big green things exploding in your face, you've still got to have your tea and do the washing.

THE HOST: Except that with the Doctor and Rose back it was all about the monsters again pretty quickly, wasn't it?

JACKIE: Ooh, I tell you, I thought I was going to get killed by a Christmas tree!

THE HOST: I'm going to stop you there and bring on somebody who's also had a Christmas visit from the Doctor – Sylvia Noble… Sylvia, thanks for coming on the show.

SYLVIA: I'm delighted to be here, Dr… er…

THE HOST: Great. So – Christmas with the Doctor – festive fun for all the family?

SYLVIA: I should say not! That wedding was a disaster from beginning to end. First, my Donna does her silly vanishing act at the altar. Off she goes to who knows where, then she's waltzing back into the reception with him, all teeth and charm, as if nothing's happened. Lovely hotel, all of our family and our friends, and Donna and her Doctor are being chased by robot Santas—

JACKIE: Ooh, I've seen robot Santas!

SYLVIA: Well, let me tell you, the mess they made! Christmas tree baubles exploding everywhere, Father Christmases shooting at us – it was just awful! And all thanks to that Doctor.

SYVLIA NOBLE
"Aliens ruined my girl's Xmas wedding"

Sunday Mirror
03/09/06 **13**

HARRIET JONES: A modern Thatcher

By VIVIEN ROOK

SOME say she will be the architect of a new Golden Age for Britain. She's clearly not best pleased when I tell her that I'll be comparing her – favourably! – to Margaret Thatcher in this piece, but Harriet Jones is too canny, too clever and far too sensible to raise any objection more vocal than an eyebrow.

But Britain's new Prime Minister, with her landslide majority, her evident political nous and her ability to tap into the concerns of real people out there, well away from the still-oh-so-male Westminster, owes an obvious debt to her celebrated predecessor.

"Oh, well, I wouldn't really want to get into that sort of comparison,' she tells me with typically pleasant

steel. 'I mean, I don't think, if you don't mind, I don't think it's terribly helpful to be comparing people in that way, especially simply because we're both women."

But she quickly and quietly changes tack to admit certain common traits.

"I think you could say that we both are immensely proud of the people of our great nation and the people of our planet, that we both would place unwavering trust in the human race. That's why it's just as important to be putting into place something like my cottage hospitals sch—

as you know, cottage hospitals not to be excluded from Centres of Excellence, which is something that will be truly beneficial to thousands of our older citizens – and, at the same time, to be working hard to ensure that our country and our great planet are properly defended."

She pauses for breath, just long enough for me to observe that she's as good at the tiny detail as she is at the bigger picture – and then she's off again.

"That's where I completely disagree, I'm sorry to say. I don't see either of those as a small thing. They're both vital for our future."

So what about the really big stuff – the imminent mission to Mars that until recently looked like an

POLICE DEPARTMENT
CITY OF NEW NEW YORK

5,000,000,023/04/17

From: Patrol Supervisor
To: Commanding Officer
Subject: Multiple arrests at New New York Hospital

1. On Saturday 15 April 5,000,000,023, officers were called to New New York Hospital by Frau Clovis, personal aide to the Duke of Manhattan. They discovered that the Hospital had been placed under emergency automatic quarantine.
2. On gaining access to the Hospital, officers learned that the Sisters of Plenitude had been farming force-grown human clones and experimenting on them to synthesize cures for diseases. Genetic experimentation of this nature is prohibited under Peace Treaty 5.4/cup/19.
3. The farmed clones had earlier broken out of their containment chambers and rampaged through the hospital, infecting patients, visitors and staff. This led to the automatic quarantine of the Hospital.
4. The emergency was resolved by a doctor, who successfully inoculated all Hospital occupants, including the farmed clones. This doctor has since absconded with his assistant, and is being urgently sought to assist police with their enquiries.
5. One distinguished patient is also missing: the Face of Boe.
6. Forensic officers uncovered evidence of the illegal use of a psycho-graft device in the Hospital basement.

JACKIE: Yeah, but the Doctor stopped them, didn't he? Pointed his sunny screwdriver at them and they ran away?

SYLVIA: Oh, he stopped them, all right. Blew them up, somehow or other. But who did he think was going to have to pay for all the damage? My poor Geoffrey, God rest his soul, that's who! Wedding insurance doesn't include alien invasions, you know! No, the father of the bride has to pick up the pieces while the bride runs off with her latest fancy man. Floating around without a care in the world, the pair of them, while London's being attacked by a giant Christmas star. Poor Geoff was worried sick.

THE HOST: So Donna left to travel with the Doctor?

SYLVIA: Oh no – home she traipsed, Christmas night, tail between her legs, and moped around the house for a year.

JACKIE: You're lucky. My Rose couldn't wait to be back off out there with him. I'd not see her for months on end.

SYLVIA: You poor dear. I met your Rose, you know – very polite young lady, even with that big gun. Took the top clean off one of those dreadful Dalek things, she did. Lovely girl.

JACKIE: That's my Rose. Didn't sit still for a minute once she was with him. Still, they'd pop back sometimes, you know, she used to bring me funny little presents from other planets, and I'd get the odd phone call—

SYLVIA: Ha! You wouldn't catch my Donna bothering to pick up the phone. No, she went off with him without a word. Sent postcards to her granddad, mind you, but she never told her own mother what they were up to.

THE HOST: And what were they up to?

SYLVIA: Well, I wouldn't know, would I? They didn't let me in on their little secrets. You'll have to ask her grandfather.

JACKIE: Ooh, they went all over, Mickey used to say she never stopped going on about it. Five billion years in the future, black holes, the Olympics, Queen Victoria, a school full of bat-people, the Coronation. They even went to France!

THE HOST: But sometimes they brought the danger home with them?

JACKIE: Yes, oh, that Martian thing on the telly!

THE HOST: That would be the Sycorax.

JACKIE: Him, yeah. The Doctor can say what he likes, I'm glad that Harriet Jones blew up that dirty great spaceship. And then there were those horrible Zybermen. They wanted to turn me into one of them! And that's when everything changed again.

THE HOST: The Battle of Canary Wharf. That's when you and Rose died?

JACKIE: You're a cheery one, aren't you? We didn't die, we just went to live… with Pete… Hang on…!

THE HOST: Let's just go back to the Cybermen.

JACKIE: God, they were so scary! Them and those Daleks. But the Doctor sorted them out. Looked like a prawn, but good in a crisis. Sent them all into Hell, and good riddance.

THE HOST: We're going to take another break now, but afterwards, we'll meet another mother whose daughter got caught up in the Doctor's world. Don't go away.

NASA

NATIONAL AERONAUTICS AND
SPACE ADMINISTRATION

July 12, 1979

TO: ▮▮▮▮
FROM: ▮▮▮▮
SUBJECT: Skylab re-entry

As requested by your memorandum, ▮▮▮▮, preliminary analysis has been completed on the Skylab debris recovered between Esperance and Rawlinna, Western Australia.

▮▮▮▮▮▮▮▮▮▮▮▮▮▮▮▮
▮▮▮▮▮▮▮▮▮▮▮▮▮▮▮▮

The thumbprint found on the ▮▮▮▮ has been positively identified. We have been instructed to make no further mention of the Doctor's role in the Skylab recovery mission.

UNIT: Sycorax – English Vocab

aboard - foraxi
and - fel
armada - staa
best - falfass
blue - creffic
blonde - bass
box - tagsalla
but - fel
bring - crel
care - passic
cattle - gatzaa
child - chafeen
choice - codsyla
christmas - craffor
clever - gilfane
compare - bec
come - cal
curse - cast
darkness - dashfellik
die - chack chiff
fleet - staa
final - bakthaa
funny - practeel
girl - cahoonic
half - gatrosca
has - pandat
invasion - Shantakra

is - si
it - stat
jump - vastrati
land - hutsa
machine - casvold
machinery
 - casvoldeera
mighty - telpo
mineral - tor
nothing - non
no - non
not - non
now - ka
offer - castreeck
our - da
or - col
own - pandat
people - gatzaa
population - foscaan
possess - codrafee
precious - pedra
property - codra
panthak
release - rastac
rock - faa
sell - vendi
so - bol

slavery - venissi
species - brendissa
stolen - stapeen
stone - cay
stride - gassac
strong - jak
summon - cal prec
(come here)
surrender - jalvaaan
sycorax - sycora
the - pel
therefore - bol
think - tass
third - potrosca
to - me
us - codrakone
very - gan
wasteland - vash
we - codrafee
welcome - padskaa
will - massac
with - met
women - pandack
word - vol
yellow - bass
you - so
your -

Balmoral Castle

October 23, 1879

The Queen thanks the Lord Provost for his communication of yesterday, which she received this morning. She quite approves the steps taken by the City of Aberdeen to hunt down this Doctor and Miss Tyler, and concurs in the Lord Provost's views. The Queen accepts entirely that the Lord Provost himself played no part in the deceptions. That the Doctor appeared before his Queen under a false identity and presenting fabricated credentials and forged documents is indeed most heinous. Yet, if our understanding of the Doctor's modus operandi is true, there may be little hope of discovering either his whereabouts or his identity. He will continue to play, as he always does, a double game, revelling in unimaginable horrors, despite all surrounding carnage, perhaps for ulterior objects. Let it be understood, however, that there shall be no overturning of the investitures of Sir Doctor of Tardis nor Dame Rose of the Powell Estate. These honours were bestowed in grateful reward for genuine service, in protecting the Queen from an unspeakable beast at the heart of a wicked conspiracy. We may none of us speak publicly of the many tales of man becoming wolf, but the Queen can vouch for their veracity. The Queen is preparing the foundation of an Institute to investigate such strange happenings and defend our borders, and its powers shall include a duty of vigilance in matters concerning the Doctor. The Lord Provost need, therefore, devote no further energies to the matter.

MYSTERY BUG STRIKES SCHOOL

UP TO seven teaching staff at local high school Deffry Vale have gone down with severe flu-like symptoms, head teacher Mr Finch confirmed last night.

"Parents should not be afraid to send all children in to school as usual," said Mr Finch. "I have made immediate arrangements to replace all seven teachers presently on sick leave, so Deffry Vale's commitment to all-round learning will be entirely unaffected."

Asked whether parents should be concerned for their children's wellbeing, Mr Finch reassured the Echo: "Absolutely not. It's true that four of the catering staff have also sadly fallen ill, but they too have been replaced, and I

Curious

am taking immediate steps to institute a new, thoroughly healthy, and compulsory, school dinner menu. In fact,

I'm confident that we'll see positive effects very quickly indeed, and perhaps discover a new educational paradigm."

AMBROSE HALL
~ Home for boys and girls. Established 1946 ~
"Suffer the little children"

EAT MORE CHIPS

DEFFRY VALE HIGH SCHOOL

SALVAGE REPORT
SUBJECT: SS Madame de Pompadour
RETRIEVAL ZONE: Dagmar Cluster

Vessel found drifting and abandoned, with no life signs, but with all warp engines running at full capacity. No Human or Robot crew on board. Extensive evidence of repair work carried out by Clockwork Robots. Elements of Human anatomy incorporated into vessel's navigational, life-support and surveillance systems suggest disastrous Robot programme malfunction. Presence of authentic 18th-century French fireplace on board inexplicable.

S.B.6 SANCTUARY BASE

This is the final report of Sanctuary Base 6.

Captain ~~Bassford~~ Walker, deceased, with honours.

Officer Chenna ~~Bassford~~, deceased, with honours.

Officer Curt ~~Bassford~~, deceased with honours.

Officer Scootori Manista, deceased, with honours.

Officer John Maynard Jefferson, deceased, with honours.

Officer Tobias Zed, deceased, with honours.

Also Ood 1 Alpha 1, deceased with honours.

Ood 1 Alpha 2, deceased with honours.

Ood 1 Alpha 3, deceased with honours.

Ood 1 Alpha 4, deceased with honours.

Ood 1 Alpha 5, deceased with honours.

Ood 1 Alpha 6, deceased with honours.

Daily Mail

GREATEST SHOW ON EARTH BEGIN[S]

L.I.N.D.A. Homework
Police Box sightings

INBOX<<<<<

FROM: Yvonne

TO: Torchwood Institute

Congratulations, all of us!

Just passing on the really good feedback from the last Ghost Shifts. Great work everyone – with ghost energy measuring over 5,000 gigawatts, and that's something we can all feel proud of. And this is something we can only build on.

Well done and stay vigilant, Torchwood One!

WELL DONE, HARRY!

Daily News **3**

by HARRIET JONES

IF anyone understands the pressures of standing up for our great country and our wonderful planet against unimaginable horrors, I certainly do.

Only twelve months ago, I was your Prime Minister, and

I faced just such a crisis as we experienced yesterday. I stand by my actions to this day, because I knew that one day the Earth would be in danger again.

I was right. And let's all give thanks that, on this occasion, we were able to call on the courage and judgement of Harold Sa...

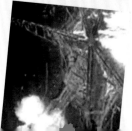

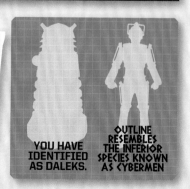

YOU HAVE IDENTIFIED AS DALEKS.

OUTLINE RESEMBLES THE INFERIOR SPECIES KNOWN AS CYBERMEN

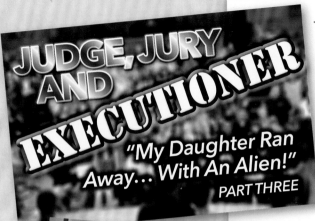

JUDGE, JURY AND EXECUTIONER

"My Daughter Ran Away... With An Alien!"
PART THREE

FRANCINE JONES
"An alien broke my family"

THE HOST: It's every mum's nightmare to hear her child has run away with an alien. We've met two mothers who it's happened to. We're now going to meet a third. And what's most remarkable is that, for all three of them, it's been the same alien.

AUDIENCE: Oooh.

THE HOST: Let's meet – Francine Jones.

FRANCINE: Hello.

THE HOST: Thanks for being with us today. Now – Martha Jones—

JACKIE: Oh, I've met Martha!

THE HOST: Martha Jones, your daughter, Francine. This is her, isn't it, Francine? Clever girl, bright future, training to be a doctor at the Royal Hope, yes?

FRANCINE: That's right. Until that day when the whole hospital vanished. My other daughter, Letitia, watched it happen. And when it reappeared, it had been to the Moon. The Doctor and Martha had saved everybody from space rhinos and a vampire.

SYLVIA: Space rhinos indeed!

FRANCINE: The Judoon. Not that Martha told us about it at the time. I saw her the next night, with the Doctor, and she let me think he was her new boyfriend. I had no idea then what they'd been doing. It was a long time before she told me. It was a long time before I wanted to listen.

Eyewitness reports from the Royal Hope Hospital continue to pour in, and it all seems to be remarkably consistent. This from medical student Oliver Morgenstern:

"I was there. I saw it happen. And I feel uniquely privileged. I looked out at the surface of the Moon. I saw the Earth, suspended in space, and it all just proves Mr Saxon right. We're not alone in the universe. There's life out there. Wild and extraordinary life."

JACKIE: Where'd he take her, then?

FRANCINE: They met Shakespeare. He wrote one of his Sonnets for Martha. Imagine that! They went to New York and somewhere called New New York – she said the traffic was terrible. The Doctor showed her spaceships and the Moon landing and a living sun and the end of the universe. She worked in a school in 1913 and a shop in 1969...

JACKIE: And you're just sat at home watching the months go by...

FRANCINE: Oh no. It was months for the Doctor and Martha, it could even have been years. But for us, back here, it was just two or three days. It was election week, remember when... that awful man... Harold Saxon... when he became Prime Minister. He was one too, you know. An alien.

THE HOST: You're saying the Prime Minister was an alien?

AUDIENCE: Oooooh!

SYLVIA: I voted for him. Seemed such a nice young man. I never understood all that – one moment he's promising friendly aliens, the next we're nearly at war with America and his wife's shot him. They never did explain it all.

FRANCINE: There's not many of us who know everything that happened. You're lucky you didn't have to live through that year.

Her Majesty has taken to her bed. She sallied forth last month in good spirits, heading to a small Glade that was well-met by sunlight. She prettily did kiss all in her retinue, vowing to return "a changed woman". And that, she most certainly did. She was espied the next day, a smile upon her countenance. She would not speak what had occured, save for encountering a "nest of creatures". But as the days passed, and her seeming expectations of another encounter dwindled, the cheer fell from her face.

Yesterday, she fell into a most ill humour. Her ladies pressed on her the need to take physic, and rushed to call for her friend Doctor Smythe. That merely stoked her furies. "I'll have none of him, nay, none of that Doctor. I'd sooner wear the King of Spain's beard." She was led away to her chamber, whereupon her agues shook forth into a fever, during which she was heard to mutter, "Ware that rogue!"

Her Chaplain was much troubled, and enquired among the soldiers who had accompanied her for what had transpired. It was given out that three men and a horse had been seen around those parts, amid much strangeness. This he confided in strictest confidence to Nursemaid, but it spread swiftly by gossip's fires among the household. When, during a lucid period, Her Majesty discovered her Chaplain's enquiries, she ordered him sent away to found a monastery in the Orknies (an end which will ill accord with his love of boisterous company).

After a while, Her Majesty's humours were rebalanced, and a hopeful expression returned. She now urgently inquired of Doctor Smythe's whereabouts. "He shall come to me," she said. "He shall. One day."

The New New York Times | Wednesday 11 March 5,000,000,053 **52**

Obituaries

The Face of Boe

'Savior of New New York' was the oldest being in the Cosmos

This legendary being – who survived the extinction of Boekind during the Fourth Great and Bountiful Human Empire then lived on for billions of years – finally died last week after a heroic 24-year effort to save the population of the New New York Undercity.

The origins of the Face of Boe remain shrouded in

SYLVIA: What do you mean? What year? It was all over in a couple of minutes.

FRANCINE: Maybe it was for you. But some of us had to live through a whole terrible year – Saxon was the Master of the world for twelve months. He killed so many millions of people, we watched Japan burn, I still can't bear to... He kept the Doctor as a sort of pet, he did such awful things to him, to all of us. He turned the world into a huge factory, making weapons to fight a war against the universe. My family was there, and we have to remember it. For everyone else, the Doctor turned the clock back. That's how good the Doctor is.

THE HOST: Is he? This is the man who took your daughter away from you.

FRANCINE: No. Martha stayed with us after that. Stayed to help us come to terms with it all.

THE HOST: This is Doctor Martha Jones, Medical Director for the Unified Intelligence Taskforce at the time of the Dalek invasion? Later to become Martha Smith, some sort of mercenary soldier?

FRANCINE: I'm not sure you should know about any of that. And she's not a mercenary. She and Mickey are freelance, helping to protect our world. But yes, she joined UNIT, a few months after Saxon, but she always came back to me when I needed her. My little girl had always wanted to make people better. The Doctor showed her how to try to make the whole world better.

THE HOST: And abducting young women was just a perk of the job for him?

FRANCINE: No, that's not—

THE HOST: Time for another short break, but we'll be hearing more from Francine, Jackie and Sylvia, plus one other very special guest. Back before you know it.

NEW YORK REVUE

STARING BARKER'S BELLES

AT THE LAURENZI THEATRE

MANHATTAN IN THE FALL

SONGS OF HOME

STARING BARKERS BELLES
AT THE
LAURENZIE THEATRE

MUSIC ORCHESTRA CONDUCTED
BY MR DEAN KNIGHT

WRITTEN AND DIRECTED BY
MR JACKSON POPE

SHOW STARTS 7PM WEEKDAYS
12PM SATURDAY MATINEE
AND
6PM SATURDAY EVENING
TICKETS AVAILABLE FROM THE FRONT
IN ADVANCE OR ON THE NIGHT

STARING LILLY MALONE

The New York Times — January 10, 1931

THEATER

PIG SLAVES IN MANHATTAN

Laurenzi Theater, Broadway

WHAT A SHOW! This is a three-hour extravaganza with 20 actors, countless extras and dancers, and a full complement of marvelously catchy show tunes. If you can imagine a fantasy of Mr. H.G. Wells with the hero rewritten as half-man, half-pig, or Mr. Eugene O'Neill's work and social concerns transplanted into a heady mix of theater and Hooverville, you will gain some idea.

As we know too well, it is a matter of weeks since a genuine series of unexplained disappearances among Central Park's dispossessed made headlines in our daily press. The writers have taken this sordid material and woven an intricately metaphorical tale, centered on the newly completed Empire State. In the ground beneath that true-life testament to American innovation, mutants in metal travel machines are conducting experiments on abducted homeless people, cross-breeding them with pigs to produce a new super-race. Our narrator-hostess is Tallulah, a showgirl whose fortunes are linked inextricably with those of Laszlo, a stagehand, and the destitute boy Frank, a young man with an instinct for charity who hungers for freedom. A run of boisterous dance numbers culminates in the arrival of a magician-doctor in a blue suit, a 'lover of show tunes', who exterminates the metal mutants, though not in time to save the Pig Slaves – except for one, who lives happily ever after with the heroine. The magician-doctor and his assistant then vanish in a blue box…

It makes its economic, as well as historic, point with some power, but that does no justice to a richly satirical musical, not least in a

BARKERS BAND BONANZA

DIRECTED BY
WHEELER

Re: Jones Plan – Update

From: Dexter@archangelnetwork.com
To: Saxon@archangelnetwork.com

Stage 1
Contact was established with Francine Jones during Lazarus demonstration. Mrs Jones now understands that her daughter is in danger, and that the Doctor cannot be trusted. (In fact, she slapped him!) Mrs Jones has also warned Martha Jones against her association with the Doctor. No confirmation of the whereabouts of Martha Jones or the Doctor after they left Southwark Cathedral.

Stage 2
Mrs Jones allowed us access to her home and we monitored incoming phone calls. Martha Jones made no calls on Wednesday, but three on Thursday. She refused to confirm whether the Doctor was with her. She accepted a dinner invitation from her mother, but failed to keep the appointment. No confirmation of the whereabouts of Martha Jones or the Doctor.

Stage 3

It was made of metal, although when I put a hand to it, it felt like skin. It felt warm under my hand, like it was paying attention to its presence, like it could feel every pore. If a pet dog, say, feels positive emotion at the presence of the master's hand, this was the opposite of that. It felt like I had touched a cauldron, inside which something was toiling and seething. The presence of my flesh offended it. And yet there was a connection.

I have seen things much like this in other dreams. The thoughts are so close in my waking brain that I cannot help but think they are related. There is always a gun, and a slit so that whatever is inside can see out. Is it a man? I think it is sometimes a man. I see him holding one eye closed so that he has no perspective, and can only see straight ahead. These things crawl forward through the mud and desolation, killing everything in front of them, illuminated from above by explosions in the sky.

The fellow feeling between those monsters and the thing I recall touching is that each stands only for its own side. The other has nothing like it. One of these can kill all.

And there is the matter of such factions being quite distinct. Not like the shades of language and culture that distinguish the great empires. The difference between you and he on this battlefield is everything, it is what great speeches are made about that I have seen in these dreams, and there is writing and writing and writing, and what's written about you, or what's written into you by those in power,

can be a matter of life and death, that's all that these vehicles or people or whatever they are care about: what you are.

There is one physical difference between the steel things and the thing which looks as if it is steel, but is somehow alive. That is the matter of illumination. The one I touched had a light like that of the sun, which came steadily from underneath it.

And I do believe I have seen this behemoth fly! It did not have a shape to fly. It was like a firework on a blaze, except that it moved aloft slowly. Slowly like a bird of prey waiting to see what was below. The shape, the metal, all confound that. But I saw it.

I recall it looking down at me, in a very familiar way. As if we had always known each other. As if this were some scorned relative or child left without protection in the wastelands. I feel like I knew its father, and tales have been told about me! A grudge that goes back a long way, to when I was different. But these creatures are never different.

I woke from this nightmare feeling tainted. As if my name and theirs are forever bound together. As if ours is a shared tragedy. I feel like I have seen them from so many different angles. Have seen them vulnerable, even. Have been with them in both peace and war.

The dream stayed with me for days. Out of the corner of my eye, as I was walking down the street, I thought I saw one reflected in a window. A combination of lights from the shop opposite, nothing more. It is as though having found these phantoms in a dream... and what do dreams mean? Nothing! There is no theory or practice that says they are anything more than what the mind has no use for! I do not know why I am writing about them so feverishly. I should stop.

I should finish my sentence, at least. It may be important to someone.

Having found these phantoms in a dream, I increasingly feel as if it is only a matter of time before they arrive. That they always arrive.

It's my home in the dreams, I know it so well, as one often knows something well in dreams without knowing it at all. It is always there, somewhere. I do not know if I own it, quite. I feel I have inherited it because all other claimants have ceased. Or perhaps that I have gained it through more dubious means. There is something dubious about it. On the outside, it is all upstanding and sombre, something to do with the law, with the police. But when I am inside it I do not think of myself as representing the authorities, I feel almost as if I am a fugitive.

Although it is a house of wonders, often when I try a wonder, it does not work, or works in a way which suggests my dream is having a game with me. It is my life all in all, to be granted a magic box and find it does not do the tricks it is supposed to! It feels like being told that one once had a part of the body that one no longer has, or an ability that has been lost. It should function. It does not. Perhaps it needs the care and attention of other people to do so. And yet that lack of function is as charming as the desire of certain folk always to sing, even though they are unable to. This building is like an old dog, perhaps it is too late to teach it new tricks now!

When I walk inside, I am always surprised. It is like a small dank door that leads into a great cathedral, hidden underground! The magic door in the hillside, behind which one can find legends and the other world that lives inside our own!

It is huge, bigger on the inside than the outside, Maius Intra Qua Extra! It should echo, but it is too comfortable for that. It is like I recall the same room when it was a child, when it was smaller. I can look down through the floor, somehow. Just by being at home I am on the peak of a mountain. And yet it is also like being inside a mother's embrace. A hardy old girl. A heart of gold. A power as great as a mother's love.

Nothing can harm me here. Unless I get lost inside.

My friends are all aboard. That is the very definition of being a friend of mine, that one has lived here with me.

I must be a gentleman of the road in my dreams, a dealer in bric-a-brac and old clothes. Because I have a gypsy caravan. I have seen myself stepping out of my home in so many different places.

It is the best thing about my dreams. It is the only reality I can fall back on. Apart from, of course, the reality of the waking world. In truth, when I am awake I rather miss it.

THE DOCTOR:

Yep. That's me. [pause] Yes, I do. [pause] Yep. And this. [pause] Are you going to read out the whole thing? [pause] I'm a time traveller. Or I was. I'm stuck in 1969.

MARTHA JONES:

We're stuck. All of space and time, he promised me. Now I've got a job in a shop. I've got to support him!

THE DOCTOR:

Martha.

MARTHA JONES:

Sorry. [pause]

THE DOCTOR:

Quite possibly. [pause] Afraid so. [pause] Thirty-eight. [pause] People don't understand time. It's not what you think it is. [pause] Complicated. [pause] Very complicated. [pause] People assume that time is a strict progression of cause to effect, but actually from a non-linear, non-subjective viewpoint, it's more like a big ball of wibbly-wobbly, timey-wimey... stuff. [pause] It got away from me, yeah. [pause] Well, I can hear you. [pause] Well, not hear you exactly, but I know everything you're going to say. [pause] Look to your left. [pause] I've got a copy of the finished transcript. It's on my autocue. [pause] I told you. I'm a time traveller. I got it in the future. [pause] Yeah. Wibbly-wobbly, timey-wimey. [pause] What matters is, we can communicate. We have got big problems now. They have taken the blue box, haven't they? The angels have the phone box.

[pause] Creatures from another world. [pause] Only when you see them. [pause] The Lonely Assassins, they used to be called. No one quite knows where they came from, but they're as old as the universe, or very nearly, and they have survived this long because they have the most perfect defence system ever evolved. They are quantum-locked. They don't exist when they're being observed. The moment they are seen by any other living creature, they freeze into rock. No choice. It's a fact of their biology. In the sight of any living thing, they literally turn to stone. And you can't kill a stone. Of course, a stone can't kill you either. But then you turn your head away, then you blink, and oh yes it can. That's why they cover their eyes. They're not weeping. They can't risk looking at each other. Their greatest asset is their greatest curse. They can never be seen. The loneliest creatures in the universe. And I'm sorry. I am very, very sorry. It's up to you now. [pause] The blue box, it's my time machine. There is a world of time energy in there they could feast on forever, but the damage they could do could switch off the sun. You have got to send it back to me. [pause] And that's it, I'm afraid. There's no more from you on the transcript; that's the last I've got. I don't know what stopped you talking, but I can guess. They're coming. The angels are coming for you. But listen, your life could depend on this. Don't blink. Don't even blink. Blink and you're dead. They are fast. Faster than you can believe. Don't turn your back, don't look away, and don't blink. Good luck.

The Last Will and Testament of the Human Race

Everything was dying. All the great civilisations gone. All that remained was us, the last remnants of the human race, stranded on the planet Malcassairo, refugees from the very end of the universe. The call came from across the stars, over and over again: 'Come to Utopia.' Originating from a point far beyond the Condensate Wilderness, out towards the Wildlands and the Dark Matter reefs, calling us in. The last of the humans scattered across the night.

We could not know what was out there. A colony? A city? Some sort of haven? The Science Foundation created the Utopia Project thousands of years ago to preserve humanity, to find a way of surviving beyond the collapse of reality itself. We hoped for a paradise whose skies were made of diamonds. And it was a false hope.

In the end days, brave men and women, doctors and professors, came to Malcassairo and sacrificed themselves to send us to Utopia. But everything there was still dying. The whole of creation was falling apart, burning. The last of humanity screaming at the dark. There was no solution, no diamonds. Just the dark and the cold. All the human invention that had sustained us across the eons turned inwards. We cannibalised ourselves. We made ourselves so pretty.

A man came, with his woman. She calls him Harry, but he says he is our Master. He has shown us how to preserve ourselves and grow stronger. He has given us a new name. He has shown us how to have fun. He has taught us how to fly and blaze and slice. He has come in his wonderful time machine to take us back home. He has told us how to gain a future in our past, to build a brand new empire lasting one hundred trillion years. He says that what we need, right now, is a doctor.

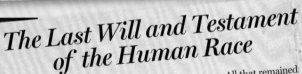

The BIG Interview

by Vivien Rook

Harriet's BACK!

I know what you're thinking. As she walks into the room, we're all wondering – will she do it? She does not disappoint. "Harriet Jones," she says, shaking my hand. And then the slightest pause. "Ex-Prime Minister."

She sits down opposite me and makes a great fuss of pouring me a cup of tea. Then, job done, she settles back and sighs, happily. She looks rested and relaxed. Gone are the sharp suits ("I jumbled them, I'm afraid") and back are the cardigans. At first glance, you wonder if this really can be the same woman who, a year ago was ousted by her own party almost overnight.

"Simply speaking, they just didn't feel I was up to it. Have a digestive," she says. "It was a bit of a surprise. After all, I had just helped save the world from an alien invasion. But then again, much the same thing happened to Churchill. Not," her face falls, "that he saved the world from alien invasion. Did he? And, I mean, forgive me if I'm comparing myself to him. Just that, you know, after the Second World War, he was chucked out of office. Poor lamb. I wonder if he was got at too?"

Harriet Jones's fall was as remarkable as her meteoric rise. Transformed from an unassuming backbencher to a stylish main player on the international stage, she's now sat firmly on the backbenches again. Her speeches in the House are occasional, her public appearances rare. But Harriet's back.

"It's cottage hospitals again, I'm afraid," she says. The slight apology is typical. "I'm putting local hospitals front and centre. There's a real distrust of those vast 'One Stop Health Solution' concrete monoliths that have been springing up – especially after the Royal Hope fiasco. It ended up on the Moon, for heaven's sake! No, we need to look at keeping it small, good and friendly. I've saved Flydale General, and there are so many charming places that are real centres of healthcare excellence that are also under threat – Leadworth, for example."

I ask her if she has the support of her party on this. She treats me to a wintry smile. "Fat lot of good that would do me, pardon my language. After I was nobbled, excuse the word, the party didn't last long, did it? I may have been an old bird, but at least I wasn't a headless chicken."

And what does she make of the current Prime Minister? This time there's real steel in her gaze. "He's a charming man, certainly. He's a very able politician." From the way she pronounces the words, I'm inferring she doesn't mean it as a compliment. "Oh, I don't. He may be just what this country needs – on paper, certainly. But what's behind him? At the risk of sounding like a crackpot, I've done some digging, and there are more questions about Harold Saxon than there are answers. His mobile telephony revolution isn't all it seems, you mark my words. Another hobnob?"

VOTED SAXON X

BUCKINGHAM PALACE

Dear Captain Harkness

Thank you for your letter of 29th December regarding the actions of the Doctor on Christmas Day in averting a great disaster for our nation and for us personally. I am delighted to confirm that my great great grandmother's sentence of exile on the Doctor and Miss Tyler has been rescinded with immediate effect.

I should also take this opportunity to thank you and your fellow officers for your own outstanding service in protecting our borders over many years. I am confident that we shall always be able to call on Torchwood Cardiff in times of grave crisis.

With cordial good wishes.

JUDGE, JURY AND EXECUTIONER

"My Daughter Ran Away... With An Alien!"

PART FOUR

THE HOST: Thanks for watching. So – an alien in a suit asks your daughter to go inside his blue box with him and see all of time and space... What does she say, Sylvia?

SYLVIA: Donna said no. The first time. Sometimes she has her feet firmly planted on the ground, she gets that from me, of course. But she's always been headstrong, that one. Packed in her job, left her flat, 'I'm going to see the world, Mum,' she says and then she's off. Only got as far as Egypt, then she was back, cluttering up the place. Came to stay for a couple of weeks, never left.

THE HOST: Never left?

SYLVIA: Well, that's what I thought, but then I'm only her mother, and that Doctor had turned her head. She took a job at Health and Safety – two days, that's all she managed before she gave that up as well. Then, one night, I was out with the Wednesday girls and all those nasty little fat creatures started just... popping out of people. Marching down the street, they were. And once they'd all gone to heaven knows where, so had Donna – upped and gone. Didn't see her for days. Dad said not to worry, he was sure she was safe. I should have guessed there was something he wasn't telling me. It was months before he told me the truth.

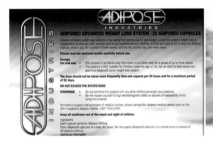

THE HOST: That's your father, Donna's granddad, Wilf?

SYLVIA: Well, of course it is.

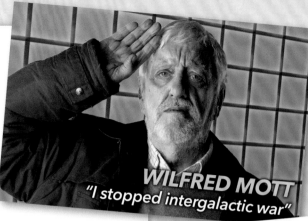

WILFRED MOTT
"I stopped intergalactic war"

THE HOST: Shall we meet him now? Here he is: Mr Wilfred Mott! Thanks for coming in, Mr Mott.

WILF: Oh, just Wilf will be fine.

THE HOST: So you knew where Donna was?

WILF: Ah well, no. I mean, yes, cos I'd seen her, hadn't I, flying through the sky in that funny old blue box with the Doctor. But I didn't actually know at the time where they'd got to, no.

SYLVIA: You said you got postcards!

WILF: I did, love, and the odd phone call, but that was a bit later. No, all I knew was that the Doctor was what Donna had been waiting for, and she'd found him. Then, when they came back to sort out that ATMOS business, she told me about Pompeii and the Ood and how she'd trust the Doctor with her life. And she was right. He's a fine man. The finest. And, excuse me, but Mrs Tyler...

JACKIE: Yes?

WILF: If I might... That Rose is your daughter, isn't she? Oh, you must be very proud.

JACKIE: Yes, I am. We all are.

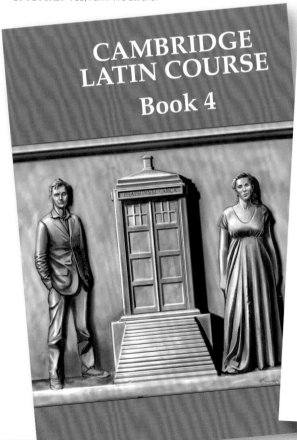

CAMBRIDGE LATIN COURSE
Book 4

Cambridge Latin Course Book 4

Translate the following sentences into Latin:

The future is changing. The sky is falling. Death. Only death.

Gods save us, Doctor!

You can't just leave them!

Come with me.

It's never forgotten, Caecilius. Oh, time will pass, men will move on, and stories will fade. But one day, Pompeii will be found again, in thousands of years. And everyone will remember you.

Thank you, Household gods. Thank you for everything.

THE OOD

ALL SALES CANCELLED.
OOD OPERATIONS NOW IN ADMINISTRATION.
IF YOU OWN AN OOD, PLEASE RETURN
HIM TO THE OOD-SPHERE.

They came from a distant world
They voyaged across the stars, with one purpose

TO SERVE

||||||||||||||||||||||||||||||||||||||

BUY ONE NOW

NOW ONLY 50 CREDITS

 ood operations

THE HOST: And what sort of things did the Doctor show Donna?

WILF: Cor, so many wonderful places and things. They fought living shadows in the biggest library in the universe! They met Agatha Christie, and them and Martha stopped some terrible war, years off in the future. But the last time I heard from her, before she came back to us, she was on a planet called Midnight. Made of diamonds, it was.

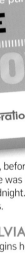

SYLVIA: And all that time, muggins here is being made to look a right clot. Phoning Veena and Susie, 'Is Donna with you?' 'No, Mrs Noble, haven't seen her for days.'

WILF: Best you didn't know, love. You'd only've got upset.

SYLVIA: Upset? Planets in the sky and all those awful Daleks—

WILF: Got one of 'em with me paint gun, though, didn't I, ha!

SYLVIA: And Donna's right in the middle of it all, having terrible things done to her mind.

WILF: Now, Sylvia, the Doctor explained all that. Donna helped save you, me, the world, the whole universe. And then the Doctor, he saved her, brought her back to us, where she belongs. And she's happy now – and pretty comfortable, thanks to that lottery ticket of his.

SYLVIA: Well, I'll thank him for that. I'll not thank him for whisking my own father off from under my nose, on Christmas Day of all days.

WILF: Do you know what, Sylvia. The Doctor risked his own life to save the whole world from that Master bloke. And then he gave his life, sacrificed himself, to save just me. Who am I, eh? Nobody important. But the Doctor would never, ever stand aside and watch another man suffer.

THE HOST: So the Doctor had put you in danger, too, Wilf, just as he had your granddaughter, and Rose and Martha.

WILF: It was an honour to stand at his side, madam, and I just hope that he got his reward... Here, who are you? How did you get us here? We shouldn't be talking about any of this. Here, are we on the telly? What if Donna sees it? She'll remember everything. It'll kill her! Who are you anyway?

JACKIE: Hey, how did I get here? I don't even live in your universe any more. Where's Pete? Where's Tony? Rose? Rose? Doctor? Are you there? Is anybody there?

(Fades to black. Closing credits.)

Hi Dad

Yes, it's really me. Not dead.

How come I'm alive? I don't know. I'm guessing the Source brought me back to life at the same time as Messaline. But they don't need me there, so here I am, out among the stars, having fun – planets to save, civilisations to rescue, creatures to defeat, and an awful lot of running to do! So much to see, so much to learn. Is that how you started?

I've no idea how to contact you, but I met this guy in this cantina, and he told me how they used to put a message in a bottle and throw it out to sea. And the best bit was somebody always found the bottle. So maybe, one day, you'll find this and come looking for me?

I'll try to make you proud of me.

Love
Jenny

ASHFIELD,
TORQUAY,
DEVON

Sir Godfrey Collins
William Collins, Sons & Co Ltd.
48, Pall Mall
London

Dear Sir Godfrey

Very many thanks for your most kind letter.

I am indeed much recuperated, and find that the
fresh air of Harrogate worked wonders. I feel
thoroughly reinvigorated and quite bursting with
new ideas.

What do you say to a murder at a vicarage? I have
a rather clever idea for a new nemesis for these
criminals and murderers, too - Miss (Donna?
Jane?) Marple, a harmless little old lady, who
has a knack for picking up the most vital clues.

I hope it will not be too long before I can get
up to London again. My major project at present
is to hunt down and destroy what is truly a
plague of wasps' nests in the garden.

Yours sincerely,

Agatha Christie

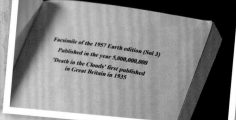

Facsimile of the 1957 Earth edition (Sol 3)
Published in the year 5,000,000,000
'Death in the Clouds' first published
in Great Britain in 1935

Take a letter, Miss Evangelista.
Subject: The Library. Dear
Professor Song. I am sure you are
aware of the famous and terrible
events that befell The Library one
hundred years ago. The computer
sealed the planet, and it has taken
my family three generations to
decode the seals and get back in –
no, strike 'get back in' – regain
access. Now that we have, I would
like to offer you a contract to

Professor Candy –
I'm not reading
this. Spoilers!

RS

THE
LIBRARY

THE LEISURE PALACE COMPANY

MIDNIGHT

FROM: THE LEISURE PALACE
TO: THE MULTIFACETED COAST

CRUSADER TOURS
1 ADULT DAY
RETURN

TERMS AND CONDITIONS APPLY

Poor Donna

http://www.royalplanetarysocietyjournal/2009_06/frontpage

The Journal of the Royal Planetary Society

The Stars Are Out Tonight
by Doctor Cedric Crossland CBE

The observations of the last few nights at first seemed impossible, a fault in a telescopic lens alignment perhaps, or maybe some of us have enjoyed one too many sherries at a Society dinner! Yet now there can be no doubt: the stars in our night sky have been simply winking out of existence.

It began quietly, too small a set of occurrences to be certain, until the entire constellation of Orion was suddenly extinguished last night. The stars are indeed going out.

Extravagant theories abound, most so nonsensical that no true astronomer could countenance them – that the on-going Triple Conjunction might somehow be 'bending space'; or, naturally, that a fleet of flying saucers is hovering invisibly above our heads, blotting out the starlight. The wildest notion, in my view, concerns a crumbling of the walls between different realities causing different universes to collapse into each other. (I think that my fellow Society members know me well enough to realise that so-called Quantum Theory has never had any appeal for me!)

1 2 3 Next

Queen's Hall, London
August 10th, 1895

Henry—What the devil was going on with that blasted tuba player this evening? Since when has a blue suit and overcoat been acceptable dress for a member of an orchestra. The fellow showed no sense of decorum, persistently grinning at members of the audience in the most insolent fashion. Tonight's promenade concert was supposed to be the start of a ten-week series, gradually raising the standard until we have created a public for classical and modern music. With these sorts of antics, we shall be lucky to last another ten hours. I suggest you arrange a replacement forthwith.

Yours,
Robert Newman

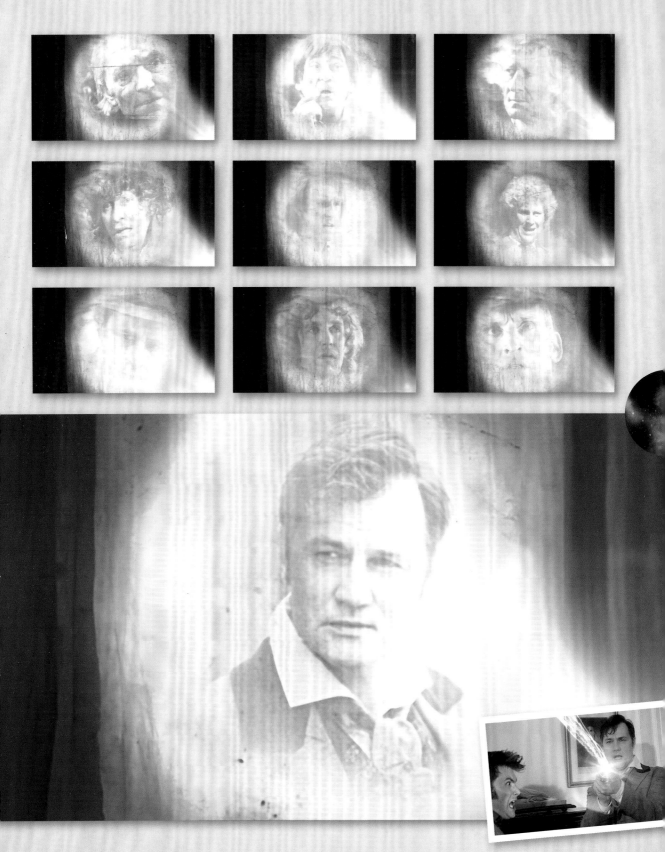

INTERNAL MEMORANDUM

From: Captain Erisa Magambo
To: Colonel Alan Mace
Re: Gladwell Road tunnel incident

Pleased to report successful conclusion: the Doctor returned the bus through the wormhole, which Dr Taylor successfully closed. All passengers safe and well, bar one human casualty, the bus driver. Minimal Code Red incursion all terminated. Local police officers debriefed and required to sign the Official Secrets Act. No other significant risk of publicity.

International gallery theft

ALL ABOARD THE MAGIC BUS

LATEST: FIRST LIGHTSPEED SHIP - PROUD HERITAGE

SUSIE FONTANA BROOKE

Susie Fontana Brooke has been successful in her mission to pilot the first lightspeed ship. Brooke entered the Space Agency at an early age, following in the footsteps of her grandmother, the legendary Captain Adelaide Brooke who led the mission to set up the first colony on Mars. A mission that ended in tragedy. A veil of darkness spread over the planet with the devastating news of a nuclear blast in 2059 which destroyed Bowie Base One, the first colony set up on Mars.

Speaking before she set out for Proxima Centauri, Brooke paid tribute to her grandmother: 'My grandmother, Adelaide Brooke, was a hero and an inspiration to so many of us, and especially to me. She was a true pioneer, who drove forward our scientific research and our goals. She believed that she had been spared, as a child, the day the Earth was stolen and moved across the universe. Her father hid her in the attic as the Dalek invasion began, and she went to the window and there, in the sky, she saw a Dalek. It stared at her. It looked right into her. And then it simply went away. She knew, that night, that she would follow it into the stars. She told nobody but my mother, and my mother told me. Now, in 2089, we are at last on the verge of realising her aims and her dreams.'

▶ Watch report

AIMS & OBJECTIVES
LIGHTSPEED SHIP

The Story of Doctor Who

2005-2010

The Tenth Doctor's tenure began in the last moments of Christopher Eccleston's final episode, *The Parting of the Ways*...

It was odd, although at least I had a couple of lines. Some Doctors have been introduced just lying on the floor... At least I had a tiny bit of a scene to do, although without Billie – Rose was a strip of gaffer tape stuck on one of the TARDIS columns so I had an eyeline.

David Tennant

... and continued, briefly, in a seven-minute scene, Born Again, *made for 2005's Children in Need telethon...*

It was one set, just a couple of hours in a morning with a very well-written scene. Because it would now form David's first outing as the Doctor, it was bound to attract a lot of attention.

Euros Lyn, director

... before getting fully under way in the show's first Christmas Day special, The Christmas Invasion. *Eventually...*

When I first read the script, it was interesting because of course I'm not in it, for a long time. There's a lot of expectation, waiting for the Doctor to wake up and hopefully save the day. So it was a curious one, reading it for the first time and thinking, 'Do I come into this?' And then, of course, when I do arrive, I don't stop talking for five pages. Lying in bed,

pretending to be ill and sweating gently for exorbitant sums of cash is every bit as easy as it looks, yep.

David Tennant

Russell absolutely understood what a Christmas special should be. It's very brave because the Doctor's off-screen for so long, but we needed to re-establish why he's so important to the world, and to Rose.

Julie Gardner, Head of Drama, BBC Wales

I had considerable doubts about the length of time the Doctor was unconscious for. But what Russell had done brilliantly was left you waiting for the Doctor for so long that, when he woke up, it was so exciting and you were so willing to welcome him that somehow the transition no longer mattered. By the time the Doctor and the Sycorax leader were having a swordfight, David was the Doctor.

James Hawes, director

DAVID TENNANT
was the Tenth Doctor

David Tennant is confirmed as the tenth *Doctor Who*, it was announced today by Jane Tranter, BBC Controller of Drama Commissioning, following the recommissioning of the second series. Tennant, whose recent credits include BBC Three's critically acclaimed drama series *Casanova*, BBC One's *Blackpool* and *He Knew He Was Right*, will star alongside Billie Piper who returns as Rose Tyler.

BBC Press Office, 15 April 2005

There was no competition and no discussion about who else it might be. We all agreed one hundred per cent that it should be David, right from the word go. No one else was ever seen or thought about.

Andy Pryor, casting director

In David Tennant's Tenth Doctor, you've got a Doctor who is nimbler, who can turn on a sixpence, who is overtly compassionate and empathetic and burdened with the responsibility of looking after all humanity.

Jane Tranter, Controller, BBC Drama Commissioning

With David, no one ever has a bad day or a cross word. He's forever happy and brings such energy to work. He is the

engine of the show, welcoming the guest stars in, welcoming the directors in.

Russell T Davies, writer and executive producer

David was a proper number one actor in the unit. He was first off the mark when they blew the whistle. His Doctor was a bit wild and volatile, which is a good thing for the character.

Bernard Cribbins (Wilfred Mott)

I'd looked at some of the old Doctors and talked about what we might achieve with the new Doctor and that he should be sexy and maybe a bit eccentric. The boys should want to be him and the girls should want to fancy him. David came to the costumiers, and I literally had two rows of clothes from different periods, suits and shapes to try on him, and pretty much from that fitting, we came up with the basic silhouette of the coat. I ordered the fabric for the coat that day, and also the ideas for the suit came from that too. We'd send stuff to Russell, and he said, 'I think it's too wide, it should be narrower.' I said, 'But he'll end up looking like a pencil!' and Russell said, 'Actually, you saying that appeals to me, I quite like the idea of a pencil.'

Louise Page, costume designer

TENNANT *on* TENNANT

It seemed so surreal, and absurd that this show which I loved so much was even back at all, and it was back so robustly. So to be asked not to have a little part in it, which was what I had been angling for, but to take over from Christopher Eccleston... it seemed absurd. And very funny.

David Tennant

I only had one question. 'Can I have a long coat?' There were a hundred sensible, practical questions I could have asked, but all I wanted was a long coat.

David Tennant

The glasses were one of those things that just kind of arose. As we put together the look, it was becoming this sort of geek-chic thing. It seemed to make sense to add a pair of specs to that. I quite like the idea of there being a speccy hero.

David Tennant

Author A.L. Kennedy on
THE CHRISTMAS INVASION

What wasn't to like amongst all the good things this episode could offer? Suddenly it felt entirely proper that Christmas should always involve a *Doctor Who* special, and it felt slightly weird when we tried to remember that it hadn't. I was a year old the last time the Doctor showed up on telly at Christmas and yet it immediately seemed this was both a tradition and a way of indicating that what was once a relatively small and sometimes rather poorly curated franchise had grown up and got important in good ways.

One of the good ways involved generosity – of budgets, of spirit, of monsters, of drama. Series One had allowed us to get used to the Doctor really being back, properly back, holding-his-companion's-hand-and-pelting-over-Westminster-Bridge back. He was here to tell us we should run – not simply because we were scared, but sometimes just for the feel of it. And now here was a great big movie-style plot with an added important costume choice and a turkey dinner, with proper humour and proper passion. Here was a chance to address the tyranny of Christmas – the enforced jollity and fruit, the clichéd weather, the threatening conifers. This was bound to become a tradition, too.

And this was our chance to be part of the first transition from Doctor to Doctor and long live the Doctor. The character had already returned and rested safely and beautifully in Christopher Eccleston's hands. Old themes had been resurrected, others initiated. And Christmas Day would see a whole new generation go through what was once the glorious childhood agony of the regenerated Doctor not knowing himself, being no use to himself, no use to anyone, cared for by those he usually cared for, threatened, weak and beautifully insane.

Would his uselessness indicate a duff actor? Or would it prepare us for affection, for a reminder of adult frailties, for a catalogue of good surprises? The Tenth Doctor fell into his new skin with a proper enthusiasm and assurance, with fury, swagger and humour. He was big-eyed, flailing, funny, deft, clever, brave – all the things we required. Tennant seemed to be both channelling his own childhood's Doctor – the Fourth – and also allowing himself to be very deeply happy in his own interpretation, his tangible communication of delight. Everything was going to be OK, we could tell – tricky lines would be galloped across like familiar music, energy would be maintained, dignity would be given to a children's entertainment with adult aspirations, potentially character-changing romps and nonsense would be given nuances and depth. Humanity would be shown as brave and wonderful and bright. It would also be proved disappointing, shoddy and violent. But essentially everything was going to be all right. The Doctor was here, and we were going to have fun. It was going to be wonderful fun.

I wake up. I talk for five pages; I press the button that nobody's allowed to press; I break the monster's staff; I haul away his whip. And then, just to top it all off, I have a swordfight with him on the wing of a spaceship. My hand is cut off; I grow it back, and then bring down the Prime Minister of Great Britain – all within ten minutes. You can't really ask for a better entrance than that!

David Tennant

Series One had brought Doctor Who *back, and made it enormously popular. But there wasn't time to sit around...*

There's very little time for pride. Pride doesn't get you past the first coffee of the day. Series Two immediately set even greater challenges than Series One – we started with our longest block yet, with a Christmas special plus two regular episodes all handled by the same director, building up to our biggest block ever, of four episodes, to compress all the Cybermen stuff into one schedule. No one's achieved four episodes since! So that kept us reaching further. And we had *Love & Monsters* bringing up the rear, possibly the most radical change to *Doctor Who*'s format ever. Plus, Billie's departure at the end! We never sat still, not for a second. The only way to stay successful is to push yourself harder.

Russell T Davies

Series Two also brought back two of the classic series' most popular characters, Sarah Jane Smith and K-9. The success of School Reunion *would ultimately lead to the popular spin-off series* The Sarah Jane Adventures...

But I have to say the K-9 that was filming on the new series, it hadn't actually advanced. David and Billie were really excited and said they wanted one, and then on the first take the dog ran into Billie, so I don't think she was so enamoured after that.

Elisabeth Sladen (Sarah Jane Smith)

I've just seen K-9 for the first time. He was zipping around on set. The only slight disappointment is that John Leeson, who does the voice, isn't here. He's having to put the voice in in post-production.

David Tennant

I was absolutely astonished to be asked back. The only sad thing, working this way, is that the fans will ask, 'What was it like working with David Tennant and Billie Piper?' And I'll say, 'I haven't the foggiest idea!' I just came to a little studio, did the voices, wrapped it all up.

John Leeson (Voice of K-9)

Director Graeme Harper had his heart set on the Cybermen sounding like Darth Vader; but because Russell told him that was totally wrong, he used to say, 'Like Darth Vader, but not Darth Vader.' When I did do what I thought was required on set, several of the actors kept saying, 'I can't understand what he's saying.' This was quite a comedown from the excitement and praise I was greeted with when I did a Dalek voice. So finally, in post-production, we did loads of different voices, working with the lovely Paul McFadden, who was always brilliant and supportive. The trouble was, Graeme couldn't tell the difference between any of the voices. We presented him with several different voices and he kept saying, 'Yes, that's the one.' Ultimately, Russell was sent the sound files and texted me to tell me which one he preferred.

Nicholas Briggs (Voice of the Cybermen)

I had the most tedious day of my life – I mean, bless Nick, but when fourteen different voices arrived, all slightly different, I nearly died. But we got there in the end.

Russell T Davies

Countless star names continued to queue up to join the guest cast...

There's a lot of wit in it which I love. I just love being Queen Victoria. It's nice shouting at people. Today's shooting involves a lot of running, which I'm not looking forward to, and this dress is the heaviest I've ever worn; it weighs the size of two sets of twins.

Pauline Collins (Queen Victoria)

The first scene up was a very interesting meeting with the Doctor. It felt on the page like it was quite subdued, just two people checking each other out. But the director said, 'Don't be afraid to go quite large.' I just let rip to see what happened. I think I surprised both me and the crew!

Anthony Head (Mr Finch)

The fact that I get to kiss the Doctor was one of the main reasons that I took the job. He doesn't really get a chance because I just snog him, and he's just pushed against the wall.

Sophia Myles (Madame de Pompadour)

The other day, I did six hours as an alien on *Doctor Who*. This will probably earn me my entire year's worth of street cred. We filmed it at the old studio in Alexandra Palace, in north London. It was very cold and the wind blew up my evening dress and rattled my pearls. I was the only actor among a dozen or so technicians and I had to respond to commands such as: 'OK Maureen, now could you give us 15 seconds of having every last drop of energy sucked out of you?' It was great. Inevitably, I overdid the screeching and cackling and, back at the theatre that night, found myself hoarse by the end of the play.

Maureen Lipman (The Wire)

What Marc Warren does so well, and it feels so natural that you don't notice the acting that's going into it, he gets an innocence without Elton Pope being geeky or unsympathetic, he gets an innocence that informs the whole of *Love & Monsters*.

Dan Zeff, director

Actor Anjli Mohindra on
SCHOOL REUNION

This is now one of my favourite Tennant episodes. It was definitely a big step to bring back a face from *Who*'s past to a new and fresh audience, but it worked brilliantly. Sarah Jane's pluckiness with Rose's confrontational 'Erm who are you?' brought about a brilliant and slightly awkward air for the Doctor to fight his way out of. New watchers of the show would of course have grown to love Rose and watching this flash-from-the-past giving her the cold shoulder was certainly risky territory handled perfectly. The constant Mickey jibes about the 'love triangle' that seemed to have formed, and the fact that the Doctor had left Sarah Jane in Aberdeen instead of Ealing, made me think, 'Ha... men!' So lovely to think that the Doctor, alien though he may be, is flawed and forgetful.

The fact that this episode was set in a school made it all the more a treat. Ah, the jokes to be had – snotty dinner ladies, 'awful' chips that you secretly still miss, etc. All very reminiscent of an actual school reunion, and the meeting of old partners and new. It is very touching that Rose's offer for Sarah Jane to join them in the TARDIS seems completely genuine, and it felt that the two of them could have formed a brilliant team in their own spin-off.

Watching *School Reunion* after having worked with our Lis gave me tingles. Seeing the way the Doctor looks at Sarah Jane for the first time since their parting reminded me of a conversation I had with David Tennant about Lissy when we were filming *The Wedding of Sarah Jane Smith*. We'd been talking about how Lissy had been the companion that David grew up watching. By this point Lis had already become a good friend of mine, but hearing David talk about her and seeing how excited he was to be working with Lis put into complete perspective how truly lucky I was to be working alongside her, and just how loved she actually was. Her gentle humility made it so easy to forget that you were in the presence of an icon.

When watching Lis as Sarah Jane I am always so keen to point out that so many of the wonderful qualities that Lis imbued her feisty character with, namely her strength and love for helping people, are true reflections of Elisabeth Sladen herself. The only thing kept at bay is Lissy's cheeky sense of humour and love of practical jokes! I guess the 'tamest' of them would be when she substituted sugar sachets for SALT ones for when Danny, who plays Clyde, was making his usual, rather sugary tea. Let's just say the costume assistant wasn't best pleased...

I wrote to Russell as a fan and said how much I loved the series. I got a letter back, and he just said, '*Blue Peter* have designed an alien for the new series and I'm trying to make the episode really special – would you like to do something in it?'
Peter Kay (The Abzorbaloff)

Early in Series Two, Tooth and Claw *had shown the foundation of the Torchwood Institute; the series climaxed with the Institute inadvertently unleashing simultaneous invasions by the Cybermen and the Daleks.*

A few months later, Jack Harkness would be back on screen in the spin-off series Torchwood, *but first the Doctor had to bid farewell to a closer friend...*

Although *Doomsday* involved a sci-fi parallel world, it's actually about a mum and dad and their daughter; about a family brought together by the Doctor across time and space. I had to leave Rose happy, that's the only ending I could possibly have been satisfied with.
Russell T Davies

Doctor Who Magazine had the new girl on the cover. I threw it across the room. I wanted to scratch her eyes out. It's like seeing your ex's new girlfriend!
Billie Piper (Rose Tyler)

Martha Jones is the first black companion, and it's a wonderful achievement, not just for me, but for casting the part black. So I appreciate that it's going to be spoken about. But the flipside is talking about 'black actor', 'black companion' all the time. If we're still doing that in 50 years' time, that's when I'd be bit miffed. I'm not upset when people address me like it now because it's something to be remarked on.
Freema Agyeman (Martha Jones)

Freema had appeared in Army of Ghosts, *not as Martha Jones but as Torchwood operative Adeola Oshodi, the role that led to her casting. Before that was announced, though, the series finale had another surprise for viewers...*

And then there was the Catherine Tate scene. That was filmed with five people. We wrapped the final day's shoot for Series Two, and everyone said, 'Cheerio.' We came back a couple of hours later, once the studio had cleared, and we filmed the Donna scene for the very, very end of *Doomsday* in top, top secret.

David Tennant

It was only after the finale went out on television that I could take the paper bag off my head that I'd been wearing around the streets of Cardiff. Before that, I couldn't tell anyone bar my mum and boyfriend.

Catherine Tate (Donna Noble)

Donna doesn't want to be there. At first, she's blaming the Doctor for the fact that her wedding day has been disrupted. She's quite a force of nature.

David Tennant

She's absolutely furious! She has no time for this madman. They start off at loggerheads, because he doesn't want this woman shouting and slapping him. But they end up quite different...

Catherine Tate

I knew from the first moment that *The Runaway Bride* would end with the Doctor saying, 'Her name was Rose,' and more particularly that it would end with the Doctor and Donna in an ordinary street, with snow... At the end, she turns away, walks back into her house...

Russell T Davies

Series Three began with Smith and Jones...

It's a great big rattling adventure. Martha's right in the middle of that, and then she meets a man called the Doctor. The whole focus of the whole episode was Martha's mad first day with the Doctor, throwing everything at her and seeing how she survived. It's really all about her.

Russell T Davies

I think it would be very easy just to create a carbon copy of Rose and just to replace her. I think what Russell's done is cleverer than that, because Martha is a very different character, and the hole she fills in the Doctor's life is a very different-shaped hole.

David Tennant

Martha Jones was about to encounter a plethora of aliens – Carrionites, Macra, Daleks, animated Scarecrows, Toclafane. Before all of those, her first day involved a vampiric old lady and a platoon of extraterrestrial rhinoceroses...

My favourite monster would probably be the Judoon; they were the first monsters I met, and I thought, as well as being scary, the work and craftsmanship on them is beautiful.

Freema Agyeman

The Judoon voice came from me studying the mask and imagining how it spoke. Then from my sore throat! The director, Charlie Palmer, thought the voice was 'funny'. I said, 'Oh, I'll try something else, then.' But he said, 'No, no, that means I like it.' It's a fun one to do, because I don't need any technical assistance.

Nicholas Briggs (Voice of the Judoon)

Doctor Who in the end is aliens or, very occasionally, which it was in *The Lazarus Experiment*, it wasn't alien. The idea was the thing that I turned into was a throwback, an evolutionary blind alley which was somehow buried into my DNA. It was a rarity for it not to be an alien.

Mark Gatiss (Professor Lazarus)

Doctor Who isn't about monsters from space; *Doctor Who* is about monsters that actually do live in your bedroom. That, for me, is what it's all about. The Weeping Angels simply regard us as transitory vermin. They're billions of years old, and we just sort of flicker around them. They shove us out of the way into the past – it's hardly a great act of evil; they're just not that bothered by us.

Steven Moffat, writer

It was great fun, completely different from anything I'd done before. But then your friends aren't too impressed. I tell them, 'I'm doing *Doctor Who*!' and they gasp, 'What's David Tennant like?' And you go, 'I dunno, he was nice for a day.'

Carey Mulligan (Sally Sparrow)

Steven Moffat's Blink *was preceded by a very different sort of story, in which David Tennant played a character called John Smith...*

Years ago, there was a range of books

called *The New Adventures of Doctor Who*, and there was one written by Paul Cornell called *Human Nature* that I think is literally one of the best *Doctor Who* stories ever written. So when we brought *Doctor Who* back, I just sat there one day and thought, 'Why are we not telling it?'

Russell T Davies

I initially tried to go too far away from the book. My first draft started with John Smith and his wife waking up in bed together. Mostly because I figured that Steven Moffat had already covered a lot of this ground in *The Girl in the Fireplace*. But Russell urged me back to the book. I don't think anyone else had read it, apart from Russell at the time of publication. I'm very pleased with the ending(s), which I didn't expect to be able to do.

Paul Cornell, writer

The Chameleon Arch literally rewrites the Doctor's biology. It changes him into a human being. There is no memory of the fact that this being was once the Doctor. The Doctor has gone, to all intents and purposes. John Smith has subsumed the Doctor's personality.

David Tennant

It was incredibly pleasing to have been part of something that got such a huge cultural reaction. When I worked on *Casualty*, nobody in my local pub honestly cared who'd written the script, but for *Doctor Who*, everyone did. I kind of knew it was good (in terms of what everyone else put into it, especially cast and director) from the read-through onwards, and surfing the reaction to it going out was a wonderful experience.

Paul Cornell

After Human Nature *and* Blink *came* Utopia, *the beginning of the epic adventure that would close the third series, bringing back an old friend...*

Jack's return to *Doctor Who* was long-awaited, not only by myself, but by the audience, I think.

John Barrowman (Captain Jack Harkness)

Captain Jack probably has the most complicated history of any character in *Doctor Who*. When you get to the massive Dalek attack in *The Parting of the Ways*, he was the last man standing. Rose then didn't just bring him back to life; she made him live permanently. So when he meets the Doctor again, it's tense. Why was he abandoned? What went on? There's a great friendship, but a new sense of distrust between them. *Utopia* deals with the Doctor telling Jack his own story.

Russell T Davies

Utopia *also brought back a very old enemy, played – at first – by Derek Jacobi. The*

revelation in the episode's closing minutes had been foreshadowed earlier in the series...

The Face of Boe's demise shifted from *New Earth* because that was the draft in which everyone dies, even the patients. At the same time, we'd just been commissioned for Series Three and I realised how huge that 'You are not alone' could be if held back till *Gridlock*.

Russell T Davies

I was gobsmacked when Derek Jacobi said, 'Oh, I love *Doctor Who*, I've watched them all, I'd love to be in it.'

Phil Collinson, producer

One of my ambitions since the 1960s has been to take part in a *Doctor Who*. (The other one is *Coronation Street*.)

Derek Jacobi (Professor Yana / The Master)

He's not just a guest star. Professor Yana is what this episode is all about. All the elements that have been laid in the series are coming together.

Russell T Davies

The Master has adopted this disguise as the Professor, but it's been so good a disguise that he's forgotten who he was. Having been this rather gentle, kind, loveable Professor, the evil side of me takes over and I start killing people...

Derek Jacobi

By the end of the episode, the reborn Master had been reborn once again...

To cast two brilliant actors as the Master, to have Derek Jacobi and then John Simm, was beyond my wildest dreams.

Phil Collinson

My little boy is obsessed with it, and that's the wonderful thing about the new *Doctor Who* – it really is a 'sit down with your family and watch it'... I'm going to impress my son, so there was no way I could say no to this. He would've never forgiven me if I'd said no.

John Simm (The Master)

I just channel-hopped and caught *The Sound of Drums*. Am I on drugs when I write these things? Sometimes I can watch my stuff and get this disconcerting draught of... well, of how it must look to other people sometimes. Of how

unplanned it all seems. Like I'm making it up as I go along. I can see how maddening it must be for some people. Especially if you're imposing really classical script structures, and templates, and expectations. The simple fact is: all those things were planned. All of them were my choice. I can see more traditional ways of telling those stories, but I'm not interested. I've made a *Doctor Who* that exists in the present tense.

Russell T Davies

Bridging the gap between the end of Series Three and the 2007 Christmas special was Time Crash...

Steven Moffat said, 'How would you feel about returning for a *Children in Need* special?' He wrote this very clever script which was as much about the Tenth Doctor remembering being the Fifth Doctor as it was about David Tennant remembering watching me on TV as a child.

Peter Davison

The record-breaking audience for the next Christmas special, Voyage of the Damned, *saw the most famous special guest yet, and featured a cameo from someone who would go on to play a major role in the Tenth Doctor's fate...*

I was a news vendor and got permission to wear my parachute regiment badge. And from that came the regular engagement as Catherine Tate's granddad. Kylie was lovely. She was great – one of the boys, just a pro. She hit her marks and was charming. When we parted I wished her good luck with an album and she kissed me on the cheek. I've been kissed by Kylie!

Bernard Cribbins

My first day on set was like stepping back in time. No, no, I mean that in the best way! I felt really at home being back in the world of TV and acting. Although I had nerves, I loved the challenge of playing Astrid.

Kylie Minogue (Astrid Peth)

And then it was straight on into Series Four, a year of Ood and Pyroviles, Unicorns and Wasps, and a return for the Noble family...

The funniest scene I've ever written in my life is when Donna meets the Doctor through the glass in *Partners in Crime*. I like being perverse in that way, it's like, 'You're worried about a comedienne being cast, you're worried this'll turn into a comedy, THIS is a comedy scene and it's hilarious, and it's Donna being funny, not Catherine.' And it's literally one of the best bits of comedy you'll ever see.

Russell T Davies

Sadly Howard Attfield, who was playing Catherine's father, had died. They then needed another male figure in that household and the producer, Phil Collinson, suggested that I might come in as Granddad. Catherine and I had mutual respect for the other person's ability and got on with the job. It was a nice little unit. I was very impressed by the team in Cardiff.

Bernard Cribbins

Also returning to the show in Series Four – for the first time in 23 years – were the Sontarans...

The first time I tried the make-up on it was very strange, because it's a gradual process. So it gets glued on to your head and, before they start making it up, it's just this rubber thing on your face. And then

the more they paint it the more realistic it looks and then it starts moving like your face does. It's a very incongruous feeling watching this different face moving in the mirror in front of you. It was quite surreal. In *The Poison Sky*, there was one sequence which was like being a kid in the playground again – shooting UNIT soldiers in a warehouse while laughing with a ray gun. That whole sequence took about ten minutes with me laughing non-stop. They'd get up and I'd shoot them down again because the camera was moving around to get a panning shot. And I thought, 'I'm getting paid to do this. I can't believe it.' It was just like playing *Doctor Who* in the playground as a kid.

Dan Starkey (Commander Skorr)

The next story introduced the Doctor's daughter, Jenny, played by Georgia Moffett – a Doctor's daughter...

She actually went for a different part originally. They rang her up and said, 'We could offer you this part, but if you just wait three months, there's a better part coming up that we'd like you to do.' She rang me up and said, 'What should I do?' And I said, 'Well, I guess if it's a better part, hang on for that.' And when it came round to that story, it was called *The Doctor's Daughter*. I think it was more to do with the name of the story than that the part was better, because it was such a perfect synchronicity for *Doctor Who* to have a story called *The Doctor's Daughter*, in which the Doctor's daughter was acting. And now she has married the Tenth Doctor and her father is, in fact, the same person, it's even weirder!

Peter Davison

Steven Moffat's Silence in the Library *and* Forest of the Dead *then gave the Doctor his first meeting with somebody who was meeting him for probably – or at least possibly – the last time...*

River Song is a time-travelling archaeologist. She's met the Doctor in the future, many futures, and has a very special relationship with that Doctor. She has her little blue book which are all her past adventures which are the future adventures of our present Doctor to come. She's somebody who holds the Doctor very dear indeed. I can't say more than that!

Alex Kingston

THE TENTH DOCTOR

As Series Four built towards its close, Russell T Davies wrote a tour-de-force for Catherine Tate...

What a mind! How do you...? The most fantastic thing about *Turn Left* was that it looked like it was always going to be that way. When I did *The Runaway Bride*, no one knew I was coming back, it wasn't even a consideration. And yet by the end of the series, it was as if it was always supposed to be. Oh that's clever.

Catherine Tate

Despite four years of relentless press attention, BBC Wales had managed to protect one or two amazing secrets...

Loads! The first appearance of Catherine Tate – then known only as 'the Bride' – was a fantastic shock. The collision with the Titanic! Bringing the Master in earlier than everyone thought, in *Utopia*, that worked a treat. I still get a visceral thrill out of that episode. But best of all, that surprise regeneration in *The Stolen Earth*. It was like the world went mad! OK, our little TV world, but that'll do me. Richard and Judy spent a whole 15 minutes discussing that! And crucially, we added almost two million onto the next week's figures. Now that's a cliffhanger!

Russell T Davies

9.4 million! The most watched programme of the week! Ha ha ha. It's *Doctor Who*'s first time in the Number One position in its whole 45-year history. It's gobsmacking. Someone should write a book about how we did it...!

Russell T Davies

Episodes 12 and 13, The Stolen Earth *and* Journey's End, *managed to bring back Harriet Jones and UNIT, at the same time as reuniting the Doctor with Sarah Jane Smith*

and friends, Captain Jack and his Torchwood team, Martha Jones, Mickey Smith and Rose and Jackie Tyler, as the Children of Time gathered to face the Daleks, led by the Supreme Dalek and Davros...

There was always a sense of drama when you had a scene with a Dalek. They're wonderful things. There was one bit in an episode where I suggested I might be able to blind a Dalek with a paint gun. That was my idea. Russell wrote it in and capped it perfectly.

Bernard Cribbins

Having fooled the audience and the press into thinking that David Tennant was leaving halfway through the Series Four finale, BBC Wales had another surprise in store the following October...

Operation Cobra! The plan for David to announce his departure live on air at the *National Television Awards*, should he win, is officially called Cobra!

Russell T Davies

I'm very excited because, in January, I go back to Cardiff to make four new specials, which will see *Doctor Who* all the way through 2009. But when *Doctor Who* returns in 2010, it won't be with me. I love this part, and I love this show so much, that if I don't take a deep breath and move on now, I never will.

David Tennant, 29 October 2008

David announced he was going and this rumour mill began, and I couldn't say what I knew, but it was a fun place to inhabit for six months, when people thought it was going to be me.

David Morrissey (Jackson Lake)

It'll all be revealed on Christmas Day. It'd be terrible to sit there on Christmas Day and have it spoiled for you. It's very

AUTHOR A.L. KENNEDY
on *David Tennant*

Reasons for entirely approving of David Tennant's Doctor.
 a) He's a ridiculously good actor and that's what the series deserves. He followed a ridiculously good actor into the role and hit the ground running. And shouting. As a kid, I would always worry about the transitions from Doctor to Doctor – Tennant continued to raise the bar and make the brand robust. He's a generous performer and, Billie Piper having found her feet with Rose in Series One, he helped to establish a great team. Love in a pre-watershed, sci-fi show watched by children was tackled with delicacy and proper passion.
 b) There was a genuine enthusiasm for the part underlying Tennant's interpretation. Whether or not he became an actor because of a childhood understanding that the part might be available when he got tall enough, he certainly grasped the essentials: the Doctor is our friend, he is horrifyingly kind, he is deeply moral, marvellously insane and you wouldn't want to cross him or hurt anybeing on his watch. If you believe in knowledge, love and humanity as transcendent powers, then he's with you and lending a hand. Tennant – because of a) – could present this precisely, energetically and with intelligence. (And the glasses helped.)
 c) In Tennant's hands the Doctor was, once again, company for kids who have to deal with an adult world.
 d) Lord knows, withstanding the semi-hysterical attention of a nation's children and a nation's peculiar grown-ups can't have been fun, but he carried it with dignity and patience. (And a bit of running about, shouting and over-dressing. Well, why not?) Good for him.

much a tease campaign, and I'm going to continue it. I have to continue it.

David Morrissey

The Next Doctor was the first of a run of specials featuring a series of one-off guest companions. David Morrissey's Jackson Lake was followed by Michelle Ryan's Christina in Planet of the Dead *at Easter, then by Lindsay Duncan as Adelaide Brooke in* The Waters of Mars...

Christina is sexy and glamorous, but she's also a tomboy and very independent. She's always chasing the next adventure, the next high. And because the Doctor is charismatic and fearless too, I think they're an excellent match.

Michelle Ryan (Lady Christina de Souza)

They are a small band of isolated scientists on Mars who are interested in finding signs of other life forms, but they aren't expecting another human being to appear. So when the Doctor turns up, he's not given the warmest of welcomes, especially by Adelaide. At first, she is suspicious of who he is but, as events begin to unfold, they have to become allies and get to know each other.

Lindsay Duncan (Captain Adelaide Brooke)

Viewers of Children in Need in November 2009 then saw a preview of the Christmas Special and knew that they'd be seeing not just the Ood but also the Master on Christmas Day. But nobody knew who else would be coming back...

The ultimate enemy for the Tenth Doctor was always going to be the Time Lords. When I handed the script in for *The End of Time*, and it had bad Time Lords, a lot of people in the office were shocked. And it's funny because I've always known – if you take me back to 2004 – I've always known that this is what the Time Lords became.

Russell T Davies

I think it was important the Doctor said goodbye to all the companions because there's a completeness about the Russell T Davies years and the Tenth Doctor years by doing that. It's a reward for the viewer as much as, in story terms, it's a reward for the Doctor.

Julie Gardner

The End of David Tennant's Time was drawing near. Fortunately, Russell T Davies

already had plenty of experience in creating and killing off amazing characters, then thinking, 'Oh, no, wait, I'd love to have had more...'

Loads of them. Maybe all of them! Harriet Jones, certainly. I'd have loved to see Elton Pope again. Ida Scott. In fact, that whole team from the Sanctuary Base, I loved them. Cassandra. That dark little Cane family in *Midnight*. Wilf! And Sylvia too! I wish we'd done more stories with Tish and Francine Jones, because they were so good together. But mostly, Rose, Martha and Donna. The Doctor rolls on, with different faces, but they're gone and probably won't ever say another word. I find that a bit sad! I'd love to write more for them.

Russell T Davies

Wilf fell in love with David's character. He was hugely affected by him. Being an amateur astronomer, he had a great feeling for space and the fact that he could join in and go into space was unbelievable. He was awestruck at having the Doctor as his friend. David and I were shooting a very small scene for David's final episode in a stable somewhere, and we had to get into the TARDIS and close the door. We did this, heard the word 'cut' and, before we got out, I said to David that the first

time I'd been in the TARDIS was in 1966. He said he wasn't even born then. That put me in my place. It was a normal day, to be honest. There were some serious scenes to be shot but there wasn't a sense of despair or anything.

Bernard Cribbins

Wow. That was David's final day filming *Doctor Who*. His last scene, at Upper Boat, dangling on wires against screen. 'I'm like an un-cool Spider-Man!' And then it was over. 'Am I free? Can I walk away?' he asked Euros, and then he disappeared, without fuss or fanfare. I was thinking, really?! Is that it?

Russell T Davies

I knew that I was finished. There was some bit of flannel about 'We'll need you back for a reference shot' – I knew that wasn't the case. I was fully aware of what the shots were, and I knew that we'd shot them all. And I just wanted to go. I just thought, 'Please don't make me come in and everybody look at me, because I'll only get upset.' But of course they did, and of course I did.

David Tennant

So long, David. You've been beyond brilliant.

Russell T Davies

ROYAL LEADWORTH HOSPITAL

Administration Office

Notice of Theft

A number of personal items were removed from the First Floor Secure Locker Room on Friday 25 June.

Would whoever is responsible please return the following items:

- 1 pair ankle-high lace-up boots (black)
- 1 pair denim jeans (black)
- 1 striped long-sleeve shirt (burgundy/white)
- 1 silk bow tie (burgundy)
- 1 tweed jacket (brown, with elbow patches)

This is not a trivial issue, and cannot be excused by the recent mass hallucination. All staff are reminded that the removal of items of personal clothing from a supposedly secure locker room is totally unacceptable.

Yes, people, these clothes are NOT COOL. Give them back!!

STOP, THIEF!

He's a pretty little thing, my lost little thief, don't you think?

Oh, I know what you'll say. But just look at him – he's taller on the inside than the outside, and, as an idea, my Doctor goes from the beginnings of the universe to its very end.

Is this one my favourite thief? Unfair! They are nearly all my favourites, with their bright little eyes and strange pelts and their endearing habits. He requires regular walks, a lot of fuss, and somewhere warm to come back to. When I am travelling very fast, he would like me to wind the window down so that he could stick his head out. But I do not have a window.

Hello!

LIZ 10's PROCLAMATION

If you are watching this... if I am watching this, then I have found my way to the Tower of London.

The creature you are looking at is called a Star Whale. Once, there were millions of them. They lived in the depths of space and, according to legend, guided the early space travellers through the asteroid belts. This one, as far as we are aware, is the last of its kind. And what we have done to it breaks my heart.

The Earth was burning. Our sun had turned on us, and every other nation had fled to the skies. Our children screamed as the skies grew hotter. And then it came, like a miracle. The last of the Star Whales. We trapped it, we built our ship around it, and we rode on its back to safety. If you wish our voyage to continue, then you must press the Forget button. Be again the heart of this nation, untainted. If not, press the other button. Your reign will end, the Star Whale will be released, and our ship will disintegrate. I hope I keep the strength to make the right decision.

FORGET   PROTEST

Got your attention, haven't I?

This thief got himself in a terrible muddle. It began when he found that first impossible girl. Her name was Ameliapond and she was going to get married to the Pretty One ten years later but there was a crack in her wall. The Doctor left her for five minutes – he had just regenerated and wanted a sit down. I'm always sad for him at that moment, and wish I could comfort him more. He gets so miserable about one thing being over and excited about another thing beginning.

This is not just true about bodies; it is the same with planets. I let him down then – I was still re/pairing/growing/decorating so we missed Ameliapond first time around and then she had to come with us as there was something wrong with her world.

The thing that was wrong with her world was me.

You are men of stone. You are blocks. You are cold. You are demons. You are darkness. You are angels. You reach out through time and you feed. Your hunger is as empty as your eyes. You are blankness. You do not think. You do not feel. You simply reach out.

Stone. They say stone remembers while time forgets. Can you live in stone? Can stone live in you? Are you living stone?

They call you the Lonely Assassins. But those who call you that know nothing of solitude, nor of assassins. To pluck out an I and separate it from all that makes it me. To cast it back into a new past, adrift and alone. To leave those behind grieving. You feed off that grief, that waste. Your meat is despair. Your drink is tears.

How many times have you done it to me. Taken me from all I love and plunged me into darkness. Watched me rebuild it all. And then cycle again. You knock me down. I rebuild. me down again. How much life have I left? friendship worth? What is that life worth if it is lived What are these words worth?

I wish I could capture you as you have captured me. But I do not. I cannot. I dare not. that which holds the image of an angel becomes itself angel.

If I could draw you perhaps you could reach out and finish me. But I dare not. I dare not. I worship my angel. It has driven me to madness and I have ridden on its wings into the darkness beyond.

For that which holds the image of an angel becomes itself an angel.

The eyes are not the windows of the soul. They are the doors. Beware what may enter there. For what if we had ideas that could think for themselves? What if one day our When dreams no longer needed us? held to be these things occur and are true, the time will be upon us. The time of Angels

00:11:25:

RORY'S STAG!

25 June 2010

Join us at the Horse & Jockey, anytime from about 6pm.

(NB: For obvious reasons, there will not be a kissogram)

No, it's OK. This book's printed on psychic paper. See, the fractals are a dead giveaway.

Madame Calvieriri

Is now accepting applications for the education, finishing and bringing on

Of the young daughters of noble gentlemen of Venice.

Orphans not a problem.

Opening address by ELDANE, leader of the Homo reptilian city beneath Cwmtaff

Representatives of Humanity, thank you for allowing me to address you. A thousand years have passed since I last spoke with any of your race. I hope, this time, we will find happier conclusions.

We are an old race – an old race, a wise race... and sometimes a foolish one. We inhabited our world for millions upon millions of years; we built and lost great civilisations; and we slept while another race built and lost great civilisations of its own. Of course, to us, that upstart race had risen and fallen while we were enjoying an afternoon nap. Well... All right, perhaps a very good night's sleep – you see how difficult it can be to keep a sense of perspective on these things?

This is the story of our planet – Earth. Of the day a thousand years past when we came to share it with you, Humanity. It is the story of the Doctor, who helped our races find common ground, and the terrible losses he suffered. It is the story of our past and must never be forgotten.

The first instinct for both Homo sapiens and Homo reptilia was for conflict – but the Doctor, as I think you know, is a difficult force to resist. Although each side held hostages, he persuaded us to negotiate. As I sat there that day across the table from the humans, the future of both species and of our beloved planet Earth rested in our hands. But as the discussions went on, I began to despair about whether we would ever find any common ground. As ambassadors for our species we all had too much to lose.

For some, on each side, however, the fear and mistrust grew overwhelming. One of our warriors died at the hands of one of yours, provoking our military commander to begin a war that could not be won. The Doctor and I were compelled to accept that this was not the time for peaceful settlement. To avert further needless deaths, it was necessary to flood the city with toxic gas, driving all my people back to our cryo-chambers.

So the Doctor sent our warriors back to their rest, on the promise of future harmony with humans. Now, as my people awaken from their thousand-year sleep ready to rise to the surface, my thoughts turn back to the Doctor. The losses he suffered then and the greater losses that were still to come.

Blue Water Box. What was it called? Swimming pool. Ah yes. I had made it nicely. I miss the swimming pool. Ripples going out in all directions when he fell into it. I tried to soften his fall with those lovely cushiony things. What are they called? Cushions? No, books. Where am I?

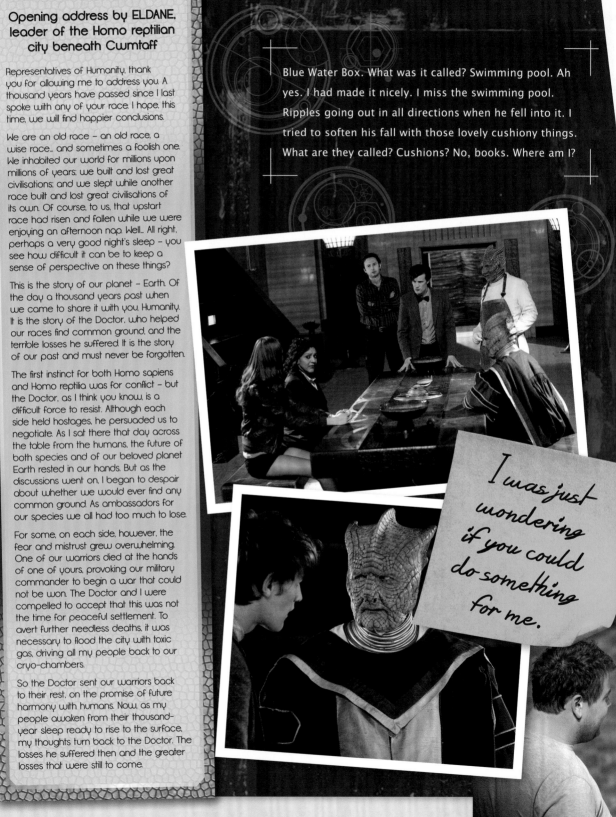

I was just wondering if you could do something for me.

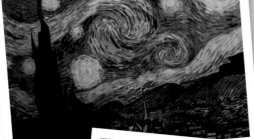

Vincent van Gogh

Painting, Oil on Canvas

Auvers-sur-Oise, France: June, 1890

Musée d'Orsay

Paris, France, Europe

Vincent Van Gogh settled in Auvers-sur-Oise, a village on the outskirts of Paris on 21 May 1890. Before his death two months later, on 29 July, the artist made about seventy paintings and a large number of drawings. This work was probably created between 1 June and 3 June. The early Gothic church in Auvers, built in the 13th century, is flanked by two Romanesque chapels. It can sometimes be glimpsed in background views of the whole village, but this is the only painting representing it in full. Van Gogh represented it as a gaudy monument that might, at any moment, launch itself from the ground, held in place perhaps only by the two paths at either side. The painting illustrates how far Van Gogh's approach differed from Impressionism: there is none of the play of light one might expect from, say, Monet. The church is recognisable, but it is neither a faithful image of reality nor a respectful depiction of faith, and this is emphasised by the ghoulish and malevolent figure glimpsed through one of the windows. It is an expression of the church, so anticipating the work of the later Expressionist painters.

van Gogh

Oil on Canvas

ur-Oise, France: June, 1890

Musée d'Orsay

Paris, France, Europe

Vincent Van Gogh settled in Auvers-sur-Oise, a village on the outskirts o
Paris on 21 May 1890. Before his death two months later, on 29 July, the
artist made about seventy paintings and a large number of drawings. Thi
work was probably created between 1 June and 3 June. Th
church in Auvers, built in the 13th century, is flanked by two Romanesque
chapels. It can sometimes be glimpsed in background views of the
whole village, but this is the only painting representing it in full. Van Gogh
represented it as a gaudy monument that might, at any moment, launch
itself from the ground, held in place perhaps only by the two paths at
either side. The painting illustrates how far Van Gogh's approach differed
from Impressionism: there is none of the play of light one might expect
from, say, Monet. The church is recognisable, but it is neither a faithful
image of reality nor a respectful depiction, and this is emphasised by the
lack of any human figures, save one soul making her way down the path
as far from the church as possible. It is an expression
anticipatin

How to act Human

Kissing ✓
Cook omelettes ✓
Get rid of bow tie No!
Watch telly ✓
Play football ✓
Go down the pub ✓
Reconnect the electrics? ✓
Make breakfast ✓
Work in an

My thief learned that, one day, I would explode. Something would make this happen (I know what causes it, of course I do). And tomorrow, yesterday, neverday, the whole universe would end – big explosion, cracks back through time. Cracks split open, universe all eaten up, worried Thief...

End of. Happens sometimes. We go down a route and there's a dead end. Somehow we reverse and continue – time is just a maze that's being shaken shaken shaken always. But one of my stories ended there – I was the last thing left in a universe I had destroyed. I was the full stop to that existence.

The Tale of the Pandorica

ONCE UPON A TIME, there was a naughty little goblin. He wore funny clothes and he had a crooked smile, and all the children liked him.

He was a very clever goblin, and he could do amazing spells. His favourite trick was to drop out of the sky into a village or town, then vanish again, then reappear a day or two earlier, looking a bit older. Nobody knew quite what to make of it, but everybody was a bit worried by him.

He wasn't really a bad goblin. He meant well. But wherever he went, things went wrong and people were hurt. Nobody could stop him doing what he wanted. After a while, the grown-ups started telling stories about him, and the stories spread from village to town to city... Soon, everyone knew to be a little bit scared whenever he popped up.

Then, one day, a good wizard called together the cleverest people in all the world and told them some bad news. The goblin's tricks were going wrong, and soon the whole world would end for ever. The goblin would not listen to the good wizard or anyone else. The only way to save everything was to build a special box called the Pandorica and trap the goblin inside it.

So the clever people worked and worked, making their special prison for the goblin. And when they had finished, they buried the Pandorica deep under the ground. To make sure that nothing could get in or out, they weighed down the ground above with the heaviest stones they could find.

And then they sent a message to the goblin.

TRANSCRIPT.

President Richard Nixon
... talking with David Frost.

FROST: Have you anything to say, Mr President?

NIXON: Look here, Mr Frost, we can go over this again and again. Watergate? A bad situation, sure. But in terms of the big picture? Peanuts. Barely a fly on a door-screen – but that's the bit of my legacy that I'll be remembered for. But you know what was really going on? I was saving the world. Oh yes. Not from nukes or commies. No. From aliens. Real, goddamn aliens.

FROST: Shall we break for lunch?

CERTIFIED COPY OF AN ENTRY OF MARRIAGE

101225

Registration District   Los Angeles

9 52   Marriage solemnized at Hollywood Chapel, Santa Monica Blvd

.	When married	Name	Age	Marital condition	Rank or profession	Residence at the time of Marriage
	Twenty-fourth December 1952	The Doctor	908	It's complicated	Doctor	A Tardis
		Norma Jeane Baker	26	The fuzzy end of the lollipop	Actress	Beverly Hills Hotel, 9641 West Sunset Blvd, Beverly Hills.

bride was given away by Jeff Christmas (father)   In the presence of Francis Albert Sinatra

OK.
Ready?

BALLAD OF CAPTAIN AVERY

He stripped the rings
from their fingers
And the flesh from their bones
He sent those fine Moghuls
Down to Davy Jones

In pursuit of their riches
He voyaged in the Fancy
A once noble captain
On a quest very chancy

But then BANGZAP we were off again
a wedding to dance at. And dancing
Song. I could smell what she was – sh
Once, I taught her how to fly. And on
Once she loved me. Once she shot me
all at the same time. I liked her, moth
day I would like to teach her to wheez
me. But the Doctor danced and River
more they danced the more trouble gr
Something wanted Thief because they
They stole River's mother, they stole R
it all so tangled. Thief and River were l
each other like wool. He had a scarf on
smelled of lavender and aluminium. I li
looked good in loops. And sometimes g
loops.

28 May Column 553

Equality Bill
Second Reading

Mr Speaker: I have selected the amendment in the name of the Leader of the Opposition.

3.50 pm

The Minister for Equality and Species Rights: I beg to move, that the Bill be now read a Second time.

For us, equality matters because it is right as a question of principle, and it is necessary as a matter of practice. It is essential for every individual. Everyone has the right to be treated fairly, and everyone should enjoy the opportunity to fulfil their potential. No one should suffer the indignity of discrimination – to be told, 'You're a Ganger, so you're less important,' to be excluded or face harassment because they are Flesh. The events at the St John's Monastery mining operation have established beyond doubt that the Flesh is alive. When we created the Gangers, we poured our personalities, emotions, traits, memories and secrets into them. We gave them our lives. We and they have the same childhood memories, just as clear, just as real. The Gangers have become people. We are talking about sacred life.

Equality is not just the birth right of every human individual, but necessary for the Gangers also. So this Government is a champion of equality—

Bernard Spencer-Davies (East Norfolk) (Con): I am extremely grateful to the Minister for giving way. I have a very serious point to raise with her, and I hope that she can be of some help to me. Studying the evidence from Morpeth-Jetsan on the St John's Monastery incident, I have come across a number of incidences of genuine human beings being callously murdered by their Ganger so-called 'equivalents'. The construction workers J. Wicks, B. Edwards, J. Lucas and H. Dicken all lost their lives. Will the Minister take this opportunity to say very clearly to real people across the country that homicide remains a crime, even when committed by these artificial creatures that she is so eager to share equal rights with?

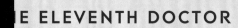

My imaginary friend

My imaginary friend is called the chiropractor and whenever someone at any point in history stubs their toe or is a bit achy, he turns up and gives them a rub.

Rory Williams (aged 10)

My imaginary friend

My imaginary friend is not called The Raggedy Doctor as I am not allowed to write about him any more because then Mrs Mitchell will get all cross and send me to see the nodding lady who smells way too much of cats. Also he's not imaginary.

Amelia Pond Age 10

My imaginary friend

My imaginary friend tells me to kill people.

Mels Zucker (Age 10)

BEWARE "THE DOCTOR"

He may USE FORCE —*Never*

He may USE HYPNOTISM *Might make you dance like a chicken!*

Yeah, got me there —He may USE PSYCHIC PAPER

And there —He may USE SONIC TECHNOLOGY

He may TURN YOU AGAINST YOURSELF *What does that even mean?*

He may ANSWER THE QUESTION

Are you sure?

Tick tock goes the clock, and all the years they fly.

Tick tock and all too soon, you and I must die.

Tick tock goes the clock, even for the Doctor.

Tick tock goes the clock, and what now shall we play?

Tick tock goes the clock, now summers gone away.

Tick tock goes the clock, and all the years they fly.

Tick tock and all too soon, your love will surely die.

Tick tock goes the clock, the cradle now be rocked.

Tick tock goes the clock till River kills the Doctor.

COMMANDER HALKE
Defeat

STON LUK...
Plymouth

LUCY HAYWARD
That brutal Gorilla

Thief became worried – he had travelled for so long that there were so many stories about him and the stories were scarf-loops and as they crossed they became confused and he was not always the hunted and the pattern ran in the water. Everyone was out to get Thief and they made River do it, drawing her to his end. But she did not do it and

Dropped stitch.

I want you to look behind you.

Breast Milk
For the baby

Grapefruit Juice
Refreshing lol!

*Blarg!!!
The one thing in the universe which cannot be improved by Hundreds and Thousands.*

*Ae.
Read this now.
Sorry about that cup of tea, Craig.*

*Don't worry. I've emptied this into the Alignment of Exidor. Let's hope I don't start an intergalactic war.
Again.*

GRAPE JUICE
1 Litre

Lasagne.
Friday Dinner.
For Daddy.

Good news. I have improved this with Hundreds and Thousands. They improve everything.

SuperValu
Lasagne
...d beef in a tomato sauce with egg pasta and a cheesy sauce
British Beef
Serves 1
400g
25-JUN

*Eurgh!
Looks like straw, feels like straw, tastes like straw.*

SuperValu
Lasagne

Are you sure it isn't straw? And anyway, who keeps straw in a fridge!

Cat food
In case next door's cat comes round

Muesli for breakfast.

This stuff is wasted on cats, Craig. It is gorgeous!!!

Dropped stitch.

5:02PM

INTERGALACTIC MINING COMPANY
INTERGALACTIC TELEX

7/1-12-09-01

STARSHIP ALASKA REPORTED LOST

☐ Last reports indicate making planetary approach in order to carry out mineral survey. Encountered what at first was thought to be severe turbulence. Then identified as some sort of force barrier. Ship rapidly disintegrated on contact. Indications are that at least one escape pod was launched. As no survivors have been heard from and the barrier surrounding the planet appears impenetrable, we do not at this time recommend the launch of a rescue mission.

WAR LOOMS

POST OFFICE

OFFICE STAMP

Charges to pay
...... s. .... d.

No. ....

TELEGRAM

Prefix.	Time handed in.	Office of Origin and Service Instructions	Words
	10.15	South London	60

Deeply regret to inform you that your husband 877543 Cpt R Arwell is missing as the result of air operation on the night of 18/19th Dec 1941 over English Channel stop Letter follows stop Any further information received will be communicated to you immediately stop pending receipt of written notification no information should be given to the press. OC Unit.

Souffle Girl –
Why is the TARDIS oven broken? It was a gift from Delia.

Cheese Soufflé

INGREDIENTS

1 tbsp flour
1oz butter
½pt milk, warmed
2oz finely grated parmesan cheese
4 large egg yolks
5 large egg whites
salt and freshly ground pepper
cayenne pepper

PREPARATION

Preheat the oven to 200C/400F/Gas6.
Prepare the basic mixture by stirring one generous tablespoon of flour into 1oz of butter melted in a heavy saucepan. Gradually add just under ½pt of warmed milk, stirring until your mixture is quite smooth. Let this sauce cook very gently and slowly, stirring frequently, for close on 10 minutes. Now stir in 2oz of finely grated parmesan cheese (or if you prefer, 1oz each of parmesan and gruyère and then the very thoroughly beaten yolks of 4 large eggs, and then continue stirring for a few seconds. Now add a seasoning of salt (always to be added after the cheese) and quite a generous amount freshly ground pepper, plus if you like, a scrap of cayenne. This basic mixture can be made well in advance.
When the time comes to make the soufflé, have the placed fairly low in the oven, and a baking sheet on the shelf. Butter 1½pt soufflé dish (the size is important). of the eggs, in a large scrupuloush

I AM HERE

Greetings from PISA, ITALY

I AM HERE

I AM HERE

RIO DE JANEIRO

The story picked up again. But this time Thief had shaken himself out of the universe. There was no Doctor in it. Even shiny metal dodgem-smell Daleks could not sniff him out. Yet he knew that this was not a happy ending to the story. Just a comma before another full stop. Thief belongs in the universe and he cannot stay out of it for much longer. (I have seen what happens in the Sad Field. It answers so many questions. Which is why IT IS FORBIDDEN.)

POLICE BOX

SILURIA

DR KAHLER-JEX   EXPERIMENTAL CYBORG PROGRAM DETAILS

//SECURITY CLEARANCE//

MILITARY SCIENCE ADVIS

EXPERIMENTAL CYBORG PROGRA
MILITARY SCIENCE UNIT

DR KAHLER-JEX
KAHLER MILITARY SCIENCE UNIT

SECU
CLEAR

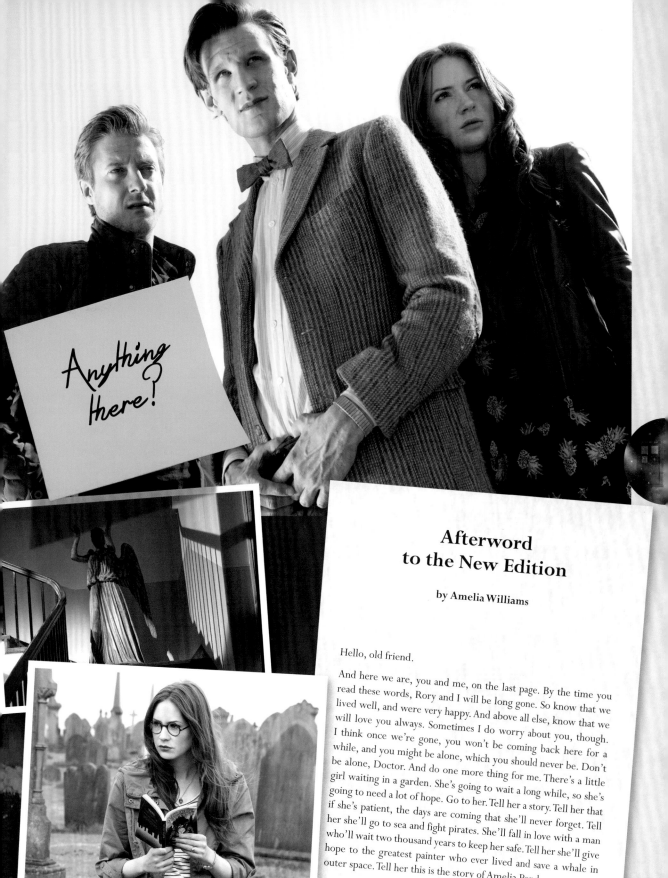

Afterword to the New Edition

by Amelia Williams

Hello, old friend.

And here we are, you and me, on the last page. By the time you read these words, Rory and I will be long gone. So know that we lived well, and were very happy. And above all else, know that we will love you always. Sometimes I do worry about you, though. I think once we're gone, you won't be coming back here for a while, and you might be alone, which you should never be. Don't be alone, Doctor. And do one more thing for me. There's a little girl waiting in a garden. She's going to wait a long while, so she's going to need a lot of hope. Go to her. Tell her a story. Tell her that if she's patient, the days are coming that she'll never forget. Tell her she'll go to sea and fight pirates. She'll fall in love with a man who'll wait two thousand years to keep her safe. Tell her she'll give hope to the greatest painter who ever lived and save a whale in outer space. Tell her this is the story of Amelia Pond.

And this is how it ends.

He does not ask me how it feels to be alone. Because he knows. Sometimes he gets scared. He always has his little strays. They stay such a short time, I wonder he names them. But when they go it always hurts him. More every time. (He used not to notice. Smell of diesel fumes and sunshine. Dodo sends him her love. He blinks in surprise.)

Now he is lonely. They grow up, they grow old, they go away, sometimes they die. But he moves on. Swimming pools come and go. I make him nicer ones, in case, one day, he comes to see them. But he does not. He keeps his head above water.

Sure?

MR STRAX'S BOOK
OF
HOUSEHOLD MANAGEMENT
COMPRISING INFORMATION FOR THE

MISTRESS,
HOUSEKEEPER,
COOK,
KITCHEN-MAID,
BUTLER,
FOOTMAN,

COACHMAN,
VALET,
PARLOUR-MAID,
HOUSE-MAID,
LADY'S-MAID,
GENERAL SERVANT,

LAUNDRY-MAID,
NURSE AND NURSE-MAID,
MONTHLY, WET, AND
SICK NURSE,
ASSASSIN,
GOVERNESS.

Also Sanitary, Medical and Lethal Memoranda.

With a History of the Origin, Properties and Uses
connected with Home Life and Defence

DUTIES OF THE BUTLER.

57. The domestic duties of the butler are to wait upon the family at mealtimes, to see to the cleanliness of everything, and to ensure all servants are properly armed. His place is at the sideboard to serve the wines, but only when called on.

58. Where the old-fashioned practice of placing either the dessert or meson blasters on the polished table, without any tablecloth, is still adhered to, the butler should rub off any marks made by hot dishes or spent cartridges before arranging the dessert.

59. Before dinner, the butler must satisfy himself that the lamps, candles, or gas-burners are in perfect order, and that the safety catches have been removed from any and all light artillery.

160. He now proceeds to the drawing-room, arranges the fireplace, closes the shutters (both wood and steel), trims any wicks as necessary and checks to ensure that the peri

JUGGED HARE.
(VERY GOOD.)

1032. INGREDIENTS.—1 hare, a strip of lemon-peel, 1/4 pint of port wine.

MODE. — First you catch your hare. This can be reasonably achieved with an impact grenade. Alternatively, a high-energy beam can be used, and, with careful management, the hare can be broiled alive before skinning and seasoning with port and lemon-peel. Do not omit to serve redcurrant jelly with it.

TIME. — Altogether 10 minutes.

AVERAGE COST, 5s. 6d.

Sufficient for 7 or 8 inefficient humans.

Seasonable from September to the end of February.

NOTE. — Should there be any left, rewarm it the next day by putting the hare, &c. in a saucen

THE DOCTOR.
CHAPTER XLIII.

2578. 'Time,' according to the old proverb, 'is money;' and it may also, be said to be life. This applies more especially to poisoning, fits, exposure to noxious gases, impulse lasers, temporal shifts; and many accidents. Human beings are a puny species. If people knew how to act during the interval that must necessarily elapse from the moment that The Doctor is sent for until his eventual arrival, many lives might be saved.

List of Drugs, &c., necessary to carry out all Instructions.

2579. In addition to a medical scanner and a meson scalpel, the household would do well to lay a little stock of the following —Antimonial Wine. Antimonial Powder. Blister Compound. Blue Pill. Calomel. Carbonate of Potash. Compound Iron Pills. Compound Extract of Colocynth. Compound Tincture of Camphor. Epsom Salts. Goulard's Extract. Jalap in Powder. Linseed Oil. Mandrel Condensors. Myrrh and Aloes Pills. Nitre. Oil of Turpentine. Opium, powdered, and Laudanum. Sal Ammoniac. Senna Leaves. Soap Liniment, Opodeldoc. Sweet Spirits of Nitre. Turner's Cerate.—To which should be added: Common Adhesive Plaster. Isinglass Plaster. Lint. A pair of small Scales with Weights. An ounce and a drachm Measure-glass. A Lancet. A

He does not want his name any more, but he cannot live without it. He knows the end is coming. He has a new little friend and she is a mystery so big inside. I DON'T LIKE HOW SHE SMELLS.

She wants to know all about him. But she is wrong. I do not like her. She's making a very big mistake. She doesn't know where he is. She is everywhere and nowhere. I don't like her inside me. Walking over my grave. Asking questions. You cannot make a soufflé without breaking things. Round things that leak. Which came first – the girl or the box?

Property of
Clara Oswald
age?
12
13
13
14
15
17
18
19
20
21
22
24

101 PLACES TO SEE

Oh. OK. Good.

RUN YOU CLEVER BOY AND REMEMBER

The Monastery of St John

Contains the
13th Century Legende
Of the Mad Monk
and the Bells of St John

The Brochure of the Long Song

(Price: 1 Treasured Possession)

Q: Why do you sing the Long Song?
A: We sing the Long Song to Grandfather, the Old God, to feed his dreams and to keep him asleep with a lullaby without end.

Q: How long has the Long Song been sung?
A: It has been sung for millions of years. Chorister handing over to Chorister. Generation after generation after generation.

Q: What will happen when the Long Song ends?
A: The Long Song will never end.

'HARM ONE OF US –
AND YOU HARM US ALL.
BY THE MOONS, THIS I SWEAR...
... BUT USE YOUR DISCRETION.'
ANCIENT MARTIAN PROVERB.

BROKEN WAS THE SWORD.
BATTLE DOUBLE-DAWNED,

THE ARMIES MARCHED SILVER SHOD
THROUGH BLOOD-DARK SPACE.

GATHERED UNDER THEIR DEATH
BANNERS AND THEIR SOUL SWORDS

THEY CRIED OUT TO EACH OTHER IN
HONOUR AND ANGER.

ON THE ONE SIDE, STRODE THE FORCES
OF GRAND MARSHAL SKALDAK,

SOVEREIGN OF THE THARSISIAN CASTE,

VANQUISHER OF THE PHOBOS HERESY,

FLEET COMMANDER OF THE NIX THARSIS.

OPPOSING THEM WERE THE FORCES OF

HE WHOSE NAME WAS STRICKEN.

BY THE MOONS THEY HONOURED
EACH OTHER,

AND THEN THEY FOUGHT.

SKALDAK, THE GREATEST HERO TO
BREATHE THE RED AIR,

AND THE STRENGTHS OF HE WHOSE
NAME WAS STRICKEN.

SKALDAK'S DAUGHTER STOOD BY HIM,

THE SAME HERO'S BLOOD COURSING
THROUGH HER NOBLE VEINS.

IT WAS HER FIRST TASTE OF ACTION,

AND BEFORE THE DAY WAS THROUGH
SHE WOULD BE

A HUNDRED THOUSAND TIMES
BLOOD-GLORIED.

TOGETHER THEY SANG THE SONGS
OF THE OLD TIMES.

THE SONGS OF THE RED SNOW.

AND THEN THEY FOUGHT.

SKALDAK ENGAGED THE ENEMY
IN THE GREAT ASTEROID BELT.
THE DAY WAS OURS.

THE ARMY SURRENDERED NOBLY
AND GAVE UP THEIR NAMES,

EACH ONE CARVING THAT OF SKALDAK
INTO THEIR FLESH

BEFORE GIVING UP THEIR OWN FOREVER

HE THEN GAVE THEM THEIR LAST
HONOUR

AND THEY WERE GATHERED UP INTO THE
ETERNAL HONOURABLE BATTLE.

BUT WHAT OF HE WHOSE NAME
WAS STRICKEN?

HIS SHIPS WERE DUST, HIS TROOPS HAD
GIVEN UP THEIR NAMES AND GONE TO
THE FIGHT ETERNAL.

WHAT OF HIM INDEED?

WITH VALIANT COURAGE,
HE TOO GAVE UP HIS NAME.

HE WHOSE NAME WAS STRICKEN
OFFERED

GENTLE SKALDAK HIS HEAD,
AND SKALDAK TOOK IT OFF TRUE,

WITH BUT ONE BLOW OF HIS SWORD.

AND SO HE PASSED INTO
ETERNAL BATTLE.

THEN SKALDAK GATHERED UP HIS FLEET

AND VICTORIOUS, HEADED FOR HOME.

BUT THE JOURNEY FOR HIM WAS A
LONG ONE.

Nothing to worry about. As you were.

They all say the same things to him. All those pets. They've done it since first I let them come inside. They always ask him. Doctor who? He never tells them. Which is a shame. As I would like to know. Just to make sure of my Thief. I have my suspicions. As though someone is standing looking over my shoulder. Which is ridiculous, as I do not have shoulders. I look away, I look back. I miss something out of the corner of my Eye of Harmony.

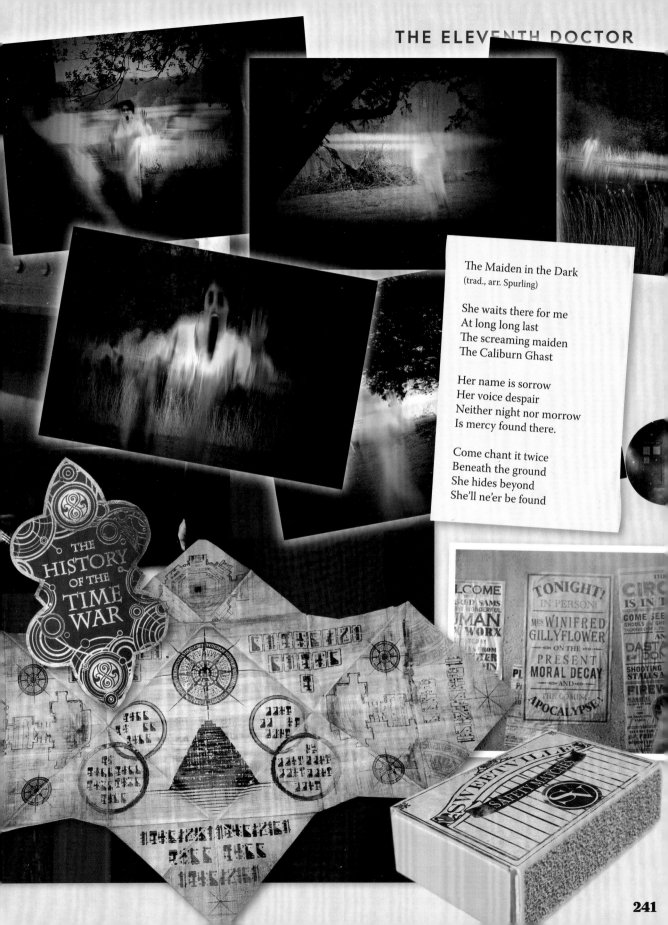

The Maiden in the Dark
(trad., arr. Spurling)

She waits there for me
At long long last
The screaming maiden
The Caliburn Ghast

Her name is sorrow
Her voice despair
Neither night nor morrow
Is mercy found there.

Come chant it twice
Beneath the ground
She hides beyond
She'll ne'er be found

THE
HISTORY
OF THE
TIME
WAR

WELCOME
TO THE
BLOOD SAMS
AND WONDERFUL
HUMAN
WAXWORX
FRESH FROM
BITTER
BERLIN

TONIGHT!
IN PERSON!
Mrs WINIFRED
GILLYFLOWER
ON THE
PRESENT
MORAL DECAY
AND
THE COMING
APOCALYPSE!

THE
CIRCUS
IS IN TOWN
COME SEE
GHOULS
TAKING OUT AN
AND
DASTARDLY
DOINGS!
SHOOTING
STALLS AND
FIREWORKS

SWEETVILLE'S
SAFETY MATCHES

Artie? What is this??

GRAVEYARD — NIGHT
It's a graveyard at night. We hear ARTIE, CLARA AND ANGIE and see their torchlights before we see them.

                    ARTIE
         Clara? Is the Doctor a ghost?

                    CLARA
                    No.

                    ARTIE
         Good. I don't believe in ghosts,
         and they scare me. Clara?

                    CLARA
                    Yes, Artie.

                    ARTIE
         I'm scared and I'm excited. Both at once. Scarecited.
         Angie, are you excited or are you scared?

                    ANGIE
                    Just bored.

The graveyard at night is a very spooky place. Statues of stone angels…

                    ARTIE
         I think one reason people don't go in graveyards at
         night is it's scarier to go into graveyards at night.

                    ANGIE
         So stupid. You're like the king of obvious.

                    ARTIE
         I am not! Maybe the Prime Minister of Obvious.
         Does Obvious have a Prime Minister?

                    CLARA
         If you two are going to fight, we're turning
                    right around, right now.

And look! It's the TARDIS. Just sitting there. Dark. Clara
approaches it. The LIGHTS GO ON! THE DOOR IS FLUNG OPEN!
And the Doctor is having a great time.

AND TONIGHT IT'S TIME FOR DANCING IN THE STARS. *ATLANTIS STYLE.* I HOPE YOU BROUGHT YOUR *POSH FROCK* BECAUSE…

                    THE DOCTOR
         And tonight it's time for dancing in the stars.
    Atlantis style. I hope you brought your posh frock, because—

He looks down. Artie. He looks over. Angie. He looks back at Clara.

                    CLARA
         I thought it would be good for them. An adventure.
    Educational. We could go somewhere fun, like Pompeii,
    or meet Shakespeare and Queen Elizabeth or something.

                    ARTIE
         Crusades or go to the Moon or meet At-zicks.

                    ANGIE
                    Aztecs.

                    THE DOCTOR
         Absolutely not! No kids in the TARDIS.
    It's a rule – a very important rule. It's rule number one.
              That's how important it is.

                    CLARA
                (to the kids)
                    Wait here.

Clara and the Doctor go inside the TARDIS,
leaving the kids outside.
                    ARTIE
                    I'm so scarecited!

Angie reaches out and takes a photo of herself
looking grumpy with her phone.

TARDIS CONTROL ROOM

The Doctor is fuming.
                    THE DOCTOR
              No Kids on the TARDIS!

                    CLARA
         Scared you'll leave them behind?
    Or they'll crash a spaceship into the Sun?

                    THE DOCTOR
              That sort of thing. NO!

                    CLARA
    Because... you don't take kids into danger.

                    THE DOCTOR
              Now you're getting it.

Hang on – how do you even know all this?

                    CLARA
              How old ARE you?

                    THE DOCTOR
                    What?

                    CLARA
         I'll accept an approximation.

                    THE DOCTOR
    Thirteen hundred and somethetysomething.

                    CLARA
    So compared to you, we're all children.
    But you've taken me into danger a dozen times now.

                    THE DOCTOR
              You're a grown-up.

                    CLARA
              Only compared to you.

                    THE DOCTOR
                    What?!?

Wait – did Clara tell you????

                    CLARA
         (throwing herself on his mercy)
    Doctor? This means a lot to me. Their mum died.
    Things are rough. Just give them a nice day out?
         They really need one. Please. For me?

THE GRAVEYARD

The door is flung open. The Doctor pulls the kids in.

                    THE DOCTOR
                 Quick! Inside!

THE GRAVEYARD AT NIGHT IS A VERY **SPOOKY PLACE.** STATUES OF **STONE ANGELS...**

Oh! Is it a comic strip? That is a lovely picture!

You know, you're really very good at this, Artie.

TARDIS CONTROL ROOM

The Doctor is running around looking for something. He knows he has it somewhere... Artie is amazed, and states the obvious. Angie allows herself one awed look at the TARDIS and then is determined not to be impressed at all.

                    ARTIE
'Scuse me. Did you know that your house is actually bigger on the inside than it is on the outside?

                  THE DOCTOR
      I did know. But well spotted young man!
              And, uh, Angie?

                    ANGIE
      I'm not stupid. I can see. It's rubbish.

                  THE DOCTOR
           No — it's bigger on the inside!
It travels in time and space! It's fantabuloso!

                    ANGIE
                   Whatevs.

But she's impressed despite herself. The Doctor opens a roundel, pulls out a pirates' treasure chest, and starts pulling unlikely things (hats for the kids and a hat for Clara too?) out of it as he talks...

                  THE DOCTOR
Kept this in reserve in case there were ever kids in the TARDIS again! We're going to Hedgewick's World! And I've got a golden ticket!

At the bottom, he finds it: A golden ticket - it looks like a gold credit card, made of real gold.

               THE DOCTOR (CONT'D)
Never used it! Always wanted to! Gets four people in for free, and right to the front of any queue, which is brilliant, because the lines for the Spacey Zoomer can go on for days. And unlimited free ice creams.

Artie looks around. Ange is taking photos with her phone.

               THE DOCTOR (CONT'D)
Hold on tight! This is going to be brilliant.

The Doctor throws switches and starts the TARDIS.

ENGINES...

HEDGEWICK'S WORLD. MOONSCAPE

TARDIS LANDING SOUNDS. We have landed on... the Moon? A moon, anyway. It's bleak. Airless. And we end up on the TARDIS as the door opens. Four heads peer out in descending order of size. THE DOCTOR'S, CLARA'S, and then ANGIE'S and ARTIE'S.

                  THE DOCTOR
Here we are. Hedgewick's World. The biggest and best amusement park there will ever be. A quarter of a million years from now. FUN!

No! No! No!!! This has to stop now. What if somebody sees it? What if your dad sees it?!

43

THE ELEVENTH DOCTOR

• Found on a cell wall in Newgate, 1893 •

Do you hear the Whisper Men? The Whisper Men are near.

If you hear the Whisper Men, then turn away your ear.

Do not hear the Whisper men, whatever else you do.

For once you've heard the Whisper Men, they'll stop and look at you.

They sing a song the Whisper Men, for a man who will not hear

For he who treads a broken road, they tell a song of grim forebode

His friends are lost for ever more, unless he goes to Trenzalore.

The girl who died he tried to save. She'll die again inside his grave.

This man must fall as all men must. The fate of all is always dust.

The man who lies will lie no more when this man lies at Trenzalore.

And my Thief stands there, surrounded by himself but so very alone. For now he knows the day is coming when he must answer the question the universe has always been asking him since the very beginning. He wants to go to the one place he cannot. The place I cannot let him go. Where I become so big and he becomes so small. But he wants to go. She makes him. I was right about her.

It is an end. But this end is not a full stop. It is a question mark.

Oh dear...

CHARTWELL HOUSE
WESTERHAM, T.N.16.

26 March 1963

My dear Mr Newman,

Forgive an approach from out of the blue.
First, my hearty congratulations on your new job
at the British Broadcasting Corporation. While
scanning The Times on my way to the obituaries
(a morbid hobby), I noticed you wr quoted as
wnting to make a whole new type of drama.

As one who has seen his fair share, I was
wondering if I cld interest you in the story of
an old, very dear friend of mine. His name is
The Doctor.

Yours sincerely,

Winston S. Churchill

The Story of Doctor Who

2010-2013

We took about 600 photographs of Matt in different clothes. From those, we came down to the tweed jacket, the trousers, the boots. At that point we knew we needed something else but we couldn't work out what it was. And then Matt said, 'Shall I try a bow tie?'

Ray Holman, costume designer

I quite like seeing versions of my costume on the high street. I think, 'Yay! People dress up as Doctor Who!' If I made bow ties cool, that's cool.

Matt Smith

Having found their Doctor, the production team had to cast the new companion – and her fiancé...

I did two auditions, one with the casting director and then the second one I read with Matt.

Karen Gillan (Amy Pond)

She's a red-headed, feisty seductress ball of wit.

Matt Smith

Probably, one of the highlights was walking onto the TARDIS for the first time. It was our first day, and we were all brand new and so scared but so excited.

Karen Gillan

I couldn't really walk into the TARDIS for the first time as an actor; I walked into the TARDIS as a child.

Arthur Darvill (Rory Williams)

The thing that blew us away about Arthur is just how funny he is. Arthur always finds the perfect moment for a gag. it's quite hard to imagine the show without him.

Steven Moffat, writer and executive producer

Rory does have an adventurous spirit. But I think when you first meet him he's

never had an opportunity to show that. Amy brings it out of him because if she's in trouble he's always going to be there.

Arthur Darvill

The first episode of Series Five had an ambitious remit – to introduce a new Doctor, a new companion, and an intriguing mystery that would run and run...

The Eleventh Hour had to do so much in such a short space of time. The Doctor has to shine – to be so completely Doctor-y from the first second. Never mind who he used to be, Matt Smith's Doctor becomes Amelia's whole world within a few minutes.

Steven Moffat

Normally when the Doctor regenerates he does that in front of someone This time we had a new companion and a new Doctor. So I came up with the idea of this little girl who meets him briefly when she's 7 and

MATT SMITH
is the Eleventh Doctor

I am very jealous of the guy who's coming next.

David Tennant

Before we commenced casting, I said, 'No, we're not going for a boy Doctor. There is no way someone the age of 27 year old could play the Doctor,' I said very grandly. And I was right. We cast a 26-year-old.

Steven Moffat

The audition process was mad. Usually with an audition you're allowed to tell people. You're auditioning for the Doctor and there's a huge legacy that comes with that. There are huge expectations. The audition process seems to fit with the show – you know, the hiddenness, and the secrecy – it makes it a bit more magic.

Matt Smith

We auditioned people, in what I'll call Top Secret Locations, but were actually slightly unpleasant hotels. We got all these wonderful actors in in deadly secrecy and got them to pretend to be the Doctor for a while.

Steven Moffat

When you get the right person, age just becomes entirely an irrelevant factor. I don't think we let ourselves believe it until about three weeks later. We all felt we had to be utterly diligent. I got an email from Steven about 4.30 one Saturday afternoon saying, 'It's Matt, isn't it? And it always has been.'

Piers Wenger, executive producer

I'd been warned that Matt was a terribly clumsy man, and for an actor who's very physical he's always breaking things. When we met, I put out my hand to shake his hand, and he put out his but forgot that he had a coffee cup in it. So my first meeting was spent dodging spilled coffee! The lovely thing about Matt is that he's a real gentleman. He behaves like a proper leading man. He creates a great atmosphere on set, he knows who everybody is and is always welcoming to the guest cast.

Marcus Wilson, producer

He's like a foal being born on a vet programme. He's beautiful and elegant and fantastically clumsy. His endearing clumsiness is actually becoming a sort of character attribute. The idea of Peter Davison was an old man trapped in a young man's body, Matt actually *is*. He's only 27 and he feels like he's about 900. He wears glasses in real life and as a result, even when he's not wearing them, he looks at you like that. He looks like a professor. He has an old soul. It's such a charming mix.

Mark Gatiss, writer

He doesn't seem to be in charge at all, and makes huge, bumbling errors, but that stimulates him to do something even cleverer, because he's such a genius. He would drive Christopher Eccleston and David Tennant's Doctors insane if he was in the TARDIS with them. He would break everything, trip over everything, his plans would be stupid, and he'd forget what he was doing halfway through. I'm loving that.

Steven Moffat

SMITH *on* SMITH

It's like any secret, it just sort of bubbles up inside you, and the longer you keep it the more mad you go, I think, and the more you're trying to suppress. I'll be in my flat and *Doctor Who* will be on and my flatmate's watching it, and I'm sat there going, 'Gah! I'd love to share with you that I'm the new Doctor, but I can't.' But it's also quite exciting and gives me a sense of mischief in that I know something that Britain doesn't know. It's exciting, nerve-wracking. I've got six months to build this Time Lord. I'm just going to concentrate on the words on the page and let the rest unfold.

Matt Smith

It's such a thrill every morning, and you're never going to know how your day's going to go. I mean, the TARDIS is always a joy, isn't it? I get to play around in a mad imaginary world *every day*, which is limitless and timeless and endless and boundless. That is as close as you get to sort of magic really I suppose. And to be at the heart of that is a thrill actually as much as anything.

Matt Smith

I think the Doctor will always be a bit of a gooseberry. But I think he'll get on with it as he normally does. He's far more interested in the structure of stars than he is in girls...

Matt Smith

It's been an honour to play this part, to follow the legacy of brilliant actors, and helm the TARDIS for a spell with 'the ginger, the nose and the impossible one'. But when ya gotta go, ya gotta go and Trenzalore calls. Thank you guys.

Matt Smith

again twelve years later. So that, for her, he's been the Doctor for ever.

Steven Moffat

A brand new TARDIS interior was unveiled at the end of The Eleventh Hour, *which led into the second episode,* The Beast Below...

We ran the set to the extremities of the studio, building around the steel frame left behind by the old Torchwood Hub. I was always keen to make the console the Doctor's altar within our cathedral of Time and Space

Edward Thomas, production designer

When I first walked on the set, I was in awe. So I just channelled that into Amy's reaction. This is her first experience on a spaceship and her first adventure with the Doctor.

Karen Gillan

She's like Wendy in *Peter Pan*. She's wearing her big silly nightie and a dressing gown and slippers. It really underlines the idea that she's gone back to her childhood. On the night before her wedding, on the night before she's supposed to grow up, she's flown off with Peter Pan.

Steven Moffat

The Doctor was summoned to his next adventure by Winston Churchill...

What I tried to do was not to do an impersonation but more try to get the essence of the individual, try to get the humour and the power... There's a huge twinkle that goes on with him, more so because of his relationship with the Doctor.

Ian McNeice (Winston Churchill)

Because there was so much 'new' in the series it felt like a good idea to renew the

The arrival of a new Doctor is a momentous occasion. It needs to be special. I've been involved with two regenerations. I co-wrote *The War Games* when Pat Troughton was condemned to turn into Jon Pertwee, script-edited *Spearhead from Space* where Pertwee first appeared and, five years later, introduced Tom Baker when I wrote his first show, *Robot*. *The Eleventh Hour* doesn't disappoint, with a stunning opening with the Doctor clinging to his wrecked TARDIS and his eerily comic meeting with little Amelia who feeds him fish fingers and custard and who later, through an interesting use of the hazards of time travel, turns into grown-up Amy. The complex plot involves the shape-shifting Prisoner Zero, and the sinister Atraxi. It plants the seeds of much that is to follow – Amy, Rory, the Silence... I particularly like the way in which the Doctor, having seen off the invading Atraxi, summons them back and delivers a magisterial ticking-off. Above all there's Matt Smith, who was clearly born to play the Doctor. With a sigh of relief you realise that the miracle of *Doctor Who* casting has happened again!

Daleks. Right from the start, I was very keen that the Daleks reflected the movie ones. As a kid, they were such a dynamic and colourful presence, and I just adored them.

Mark Gatiss

Walking into the prop room and realising we only had three Daleks – they're our Big Bad and we had three of them. How could I justify asking for half a dozen more? I thought, 'I'll claim it's a new race of Daleks.'

Steven Moffat

I was immediately tickled by the idea of a domesticated Dalek asking someone if they wanted tea. And the Doctor's mounting frustration as these horrible killers play by the rules of English etiquette!

Mark Gatiss

The Daleks were not the only returning monsters in Series Five. The Time of Angels brought back the Weeping Angels, along with a certain time-travelling archaeologist...

I had loads of Angels ideas I never got to use in *Blink*. So I fancied something more action and spookiness based, to see what else they could do. Stand still in different places, as it turned out.

Steven Moffat

When I started with David Tennant, obviously I thought that was just a one-story deal, particularly because River Song got killed off at the end. I didn't imagine for a second that I'd be asked back.

Alex Kingston (River Song)

As I wrote *Silence in the Library*, what started as a gimmick began to grow in my head. The story of who she could be, and how and why. It's a good story, and there are surprises, so why not tell it? Good mysteries are easy.

Steven Moffat

Rory's first episode as a companion saw the Doctor break into his stag-do and take him and Amy to Venice...

The brief I was given was to write a big romantic romp. *Doctor Who* works at its best when very human relationships are being played out against this huge background. It was great fun to set a domestic argument from 2010 in 1580.

Toby Whithouse, writer

Ah, the look of the Vampire girls. I've never seen the crew more occupied and attentive! They looked like 1980s glam-rock stars. Come back – you're always welcome.

Matt Smith

Having confronted bloodsucking teenage girls in Venice, the Doctor, Amy and Rory next faced a rather different threat...

So many of the monsters in *Doctor Who* are computer-generated, so to have a whole bunch of old people with Zimmer frames and walking sticks chasing us was quite scary.

Arthur Darvill

There's something quite scary about old people, particularly if you're young. It's partly to do with the teeth, which is why the Eknodines emerge from their mouths.

Simon Nye, writer

First seen in 1970, the Silurians returned for The Hungry Earth *and* Cold Blood, *episodes that would have far-reaching consequences for Rory...*

I loved Alaya because she was really, passionately lizard. And then of course Restac was just mental. There's just nothing that stops her.

Neve McIntosh (Alaya / Restac)

First there was a rumour that Rory was going to die, and before that was set in stone there was a rumour that he was going to come back to life. So I got that script and thought, 'OK, this is cool, I come back to life.'

Arthur Darvill

Amy really hides her emotions a lot. She's really guarded, so it was nice to do something where she let that guard down completely.

Karen Gillan

Richard Curtis penned an unusual episode which saw the Doctor and Amy saving Vincent van Gogh from an invisible monster...

Van Gogh is pretty much the only famous artist in almost any medium who had pretty much no acknowledgment whatsoever during his lifetime. I loved the thought of making him happy.

Richard Curtis, writer

The real meat of this story is the Doctor meeting someone that he can't save. He can't save people from themselves. The demons that assail Vincent are far beyond the Doctor's reach.

Steven Moffat

Gareth Roberts had previously taken the Doctor to Shakespearean England, to an alien desert and for cocktails with Agatha Christie. Now he trapped the Time Lord in a small suburban flat and gave him his biggest challenge of all – to pass for normal...

It was an idea I had years and years ago. The story's about the Doctor having to go undercover as an ordinary human being for a few days and become a young guy's flatmate.

Gareth Roberts, writer

I'd *love* to share a flat with the Doctor! What would drive me mad? Threats on my life, aliens, Cybermen walking in, strange little creepy girls at the top of staircases... So much, but I'd definitely roll with it. He'd be a *great* flatmate. The best – never there, doesn't really eat...

Matt Smith

Series Five drew to a close with a return not just for River Song but for a huge alliance of the Doctor's foes...

Episode 12, when the Doctor's dragged into the Pandorica – that's a real highlight for me.

Matt Smith

Every episode had been building up to that moment, so I had to make sure that I didn't blow it. I don't think anyone could have worked out exactly what happened next. It took me a while...

Steven Moffat

The second half of *The Big Bang* only came in three weeks before we started shooting and it had a wedding in it! We didn't know about that, so we had to find a wedding venue. Steven Moffat will only hand in stuff that he's happy with, and often his first drafts are near-perfect, but they can be rather last-minute. *Doctor Who* can be a fly-by-the-seat-of-your-pants kind of show, but that's what makes it exiting.

Toby Haynes, director

The tricky thing was that I had to write bits of Episode 13 before I'd written Episode 12. But it seems more complicated than it actually is, like all good tricks. Of course you have to pay attention, but why the hell not? I haven't actually encountered anyone who didn't get it, only people who explain to me that other people won't have got it. 'A lot of people won't have understood that,' they say, then always add, 'But I got it, of course.'

Steven Moffat

New producer Marcus Wilson came on board for the 2010 Christmas special...

I was in denial when I started. *A Christmas Carol* was an immense episode and I was going, 'How the hell are they going to do this?' And then you see it on set and it's reassuring; you see how you become part of it and decide how you'll do it. My job is basically to put Steven Moffat's vision on screen. The relationship Steven and I have is that we're almost testing each other. He says, 'I want to do this' and I go, 'Yeah, we can do that, what about this as well?'

Marcus Wilson

It's sometimes surprising what they can pull off – and what they can't pull off. They'll say, 'No we can't do that cocktail party at night, it's ridiculous, lots of extras, but that bit where the giant mutant space badger hatches in the middle of Big Ben? We can do that!'

Steven Moffat

Series Six promised shocks, mysteries and – in the opening minutes of the first episode – a big, impossible conundrum. And maybe even some answers...

All the answers are coming, I promise. Including the answers to questions people haven't even thought to ask yet.

Steven Moffat

The Doctor is faced this season with a set of choices that are impossible for him to sit on the fence about. It makes him vulnerable. But he's still the same Doctor, he's still the mad bonkers professor.

Matt Smith

We're going straight into the Silence, and what they are. A much bigger mystery and a bigger story is possible now.

Steven Moffat

So much happens in 20 pages you think, 'My god, this can't be happening, the Doctor can't be dying in the first 15 pages!' But he is. But how do you get back? I mean, I've yet to find out...

Matt Smith

The look of the Silence was an amalgam of existing imagery – like we've seen them in the corner of our eye for centuries.

Steven Moffat

There was also the mysterious appearance of a woman with an eye-patch. She'd be back...

They didn't tell me exactly when these little pop-ups would come. The first episode I wasn't in, and I just thought, 'Perhaps I won't come in till much later,' and then I suddenly popped up. So hopefully I'll just keep popping up and intriguing everyone until I burst in!

Frances Barber (Madame Kovarian)

With the Silence apparently defeated, the Doctor, Amy and Rory set off to meet pirates, a Siren and clones made of Flesh. And the Doctor's 'wife'...

There were hundreds of things in *The Doctor's Wife* that never made it in. The funniest were the scenes I wrote with Amy Pond versus Nephew in the TARDIS swimming pool. They wound up getting cut because Karen Gillan can't swim.

There was also Rory getting locked in the Zero Room and informed that the whole point of a Zero Room is that you are absolutely cut off from all influence elsewhere in space and time. Which is great for Time Lords, but a human being will go mad in approximately fifty seconds. The only way out is a switch which, because Time Lords can levitate in a Zero Room, is right up at the top of the room... The budget did not actually go to a Zero Room. Poor Steven Moffat fought for my Zero Room scene – 'What if we just made it a black curtain round a space?' They told him, 'It'll just look like a curtain,' and he got talked out of it. I was the one going, 'A curtain! Anything! Give me my Zero Room scene!' But we would have lost it anyway: the first cut lasted an extra fifteen minutes.

Neil Gaiman, writer

I cried when I read the end. Neil Gaiman's words were so beautiful.

Suranne Jones (Idris)

There was a very surprising twist in store for Amy at the end of the next story...

Steven decided he wanted Amy to be Flesh and began working that story back through the earlier scripts. I wasn't asked to write that twist ending until very near shooting. So I think Steven only had it fully worked through at that point – in that Moebius strip he calls a brain.

Matthew Graham

The first half of Series Six ended with another epic – the Doctor was going to rescue Amy. At any price...

Ambitious scripts? There's been a few I've winced at. I remember reading *A Good Man Goes to War* and going, 'Bloody hell, it's *Star Wars*.'

Marcus Wilson

The Doctor's cashing in centuries of kindness – which, of course, he should never do. He realises no one should have this much influence. Not even him.

Steven Moffat

Neve McIntosh returned, playing a crime-fighting Silurian, and the episode also introduced a scene-stealing Sontaran...

which I knew, I might add.

Matt Smith

Later that year, the series resumed with the ambitiously titled Let's Kill Hitler...

A regeneration rom-com, guest-starring Hitler. It's what the world has been waiting for!

Steven Moffat

When I read 'Rory punches Hitler in the face', I was a very, very happy man.

Arthur Darvill

As the series continued, the TARDIS crew were confronted with an older Amy and, in The God Complex, *their worst fears...*

I don't age well, I've learned. What was quite depressing, but in a weird way nice, was taking the prosthetics off and seeing a young face underneath. But then I started thinking, 'When I'm actually that age, I can't take it off!'

Karen Gillan

It was Steven Moffat's idea that we should hint at the Doctor's own room in *The God Complex*. There was an early version of the script where we actually saw what was in there. But what's scary for one person isn't scary for another. That's why

When we have other guest actors on, it usually takes a while for them to get used to me. You've got this strange potato-man in the corner coming to life and threatening them.

Dan Starkey (Strax)

A Good Man Goes to War *promised to explain the mystery of River Song...*

It was a bizarre read-through... I thought, 'Steven Moffat has rushed the end of this...' We got to the end, and it really didn't make any sense. It made for a slightly strange atmosphere.

Arthur Darvill

And then Steven Moffat said, 'This isn't the real ending; you'll find that out later...' So we had a fake ending, even at the read-through.

Neve McIntosh (Madame Vastra)

I knew, because Steven had given me the script that he always intended to shoot. But nobody else did, including Karen and Arthur. When we actually shot that moment, the crew wasn't expecting me to say what I said. No one knew until that moment.

Alex Kingston

A great cliffhanger, a homage to *Star Wars* at the end there. 'I am Melody Pond, I am your daughter.' None of

```
AMY LOOKS TO THE COT. THE
   GALLIFREYAN SYMBOLS.

           AMY
Still can't read it. Tell me what
    it says. Just tell me.

        RIVER SONG
You have to see it for yourself.
Because it's the key to everything
 - it's why all this is happening.
It's what this base is really for.

   RORY ALSO STARING NOW.

          RORY
        What is it?

        RIVER SONG
   The Doctor's real name.

ON THE GALLIFREYAN LETTERING.
ON AMY AND RORY, STARING. AMY'S
EYES WIDEN, AS SHE STARTS TO
         UNDERSTAND.

           AMY
       … Oh my God!

      END CREDITS
```

the Doctor sees it but we don't, so that it's left to the viewer's imagination.

Toby Whithouse

The Doctor was about to die. But first, he went to visit an old friend...

Craig has an ordinary life most of the time. He's like the anti-River Song. But he loves the Doctor and is eternally grateful to him, so I'm sure they'll meet again.

Gareth Roberts

One of the great joys for me in Series Five was how successful and how beloved the episode *The Lodger* was. I just said, 'Can we do it again?'

Steven Moffat

The Cybermen came into it because I wanted a sense of history for the Doctor's final adventure before he keeps his date with destiny.

Gareth Roberts

When Steven Moffat said the script needed a more broken-down and damaged look for the Cybermen, we laughed and told him, 'Well, they already are!' These suits have had a lot of use over the years, and need constant repair.

Neill Gorton, Millennium FX

Series Six ended in a universe stuck at 5.02pm, with pterodactyls, pyramids, steam trains and two armies...

I was a bit nervous, because I know my own love of Byzantine complexity. I worry that I do it too much. I have to keep pulling myself back...

Steven Moffat

Ultimately, River married the Teselecta. I can absolutely say with my hand on my heart, 'I married the Doctor'... but did the Doctor ever marry me?

Alex Kingston

So now the Doctor has a wife whom he married in an alternative timeline while miniaturised inside a robot replicate of himself, who goes on to have a reverse-order relationship with him, while serving time for his murder, before dying to save his life, before he even meets her. Makes *On Her Majesty's Secret Service* seem like a decent honeymoon.

Steven Moffat

Next up was the 2011 Christmas special, before Series Seven unleashed another mystery...

The Doctor's project is to erase himself from history, because there are only so many times you can stand and boast at Stonehenge. We've had a lot of fun with the Doctor as a quasi-celebrity – you're this wandering gypsy scientist and suddenly you discover you're a legend. What's this going to do to you?

Steven Moffat

Steven wanted a series of movies. The brief was 'What would be the movie poster tag line?' He kicked it off with *Asylum of the Daleks* – what scares the Daleks?

Marcus Wilson

We'll have more physical Daleks in the room than ever before. The running total is somewhere between 20 and 30 real ones. We're collecting every Dalek known to man.

Caroline Skinner, executive producer

We basically went to key suppliers like The Mill and said, 'What would you like to do? What can you do well?' And The Mill said, 'We'd love to do dinosaurs.' What I hadn't planned for was the combination that Steven would cook up in his brain: dinosaurs, but on a spaceship.

Marcus Wilson

I'd pitched Steven the idea of the Cube invasion, which he'd bought straight away... and then I went, 'Oh, I'll probably need UNIT. Can I have UNIT?' If there is an alien invasion, you're going to need people to deal with it... It's a really useful dramatic mechanism as well as being great in terms of the show's continuity.

Chris Chibnall, writer

It's such an honour to be part of this incredible tradition.

Jemma Redgrave (Kate Stewart)

The very last shot that we did was Matt, Karen and Arthur stepping into the TARDIS for the final time, and clearly that was a very particular moment in *Doctor Who*'s history...

Douglas Mackinnon, director

While The Power of Three *was the last episode Karen Gillan and Arthur Darvill filmed, Amy and Rory's departure actually came in the next episode,* The Angels Take Manhattan*...*

One of the on-going tragedies of *Doctor Who* is that we see him get so close to his friends. The Doctor, Amy and Rory have become such a little family unit, and you think, 'Oh, it'll be like this for ever.' At a certain point, like Wendy and Peter Pan, they have to go away and grow up.

Steven Moffat

We wanted to create that sense that you shouldn't miss the last days of the Ponds. But we wanted the manner to be

a surprise. For the climactic scenes in the graveyard, we had green screens to block the paparazzi from seeing what was being filmed.

Marcus Wilson

I can exclusively reveal that most things like *Doctor Who*, on closer inspection, may not make complete sense. They make emotional sense, they can inflame and excite you, but I'm not absolutely sure – and I say this as their creator – that the Weeping Angels are an entirely sensible decision on the part of evolution.

Steven Moffat

During a mid-series break, production shifted to the BBC's new studios at Roath Lock...

We had a great home at Upper Boat. The TARDIS there had been designed into the fabric of the building so we knew we couldn't take it without damaging it severely. We said, 'We're going to have problems, so why not start again from scratch?' And a new start worked well story-wise, with the Doctor moping away on his cloud for 200 years.

Marcus Wilson

For the very, very first time we've got a TARDIS in 360 degrees. If you look at that very, very first episode, *An Unearthly Child*, when they go into the police box it's super sci-fi, so we've gone back to a sci-fi TARDIS. It's a machine, it's not magic.

Steven Moffat

The 2012 Christmas special introduced a number of elements that would prove important in the second half of Series Seven. Including at least one very dead character...

It was funny, because we shot the stories out of sequence. So first of all I got the script for *The Crimson Horror*, and it was obvious that Strax is alive, he's serving Madame Vastra and he seems OK with that... Steven Moffat said, 'Yeah, don't worry, it will be explained. Sort of.'

Dan Starkey

For the first audition, I read the scenes and prepared them in a certain way, but as soon as you're approached by Matt all of that goes out of the window.

Jenna Coleman (Clara Oswald)

We have fun, don't we? That's sort of the main thing. There's also a rhythm to Steven's writing, and Jenna just immediately got it.

Matt Smith

We were going to have to do a modern-day story, meeting Clara yet again, and Marcus Wilson said, 'Let's do *The Bells of St John* as a proper London thriller, as close as we can get to James Bond.'

Steven Moffat

At the end of the tone meeting, Steven said, 'Is no one going to say anything about the fact that I've asked you to fly a Boeing 747 across London?' And we said we could do that.

Marcus Wilson

Obviously, for Clara, this is a completely clean slate, she is meeting the Doctor for the first time. But the dynamic is so different because there's nothing he hates more than an unsolved mystery.

Jenna Coleman

Doctor Who's about collaboration and a huge love from the crew for the show – doing all-nighters and working incredibly hard because they want it to be good. Good enough is never enough. *Cold War* is a good example of that. We were supposed to be shooting another script and then it was brought forward. That submarine was literally built in two weeks where it would usually take months.

Marcus Wilson

I've always loved the iconic Ice Warriors and have been badgering to bring them back for ages. And now they're on a sssssssubmarine! With Russians!

Mark Gatiss

Mark Gatiss started pitching a couple of very, very clever ideas about what we could do with an Ice Warrior, and I went for it. Sometimes you think a design should be changed because it's so familiar; that one's slightly less familiar, so we just made a super-version of the original.

Steven Moffat

Having shown viewers what lurks inside an Ice Warrior's armour, the show now explored the innards of another of its icons before giving the Cybermen an upgrade...

Actor Katy Manning on
THE CRIMSON HORROR

I sat there and I hardly blinked. This just worked. I'm absolutely bonkers about Matt. He has a wonderful physicality as an actor – always doing something clever with his body and his face. He's never still. He's created this wonderful thing, like he's taken all of the Doctors, and put them into a mixing bowl. He's just magical. And I am loving Jenna. I just liked the simplicity of her relationship with the Doctor. No great complexities – they just looked so nice together. I wasn't really that surprised to see she was good at running in a frock. When you're a *Doctor Who* companion, you have to climb mountains in miniskirts and scale oil rigs in platform heels. It's all part of the job. But she does do wordless surprise amazingly. Their relationship isn't in words – it's in looks and moments and connections. It reminds me a little bit of me and Jon, dare I say.

And oh – hello, Diana Rigg! She did a fabulous job. She made the most out of that character, underplaying it just enough. And when the little creature that was attached to her chest crawled away across the floor it was really rather sad. It was a lovely touch having Rachel Stirling as her daughter. She had quite a difficult part to play, with her love for her 'Monster'.

I liked very much having two fabulous aliens working together with the Doctor – a Silurian Miss Marple, and the Sontaran was a bit like Oddjob in the Bond movies. And they're wonderful – those masks are so beautifully applied. You don't think for a second there's a person there.

Saul Metzstein did a great job of the direction. You look back at the old series, and it's like your favourite sweater, it doesn't matter how many holes there are in it, you still love it. But we have moved on, and to be able to produce this kind of television now is amazing. There's so much more to play with now, but the love and the passion that goes into making *Doctor Who* is just the same. I'm watching it and absolutely loving it, just like in the old days.

Journey to the Centre of the TARDIS. It was just the title alone, I guess. You will go to the heart of the TARDIS, you will see more of the TARDIS, more properly than you've ever seen before.

Steven Moffat

I sent an email off to Steven Moffat and said that it seems weird that we've never had an Evil Doctor, inside the head of the Doctor, arguing with the Good Doctor. The chess game is the perfect way to do it. Once I did that, it took over the entire episode. I hadn't realised when I was writing it that this meant Matt had to learn twice as many lines as normal. I got to see some of the rushes – Matt swears like nothing I've ever any actor swear, playing chess with himself and missing a line and losing it and getting so gloriously, magnificently sweary.

Neil Gaiman

The Series Seven finale will hopefully change the way people look at *Doctor Who*.

Marcus Wilson

My aim for it is to have slightly more than you think could possibly happen in one episode. Slightly more treats than you think you could be allowed... And the Doctor's great secret will be revealed... And actually will. I'm not lying. Unless I am lying, and I'm lying when I said that.

Steven Moffat

On Saturday 23 November 2013, Doctor Who's 50th anniversary, a very special episode will be shown on BBC One...

You will not be disappointed.

Matt Smith

Well, that's what we'll put on the poster, then.

Steven Moffat

I read it and I clapped at the end. I think it's hilarious and I think it's epic and I think it's fast and I'm telling you nothing more. It somehow manages to pay homage to everything and look forward and that's the genius of it.

Matt Smith

The Zygons are just the villain we shot outside. I'll be honest with you, what you know about *Doctor Who* is entirely conditioned by which bits we have to shoot outside. We just tell you what we have to, when we have no choice. If we could make this on the dark side of the Moon and tell you nothing at all, I'd do it. And I'd also lie to you prodigiously and regularly right now if I felt it would help keep a secret. Watch me.

Steven Moffat

Filming brought central London to a halt as a TARDIS flew above Trafalgar Square...

We actually got swung on a crane from side to side, and then I was fully harnessed and belted in. When else are you going to get a chance to do that in Trafalgar Square?

Jenna Coleman

I loved it. I had to persuade them to let me go up. We had one shot at it, that was it. And it was great. It was 90 foot up. And you can see everyone.

Matt Smith

It was quite a complicated thing to set up. You're taking two well-known actors into the centre of London and a blue box that a few people might recognise... We spent a lot of time working with City of London, Transport for London, Westminster City Council and lots of different agencies to coordinate everything. They were brilliant. It was the first time the TARDIS has been lowered into Trafalgar Square!

Marcus Wilson

I always wonder, like when we were in Trafalgar Square, how do people find out we're there? There were so many people dressed up as Doctors. Somehow they find out, get dressed up as the Doctor, and get down to set.

Jenna Coleman

I remember *The Five Doctors*, when I was 12, being about the most exciting thing that had ever happened, so to be part of something that will have the same excitement for a new generation is a thrill.

David Tennant

The Five Doctors? I really like that episode. I think there is an expectation that our anniversary will be like that but bigger. But we don't have five Doctors. I think I'd be dizzy with five. At the moment it's quite a serious thing to be on set and to have two!

Matt Smith

With *Doctor Who*, the moment you get the job, people are asking when you'll leave; the moment you leave, people are asking when you're coming back. I think people believed I'd been lying for months if not years about knowing whether this was happening or not, but it genuinely has been quite last-minute.

David Tennant

You're going to get every kind of retrospective in the world when it comes to the 50th and you're not going

to be short. To make this show just a walk-down, just a tribute to the past, a backward glance, would be like one of those end-of-year shows: 'That was the year that was! Look back and feel slightly old and sad.' Don't do that! Of course, it's a celebration of the legend of *Doctor Who*, but more importantly it's ensuring there's going to be a 100th anniversary.

It's a hugely important story to the Doctor. That was my mission statement. Very, very rarely in *Doctor Who* does a story matter to him very much at all. Obviously he runs around, defeats mutants, meets a space badger, saves a civilisation, causes epiphanies to happen for everybody he meets, rushes back to the TARDIS and forgets everything about it. If you asked him he might have a vague memory of the badger, and that's it.

My intent was to move it forward, to have a show that's equally about the next fifty years of *Doctor Who*. Attaching the word 'fifty' to anything... I almost tried to rip the logo off, saying, 'Why is that good?! That show you're watching is really old!' Why is that a great thing to say? It's about proving we've got many, many more stories to tell, and in a way, being able to say the story really starts here. People ask me how am I going to please the regular audience, and I say I'm actually on a recruitment drive to get people who've never watched it before to watch *Doctor Who*. That's what matters. There are some people out there who've never watched it before, God help them. You want them to think, 'Oh, I've been missing out, I'm going to join in now.'

If you're going to celebrate *Doctor Who*, you're celebrating the Doctor – well, why not tell his story? What's it like for him? What's it like being him, what defines him, what defines what he is? How do you make that a mighty moment in his life? What would be the Doctor's most important day, what would be the show that would change him as a person for ever, alter the course of his life? That's what's big enough to do for the 50th, rather than just have a parade of the greatest hits. Never mind that space badger one; this is the adventure that he really remembers, and thinks, 'That was the day everything changed.'

Steven Moffat

Two guys, two sonics, two TARDISes. I've described it as sort of having Stan Laurel and Stan Laurel, and not having Hardy anywhere.

Matt Smith

What's been quite interesting is to find the moments when our two Doctors intersect, and then the moments when they do things rather differently. The fun is in the gap between the two. They switch between praising each other's ingenuity to trying to undermine it at every opportunity. You sort of swing from being quite pleased with yourself to being infuriated at your own inadequacies, and I guess that's kind of writ large, isn't it, if you meet yourself.

David Tennant

It's one of those things that *Doctor Who* can do. You actually can have another Doctor revisit. I tried to imagine what it would be like to interact with your younger or older self, and I concluded that I'd absolutely hate it. I mean, there's just nothing good about it. My younger self would be a prat

and my older self would just be even uglier. Imagine the lack of hope you'd have the moment the 30-year-old me came into the room and saw the 51-year-old me and went, 'Really? Is that as good as it's ever gonna get?'

I didn't write the show like that. That would've been depressing.

Steven Moffat

I thought, 'Oh, this'll be great.' As the day approaches, I then think, 'What if Matt feels like I'm stepping on his toes? Or what if I can't remember how to do it? Surely I'm too old to be doing this now?' The first day, Matt wasn't there. So the first day, it was just me. It was like, 'Oh, yeah, I sort of remember this.' And then the next day it becomes something different again because we were together. Mind you, there's not as many lines to learn when there's more than one of you.

David Tennant

One of the comments that David and Matt made to each other after the read-through was 'It's really weird to hear somebody else doing this, because I keep thinking, "Oh, is that how you're meant to do that bit?"' You have to say, 'No, no, could you please both do it different ways?' While the flourishes change between the Doctors, the essential Doctor is just the Doctor.

Steven Moffat

Our first day on the TARDIS, we were greeted by the new Director General of the BBC... Maybe that's what always happens? I don't know, maybe that's a *Doctor Who* anniversary thing?

David Tennant

I had one costume, and I think they got one from an exhibition. And I think they found a stuntman one. So we've got two and a big one. It's slightly alarming – if they get ripped, there's not a lot of replacements.

David Tennant

In the first years when *Doctor Who* came back, everyone just became a fan. People stopped me in the street with the most abstruse questions – and they're real people, they're not fans like me – and I'm thinking, 'You're not supposed to know that stuff, that's supposed to be mine!' It's very, very easy to keep *Doctor Who*

JOHN HURT...
is the Doctor?

Acting Royalty. One thing we wanted with the 50th Anniversary was to say, 'Let's have acting royalty in this show; let's have an actor who almost represents the stature of *Doctor Who*.' So to have John Hurt here and for him to be so enthusiastic and so nice is thrilling. And you know, he's amazing.

Steven Moffat

It's amazing to have an actor of his calibre around. He can make moments out of nothing. its extraordinary. He's doing proper acting, I'm just sort of waving my hands a lot.

Matt Smith

When we do scenes with John, I look at him and I just feel I'm pulling the biggest faces in the world.

David Tennant

Literally. With John Hurt just moving his eyes.

Matt Smith

accessible, because it's designed to be. The format can be summed up in such a short sentence even after all this time: it's a man who can travel anywhere in time and space in a box that's bigger on the inside. That's all you need to know.

Steven Moffat

I can't imagine what will happen to *Doctor Who* in the next fifty years. I would say with absolute confidence it'll still be around; heaven knows in what form, heaven knows if there'll be interruptions at some point. It's a massive thing. If letting it die in public sight and leaving it off the air for 15 or 16 years didn't work, then what the hell's going to work? It's indestructible.

Steven Moffat

For Alasdair and Mrs Bradley   *For Lucy, Kieran and Jacob*

ACKNOWLEDGEMENTS

This book would not have been possible without Tom Wicker, Darren Scott, Tim Leng, Andrew Pixley, Justin Richards, Nicholas Payne and Lizzy Gaisford, Stephanie Milner and Georgie Britton, Katie Player, Matt Nicholls, Eliza Nimon, Alice Macaire, Gillane Seaborne, Helen Raynor, Gary Russell, Michael Stevens, Tom Spilsbury and John Ainsworth, Derek Ritchie, Richard Cookson and Edward Russell. Thanks also to Waris Hussein and Patrick Mulkern for showing us the camera scripts for the very first serial in 1963, and to the *Doctor Who* Art Department for many other assets. As always, deadlines end, papers are dropped, plans are changed, and we've been unable to include many glorious items. One day. Yes, one day.

Special thanks to everybody who found time to contribute and/or to be interviewed: Colin Baker, Carole E. Barrowman, John Barrowman, Sir Tim Berners-Lee, Nicholas Briggs, Nicola Bryant, Paul Cornell, Bernard Cribbins, Russell T Davies, Peter Davison, Richard Dawkins, Terrance Dicks, Clive Doig, Neil Gaiman, Mark Gatiss, Waris Hussein, A.L. Kennedy, Tom MacRae, Katy Manning, Richard Martin, Paul McGann, Harry Melling, Steven Moffat, Georgia Moffett, Anjli Mohindra, Kate O'Mara, Marc Platt, David Roden, Gary Russell, William Russell, Robert Shearman, Andrew Smith, Dan Starkey, Donald Tosh, Lalla Ward, and Marcus Wilson. Jenna Coleman, Steven Moffat, Matt Smith, David Tennant were interviewed during filming for the 50th Anniversary Special.

Sadly, many of *Doctor Who*'s earliest cast and crew are no longer with us, while some were unable to fit us into their schedules. But the show is probably the most comprehensively documented production in television history, and there is now an enormous archive of interview material for fans to enjoy. Compiling the 'oral history' presented in this book, we have been indebted to:

Peter Haining, in *Doctor Who: A Celebration* (1983), *Doctor Who: The Key to Time* (1984) and *Doctor Who: 25 Glorious Years* (1988), gathered up interviews with William Hartnell, Terry Nation, Patrick Troughton, Terrance Dicks, Jon Pertwee, Roger Delgado, John Nathan-Turner, Janet Fielding, Peter Davison, Stratford Johns, Bill Cotton, and Richard Briers, while Matthew Waterhouse gave an insight into the 1980s in *Blue Box Boy* (2010), and Gary Russell and Philip Segal's *Doctor Who: Regeneration* (2000) remains the best exploration of the 1996 television movie with Paul McGann. Malcolm Hulke's *Writing For Television* (1974) contains a fascinating series of insights from Sydney Newman, Dennis Spooner, Robert Holmes, and Hulke himself. More recently, Gary Russell spoke to Russell T Davies, Julie Gardner, Jane Tranter, Phil Collinson, Paul Cornell, Mark Gatiss, Edward Thomas, Neill Gorton, Mike Tucker, Steven Moffat, Helen Raynor, Joe Ahearne, Euros Lyn, James Hawes, Andy Pryor, Louise Page, and Dan Zeff for *Doctor Who: The Inside Story* (2006), and *The Brilliant Book of Doctor Who* has talked to Steven Moffat, Matt Smith, Karen Gillan, Edward Thomas, Toby Haynes, Neill Gorton, Matthew Graham, Toby Whithouse, and Tom MacRae.

Magazines and fan publications such as *Radio Times*, *Gay Times*, *SFX*, *Television Today*, *DWB*, *In-Vision*, *TARDIS*, *Fantasy Empire*, *TV Zone*, *Starburst*, *Space Voyager*, *Fan Aid*, *Arkensword*, *The Frame*, *Time Meddlers of Vancouver*, *Tranquil Repose*, *The Colin Baker Interview* and, of course, the irreplaceable *Doctor Who Magazine* have conducted countless interviews over the years with the likes of Sydney Newman, Peter Brachacki, Barry Newbery, David Whitaker, Raymond Cusick, Dudley Simpson, Douglas Camfield, John Wiles, Jackie Lane, Michael Craze, Innes Lloyd, Gerry Davis, Deborah Watling, Patrick Troughton, Pauline Collins, Michealjohn Harris, Peter Bryant, Victor Pemberton, Jack Lovell, Terrance Dicks, Michael E. Briant, Wendy Padbury, David Maloney, Derrick Sherwin, Ian Scoones, Malcolm Hulke, Jon Pertwee, Christopher Barry, Caroline John, Robert Holmes, Richard Franklin, Roger Delgado, Brian Hayles, Bob Baker, Ian Marter, Philip Hinchcliffe,

Graham Williams, Anthony Read, Mary Tamm, Douglas Adams, Christopher H. Bidmead, Anthony Ainley, John Nathan-Turner, Eric Saward, Beryl Reid, Peter Moffatt, Mark Strickson, Gerald Flood, Richard Hurndall, Graeme Harper, Colin Baker, Nicola Bryant, Philip Martin, Bonnie Langford, Pip and Jane Baker, Matthew Jacobs, Yee Jee Tso, Christopher Eccleston, Penelope Wilton, Steven Moffat, Mark Gatiss, Anthony Head, Kylie Minogue, Michelle Ryan, Lindsay Duncan, Ray Holman, Karen Gillan, Arthur Darvill, Ian McNiece, Alex Kingston, Neve McIntosh, Gareth Roberts, Frances Barber, Suranne Jones, Caroline Skinner, Chris Chibnall, Jemma Redgrave, Douglas Mackinnon, Jenna Coleman and Michael Pickwoad. *The Doctor Who Handbook* (Telos), the online *Doctor Who Interview Archive* and the matchless Andrew Pixley have between them compiled a treasure trove of conversations with *Doctor Who*'s stars and creators from all these publications and many more. We are also grateful to Darren Scott for providing his impressive catalogue of interview transcripts. All were invaluable in putting together the story of *Doctor Who* presented in these pages.

There have been numerous promotional appearances on BBC television and radio programmes, from *Desert Island Discs* (William Hartnell) and *Pebble Mill at One* (Patrick Troughton) to *Breakfast* (Colin Baker, David Morrissey) and *Newsnight* (Andrew Cartmel). BBC DVD's exhaustive range of supporting features have included contributions from Maureen O'Brien, Peter Purves, Anneke Wills, Derrick Sherwin, Peter Darvill Evans, John Freeman, Kevin Davies, Gary Russell, Alan Barnes, Justin Richards, Steven Moffat, and Arthur Darvill. We are grateful to Ed Stradling for supplying access to material he has filmed. *The Story of Doctor Who* (BBC, 2003), interviewed Verity Lambert, Carole Ann Ford, Frazer Hines, Barry Letts, Nicholas Courtney, Wendy Padbury, Katy Manning, Elisabeth Sladen, Tom Baker, Louise Jameson, Sarah Sutton, Peter Davison, Janet Fielding, Mark Strickson, Nicola Bryant, Colin Baker, Sophie Aldred, and Sylvester McCoy.

Doctor Who's return in 2005 was accompanied by BBC Three's much-missed behind-the-scenes programme *Doctor Who Confidential*. Over six series and many specials, *Confidential* spoke to just about everyone who's ever been involved with the new series of *Doctor Who*, including Lorraine Heggessey, Christopher Eccleston, Billie Piper, Russell T Davies, Julie Gardner, Edward Thomas, Phil Collinson, Noel Clarke, Camille Coduri, Neill Gorton, David Tennant, Pauline Collins, John Leeson, Sophia Myles, Peter Kay, Freema Agyeman, Carey Mulligan, John Barrowman, Derek Jacobi, John Simm, Catherine Tate, Steven Moffat, Matt Smith, Piers Wenger, Ray Holman, Karen Gillan, Arthur Darvill, Toby Whithouse, and Richard Curtis. The team behind *Doctor Who Confidential* went on to make BBC America's ambitious 11-part series *The Doctors Revisited*, interviewing, among many others, William Russell, Tom Baker, Louise Jameson, Mark Strickson, Janet Fielding, Colin Baker, Nicola Bryant and Sylvester McCoy. Some quotes from these programmes appear in this book.